A Philosophy of Recipes

Also Available from Bloomsbury

A Philosophy of Recipes

Making, Experiencing, and Valuing

Edited by Andrea Borghini and Patrik Engisch

BLOOMSBURY ACADEMIC

LONDON • NEW YORK • OXFORD • NEW DELHI • SYDNEY

BLOOMSBURY ACADEMIC
Bloomsbury Publishing Plc
50 Bedford Square, London, WC1B 3DP, UK
1385 Broadway, New York, NY 10018, USA
29 Earlsfort Terrace, Dublin 2, Ireland

BLOOMSBURY, BLOOMSBURY ACADEMIC and the Diana logo are trademarks
of Bloomsbury Publishing Plc

First published in Great Britain 2022
Paperback edition published 2023

A catalogue record for this book is available from the British Library.

A catalog record for this book is available from the Library of Congress.

Library of Congress Control Number: 2021947577

ISBN: HB: 978-1-3501-4591-7
          PB: 978-1-3502-7033-6
          ePDF: 978-1-3501-4592-4
          eBook: 978-1-3501-4593-1

Typeset by Integra Software Services Pvt. Ltd.

To find out more about our authors and books visit www.bloomsbury.com
and sign up for our newsletters

Contents

Figures

Acknowledgments

The idea of a volume on recipes and philosophy originated with the conference "Framing Recipes: Identity, Relationships, Norms" organized by Andrea Borghini and Francesca Mastrovito and held on December 4 and 5, 2018, at the University of Milan, Italy. We heartfully thank Francesca, the students who helped run the conference, the conference speakers, and all of the attendees for their insights. We also wish to thank Lily McMahon and the Bloomsbury editorial staff for believing in our project and following it patiently, professionally, and cordially. Thanks also to Sharon Casu for her help with the index. From Andrea, a special acknowledgment to Min and Lelio, for the courage and energy they provide on a daily basis. All the phases of production for this volume are deeply indebted to the social network of Culinary Mind: we wish to thank everyone who has actively taken part in it since 2017. This research was also funded by the Department of Philosophy "Piero Martinetti" of the University of Milan under the Project "Department of Excellence 2018–2022" awarded by the Ministry of Education, University and Research (MIUR).

Introduction

A Philosophy for Recipes: Questions and Methods

Andrea Borghini and Patrik Engisch

This collection of chapters engages with the philosophical exploration of a founding concept within culinary cultures—recipes. Along the way, other concepts take central stage too, including taste, representation, memory, and intellectual property rights.

Recipes and cookbooks have received significant attention in recent scholarship, and to date a reader finds several distinguished academic volumes demonstrating their cultural significance (an initial and non-exhaustive list includes Bower 1997; Theophano 2002; Floyd & Forster 2003; Elias 2017; Leong 2018). The present volume adds a missing and unexplored perspective, approaching the topic from a philosophical angle.

The collection distinguishes itself on three main counts from other volumes within the growing field of the philosophy of food (for a brief and updated overview of the field, see Borghini & Piras 2020a). First, its concern with the theoretical aspects, broadly understood, of the philosophical questions posed by food. Second, its focus on the philosophically underexplored notion of recipe and on a host of issues related to it. Third, its interdisciplinary perspective. We shall elaborate on each of these aspects below before offering a brief overview of the chapters contained in the volume.

The Role of (Theoretical) Philosophy in the Study of Food

Food, in the mode of production or consumption, is everywhere, all the time. Hence it is not surprising that it raises conceptual and value-laden issues that call for philosophical exploration. What makes researching this field of study particularly exciting is the many remarkable topics still awaiting examination. As strange as it may seem, until a few years ago the philosophers who pondered on the nature of recipes (Borghini 2015; Borghini & Piras 2020b) or the existential significance of hunger (Borghini 2017) could be counted on one hand. It is, thus, not unusual to run into some brilliant case study or a philosophically fruitful question.

Yet, how should the philosophy of food be approached? Analogous to the philosophy of medicine, the philosophy of physics, the philosophy of biology, and the philosophy of art, the philosophy of food studies issues that arise from the consideration in its specific domain of entities and practices—food, eating, the edible environment, and their significance to the human condition. Furthermore, in line with these other philosophical sub disciplines, the philosophy of food offers a privileged angle for dealing with fundamental issues that pertain to its domain.

The array of topics that are potentially of interest to philosophers of food is wide (for a list, see Borghini & Piras 2020a). Some of them have already been singled out and are extensively discussed. These include the ethical commitments we have to other animals; the environmental impact of food production and consumption; and the place of food in an analysis of aesthetic experience. Other topics, however, have only recently come into focus or are still awaiting proper attention from philosophers. These include a series of theoretical questions concerning food: What is food? What is an ingredient? What are recipes? What is the relation between recipes and the dishes they help deliver? There are also questions pertaining to consumption: What is hunger? What is appetite? What should a solid scientific theory of metabolism look like?

These more theoretical questions are, essentially, conceptual ones. They lay the foundation for a philosophical analysis of the most basic concepts of the culinary domain and of the possible relations between these concepts. The goal of this volume is, thus, twofold: first, to offer a philosophical exploration of recipes from a theoretical perspective that can set an example for future studies and, second, to present chapters by non-philosophers that should stimulate further philosophical inquiry and that show the fruitfulness of a contamination between philosophy and other disciplines, at least when it comes to food.

Recipes and Philosophy

Why do recipes constitute a good entry point into the theoretical study of food for philosophers? Because recipes are the most central tool that mediate our relation to food. They represent and archive culinary cultures and, as such, have accrued over millennia a theoretical (on top of a practical) complexity that pertains to few other culinary concepts.

Recipes enjoy a special status in contemporary culture. First of all, they provide the *forms* that food consumption can take, inside and outside of the home. Menus at restaurants, cafes, and from street vendors consist of named dishes with a list of ingredients, functioning as proxies for recipes; within the kitchen, a chef has to be able to teach the staff how to cook items on a menu, and recipes are an invaluable tool for achieving this. Home cooking is no less based on recipes: when someone prepares food at home, they most often do so by following, modifying, or imagining a recipe.

Most communication about food also rests on an understanding of recipes. Dietary guidelines tend to be given or at least exemplified in terms of recipes. Food criticism relies on an understanding of how a recipe *ought to be*. Cookbooks form a major sector of the publishing industry. TV shows and the media treat recipes in a manner more and more akin to items of popular culture such as songs and movies. Recipes also deserve legal and cultural protection: those associated with so-called geographical indications (e.g., Champagne and Parmigiano cheese) are protected by intellectual property rights, and UNESCO's Intangible Cultural Heritage list now contains culinary cultures or gastronomical meals, which are arguably structured in terms of recipes.

Despite the increasing societal interest in scientific findings about nutrients and other abstract components of foods, to date recipes are not central to explaining the relevance of eating to human cultures, socio-political agency, trade relationships, personal identity, religious identity, and much more. The rise in societal value of food, thus, goes hand in hand with the increase in value accorded to recipes.

Philosophy offers a unique perspective on recipes. Unlike other subjects in the humanities, the primary aim of a philosophical analysis is to delve into fundamental and normative questions, which serve to generate models for framing our discourses and discussions on recipes. Some of these questions are more theoretical in nature. For instance, what fixes the identity of a recipe? Its taste? Its ingredients? The process of production? Its relationship to a specific group of people? Are there recipes that have not been named yet? Can you make a recipe by accident? Do recipes play a role in the representational power of food? Whilst others are, instead, more value-laden in nature. For instance, who possesses the authority to fix the identity of a recipe, for example, to turn it into a geographical indication? When is it that making a recipe constitutes a form of cultural appropriation? Which aspects of a recipe can have intellectual property rights and why? The models emerging from the analysis of these topics can serve to frame sensitive ethical, political, legal, socio-economic, and cultural issues that make reference to recipes. They also provide unique tools to foster self-understanding of our eating and drinking practices.

Our Approach

This collected volume examines recipes from a philosophical point of view. Scholars have thus far amply illustrated the value of studying recipes through multiple lenses, including those of literature, history, anthropology, and law. Yet, with the exception of a few philosophical papers (e.g., Heldke 1988), philosophers did not delve into the analysis of recipes until a few years ago. The first philosophical paper addressing the issues covered in this volume was Borghini (2015) and we may furthermore cite the recent journal issue (Borghini & Piras 2020b). Thus, a volume on this topic is much needed to generate a plurality of perspectives and a debate, which will continue in journals, books, and conferences in the years ahead.

Why take a multidisciplinary perspective in a book that has a philosophical aim? First of all, a lot of disciplines may feel that there are philosophical issues arising in their studies with respect to food. In that sense, philosophers do not preselect what is philosophically relevant but, rather, answer to external demands. In this volume, collaboration with colleagues from other disciplines serves the role of singling out such philosophical issues.

Second, the study of food is constitutively interdisciplinary, as urged by Carlo Petrini:

> It is the gastronome's responsibility to become learned: not a botanist, not a physicist, not a chemist, not a sociologist, not a farmer, not a cook, not a doctor. All he needs is to know enough of these disciplines to understand what he eats. He must have some of the knowledge of each of those specialists, as far as food is concerned. And he must not be intimidated if experts look down on him as an amateur. Better to have a smattering of botany so that you can recognize a particular variety of plant, so that you know how, where, and by whom it was grown, how it was preserved and cooked, whether it can be bad for your health or not, and so that you can enjoy it more consciously. The alternative is the perfect biotechnologist, happy to eat a genetically modified organism that is harmful to farmers and the environment—a substance manipulated by the food industry, warmed up in a saucepan, and sadly lacking in taste. (Petrini 2013: 207)

In other words, we believe that a philosophical analysis of recipes cannot be taken up in isolation from the insights provided by other disciplines. For this reason, contributors to the volume are experts on some food issues that bring to the table key conceptual elements to advance future (philosophical) discussion on food. For instance, consider Barbara Haber's chapter in this volume. On the surface, it does not engage with philosophical questions. However, it highlights the role that imagination (as opposed to belief or knowledge) serves in a certain conception of recipes, offering an important entry point for assessing the epistemological values of recipes. Another neat example is Johanna Mendelson Forman's contribution, which underscores ethical and socio-political uses of recipes as found in social gastronomy, gastrodiplomacy, and culinary diplomacy.

The Chapters

The idea of the volume as well as many of its chapters originated during a conference held at the University of Milan, Italy, in December 2018, organized by Andrea Borghini and Francesca Mastrovito within the Culinary Mind network. The final structure of the volume, however, was substantially reconceived by the editors. It contains seventeen chapters in total, clustered into three themes—Making, Experiencing, and Valuing. In the remainder of this introduction we briefly summarize each contribution. Each part of the volume opens with some introductory remarks on the specific theme.

Part One: Making

Andrea Borghini's "Seven Philosophical Questions about Recipes" connects all the different chapters in the volume while presenting a series of conceptual questions about recipes that call for further scholarly attention. Borghini contends that, though a serious analysis of these questions must rest on a cross-disciplinary effort, philosophers are particularly suited to lead efforts to address them.

Sanna Hirvonen's "Recipes Without Maker" is concerned with the metaphysical nature of recipes. Hirvonen outlines two broad theoretical options, a constructivist and a realist one. She then argues against the constructivist theory of recipes elaborated in Borghini 2015 and in favor of a realist conception according to which recipes come in to existence automatically as the result of the preparation of a dish, whether or not they are being made public in any form.

Davide Bordini's "The Taste(s) of a Recipe" investigates the relation between recipes and taste. He argues for the thesis that though a recipe can serve as a guide to a certain taste, a certain taste is not essential to a recipe. Instead, he proposes a view of the relation between recipes and dishes that allows the same recipe to be associated with different tastes.

Andrea Borghini and Gabriele Ferretti's "Dip It before You Eat It! On Recipes and the Architecture of a Dish" explores a new avenue to show that recipes enable and can be used to perfect the relationships between cooks and diners. The authors' concern is with the means a cook can employ to communicate to an average diner that a dish should be consumed in a certain way. In particular, the chapter focuses on those characteristics of a dish that can be designed by a cook so that it affords certain procedural knowledge to the diner. The authors call those characteristics the *architecture* of the dish. A dish, when viewed through an architectural lens, conveys a fundamentally *narrative* framework, with specific perceptual and practical aspects, which the authors describe by drawing upon the literature in cognitive science on practical knowledge and affordances.

Merry White's "Body, Tool and Technique: Elements of Work in the Japanese Kitchen" offers a contrastive anthropological look at the role that the notion of recipe plays, or rather fails to play, in Japanese culinary culture. As White shows, Japanese food preparation rests less on abstract formulas than on more concrete notions such as understanding of the ingredients, training of the body, and the mastery of specific tools.

Maya Hey's "On Attunement: Fermentation, Feminist Ethics, and Relationality in Sake-Making Practices" argues that fermentation provides a way to practice human and more-than-human relationships in repeated ethical encounters. Her argument draws on data generated during ethnographic fieldwork conducted at the sake brewery Terada Honké. Relying on the notion of attunement, she articulates how the brewers must tune into their senses and their sense of self in space—which, cumulatively, help to shift attention away from any one human individual toward a more collective, multispecies ethic.

Part Two: Experiencing

Carolyn Korsmeyer's "Historical Dishes and the Search for Past Tastes" focuses on the practice of preparing dishes following retroengineered recipes retrieved by chemical analyses of remains of foodstuffs. In particular, Korsmeyer focuses on the question of whether food obtained through the application of these recipes could be faithful guides to tastes of the past and argues for a form of historicism of perception.

Patrik Engisch's "Recipes, Tradition, and Representation" takes a fresh look at a vexed interrogation in the philosophy of food—whether recipes and their instances, namely, dishes, can have any representational power. Engisch argues that once a certain conception of recipes is in place, complemented by a certain conception of traditions, it becomes plausible that certain recipes, traditional ones, and their instances, traditional dishes, can be said to represent past living conditions.

Cain Todd's "Authenticy, Style, and Recipe in Wine" argues that style in wine can be thought of as a particular modification of wine recipes. Todd's chapter begins by showing that, in contrast to food, a generic notion of a recipe does not do much to illuminate the nature of wine and its appreciation; rather, it is more helpful to think of wine in terms of style. Having established this point, Todd then contends that one of the main values associated with style, authenticity, can be articulated by thinking about the relationship between wine and recipes.

Barbara Haber's "Writing Cookbooks behind Barbed Wire" tells the story of thousands of American civilians living in the Philippines during the Second World War and that were rounded up by the Japanese and thrown into internment camps. Little food was provided and as conditions of near starvation grew worse, prisoners obsessed more and more about food, dreaming of it at night and fantasizing about it during the day, eventually collecting, creating, and exchanging recipes.

Akiko Frischhut and Giuliano Torrengo's "A Puzzle About Aftertaste" takes on the guiding role that recipes play with respect to taste and expands it to include the phenomenon of aftertaste. They argue that the latter constitute a specific class of aftersensations that, unlike after images, are appearances of the objects from which they causally derive.

Part Three: Valuing

Lisa Maree Heldke's "Recipes for Theory Making" is about philosophical inquiry and cooking. Heldke suggests that thinking about cooking can illuminate our understanding of other forms of inquiry. Specifically, she thinks it provides us with one way to circumvent the dilemma of absolutism and relativism. The chapter is divided into two sections. In the first, Heldke sketches the background against which her project is situated. In the second, she develops an account of cooking as inquiry by exploring five aspects of recipe creation and use.

Rafi Groslyk and David Kyle's "The Recipes of Genius on *Chef's Table*" offers insights into the creative process of dish development by those who are conceived as culinary geniuses—chefs who implicitly depart from any prior recipe or even prevailing techniques. They describe four primary "recipes" (cultural scripts) of contemporary creative and talented chefs. Using content analysis of the Netflix series *Chef's Table*, they argue that the narratives of culinary genius serve to reinforce winner-take-all ideologies of a global meritocracy through a highly individualistic framing of the creative process and represent the ideal of the privileged individual genius.

Enrico Bonadio and Natalie Weissenberger's "Food Presentations and Recipes: Is There a Space for Copyright and Other Intellectual Property Rights?" provides an overview of the potential use of intellectual property rights in the context of protecting culinary works. Drawing on case-law emanating primarily from the United States and Europe as well as academic work in the area and the viewpoints of industry insiders, they show that a clear schism emerges between those who believe culinary art should be protected to the same extent as other art forms, and those who believe endowing such protection upon something as culturally significant as food would go against the very principles the culinary community is founded on.

Anne Barnhill and Matteo Bonotti's "The Ethical Dimensions of Recipe Modification" discusses four examples of recipe modification in high-income countries, such as promoting healthier versions of recipes, offering modified versions of recipes to accommodate people with dietary restrictions, or restaurants offering modified versions of culturally significant recipes. They then turn to ethical issues raised by these forms of modification such as cultural appropriation, political legitimacy, gentrification, and ethically motivated shifts toward plant-based diets.

Johanna Mendelson Forman's "Is Social Gastronomy a Recipe for Peace?" is concerned with the role that recipes can play in connecting people. Focusing on social gastronomy, using food as a means to achieve a specific social impact, she shows that food has evolved beyond the dining room to become a means of engagement leading to employment and social integration and a tool for resolving disputes as groups exercise modern-day commensality.

Benjamin Aldes Wurgaft's "A Philosophy of Meat in the Early Twenty-First Century" examines a new recipe for so-called cultured meat. Its promoters argue that it will help us to eliminate the scope of industrial animal agriculture, and thus ameliorate the environmental damage and animal cruelty it causes. However, Wurgaft argues, the utilitarian moral framing of cultured-meat promoters obscures many valuable philosophical questions about the differences between human and non-human animals, and about human nature that meat—derived from animals or cell-cultured—raises.

Part One

Making

Introduction to Part One: Making

Recipes are at the core of culinary cultures and can guide all actors involved in them. Food producers often prepare their products for a certain recipe (e.g., a pre-packaged bag of salad or a fish fillet cut to be fried in a pan); cooks follow a recipe to prepare the food; diners often organize their diet and their specific meals based on recipes, which suggest the order (e.g., the main dish before dessert) and the quantity (e.g., a larger main dish than dessert) of the food to be consumed.

The historical and cultural role of recipes has been widely studied, as indicated in the Introduction to this volume. But, many conceptual questions regarding recipes had never been systematically addressed until a few years ago (see Borghini 2011 and 2015, and the papers in Borghini & Piras 2020 for early contributions in this area). For instance, under what conditions can we say that a recipe comes in to existence? For example, can you make a recipe by accident? What if—unknown to the person who claims to have invented a new recipe—a strikingly similar one was already known to some other culture? Under what conditions can we say that two recipes are, in fact, the same? To answer these questions, we must presumably get clear on a host of related issues, most importantly the role that individual aspects—such as taste, ingredients, tools, contexts of consumption—play in determining the identity of a recipe.

From a philosophical angle, then, a study of recipes calls first of all for the application of the conceptual tools of metaphysics and social ontology to rethink culinary items. The first three chapters of this part of the volume make a contribution precisely in this direction.

In Chapter 1, Andrea Borghini connects all of the different chapters in the volume while introducing some open conceptual questions about recipes that must be addressed in the coming years, if we want to improve our understanding of these culinary items in designing diets (e.g., improving communication between nutritionist and patients), identifying culinary cultures (e.g., adequately representing diverse cultures), settling legal disputes about food labels or recipes (e.g., labeling of vegan meats and dairies), and so on. The questions discussed include: Are recipes procedures or culinary items? What is the relationship between a recipe and its representations? How do recipes come to be, go out of existence, and what keeps them in existence? Are there any indispensable elements in a recipe? Who has the authority to determine the existence and the identity conditions of a recipe? Borghini contends that, though a serious analysis of these questions must rest on a cross-disciplinary effort, philosophers are particularly suited to lead efforts to address them.

In Chapter 2, Sanna Hirvonen takes issue with the kind of things recipes are. Here, there are two main options. First, they could be socially constructed entities, that is, entities that come into existence as the result of human *fiat*. A good example of such an entity is marriage. Indeed, that two people to form a married couple is the result of a human *fiat* pronounced by an authorized person. Recipes, according to this first option, would be analogous to marriages: they come into existence as a result of a (authorized) person declaring that something is a recipe.

A second option—call it realism—would be to conceive of recipes as entities that don't need human *fiat* to come into existence. It is important, however, to distinguish the idea that something doesn't require human *fiat* to come into existence from the idea that something doesn't depend at all on humans. Take the Moon. Not only does it exist independently of any kind of human *fiat*, but it is completely independent of human beings too. Had the universe developed differently such that there would be no humans, the Moon would still be as it is. Now compare this with human heartbeats. They do exist and do so independently of human *fiat*. Yet, heartbeats do depend on us, as without humans there would be no human heartbeats. Accordingly, someone wishing to argue in favor of a realist theory of recipes could mean either one of two things: that recipes don't need human *fiat* to come into existence and are independent of us or that recipes don't need human *fiat* to come into existence, but are still somehow dependent on us. According to Hirvonen, the latter form of realism is true of recipes. She argues that recipes are dependent realist entities insofar as they merely are automatic by-products of our cooking practices.

In Chapter 3, Davide Bordini explores further the metaphysics of recipes and discusses the role of taste in fixing their identity. A controversial albeit tempting thesis may be to think that the identity of a recipe should, at least in part, be determined by its taste. In other words, at least part of what it is to be a certain recipe is to be conducive to the generation of food that tastes a certain way. Indeed, why in the first place would we have an interest in recipes if there wasn't this connection between recipe and taste? According to Bordini, however, this idea is mistaken: if there is a connection between recipes and taste, it is not, surprisingly, one that fixes their identity conditions.

A different question one might ask about recipes is the following: what can recipes possibly do? In other words, what range of features of a dish can a recipe determine? In the next chapter, Andrea Borghini and Gabriele Ferretti take up this question from a specific angle, by exploring a new avenue to show that recipes enable and can be used to perfect the relationships between cooks and diners. In fact, recipes are implicitly used as a tool by cooks to communicate to an average diner that a dish should be consumed in a certain way. In their contribution, Borghini and Ferretti focus on those characteristics of a dish that can be designed by a cook so that it affords certain procedural knowledge to the diner. The authors call those characteristics the *architecture* of that dish. A dish, when viewed from an architectural lens, conveys a fundamentally *narrative* framework, with specific perceptual and practical aspects, which the authors describe by drawing upon the literature in cognitive science on practical knowledge and affordances.

The last two chapters of this section, finally, have a different aim. Overall, their goal is to somewhat challenge the assumption that recipes play a universal role with regard to the replication and dissemination of dishes (individual, consumable food items) and, thus, bring into conversation the conceptual work of the first four chapters with cutting-edge field research. Written by, respectively, an anthropologist and an ethnographer, these chapters both focus on Japanese culinary culture and serve as a wonderful demonstration of the complexity of the relation between ingredients and foodstuff.

Merry "Corky" White's chapter, first, focuses on the relation, or lack thereof, between recipes and dishes in the Japanese kitchen. As she makes clear, recipes do exist in the Japanese kitchen and the cookbook business is as thriving in Japan as elsewhere. However, she argues that within the Japanese culinary kitchen, the emphasis is less on the creation and realization of recipes and more on the idea of—to put it metaphorically—somehow becoming oneself a recipe. In other words, she argues that the abstract role played by recipes in other culinary cultures is replaced in the Japanese context by other more concrete notions, like the training of the body, the internalization of a procedure, the mastery of specific tools, and the assimilation—up to the point of their becoming a second nature—of more or less general principles of Japanese cooking. These include principles about preparation, but also about the implementation of a multisensory approach to dining, with an emphasis on textures and colors. As White explains, however, this perspective is less about the production of Japanese food than about the culinary incarnation of a certain Japanese ethos according to which mastery is not about consistency in applying formulas or recipes but rather about being tuned in to outside demands, such as the ones of food itself.

In the final chapter of this first part of the volume, Maya Hey turns her ethnographer's eye to a specific Japanese case study, namely the working of the natural sake brewery Terada Honké. She highlights the entanglement of the different affective and value components that go into the production of the drink and, in particular, emphasizes the symbiotic relation that obtains between the brewery, the microbial life it hosts, which is an integral part of the process of production of the sake, and the workers themselves.

The central concept Hey uses is *attunement*, with the idea that producing sake at Terada Honké is less a matter of following a recipe than being attuned to a certain process and to the microbial life that permits the natural fermentation of the end product. The notion of attunement provides a lesson for the theory of recipes, as it shows that, at least in this instance, producing food is not a mere matter of imposing a form on ingredients, but of getting attuned with ingredients, such as microbial life (for a parallel discussion focusing on beer, see the chapters in Hales 2007, especially ch. 8).

Further Reading

Borghini, A. (2015). "What Is a Recipe?" In: *Journal of Agricultural and Environmental Ethics*, 28: 719–38.

Borghini, A. and Piras. N. (2020). "The Philosophy of Food: Recipes Between Arts and Algorithms," In: Special issue of *Humana.Mente*, 13 (38).

Engisch, P. (2020). "Recipes and Culinary Creativity: The Noma Legacy." In: *Humana. Mente*, 13 (38): 61–82.

Hales, S. (2007). *Beer and Philosophy. The Unexamined Beer Isn't Worth Drinking*. Malden, MA: Blackwell.

Korsmeyer, C. (1999). *Making Sense of Taste*. Ithaca, NY: Cornell University Press.

Strohl, Matthew (2019). "On Culinary Authenticity." In: *Journal of Aesthetics and Art Criticism*, 77 (2): 157–67.

Seven Philosophical Questions about Recipes

Andrea Borghini

Introduction

A restaurant menu, the guidelines for a low-carb diet, a legal dispute about vegan dairies, the first-ever episode of a TV show dedicated to food starring Julia Child—all the items on this apparently disordered list share the use of recipes and remind us of how pervasive they can be in our culture. The list is of course incomplete and the chapters in this volume bear witness to that: we discuss recipes with friends, we read about them in fiction novels, we fancy them in books about the future of food, and we can presume that recipes play a key role in our evolution too.

Everything about food, including recipes, has attained overwhelming attention at all societal levels and on a global scale in the past two decades. By now, food is a key vector for social and diplomatic initiatives (see the chapter by Mendelson-Forman in this volume); it is used as a form of entertainment on TV (see the chapter by Grosglik & Kyle in this volume) and on the Internet (e.g., by sharing food experiences through social media or watching *mukbang*); moreover, cooking and dining can arguably be regarded as forms of public art (see Borghini & Baldini 2021).

In short, recipes and other food items carry crucial soft power in global societies. With power, come ethical and socio-political responsibilities. To allocate them, we must also have a grip of the employed concepts. It is here at the intersection of a theoretical work intertwined with value-laden issues that I believe the work of philosophers is most needed (for a series of parallel approaches unrelated to food, see Burgess, Cappelen & Plankett 2020).

In this chapter, I map out some core philosophical questions that recipes elicit in an effort to collaborate with scholars studying the multiple roles of food in global societies—aesthetic, socio-political, environmental, ethical, legal, cultural, medical, economic, educational, and so on.

Are Recipes Procedures or Culinary Items?

I shall begin with the divide between two radically different conceptions of recipes that I propose to label *procedural* and *culinary*. Hence, the question:

(1) Are recipes procedures or culinary items?

According to the first conception, a recipe is a *procedure* to deliver an end result—a consumable item, a certain kind of food. The distinguishing feature of this conception is that there is a fundamental ontological distinction between recipes and the foods they deliver: we consume, taste, and buy foods, but we cannot consume, taste, and buy recipes. Recipes—under the procedural conception—are not strictly speaking culinary items; rather, they are tools to deliver culinary items. In the same way that one needs an espresso machine to make a cup of espresso coffee, one needs a recipe for japchae to make a bowl of it.

The procedural conception can be elaborated in a number of directions. To illustrate, here are three important theoretical junctions for its development. (i) We have procedures of all sorts and only some of them will count as recipe-procedures—yet, which ones? For instance, "Go to the woods, pick some wild berries, and eat them" may not be regarded as a recipe-procedure, but some other form of procedure related to food consumption. (ii) Specific recipes will be tied to specific procedures—yet, which ones? Consider the following procedure: "Mix some wheat flour, water, a pinch of salt and some baker's yeast, let the whole thing rest for a couple of hours and cook in the oven for 45-60 minutes." Is this a recipe-procedure for bread? One may argue that it is not specific enough and, thus, should rather be seen as a more generic procedure linked to some specific recipe-procedures (we will return to levels of generality with the sixth question). (iii) Which forms of representation are suitable for recipe-procedures? Plausible candidates may include recipe books, videos, people's memories, and computer programs, but are all representations suitable? Should we regard them as equally valuable in representing a recipe?

The second conception of recipes—the culinary conception—differs from the procedural one because it sees recipes as culinary items, that is, as entities that have taste profiles, that can be consumed and experienced. The divide is, thus, ontological: according to the culinary conception, one cannot tell apart procedure and food because the two aspects are ingrained in several respects. In fact, procedures often do not end once the food is ready to be consumed, but involve also consumption itself (see the chapter by Borghini & Ferretti in this volume for additional examples on how recipes and consumption are ingrained). For example, at an ice-cream parlor preparing the ice cream to be scooped into a cone, making the ice cream, and preparing the cone go hand in hand; or, think of the signature recipe by Noma chef René Redzepi "The Hen and the Egg," in which the food preparation is completed at the table with the help of the guests. Moreover, when consuming food we are not blind to procedures, as if we could easily separate the two. The values we attach to specific foods most often depend on the procedures: this is true not only for aesthetic values but also for environmental, economic, social, affective, and other varieties of values. While it is perfectly intuitive to define— say—an hot-air balloon, regardless of the specific procedure employed to produce it, when it comes to food, we do value how it was made. Thus, procedures for making food often encompass the food consumption, while the food consumption is often understood in association with the procedure. This intertwinement is at the core of the culinary conception of recipes.

The divide between the two conceptions of recipes can be illustrated through certain semantic issues regarding the names of culinary items. Consider, for example, the term "japchae." Does the term name a recipe, or does it name the culinary items delivered by a plurality of recipes? According to the procedural conception, it is the latter: we have plenty of procedures to make japchae and those are its recipes; thus, "japchae" stands for all food items that are delivered through such procedures. According to the culinary conception, instead, it is the former: "japchae" stands for a recipe. So, for the culinary conception, from a restaurant menu we order recipes, which we understand will come in one or more instances (e.g., three bowls of japchae, one for each diner); for the procedural conception, instead, we order foods and we may or may not be told what the recipe to make such foods was.

Both conceptions find some appeal in everyday ways of talking about recipes. Procedures seem to come under the spotlight when we compare recipes with a specific end result on the horizon. A vegan recipe for Genoese focaccia bread, for instance, aims at producing a food that meets the standards of Genoese focaccia even though it is made from different ingredients (no animal fat) and with slightly different procedures. Here the procedure is regarded as a tool, which is used to get to a certain result. However, when we discuss the cultural heritage of the people from Genoa and surrounding areas, and we include focaccia bread among the culturally inherited items, it is equally intuitive that we are protecting both the procedure and the food, where the two are indissolubly intertwined.

A first task ahead is, then, to devise adequate conceptual avenues to resolve the tension between the two conceptions of recipes.

Are Recipes Types or Tokens?

When it comes to food some people like repetition. For example, as narrated by Joe Pinsker in a recent article for *The Atlantic*, "Vern Loomis, a retired structural draftsman in West Bloomfield, Michigan, had a standard office lunch: a peanut-butter sandwich, with various fruit, vegetable, and dessert accompaniments. He ate this, he estimates, nearly every workday for about 25 years" (2019). But, one may ask, was Loomis's daily lunch really always *the same*?

The answer is, quite obviously, "No." The fruits might change, ditto for the vegetables, or the type and quality of the bread and of the peanut butter. Not to mention that Loomis's himself—his taste, his appetite, his mood—was not always the same, and that over time the office environment changed too.

This negative answer, however, holds only if one gets particular about Loomis and his food. But, should one? After all, it seems perfectly alright to refer to Loomis in the article as the same person throughout those twenty-five years; why should one have a different mind about the food?

The two opinions just stated exemplify the second conceptual question that surrounds recipes (see Borghini 2010):

(2) Should we regard recipes as tokens or types?

To illustrate with another simpler and imaginary example, suppose that during those twenty-five long years, Loomis would make himself two eggs sunny side up every morning for breakfast—did he thereby make *the same recipe* every morning?

The answer to this question seems unavoidably linked to a more fundamental one: when is it that two recipes are the same? Whether we think of recipes as procedures or as culinary items, no two procedures and no two culinary items will be exactly the same, strictly speaking. Yet, they will be the same, if we speak "loosely," as Chisholm famously put it (1969). So, the issue seems to be whether, when we speak of recipes, we are speaking strictly or loosely.

As we address the question of whether recipes are types or tokens, another set of issues unavoidably come into play. This is the relationship that there is between a recipe and the food that is associated with it. If Loomis was cooking two eggs sunny side up every morning, every morning he was making some food (which presumably he would consume before leaving home). So, the recipe for sunny side up eggs he was following, whether a type or a token, was leading up to some specific food. Call this food a *dish* e.g., a two eggs sunny side up on a plate, in the case of Loomis's breakfast).

The specific stance one wants to take about whether recipes are types or tokens may, in fact, depend on how one sees the relationship between dishes and recipes. Here are some hints, which await further theoretical development: (i) Can the same recipe lead to more than one dish? It can, only if it is a type, so that the same type of procedure or culinary item can be delivered in multiple different instances. (ii) Can the same dish have more than one recipe for it? It can, only if the identity of the dish is not strictly tied to a specific recipe that delivers it. (iii) Can there be a dish with no recipe? This question requires discussing to what extent the idea of a dish is imbued with cultural elements, in particular whether in the absence of a procedure—no matter how simple (e.g., eating cherries directly from the tree)— we would still be willing to retain what we consume as a dish or even food (for a discussion of this point, see Hirvonen's chapter in this volume and also Borghini & Piras 2020c).

I have emphasized here the purely theoretical sides of these interrogatives. The conceptual density, however, should not betray their importance for matters of everyday relevance. To illustrate, the repeatability of recipes is key to assess intellectual property right issues regarding them (see the chapter by Bonadio & Weissenberger in this volume) and to shed light on the cultural significance of so-called signature recipes (see Bacchini 2020 as well as Borghini & Gandolini 2020).

What Is the Relationship between a Recipe and Its Representations?

If we read them at face value, most recipe books seem to be written with the (implicit or explicit) assumption that recipes are types—not tokens. In fact, a recipe book (implicitly or explicitly) pretends to guide a reader in delivering (or imagining to deliver) certain dishes. Similar considerations may hold for TV shows instructing viewers on how to make certain dishes, starting at least with Julia Child's first-ever episode of a TV show entirely dedicated to cooking, which first aired on February 2, 1963, and featured *boeuf Bourguignon*. Clearly, not all TV shows devoted to food and not all social media acts dealing with food aim to represent recipes (see Grosglik & Kyle's chapter in this volume and also Pollan 2009), but, many do. Here, however, arises our third conceptual question:

(3) What is the relationship between a recipe and its representations?

I illustrate the difficulty of this question by considering three aspects of a representation: the medium, the degree of adequacy, and the representability of the recipe.

(i) *The medium.* To appreciate the complexity of question (3), we shall first reflect on the relevance of the medium for determining the identity of a recipe. Recipes have been represented via different media. These include writing (e.g., recipe books, novels, private journals), videos (e.g., in TV shows, documentaries, social media, private videos), and speaking (e.g., in rhymed recipes, word of mouth). Is the identity of a recipe dependent on the specific media used to represent it? If Julia Child would have made a radio show, rather than a TV show, would her boeuf Bourguignon recipe have been the same as the one we see in her video?

For a parallel, consider a song—say African Jazz Mokili Mobimba—relayed through different media—a vinyl record, a CD, or a live performance—by the same band. No matter the medium, we regard the song as the same. This is not to downplay the significance of the medium to the overall value of the auditory experience, but the crucial point is that the medium is not in and of itself a discriminating element for the identity of the song. Could we say the same about recipes? Probably not, as the introduction of video recordings of recipes brought a depth of representation that sets apart the cooking instructions relayed in video from those provided in writing or speaking. This is just a hint, though, as the matter deserves closer attention.

(ii) *The degree of fidelity.* The conceptual questions regarding the link between recipes and their representations are not exhausted with a consideration of the media. In fact, it is typically far more disputed whether a certain representation of a recipe conveys information to the reader that is sufficiently detailed and accurate enough for (actual or imagined) replication. Borrowing a metaphor employed to describe the quality of the reproduction of music sounds, I call the type of information its "degree of fidelity." So, high-fidelity recipes are those that convey excellent quality of information, which is detailed and accurate, while low-fidelity recipes are those conveying poor quality of information, which is missing in crucial respects and possibly misleading.

Although the representation of recipes has become relatively standardized in a format providing a list of ingredients followed by some guidelines, the degree of fidelity can vary greatly. America's Test Kitchen recipe for hardboiled eggs is highly detailed (America's Test Kitchen 2018), to the point of possibly being intimidating, while other books may leave much room for discretion, for example, by providing a wide range of cooking time, or by leaving unspecified the initial water temperature or the type of pot to be used.

The degree of fidelity exercises a normative pressure over the reader, suggesting how a recipe *ought to be* reproduced and, thus, influencing its development over time.

For this reason, it is a critical element for understanding and possibly predicting how recipes evolve over time and across different communities. Although implicitly it has come under the scrutiny of scholars working on the history of recipes (see, for example, Floyd & Forster 2003; Elias 2017), it deserves a closer theoretical analysis to be systematically used across various fields of study.

(iii) *The representability of the recipe*. Many recipes are passed down over generations and circulated between peers, but are all recipes representable? Supposing that they are, does representability imply transmissibility? Case studies to be considered for this discussion include: signature recipes, that is, those that can be arguably made only by certain people because of their special skills (think of Jirō Ono's sushi); recipes whose identity is rooted in improvisation (for a parallel, see Bertinetto 2020); recipes that owe their identity to special ingredients (e.g., a rare fish that will never be eaten again) or special contextual conditions (e.g., *your* wedding cake).

Obviously, we can film Jirō Ono making sushi as well as a cook improvising a recipe or preparing a wedding cake. As for the recipes involving special ingredients or environmental conditions, we could still have specifics for them. Finally, Jirō and the cook improvising a recipe may write down some guidelines for others that aim to follow their steps. This line of reply seems fair. Yet, having a video recording or some guidelines does not, in itself, guarantee that the recipe is transmissible, because there may be no one in the future with Jirō's abilities and because one may argue that the whole point of improvisation is that its repetition is a different sort of action. As for the recipes involving special ingredients or conditions, they would not be replicable in light of such "material" constraints. Hence, some recipes seem not to be transmissible, for limitations related to expertise, the type of action involved, and material circumstances.

One may at this point try to push the line further and argue that, for some recipes, we cannot even produce an adequate representation. Can you really represent Jirō's abilities of sushi making, his expertise? What would such a representation look like? (Ways of answering these questions may be suggested by the debate on the relationship between know-how and knowledge; see Pavese 2016, 2018.)

To be called into question are, then, the ideas that *all* recipes must be transmissible and representable because for some recipes, no matter what your conception is, there may be no possible avenue for transmissibility or representation.

How Do Recipes Come To Be, Cease to Exist, and What Keeps Them in Existence?

The next question on the list is taken straight from the standard repertoire of questions that philosophers pose about any sort of thing that comes under their scrutiny. If there are recipes, what governs their existence? More precisely:

(4) How do recipes come to be, cease to exist, and what keeps them in existence?

There is a quick way out of this question, namely the so-called Platonism about recipes (see Borghini 2015), according to which recipes do not come to be and never cease to exist—they are eternal, like some people say that sets, geometrical proportions, or numbers are eternal. Platonism about recipes, however, faces some important challenges. Most notably it must provide an explanation of the fact that we do not have high-fidelity representations for recipes, while we do have some neat representations for sets, numbers, and geometrical proportions. Thus, for the latter it seems more plausible to argue that they enjoy an ideal, eternal status of existence, but can we say that about recipes? This is not enough, of course, to discard Platonism about recipes, but it may be enough to suggest that we should also consider alternative options.

It is useful to build a discussion about the modes of existence of recipes by way of different sorts of examples. I consider three here.

(i) *Recipes by accident.* The first set of examples I want to consider serves to reflect on how recipes come into being and deal with episodes where a recipe originates from some accidental procedure. Imagine a time in the past when no human had a recipe for eating corn and no human had tried it and imagine a community living in an area surrounded by corn fields. One day a fire erupts in some corn fields, right when the kernels on the cobs are ripe. The people visit the field after the fire and find some cooked corn. Attracted by the sweet smell, they try it, discovering that it is delicious and nutritious. Did the community just witness an accidental execution of the recipe for corn on the cob?

While this example is fictitious, the literature on recipes is filled with tropes regarding amazing foods that were supposedly discovered by accident. The putative list includes nachos, popsicles, sandwiches, potato chips, brandy, cheese left in a cave, and many more items that may be among your favorites. The key issue for present purposes is: when exactly did the recipe come into existence?

If we keep to one side the Platonist answer (i.e., the recipe existed all along), we are left with two main options. The first is that the recipe came to exist by accident—for example, the fire, literally speaking, made corn on the cob for the first time. The second is that the recipe came to exist only once someone traced what happened (e.g., the fire cooked the fruits of the corn plants) and singled out that process as a recipe-making process. This second option has further ramifications, which we shall explore in a moment.

The issue at stake is by no means abstruse. If recipes can be executed also by non-human agents, we have a straightforward argument to claim that a machine can make the same recipes that humans can make, regardless of whether machines can "reason" like humans do (see Tuccini et al. 2020). This may well be a delicate topic to discuss in the years to come, when meals (including, e.g., traditional dishes) may be prepared by non-human agents.

(ii) *Unnamed recipes.* Let us now focus on the second camp described above, according to which recipes exist only once someone traces the recipe-making process. We can use a second set of examples to show that this camp can be further divided down into quite distinct positions.

Massimo Bottura famously named one of his signature recipes *Oops I dropped the lemon tart!* after dropping the lemon tart in the kitchen. Now, imagine a parallel cook that, on the same evening that Bottura comes up with his new signature recipe, drops their lemon tart in the kitchen and decides, nonetheless, to serve it to the client, after explaining that, unfortunately, the lemon tart had been dropped (but that it was nonetheless safe to eat). Bottura gave a name to his recipe, thereby completely changing the expectations of the diner and perhaps the meaning of the dish that was being served to them; the other cook did nothing of the sort, they simply offered their excuses to the client and decided not to charge them for the dessert. For present purposes, the question is: did the two cooks serve the same recipe?

Cases where different communities prepare foods from nearly identical recipes, albeit using different names for them, are relatively widespread. For instance, farinata, fainè, cecina, and socca may be regarded as linguistic variants of the same recipe. But, should they? Or should they be regarded as different recipes?

These examples remark the putative relevance of performative acts in determining the existence of a recipe: until Bottura named his recipe, such a recipe arguably did not exist (see also Borghini 2015 on this). At the same time, while performatives may be regarded as sometimes necessary, they are arguably not sufficient in determining the existence of a recipe—otherwise one could turn, say, a bowl of japchae into a pizza margherita just by changing its name. Also, not everyone can be in charge of the performative act: just like for works of art, only the artist (typically) has the power to determine the name of the artwork, so with recipes only certain people have the authority to determine their name (I will come back to this in the last question I will examine).

(iii) *Recipes without dishes.* A third set of examples would serve us to reflect on the conditions under which recipes may continue to exist or cease to exist. As Haber (in this volume) suggests, recipes are sometimes used not to actually prepare foods, but to imagine ways of preparing and consuming foods that perhaps no one will ever eat. From here, it's just a short step to ask whether there are recipes for dishes (i.e., foods that we can eat) that do not yet exist, and whether there are recipes for inedible dishes. These questions parallel those regarding sounds that we cannot hear or that do not exist (Cray 2016) and architectural plans for buildings and cities that cannot exist or that we cannot inhabit (e.g., like those described by Escher or Calvino).

The matter is delicate because if we admit that there are recipes that cannot deliver a dish, then the existence of a recipe is independent of whether or not it is actually executed. A recipe could come to be and continue to exist regardless of whether someone cooks it. Yet, we could ask, is it indispensable that someone keeps thinking or talking about it? In other words, should the recipe be part of a culinary world, regardless of whether people (can) cook it or not?

The three sets of examples examined bring to the surface conceptual issues that have received sparse attention in the literature on recipes and that urgently need to be addressed, if we aim to create a solid common ground for conversing about value-laden themes related to recipes and culinary culture.

Are There Indispensable Elements in a Recipe?

To some it may seem even obvious that an ice-cream cone must be served in a cone, or that French fries must be made from potatoes. These examples illustrate the fact that people tend to associate certain recipes with some obligated passages. Other times, the obligation is somewhat enforced. To protect the integrity of *pesto alla genovese*, the

Consorzio del pesto genovese requires, among other things, that the basil used for the recipe be from the cultivar "basilico genovese." Yet, most diners cannot access such a cultivar on a daily basis; hence, they cannot claim to be making pesto alla genovese, at least according to the Consorzio.

Considerations regarding ingredients and procedures lead to our fifth question:

(5) Are there indispensable elements in a recipe, that is, elements without which the recipe would be disrupted (see Borghini 2011)?

Notice that the question asks about indispensable conditions for a specific recipe; we could raise also a parallel and more general question, namely, do all recipes have some indispensable elements? For example, the fact that they have to have some ingredients or that they have to lead up—if properly executed under favorable conditions—to a food. I discussed many conceptual nuances of this question in the previous section, when considering the elements that are key to the existence of recipes.

Question (5) finds parallels in other fields too. Can you execute Chopin's first piano concerto without a piano? Can you do it without a conductor? Or without cellos? When it comes to recipes, there are many plausible candidates to be counted as indispensable. Taste is a tempting initial option to consider. Bordini (in this volume) discusses at length the prospects of taste being considered as indispensable, reaching a skeptical conclusion (and, on this, see also Korsmeyer's chapter on recipes providing a taste of the past). Cognate notions of taste that may be regarded as key include after-taste (see Frischhut & Torrengo's chapter in this volume) as well as style (see Todd's chapter in this volume). Other obvious candidates are ingredients, as the examples of an ice-cream cone and French fries suggest. But, even with ingredients, one may wonder whether they seem only contextually indispensable. Does it take an animal to make meat or to make a dairy product? Possibly not (see also Wurgaft's chapter in this volume) and I shall leave the issue open. But, we could fancy that it does not take a "real" cone to make an ice-cream cone and it does not take "real" potatoes (*Solanum tuberosum*) to make French fries.

What about other candidates? We may cite the setting, as certain foods are meant to be shared from a plate (e.g., injera), or eaten with hands or with special tools (e.g., a crab cracker). Other foods—such as street food—may seem to depend upon place. Another interesting element is the *role in a meal*. For instance, a wedding cake plays a very specific function within a special meal, at least within some culinary traditions (see Charsley 1997): it must come at the end of the meal, be cut by the couple, and be served to all guests. Without performing such functions, the cake cannot be considered a wedding cake. Or consider *canapés* and *amouse bouches*, which are conceived to be served at the beginning of a meal. Of course, a cook may serve these items at later stages of a meal, but the question is: would they still be the same recipe?

Other interesting cases emerge when we consider recipes that have a value based on the action that the cook has to perform. For instance, this is the case with "handmade and homemade" recipes, which tend to be bestowed a special status. Thus, for instance, handmade and homemade tagliatelle may arguably be regarded as something other than machine-made tagliatelle bought from a supermarket: the two recipes share only part of their name, ditto for the dishes that they deliver. To offer another illustration, in the Japanese culinary context, what matters is not the end product, but rather the type and quality of the effort produced in delivering such an end product (see White's chapter in this volume). Finally, we may cite the case of fermented foods, whose recipe crucially rests on a certain relationship between the food and the producer (see Hey's chapter in this volume, which discusses the practice of making sake).

All these examples suggest that culinary cultures are filled with apparent obligations, norms directing diners as to how, when, and with whom to consume the food and even how to produce it. But, the normative demands that people can make on a recipe are not by themselves proof that we are conceptually bound to claim that the recipe cannot exist unless those demands are met. The fact that most people expect an ice-cream cone to be served in a cone may not be enough to prove that, unless it is, it is not any longer an ice-cream cone. How far should one go? Is one willing to claim that a bowl of amatriciana could be served in a pill, which provides an analogous gastronomic experience to the "real" pasta? As these points demonstrate, a thorough investigation into the relationship between culinary norms and conceptual limits of the culinary entities involved is needed.

Is It Possible to Arrange Recipes into Taxonomies?

There are so many recipes that it becomes imperative to try and sort them out in some way or other. Recipe books, repositories, and archives typically organize them by kinds, such as soups, salads, sandwiches, or desserts. But we could also group recipes based on many other criteria: the procedures that they share (e.g., whether they require, at some point of the process, frying, baking, or freezing the food); the types of ingredients that they involve (e.g., vegan recipes, seasonal recipes, regional recipes); their nutritional values (e.g., low-calorie recipes, low-sugar recipes, energy-boosting recipes); their socio-economic profile (e.g., family recipes, gourmet recipes); their national profile (e.g., Mexican recipes, Lebanese recipes); and so on.

In fact, these attempts at ordering the universe of recipes may contribute to generating the opposite impression—that such a universe is actually an ontological jungle. Is there any hope to find some order in this jungle? Or, to put it more formally:

(6) Is it possible to arrange recipes into taxonomies?

Consider, for example, pizza. Talking about the eating preferences of Min, a speaker may note: "Min likes pizza, especially marinara, with extra red pepper." By uttering this sentence, the speaker is actually utilizing some implicit taxonomy: among all pizzas (the most general taxon), Min likes pizza marinara (a taxon included under pizza) and, among the latter, Min likes pizza marinara with extra red pepper (a taxon included under pizza marinara). Now compare this sentence with: "Min likes flowers, especially mimosa (*Acacia dealbata*) flowers, with large and bright flower-heads." The latter would describe Min's preferences with respect to a specific taxonomic ordering: among all plants producing flowers, Min likes mimosa, in a specific moment of its seasonal development. Could we bring recipes to be arranged in taxonomies that are as cogent as those used for living entities?

Biological taxa supposedly track down causal features of living entities (even though the extent within which they do so is questionable; see, e.g., Ereshefsky 2000). Which causal features could taxonomies for recipes track down? We do have some plausible candidates here, emerging from the hard sciences: metabolic processes; cooking techniques; environmental impact; material features of the end product, such as consistency, perishability, taste-properties. Depending on the reasons we have for employing a taxonomy, we can pick one set of those causal features or another.

This set of causal features of recipes, however, leaves out important roles that recipes play in our lives. Recipes are shaped by and shape socio-economic conditions, identities that connote political orientation, religion, gender, race, community, ethical values, aesthetic values, and so on. It is important, then, to include also taxonomies that track down the causal features of soft sciences.

The answer to question (6), hence, may begin by remarking that we can arrange recipes in taxonomies based on some set of causal features borrowed from hard and soft sciences. Which sets of features are to be avoided and which ones seem most promising, however, remain to be ascertained.

It is worthwhile also to mention at least another conceptual difficulty related to taxonomies, namely the fact that they vary from one culinary context to another. To stay with the example of pizza, the taxonomies of pizza one finds in menus in Italy and in the United States arguably do not align. While in Italy a marinara is regarded as a low-level taxon of pizza (the equivalent of a species in the Linnean hierarchy), in the United States a marinara could be made in one of many styles—for instance, New York-, Chicago-, Miami-, New England-, Buffalo-style (each of which would be the equivalent of a species in the Linnean hierarchy). Or, consider cookies. In the United States, *biscotti* and cookies are two separate taxa, both falling under biscuits; in Italy, instead, biscotti and cookies are part of the very same taxon. Other typical misalignments may regard the culinary role of the food, for instance, whether a tomato is regarded as a fruit or as a vegetable in the specific context, or whether a cheese is regarded as a dessert or as an appetizer.

These sorts of distinctions become important once we trade food products between countries. Thus, for instance, a company producing biscotti in Italy, where they are also referred to as a type of cookie on the packaging, cannot arguably refer to them as "cookies" in the United States market.

Who Has the Authority to Determine the Existence and the Identity Conditions of a Recipe?

In March 2015, BuzzFeed published a video of just over three minutes titled "Mexican People Try Taco Bell for the First Time," which as of March 7, 2021, has been watched over 19 million times just on the *YouTube* channel run by BuzzFeed. In this unverified video, a number of Mexicans scrutinize Taco Bell's tacos, discussing their taste and authenticity, while eating them for the first time. The recording is part of a popular series of videos dedicated to questioning the cultural authenticity of food served in well-known restaurant chains. The intended tone of the series is entertaining. But, they betray an underlying delicate question: who has the authority to decide whether or not Taco Bell makes tacos? Could Mexican people object to the fact that Taco Bell claims to be selling tacos? Could they object to the very name Taco Bell? Hence, a more general question that deserves closer theoretical attention:

(7) Who has the authority to determine the existence and the identity of a recipe?

To further illustrate the importance of the matter, we can consider also the case of geographical indications, for example, products such as Champagne, Parmigiano Reggiano, Darjeeling tea. In these instances, producers must conform their recipes to a series of guidelines referred to as a "disciplinary of production" established by a consortium. The body has the authority to determine whether the end product deserves to be called "Champagne," "Parmigiano," or "Darjeeling." Now, elaborating on the videos by BuzzFeed and to play the devil's advocate, one may note that Mexican cuisine is protected under the UNESCO List of Intangible Cultural Heritage and, therefore, Mexican traditional recipes—such as tacos—should be protected (see also Engisch's chapter in this volume on the representational powers of traditional foods). If the label "Champagne," at least within the boundaries of the European Union, can be reserved only to wines produced according to certain standards, why not claim that also the label "tacos" should be reserved only to foods produced in accordance with certain standards?

An entry point into questions of authority rests on the concept of authoriality: who can be regarded as the author of a recipe, and in what ways are authors linked to the exercise of an authority to determine the identity of a recipe and of its end product? Borghini & Gandolini (2020) suggest that authoriality takes four different forms, based on the kinds of recipes that are under consideration: (i) *open recipes*, like pizza margherita or soft vegetarian tacos, where the authoriality seems to be open to interpretation for potentially any user; (ii) *geographical indications*, where each member within a consortium is bestowed special authority; (iii) *brand recipes*, where the recipes to make a certain branded product (e.g., Nutella or Coca-Cola) may be kept secret and managed by the company through the branding of the end product; and (iv) *signature dishes*, where the chef—not even the line cooks—is arguably the ultimate author of the dish.

Regardless of how many and what kinds of authors a recipe may have, another issue remains: how is such authority exercised? Borghini (2015) suggests that a recipe requires a performative utterance on the part of the cook. Yet, do performatives require a public context? What if the cook is the only one who will ever see the food? Think, for instance, of the case of a prisoner on an island who is cooking a last meal, having no possibility of leaving a trace of what they cook. Or, imagine a cook who possesses no linguistic abilities having grown on a deserted island but who ends up being a really good cook. Hirvonen (in this volume) rightly questions the need for a performative to claim the identity of a recipe, and more needs to be said in regard to this point.

Disentangling the riddles of authoriality and authority is key to resolve a wide range of disputes involving recipes and food, including those concerning cultural heritage and cultural appropriation (see the chapter by Barnhill & Bonotti in this volume), and intellectual property rights over signature dishes (see the chapter by Bonadio & Weissenberger in this volume).

Conclusion

The seven questions I have presented here do not of course exhaust all the conceptual issues that have arisen and that will arise about recipes. Rather, they absolve three other functions. First, they prove that recipes and culinary items can be a rich terrain of study not only for ethicists, aestheticians, or political philosophers but also for philosophers with a theoretical inclination. Second, they model a role that theoretically inclined philosophers can play within the broader community of scholars and practitioners who are invested in studying food, namely, to rethink and negotiate key conceptual aspects. Finally, they suggest in what ways the chapters contained in this volume jointly contribute to foster the study of recipes from a philosophical angle.

Recipes Without Makers

Sanna Hirvonen

Introduction

Recipes are a cornerstone of all culinary cultures. They enable people to cook a variety of dishes, and they are essential in transferring that knowledge from location to location and from one generation to the next. Many learn cooking by observing, but recipes allow us to also learn to make dishes that come from outside of our own cultures. Many of us nowadays feed ourselves with an entirely multicultural diet because we now have access to recipes from all over the world.

When we think of recipes, what typically comes to mind is either a written recipe, say, in a cookbook, or a verbal narration of how to create a dish. As a first approximation for what recipes are, we can say that a recipe describes the steps in the cooking which results in a type of dish. The existing theories mostly agree in broad outlines as to what recipes are, but important questions remain about their identity conditions. For example, are recipes akin to works of art in that they have authors or makers? When are two dishes instances of the same dish? How much can a recipe change before it becomes a different recipe, and who gets to decide what changes are allowed?

These questions might seem abstract, but we need to answer them to better understand what recipes are. That matters because of the rising importance of recipes in societies. For example, let us consider the cookbook industry. Sales volumes of printed cookbooks are increasing, and cooking websites have an ever-growing number of users. However, a large number of cooking websites recycle the same recipes that often originate in famous cookbooks, or they are variations or simplifications of such recipes. Is that ok, or should it be considered plagiarism? What about cases where a chef takes traditional or preexisting recipes from another culture and publishes them in a cookbook? Is there such a thing as cultural appropriation of recipes?

A theory of recipes may also have consequences on policy matters in the food industry. For example, the European Union protects regional ingredients, beverages, or dishes by forbidding others to use their names, which is why, for example, the name "Feta" can no longer be used for cheeses made outside of certain Greek regions, or why only the sparkling wines made in the Champagne region can be called "Champagne." These decisions may partly depend on what is considered to be the recipe for Feta or for Champagne, and thus whether it would be possible to replicate them in other regions.

To advance our understanding of recipes, a question we will focus on is how do recipes come into being? In this chapter I formulate a realist account of recipes and compare it to a constructivist account by Borghini (2015). Constructivists hold that the existence of recipes constitutively depends on a human *fiat*. So just as naming comes down to performative utterances like I name this ship *the Titanic*, the identity of a recipe is likewise dependent on a similar performance, once certain other conditions are met.

A constructivist theory would seem to have a simple answer to the question of the authorship of recipes. However, in this chapter I argue that constructivism faces challenges in making sense of some of our intuitive understanding of recipes. In particular, I argue that there are cases where someone intends to imitate an existing dish and fails but thinks they have succeeded. The resulting dish and the recipe for it may now come to live a life of their own, resulting in a novel recipe that originally came into being without the performative act that the constructivist argues is constitutively necessary.

As an alternative to constructivism, I defend a realist account of recipes and dishes. A dish's identity depends on its core ingredients and its flavor profile, texture, temperature, and look, and a recipe's identity depends on the identity of a dish. So, whenever a novel dish comes into being—in other words a dish whose ingredients and flavor profile are different enough to some previous dish—a new recipe also exists.

I should emphasize that there has been very little work on the nature of recipes, so constructivism and realism are by no means the only alternatives available. However, they represent two opposite points of view with constructivism emphasizing the role of human intentions and actions in recipe creation, whereas realism highlights how recipes depend on dishes themselves. Hopefully the discussion here will serve to map out some of the core positions and issues for the future study on recipes.

What Are Dishes?

Dishes as Anything Edible vs. Dishes as Preparations

Let us begin by clarifying the terminology we will use. In ordinary language the distinction between recipes and dishes is not always clear, as in "You're stuck inside from the coronavirus quarantine and want to stress bake. Here are recipes you can make when you don't have eggs, milk or butter" (Moniuszko 2020). However, strictly speaking recipes describe how to prepare a *dish*, and a dish is the resulting edible product—thus, if you are cooking, you are not making a recipe, but a dish. (Note that our discussion will equally apply to beverages, but for the sake of convenience we will include them under the term "dishes.") A third component we need is cooking: a dish is the stuff that results from cooking. As a starting point, let us say that a recipe is something that describes how to cook a type of dish. We should also distinguish between dish types, for example, *Pasta Carbonara*, and dish tokens, that is, concrete instances of *Pasta Carbonara*.

So, what are dishes? That is a difficult philosophical question in itself, so I cannot offer a full account here, but we will distinguish between some useful alternative accounts. It should be noted that since dishes and recipes are intimately connected, a complete theory of recipes should be ultimately paired with a complete theory of dishes. Borghini (2015) relies on a permissive view of dishes according to which anything edible to some agent is a dish for that agent. In other words, something can be a dish for an agent in a certain context but not for another agent, or not even for the same agent who is in a different context. The context sensitivity is needed to account for variability between different kinds of agents, for example, a dish for a dog may not be a dish for a human. What counts as a dish is also dependent on cultures since many humans eat things that others do not even consider edible.

The problem with the view that takes anything edible to be a dish is that it does not distinguish between mere foodstuff and dishes, which intuitively do differ. A more restricted view of dishes holds that for an edible thing to be a dish, some preparation must be involved. I think that definition is more in line with our intuitive notion of a dish. The problem is that not any preparation which leads to an edible result is a dish. Take salt dough for example. Salt dough requires preparation and it is edible, but it is not meant to be eaten and therefore intuitively it is not a dish (at least for humans). To rule out salt dough from the class of dishes, we may try to limit the range of preparations into those that aim to make foodstuff somehow *better to eat*, say, by making it safer, healthier, tastier, or more pleasant in other ways.

Here is an example of preparing a foodstuff so that it is better to eat from the animal world. The Japanese macaques on Koshima island used to eat their sweet potatoes unwashed, until in 1953 a female macaque started washing her sweet potatoes to remove the sand. Somehow the practice spread and soon a large part of the population was washing their sweet potatoes. An intriguing further development came when the monkeys started washing the sweet potatoes in salty water, apparently for the simple reason that the added salt made them taste better (Hirata, Watanabe & Masao 2001). I would like to suggest that whereas a sweet potato is merely foodstuff, a washed sweet potato is a dish for the Japanese macaques since it has been prepared to make it more pleasant to eat.

However, we need to sharpen the idea of what makes something better to eat. For example, vitamin pills are prepared out of edible ingredients so that they are healthy, and they are made to be consumed by way of eating (especially the ones that need to be chewed, not just swallowed). But they do not seem to be a dish. One might think that it is because they offer no energy; but a portion of shirataki "zero calorie" noodles seems like a dish even though it contains no calories. One might eat shirataki noodles to get the pleasure of eating without gaining energy, but not every dish is pleasurable to eat either. When people face famine, they eat, for example, bark, and a bowl of bark soup seems to be a dish even if we assume that the eating is not pleasurable. Perhaps there can be contexts where something similar to vitamin pills would count as dishes, for example, in a spaceship or in a future similar to the world of the 1973 film *Soylent Green* by Richard Fleischer.

One option is to take the "better to eat" to be dependent on both a context and an agent so as to define it as *better according to the agent in question* (in a particular context). That sounds more promising since dishes can serve a multitude of possible aims. Thus, one may prepare foodstuffs into a dish whose aim is, for example, to nourish healthfully, to fatten someone up, to provide pleasure from flavors or textures, to cool one down, to give spiritual comfort, or to provide the nostalgic comfort of home. We have already assumed that a dish for one person may not count as a dish for another, for example, when it contains insects that the other one does not even consider to be food. So, we can extend that context dependence also to the preparations, so that whether a preparation makes something better to eat depends on the context.

To summarize, we have seen two possible ways to think of dishes: dishes as anything edible, including simple foodstuffs such as an apple, or dishes as foodstuff that is prepared in some way that makes it better to eat according to the context in question. Both ways of thinking of dishes are equally valid; however, later on we will see how the choice of a theory of dishes plays out in theories of recipes.

Dish Internalism vs. Externalism

Sometimes the preparations for a dish may not change the physical properties of the foodstuff in question. For example, there are dishes which should not be eaten before a religious or other kind of ceremony is performed, and that may be considered to be part of the necessary preparation for the dish to be ready. It is useful to make another distinction regarding theories of dishes that is independent of the distinction between dishes as anything edible (to someone) versus dishes as preparations which make something better to eat (according to someone). Let us distinguish between what I call *internalist* and *externalist* views of dishes or points of views on dishes (with apologies to philosophers for introducing another internalism–externalism distinction). When we identify a dish from an internalist point of view we are considering only its intrinsic properties. When we identify a dish from the externalist point of view, we are also taking into account its relational properties, for example, the way it was prepared and served, where its ingredients come from, who made it, and so on.

These two different ways of identifying dishes also imply a difference regarding how we know about the properties of the dish. To find out some of the properties of a dish in the internalist view we can look at it and eat it, or perhaps analyze it in a lab, but for ordinary purposes our senses of taste, smell, touch, vision, and to some extent hearing provide plenty of information about the dish's intrinsic properties. In the externalist view the dish's properties may extend far and wide and require a broader understanding of how the dish relates to its makers, to the culture of the people who make it, to its environment in terms of its ingredients, or to its own origins regarding its recipe.

Let us summarize the conceptual analysis we have done. When we are thinking of recipes for a dish, we should clarify at least whether we are talking about dishes in the permissive sense where anything edible counts as a dish, or in the more restricted sense where some preparation is needed. Once that choice is made we need to specify whether we are talking about dishes from the internalist or externalist point of view.

Finally, we should be mindful of dish types vs. dish tokens. For example, if we talk about two different concrete dishes, aka dish tokens, that have the same intrinsic properties, we may say that they are instances of the same internalist dish type. But those same dish tokens may not be instances of the same externalist dish type, for example, if their ingredients come from different countries.

In what follows I develop a theory of recipes for dish types where dishes are understood to require some preparation and they are identified as in the internalist view. It is not because I think dish internalism is in any way superior to dish externalism, but because dishes identified via internalism are simpler and make for less complications in the theory. It is better to start with a simple theory that can then be extended and modified to also cover dishes as identified by dish externalism.

Constructivism and Realism about Dishes

Let us now turn our attention to recipes. Earlier I said that recipes are roughly speaking descriptions of the cooking process that result in a type of dish. Indeed, this definition is rough, as "description" is too narrow and applies mostly to written recipes. When someone is cooking on the basis of a recipe, we can distinguish two essential elements: the actual cooking process (that follows the recipe) and the final dish, which in part also determines what the recipe was, and whether the recipe was successfully followed. When we think of several instances of cooking following the same recipe, we have cooking types. A recipe can be thought of either as a cooking type or as the information that the cook follows in their cooking. The information can be thought of as an abstract object, akin to a musical work or the content of a book, or as the way it is stored for example as the *conceptualization* or a mental representation of how to prepare a dish. In this chapter there is no space to go deeper into the question of the metaphysical nature of recipes, but it is useful to be aware of the ways in which recipes can be thought to exist. I will treat recipes as conceptualizations had by agents or as cooking types, which I take to be two sides of the same coin. Let us now focus on the following question: when do recipes come into being?

Borghini develops a constructivist account of recipes whose core idea is that recipes are constituted by human *fiat*: "what matters [for the identity of a recipe] is that whoever produces the recipe recognizes it as such" (Borghini 2015: 724). The producer of the recipe—usually the cook—must go through a process of identification, that is, of identifying something of a suitable nature as a recipe. That process is typically performed via a speech act. Borghini takes the identification of a recipe to be a *performative utterance* that brings into life a social entity. A recipe is thus brought about by, say, uttering "I call this the *Lockdown pantry pasta*," or by writing down the name of the recipe. Borghini is careful to add that although the human fiat is necessary for a recipe to exist, there are further necessary conditions related to the expertise of the cook.

Borghini holds that constructivism is the right theory of the identity of dishes as well. In other words, whether a dish exemplifies a certain recipe (say, a *Coq au vin*) constitutively depends on the declaration of intention of the cook, though it will have to fulfill certain conditions set out by the recipe as well. He compares the dependence of the identity of dishes and recipes to the identities of musical performances: whether something is a cover of a song or not depends partly on what the players intend to be playing, though obviously it will also depend on whether they have the skills to play the song in question. That is constructivism in a nutshell. We will see more details of it later, but let us first look at realism about recipes and dishes, which takes a very different approach to both.

Whereas constructivism takes the identity of recipes and dishes to be constitutively dependent on human agents, the realist view developed here gives center stage to cooking and the final dish. We identify a dish in an internalist way based on its ingredients and its gustatory properties, like its flavor profile, texture, temperature, and look. A recipe's identity derives from both the internalist identity conditions of a dish and the way it was cooked. Thus, if two tokens of dishes are of the identical type from the internalist point of view and they were cooked the same way, then their recipe is the same.

A theory of recipes and a theory of dishes are two separate topics, but due to their intimate relation it is natural to think of them in a similar way. Thus, even though the realist theory of recipes is not inherently committed to a realist theory of dishes, let me show how it would go. First, the identity of a dish is determined as described above from an internalist point of view. Thus, two concrete dishes are an instance of the same dish type if their core ingredients are the same and they have the same core gustatory properties. I should emphasize that "the same" should be taken to be context-sensitive: for example, if a chef in a restaurant teaches their staff how to prepare a dish, they expect them to be able to reproduce it to a very high degree of similarity. However, if you and I are planning to cook the same dish in our respective homes, we may take the dishes as being of the same type even if there are some variations in the quality of our ingredients and the final flavor profiles of the dish (say, you might prefer it saltier than me, or you chopped the vegetables in a slightly different way).

Now, someone might worry that the realist account developed here has made recipes too far removed from our intuitive conceptions of what a recipe is. One may object as follows: the prototypical recipes are not abstract entities (cooking types) or merely in someone's head, but they are written down or spoken out, they have names, and they might even have more culinary value than someone's random conceptualization of how they combined the leftovers in their fridge into a quick lunch dish. If any old dish has a recipe, what distinguishes those recipes from the kind of recipes we learn or share?

These challenges rely precisely on those intuitions that support constructivism, namely that a recipe exists only if someone so intends and thereby does a suitable performative act, like giving the recipe a name and writing it down or making a YouTube video of it. However, I think the only difference between those recipes and the ones that were never written down or passed on is simply that some are made public, some are not.

We can imagine a solitary master chef who has created dozens of delicious recipes that would be absolutely worth sharing but she just does not care to do so. Her recipes remain in her head as mere conceptualizations and she never names any of them. But they are still recipes—information about how to prepare a dish or cooking types. We need to be careful not to confuse creating a recipe with marking down or naming a recipe. Creating a recipe happens when the cook has decided and completed all the steps in how to prepare the dish. They may also mark down the recipe or name it, but according to the realist theory advanced here those acts are not acts of creation. An unnamed, unwritten recipe is still a recipe.

The point about culinary value is related. Naturally, the better the dish, the more reason there is to write down the recipe to remember it and to share it. Typically, the better a recipe is, the better known it is. So again, the dishes that are prepared just once because they turned out to be not very good do have a recipe, but there simply are not enough reasons to keep a record of them or to share them. But bad or forgotten recipes are still recipes.

One of Borghini's reasons for defending constructivism is that he thinks realism cannot explain some of our intuitions in certain cases. One problem relates to a cook's authority over the recipe:

> Mild realism falls short of capturing the identity conditions of a good number of important recipes. For instance, some recipes—e.g. a chef's salad or a house pizza—owe their identity to the sort of person preparing them rather than to the ingredients or the procedures. In general, the idea that a recipe depends on the fiat of the cook is entirely in keeping with practice, but mild realism is unable to accommodate any case of this sort. (Borghini 2015: 724)

Borghini's point here is that as the author of the recipe the chef has more authority than anyone else regarding the recipe, which gives them the power to modify it to a certain degree. Thus, say a house pizza can be considered to remain the same even if the chef somewhat tweaks it.

My realist take on the case is somewhat different. We should again mind the distinction between creating recipes and naming them. For example, a restaurant may always have a dish called "Chef's salad" on their menu even though its recipe changes every week. What that shows is the name "Chef's salad" is ambiguous between a variety of salads, each of which has their own recipe. According to the theory developed here, the recipe comes first, and if the cook is so inclined, they can name it. The naming itself may well require a performative act, but for a recipe to be named it must already exist. The problem Borghini's example illustrates, however, goes beyond the more superficial question of what's in a name to what modifications to a recipe are considered acceptable. We return to the question briefly later.

The Identity of Recipes

We have seen that according to constructivism, a recipe comes into being when its author does a performative act such as naming the recipe, announcing its existence, or writing the recipe down. The identity of the recipe depends in part on the author's decision, so that a Chef's salad may have acceptable modifications while still remaining the same recipe. However, there are other conditions for the identity of a recipe that we will look at in this section.

Earlier I said that recipes are cooking types or conceptualizations of how to prepare a dish, but we did not yet discuss whether a recipe can exist without the dish in the realist account. It might seem possible: after all, one can invent a recipe first and then try it out. However, I think what really happens is that one has an idea for a recipe, then one goes on to test the idea by preparing the dish, and only once the dish is ready does the full recipe exist. That is because the imagined recipe is not yet complete enough to count as a recipe. Let me try to explain that more clearly.

One important issue to notice about the relation of recipes to dishes is that any ordinary recipe, like a recipe in a cookbook, is always an incomplete description of how to cook a dish. Let me list some factors that matter for the final dish which are typically left out of a recipe (see also Borghini [2015: 729–30] for some further factors):

1. The temperature at which the preparation should happen, e.g., what counts as room temperature, "warm" or "cool" (as in keep the dish in a cool place until served). Room temperatures will be very different in say, a barely-heated British apartment in the winter and a kitchen in the subtropics in the summer. A good example of that is the common simplification that red wine should be served at room temperature; however, the intended room temperature is around 15–19 degrees Celsius (59–66 degrees Fahrenheit), which is much colder than the standard room temperature in a lot of countries or during warm seasons.
2. The cooking temperature of the stove. Typically, a recipe will say something like "cook on medium heat." But there are massive differences between what is low, medium, and high heat on different types of stoves. For example, wok recipes say "cook on high heat," but actual wok burners are much more powerful than the standard burners in European stoves.
3. The exact type of cooking vessels and utensils. For example, the size, thickness, and type of frying pan, cooking pot or oven dish will massively impact basically all of the aspects of how the ingredients cook.
4. The size of the ingredients. For example, one large potato can be the equivalent of four small ones, one large courgette the equivalent of three small ones, and so on.
5. The variety of vegetables or fruit used and their exact level of ripeness. For example, compare a barely red, hard tomato grown in a North-European greenhouse to a ripe San Marzano, or think of the "ripen at home" fruits and veggies that will never attain the flavor and texture of properly ripened ones. Or think of all the recipes that call for, say, "green chilies" without specifying which species it should be.
6. The level of quality and freshness of spices and condiments. For example, the average supermarket versions of spices and condiments are often a pale imitation of the genuine items.

These are some of the features that are crucial to the identity of a dish, but which are not mentioned in a typical written recipe. Neither are they part of a newly invented but not yet tried idea for a recipe. A recipe is always a recipe for a particular dish, but if the recipe is incomplete it can give rise to several different dishes. That is why I hold that a recipe's existence and identity depend on the existence and identity of a dish. In this respect Borghini agrees:

> Unlike movies, literary works, and certain musical works, it seems that recipes are *not* autonomous entities, but are vicarious of dishes. [...] it is impossible to spell out recipes in details that would match a full-fledged dish. If so, then it is allegedly impossible to gain full acquaintance with a recipe, unless we have experienced a dish instantiating that recipe. [...] I am contending that until a recipe has not been realized, we can only speak of it as an entity that could exist in potency, but that is not yet existing. [...] A recipe is existentially linked to some dish instantiating it: no such dish, no recipe. Knowledge of the recipe hence requires acquaintance with some dish instantiating it and, typically, a process of apprenticeship that would fine-tune our acquaintance. (Borghini 2015: 730–1)

To illustrate the points about acquaintance with a dish, if a chef in a restaurant wants to teach the kitchen staff a recipe, they do much better if they show how to cook it and have the staff taste the dish than if they write the recipe down. If the staff have not tasted the dish, they are in a sense working blind. Borghini further argues that to imitate a dish, one needs not only acquaintance with it but also expertise in the relevant abilities. Cooking is a skill that requires apprenticeship, and different dishes may require specific skills that need to be learned. Given that I take recipes to be conceptualizations of how to prepare a particular dish, if one observes the making of a dish and tastes it but lacks the skills to make it, one does not yet know the full recipe for it. Knowing a recipe means knowing how each step in the preparation is performed. That is why classic French cookbooks do not only have recipes, but they teach a large number of techniques that must be mastered to be able to follow the recipes.

Thus, if there is no dish, there is no complete recipe. What about the other way around: can there be dishes without a recipe for them? Borghini holds that not every dish has a recipe, since he thinks that a crucial precondition for a recipe to exist is the *repeatability* of a dish: "a recipe—in first approximation—comprises the array of repeatable aspects of a dish whose replication would deliver a dish of the same sort" (Borghini 2015: 722). This has the following consequences:

> Not every dish need exemplify some recipe. In principle, the procedure that delivers any dish has some aspect to it that could be replicated. However, some dishes—and the procedures that deliver them—remain neglected. It may be because they are unappealing; but, more circumstantial reasons could intervene too, for instance the conditions in which the dish is prepared may be truly exceptional (e.g. a dish prepared while stranded on a highway or during an expedition to the Antarctic) and replicating it is not worth it. Thus, only selected dishes enter the ranks of recipes. (Borghini 2015: 722)

That is a natural thing to say from the constructivist point of view, which holds that a recipe exists only if there is a cook who performs the appropriate act that brings a recipe into existence. If the cook knows that the dish cannot—or should not—be replicated, they will not create the recipe.

Can there be dishes without recipes in the realist account? Given that we take dishes to be prepared foodstuff, in most cases recipes and dishes connect in a natural way: since a dish must be prepared somehow, normally it also has a recipe, which is the conceptualization that specifies the preparation. For example, the Japanese macaques' dish of a potato washed in saltwater has a recipe, which is the conceptualization of the process (however, it is conceptualized by the macaques) or simply the cooking type, the action type of washing a potato in saltwater.

However, a preparation cannot always be fully conceptualized so that repeating the steps (the cooking type) would result in the very same dish, identified from the internalist point of view. For example, the essence of spontaneous fermentation is that the dish under preparation (typically a beverage such as beer or wine) is left to catch wild strains of yeast or bacteria that are floating in the air, reside in the barrel used, or come as a by-product of some of the ingredients used. When the process is repeated the resulting product may never taste exactly the same as the previous batch since how the product changes is up to the environment and outside of the control of the maker. Does that therefore mean that such products do not have a complete recipe, since the very same dish as identified by its flavor profile cannot be recreated?

On the other hand, in the above kind of cases there is a complete recipe in the sense of a complete information or conceptualization of the process itself; there is a cooking type that can be repeated; it just leaves some aspects of the process up to the environment. So, what should we say of cases where the recipe specifies the full cooking process, but nevertheless the dishes that result from it may not be of the exact same type because the recipe intentionally lets the environment influence the result? In such cases we might think of the recipe not as a perfectly specific recipe for a particular dish, but more like a recipe template that results in various different dishes. In fact, a lot of recipes leave room for choice regarding the exact ingredients used, which makes them also rather like templates to be filled in.

Thus, rather than thinking of recipes simply as complete or incomplete, we can think of recipes in a hierarchical way, akin to the taxonomic hierarchy in biology (thanks to Andrea Borghini for the analogy). Complete recipes are like species: for example, a specific version of Swedish meatballs, say, the one made by Sven's grandmother, is one species, and the one sold in Ikea is another species. "Swedish meatballs" is akin to genus, which belongs to the family of meatballs that would include Middle-Eastern *kofta*, Italian *polpette*, *bola-bola* from the Philippines, and so on. When we learn public recipes, we typically learn either complete recipes, aka recipe species, or recipe templates that belong to a genus, which leave some choice over the details. Once one has fixed the details, the resulting dish is an instance of a recipe species, a complete recipe.(see Hirvonen n.d. for more on the incompleteness of recipes).

Let me illustrate the idea with our example of spontaneous fermentation. Suppose we have a recipe for ale that includes spontaneous fermentation. Given that the resulting ale may always vary in flavor, we should think of its recipe as a recipe template, a recipe genus. Each time the recipe is followed it results in a specific ale, which theoretically speaking has a recipe; it is the information about the cooking process, including the environment. However, in practice the particular recipe can never be repeated because there is no way to insure that the environment will ever be the same. Perhaps the notion of a recipe used here is very abstract, but it emphasizes the inherent relation of a particular dish to its recipe.

One reason why realism is especially appealing is its ability to explain the feeling we have that certain traditional, classic dishes and their recipes have changed and, at worst, have become fakes. Oliver (2007) describes how the beer industry has replaced most of the traditional ways of brewing by novel ingredients and methods that are cheaper and more reliable, but flavorwise the results are vastly inferior and in other respects too they are very different from the original beers. One of the famous companies that gave up the tradition of cask-conditioned brewing and replaced it with filtered and artificially carbonated fizzy beer was Guinness:

> Guinness pioneered this neat trick in the 1960s. Until then Guinness had been a cask-conditioned beer. When cask-conditioned beer is pumped quickly into a glass, the beer mixes with air. Nitrogen forms small stable bubbles and air is mostly nitrogen. So this gives a beer a tight creamy head. I think you can pretty much see where this is going. Nitrogen was dissolved into the beer, which was then forced out of the special new Guinness spigot at high pressure. This caused the nitrogen to break out of solution, and *voila*, a tight creamy head on a very lightly carbonated glass of Guinness. (Oliver 2007: 39)

Realism can easily explain why a connoisseur of Guinness who was used to it being cask-conditioned would be very disappointed and upset by the change: Guinness went and changed the recipe while still calling the beer by the same name. Constructivism does more work to explain what goes on in such cases, since presumably the Guinness factory is the chef and the authority over the recipe of Guinness, and thus they are permitted to modify the recipe. The intuition that the contemporary Guinness is fake Guinness is hard to make sense of in the constructivist picture.

Recipes Without Makers

To summarize, the core difference between constructivism and realism is the role of the chef (or chefs) with respect to the coming into being and nature of a recipe. According to constructivism, a recipe exists in virtue of the *fiat* of the chef (assuming they fulfill some other conditions) and they also have authority over the way the recipe can be changed. Realism leaves the chef out of the picture and takes recipes to be the type of cooking process (or the information about it) that results in a particular dish. We have also seen that knowing a recipe requires much more than following a public recipe and doing one's best in cooking the dish, due to the typically incomplete nature of public recipes. One way recipes change or arguably come into being is when someone follows an incomplete recipe (or unsuccessfully follows a complete recipe) and then continues to make the resulting dish in their own way afterward. So, what happens in such cases according to constructivism and realism? Let me illustrate the problem with a story.

A Recipe Without a Maker

In the ancient times before Internet there was a small, isolated Northern country, call it Norland, whose inhabitants very rarely if ever had any interactions with Italy, Italians, or Italian food, including pizza. Norland did not import food, so they grew their own tomatoes in greenhouses under lamps. They had heard of mozzarella and produced their own version of it, which, however, had little to do with the real mozzarella in terms of its flavor or texture. One day a Norlander, call him Arvid, is emptying his grandmother's attic and finds a recipe of Neapolitan Pizza Margherita. Arvid doesn't know what it is but decides to give the recipe a try.

Arvid goes to his local grocery store and buys the ingredients: local tomatoes, local mozzarella, etc., and proceeds to cook the dish in his old gas oven. However, Arvid lacks acquaintance of how Neapolitan Pizza Margherita's texture and flavors should be, he lacks knowledge and skill in preparing the crust, the ingredients used are too different from the intended ones, and the oven is much too weak. All in all, the flavors and the textures just aren't right at all, so the result is not similar enough to a genuine Neapolitan Pizza Margherita to count as an instance of it. But Arvid doesn't know that because he has never eaten a genuine Neapolitan Pizza Margherita, and he loves the pizza he made.

He offers the dish to his friends who like it, and they ask him for the recipe. In a few years the country abounds with homes and restaurants making the said dish, known as "Neapolitan Pizza Margherita," which, however, bears little resemblance to the Neapolitan Pizza Margherita. Norladers also like to experiment, so it is common to add things like reindeer, elk, or salmon as extra toppings.

We are assuming that the new pizza is not an instance of the Neapolitan Pizza Margherita. So, what is the recipe that the Norlanders got from Arvid? My take on the story is that a new recipe has come into being without any performative having taken place—all Arvid tried to do was to make a Neapolitan Pizza Margherita, but he failed, and his failure created a new dish and a new recipe. Whereas Arvid's first making of a pizza could be considered a failed attempt at a Neapolitan Pizza Margherita, he accepted the resulting dish as a perfect result. From then on, he intended to replicate *the pizza he made*, and his pizza provided the dish that the other Norlanders were later trying to imitate. Arvid's recipe shares its name with (Neapolitan) Pizza Margherita, but otherwise the two dishes are very different.

This case illustrates the core difference between constructivism and realism. Given the emphasis constructivism gives to the chef's *fiat*, it is hard to see what is going on in the case. One option is that according to constructivism, the Norlanders are continually and unsuccessfully trying to cook Neapolitan Pizza Margherita, of which there is only the original recipe. Since Arvid thinks he is merely following the original recipe, he will never make a performative utterance aimed at creating a new recipe. Realism in contrast identifies a dish based on its core ingredients and flavors, and a recipe is the way to cook the dish. Since there is a large difference between Arvid's pizza and Pizza Margherita, the two dishes are different, and so are their recipes. The recipe Arvid used was to some extent incomplete since it did not specify the quality of the ingredients, the type of oven to use, and so on. Consequently, Arvid created a complete recipe, Arvid's Pizza Margherita, which became a favorite of Norlanders.

If realism is true, recipes come into existence quite easily. I think looking at actual recipes and their origins speak in favor of that too. The world is nowadays full of different types of pizzas, but they all had the same origin. Are they all really pizzas? We are all familiar with the arguments over what counts as a pizza and what does not: "You cannot put pineapple on a pizza," "You can't make pizza if you don't have a pizza oven," "Pizza must have a thin crust," and so on.

When there are many variations of one recipe, rather than to argue which ones are the real thing and which are not, we can rather consider them as subtypes, as in the biological hierarchy. For example, pizza has so many subtypes that it can be considered to be an order. The members of its family are, say, New York style pizza, Neapolitan pizza, Chicago pizza, and so on; the genera of each family are types of pizza toppings such as Pizza Margherita, Primavera, and so on, and finally, the species are particular versions of those, for instance Arvid's Pizza Margherita. In other words, "pizza" refers to such a high-level category that it leaves open much of its characteristics. If one specifies the family of pizza, say Neapolitan pizza, we still only get a recipe template, an incomplete recipe that merely specifies the core features of all Neapolitan pizzas. Complete recipes are specific dishes, like Montrose Pie, a pizza with bananas by Reds Pizza in Santa Monica, California.

The final topic we should address is traditional recipes that have acquired a legally protected geographical status in Europe, for example, cheeses such as *Gorgonzola*, *Comté*, or *Feta*, various kinds of regional products like types of honey, wine, liquors, or bread, and even parts of dishes like the sauce *Amatriciana Tradizionale*. Borghini argues that the reasoning behind such protected geographical statuses relies on realism. However, I think that is the case only if one accepts what we have called an externalist view of dishes, which seems to correspond to what Borghini calls an *extended concept* of a recipe or a dish:

> When speaking of a dish or a recipe, at times we refer merely to the item that is consumed—say, a slice of pizza; in other contexts, however, we refer to that item *plus* the relevant events that brought to its realization; the relevant events, in turn, may be limited to the action of the cook (say, all the toil and labour that went into preparing the slice) or, rather, the events may comprise a more extended series (e.g., the farms where the grains, the tomatoes, and the milk were produced). I call the latter the *extended concept* of a recipe or dish. (Borghini 2015: 722)

If one conceives of dishes in the externalist way with quite strict standards of what counts as the same dish, then a realist can argue that, say, Feta cheese can only be produced based on the milk of sheep or goats from specific Greek regions because that is the core ingredient used in making Feta. However, I think that most recipes can be reproduced relying merely on the internalist view of a dish—its flavor, texture, temperature, and look—thus ignoring where the ingredients come from. Sometimes the origin of an ingredient is essential to its having the right flavor, in which case the recipe requires the use of the ingredient with a particular origin, but the origin plays a role only insofar as it has a notable impact on flavor.

In short, realism could be used to defend the protected geographical status of certain dishes, but only when there are good reasons to think that the region where they are produced makes a difference to the dish's flavors, or if one relies on the externalist concept of a dish, which is problematic in many ways. However, there are lots of reasons to have a protected geographical status for dishes and produce that go well beyond the idea of protecting a traditional recipe. Whether we choose constructivism or realism as the best theory of recipes is not enough to adjudicate whether dishes should be protected based on their geography.

Conclusions

The aim of this chapter has been to present a viable alternative to constructivism about recipes. Realism grants recipes life irrespective of their social existence: what matters is that someone has created a novel dish, and a recipe is the information/ conceptualization of how to prepare the dish, or a cooking type that results in the dish. Some recipes become public recipes by being written down, named, and shared. Public recipes may go on to have a long, famous life, and they most likely also give rise to several new recipes that start out as either failed attempts at the original or as intentional modifications of it.

Constructivism gives more emphasis to the selection process by cooks, by taking them to have the power to decide which among the dishes they have cooked get to have a recipe. However, I argued that there are some recipes where it is less clear how the constructivist would explain their coming into existence. I gave the example of recipes without makers, illustrated by the story of the Norlandish Pizza Margherita which came into being by accident but went on to live an illustrious life.

No doubt both constructivism and realism capture some aspects of what we take recipes to be, and to decide between them or possible other theories will require much more space than we have here. I have provided some groundwork for future theorizing as well as a realist account, which takes the identity of a recipe to depend on the cooking process which leads to a particular dish. The recipes existence is thus strongly dependent on the process of cooking and on the dish. Recipes can also come to have a social life in the form of public recipes, but I take that to be a non-essential part of the true nature of recipes.[1]

3

The Taste(s) of a Recipe

Davide Bordini

Introduction

Taste plays a marginal role, or no role at all, in discussions about recipes and their identity. This is surprising, given the importance of taste in our everyday food practices and in motivating our food choices (see, e.g., Liem & Russell 2019). In this chapter, I want to bring taste to the foreground. The broad question I have in mind concerns the relation between recipes and taste. This is a huge question, so the focus will have to be narrowed down to something more specific and tractable.

A useful starting point is the following story about recipes and taste:

> When we cook, we aim for (re)producing certain gustatory experiences we give value to and making them available at different places and times. Recipes are what allows us to do that. They are *guides* to taste: to get the desired gustatory experience, we just have to (re)produce a proper instance of the right recipe—or *find* the right recipe. For example, you like the taste of saffron *risotto* and really want to enjoy it again at home for dinner tonight. What do you do? Well, you cook it: you (re)produce a proper instance of saffron *risotto* and thereby you get to enjoy once again that taste you were desperately craving for. Now, in virtue of what do recipes guide us to taste? Easy: taste is a distinctive trait of a recipe—i.e., something that contributes to its identity or is otherwise strongly related to it. In other words, a recipe is *essentially* related to a certain taste, and this explains the association between the two. Take again our example: saffron *risotto* is essentially related to a certain taste. So, there cannot be something that counts as an instance of saffron *risotto* that does not deliver that gustatory experience. And this is why I just need to reproduce an instance of saffron *risotto*, to get that experience.

At first sight, all this sounds quite natural and intuitive. But is it also true? In particular, is it true that a recipe possesses its taste essentially? In this chapter, I address this question and offer a negative reply to it. Do not get me wrong: I do not mean to deny that recipes and taste are somehow associated—I just do not think that they are related in the way suggested above. My aim, then, is to lay the ground for an alternative approach to account for that association. In short, my final suggestion will be that the main source of the association between recipes and taste is not to be found in recipes themselves and their essences, but in dishes.

Here is how I will proceed. I will start with some clarifications about dishes, recipes, and taste. This will provide the preliminary grounds to better formulate and understand the question that I am raising here (section "Recipes, Dishes, and Taste"). Next, I will offer a more precise characterization of the specific view that I want to target. I will sketch and discuss different versions of it and argue that they are not convincing (section "Essentialism"). I will then point out some general lessons concerning recipes that can be drawn from our discussion and will set the grounds for an alternative picture (section "Lessons and a New Starting Point").

My discussion will be largely conducted by reasoning from first principles. This is because, to the best of my knowledge, the idea I criticize here has not been explicitly formulated in a fully articulated philosophical view. As weird as this might sound, it is not an unusual situation in philosophy of food, especially when it comes to theories of recipes—a largely neglected and unexplored area, where a huge amount of work is still ahead of us in terms of mapping the logical space (Borghini's [2011, 2012, 2014a, 2014b, 2014c, 2015] research on the topic is a notable exception). With this chapter, then, I want to give a double contribution: in addition to providing philosophical reasons to dismiss the idea that a recipe is essentially related to its taste, I offer a philosophical articulation of that very idea, thereby furthering the mapping of the logical space.

Recipes, Dishes, and Taste

Recipes and dishes. I borrow this distinction from Borghini (2015). Consider, for example, a slice of *pizza*. Intuitively, there are two ways to look at it. A slice of *pizza* can be understood as *that* concrete object that is *now* in my kitchen and I am ready to eat. Or it can be understood as the array of the *repeatable aspects* whose repetition would deliver a slice of *pizza* of the same sort. When understood in the first sense, our slice of *pizza* is a dish; when understood in the second sense, it is a recipe.[1]

Following Borghini, my understanding of what counts as a dish is very broad and permissive: "anything that is ready for someone to be eaten up" (2015: 722) or drunk counts as a dish. So, dishes are not just the sorts of thing that are cooked in restaurant or at home; cheeses, fruits, chocolate, cookies, drinks, etc.—they all count as dishes.

Taste. First of all, by "taste" I do not mean to refer to our aesthetic judgments concerning food—namely, the sort of statements we make about something tasting good or bad. Rather, what I have in mind are *taste properties*: a certain class of qualitative properties that we typically attribute to foods and drinks and we experience by using our sense of taste, specifically, by eating or drinking.

Secondly, strictly speaking, only five basic gustatory properties count as taste properties: sweetness, sourness, bitterness, saltiness, and umaminess. However, my use of "taste property" here will be broader to include also what are typically referred to as flavors, namely, properties such as aroma, fruitiness, herbalness, meatiness, and smokiness.[2]

Thirdly, I have talked about the taste of a recipe, and this might sound weird. After all, one might think, recipes are abstract entities and, as such, they are not the kinds of thing that *have* taste, strictly speaking. These doubts are legitimate, so let me say something more to better qualify this. When I say that a recipe has a taste, I do not mean to say that it tastes salty or fruity, and so on—this is the way in which a *dish* has a taste; recipes do not have taste in *this* sense. Rather, what I mean is that recipes are somehow associated with some set of properties that determine a certain type of *gustatory profile*. Such a type of gustatory profile is what I mean here by "taste of a recipe." From now on, I will use expressions such as "taste of a recipe," "type of gustatory profile associated with a recipe," "taste properties associated with a recipe" interchangeably, unless otherwise specified. Is there a unique type of gustatory profile for every recipe or can there be more? This is an important question and is part of what I am going to discuss here. So, I leave it open for now.

With this at hand, we are now in the position to have a better grasp on the very general background question that motivates this chapter: how should we understand the relation between a recipe and some type of gustatory profile that is (usually or typically) associated with it?

The hypothesis anticipated in the introduction is that we have to look at recipes themselves to find the source of this association. Intuitively, the thought is that a recipe possesses a certain type of taste *in its own right*, just by being the recipe it is—namely, independent of its being related to any other thing, dishes in particular. This is because—the thought goes—a certain type of gustatory profile constitutes the very essence of a recipe or is otherwise strongly related to it. In short, a recipe has its taste *essentially*. Call this *essentialism*.

This brings us to the more specific question I want to directly tackle: is (some version of) essentialism true? In other words, is it true that recipes possess their taste essentially? As anticipated, I will reply negatively to this question.

Essentialism

In this section, I discuss essentialism. First, I will construe the view in its general form. I will do that somewhat dogmatically and schematically, as my aim here is just to introduce the view and not argue for it. Then, I will articulate the different specific subversions of essentialism and consider them in turn. As I will argue, none of them offers a convincing account of the relation between recipes and taste.

General Essentialism

The core ideas behind essentialism are two: (i) recipes have an *essence* that fixes their identity; (ii) they have a taste *autonomously*, just by having that essence—*nothing else* is required; dishes, in particular, are not required. With this in mind, essentialism in its general form can be captured as follows:

1. Recipes are *kinds* of gustatory objects (dishes).[3]
2. Recipes have an *essence* that fixes their identity, once and for all: a recipe R and a recipe R* are one and the same recipe if and only if R and R* are the same with respect to a certain set of essential properties.
3. Recipes are *autonomous*: they do not need anything else—in particular, they do not need dishes—to have the properties they have, be what they are, and exist.
4. This conception thus attributes metaphysical *priority* to recipes (the abstract kinds) over dishes (the concrete instances). So, *recipes come first*: they are prior to, and exist independently of, dishes—facts about recipes are not determined or explained by facts about dishes but determine or explain facts about dishes.
5. Given their priority, recipes dictate what properties their instances (dishes) cannot fail to have. So, the essence of a recipe R, in addition to fixing R's identity, will also dictate what properties a dish must have to be an instance of R. This provides us with a criterion to identify the dishes instances of R: *all and only* the dishes that are instances of R have R's essential properties, or some corresponding properties, which can be linguistically expressed by the same predicate. If P and Q are the properties that constitute the essence of, say, the *carbonara* recipe, then all and only *carbonara* dishes will have P and Q, or some corresponding properties, which can be linguistically expressed by "P" and "Q." Moreover, *carbonara* dishes have P and Q only *derivatively*, *qua* instances of the *carbonara* recipe.
6. It follows that a recipe has its taste just by being the recipe it is, namely, just by possessing a certain set of essential properties. By contrast, dishes have their taste only *qua* instances of a recipe. Recipes, thus, are the *primary* bearers of taste, while dishes have a taste only *derivatively*.

The claim in (6) that a recipe possesses its taste just by possessing a certain set of essential properties can be spelled out in different ways. On one understanding, it means that taste properties are (among the) essential properties of a recipe, thus (partially) contributing to its identity. On a different understanding, it means that the essential properties of a recipe, though they are not taste properties themselves, determine the taste a recipe possesses. This delivers different essentialist options. Let us examine them in turn.

Strong Essentialism

According to the strongest version of essentialism, taste properties constitute the essence of a recipe—they *entirely* determine its identity. On this view, then, the identity criterion for recipes is sameness with respect to taste—same taste, same recipe; different taste, different recipe. More precisely, R and R* are the same recipe if and only if they are the same taste-wise.[4] So, what makes, for example, *carbonara* the recipe it is in its *carbonara* taste. As a consequence (see point (5) above), *all and only* the *carbonara* dishes will have the same unique carbonara taste.[5] More generally, all and only the dishes that are instances of the same recipe R have the same taste. This means that there cannot be a dish that has, say, a *carbonara* taste but is not an instance of *carbonara*. This is highly implausible. To see why, consider the following case:

> *The matzo pill.* Matzo is the unleavened flatbread consumed by Jewish people during Passover. Suppose that, for some reasons, one day some genius scientist comes up with a chewable pill that perfectly replicates all the taste properties of a matzo that you would eat during a Passover *seder*. So, the matzo pill tastes just like a piece of matzo bread—they are indistinguishable and, indeed, the same taste-wise.

If strong essentialism is true, then we should conclude that (i) the matzo pill is an instance of matzo and (ii) the recipe of the matzo pill and that of matzo are just one and the same recipe. Intuitively, however, this just seems false, and we should probably reject a theory that forces such counter-intuitive conclusions upon us. Plausibly, the matzo pill is *not* an instance of matzo, as well as the recipe of the matzo pill and that of matzo are *not* one and the same recipe.

Two More Plausible Versions of Essentialism

Moderate Essentialism

At this stage, the essentialist can weaken their view and maintain that taste properties alone do not exhaust the essence of a recipe—they are *among* the essential properties of a recipe, but *not* the only ones. This move generates *moderate essentialism*, according to which taste is a necessary but not sufficient condition for the identity of a recipe. As a consequence, on this view, it is still true that *all* the instances of a recipe R have the same taste T, but it is no longer true that *only* the instances of R have T.

Of course, to be complete, this version of essentialism has to tell us what other properties, along with taste, constitute the essence of a recipe—perhaps, the most natural option would be to combine taste with ingredients and/or production procedures. However, at this stage, the main worry does not concern the specific set of necessary conditions that are jointly sufficient for the identity of a recipe, but the very plausibility of treating taste as a necessary condition for the identity of a recipe. In a nutshell, it seems that the same recipe might allow for a great deal of variations in taste—dishes that we would intuitively take as instances of the same recipe often taste very different. This does not just mean that some of them taste good, while some others taste bad; it means that their gustatory profiles differ significantly, to the extent that they seem to be of different types. Consider, for example, *pizza margherita*—it allows for a good number of variations in taste. To be sure, a pie of Neapolitan *pizza margherita* and a pie of, say, Pizza Hut or Domino's *pizza margherita* taste quite different. Both might taste good, but they do seem to have two different types of taste. This variety of taste-types associated with the same recipe militates against imposing taste as a necessary condition for the identity of a recipe.

The moderate essentialist might try and overcome this difficulty by individuating a minimal set of taste properties that remain constant across variations and, on these grounds, define a necessary condition for the identity of a recipe. The problem with this proposal is that this set is quite hard to pin down. In particular, the range of variations is so wide that reasonable doubts arise as to whether we are going to end up with the necessary condition we need—specifically, something less trivial and more informative than just having a *pizza margherita* taste. Moreover, it is quite hard to see what a *pizza margherita* taste—understood as the minimal set of taste properties that are supposed to be common to all *pizza margherita* dishes—would be exactly. Actually, it is legitimate to doubt that there really is any such thing—at least in some interesting sense. After all, a Neapolitan *margherita* pie and a Pizza Hut or Domino's *margherita* pie do not really seem to have a lot in common taste-wise. Granted, both are probably salty, oily, cheesy, etc. But many dishes share these very basic taste properties, without sharing a *pizza margherita* taste. So, in this case, the necessary condition we are imposing does not just reek of triviality, it is also quite obscure.

A better option is to contend that *pizza margherita* is not a single recipe but a *family of recipes*: Domino's *margherita* and Neapolitan *margherita* are not the same recipe—they are in fact *two* different recipes that belong to the same family. Each member in the family is a recipe on its own and is qualitatively different from the others, though somehow parented to them. The natural move is to capture this in terms of a determinate–determinable relation—Domino's or Pizza Hut *margherita* and Neapolitan *margherita*, then, would be different *determinates* of the same *determinable*. The next move is to maintain that this reflects and is ultimately explained by the relation between the different tastes in question. The thought is, the taste of Domino's or Pizza Hut *margherita* is qualitatively different from that of a Neapolitan *margherita*: they are different determinates of the same determinable, *pizza margherita* taste.[6] Importantly, the latter might be construed as something that does not need an exhaustive list of descriptive features to be identified—possession of the right *recognitional concept* might suffice (Evans 1982; Peacocke 1992; Loar 1997). This would guarantee that instances of the determinable *pizza margherita* taste can be spotted without having to indicate the distinctive features of such a taste.

The viability of this way of construing moderate essentialism relies on (a) the plausibility of treating *pizza margherita* as a family of recipes, (b) modeling the relations within the domain of taste in terms of determinate–determinable relations, and (c) the possibility of extending this treatment to cases other than *pizza margherita*. I will not discuss this here. To my mind, the main reason to drop moderate essentialism comes from a different and more general problem that affects *all* versions of the view. Before getting to that (subsection "Against Essentialism"), let me introduce the last and weakest version of essentialism.

Weak Essentialism

An alternative option is available to the essentialist. They can maintain that even though taste itself does not fix the identity of a recipe, it strictly depends upon the essential properties that fix its identity—these properties being ingredients and production procedures. In short, the idea is: same ingredients and procedures, same recipe, same taste; different ingredients or procedures, different recipe, different taste. This is *weak essentialism*.

Weak essentialism combines the following two claims:

(Identity)   The identity of a recipe is fixed by a certain combination of
                    ingredients and production procedures.
(Determination)   The combination of ingredients and procedures that fixes the
                    identity of a recipe R also determines the taste of R.

(Identity) provides us with the identity criterion for a recipe R: a certain combination of ingredients and procedures. (Determination) adds that such a combination of ingredients and procedures is what makes a certain gustatory profile the taste *of* R, as opposed to the taste of another recipe. For example, *carbonara* is individuated by a certain combination of ingredients (*guanciale*, eggs, pasta, etc.) and a set of procedures that specify how to deal with those ingredients, put them together, and cook them properly. This combination, which fixes the identity of *carbonara*, also makes it the case that *carbonara* is associated with some type of gustatory profile and not others. Such a gustatory profile is the taste *of carbonara* (as opposed to that of, say, saffron *risotto*) because it is determined by the combination of ingredients and procedures that fixes the identity of *carbonara* (and not that of saffron *risotto*).

There are different ways to object to this view. Here is one example. Via the determination claim, weak essentialism establishes a strong relation between ingredients and procedures and taste. This, in turn, assumes that taste properties are at least partially dependent upon the physico-chemical properties of the ingredients. So, one way of attacking the view consists in challenging this assumption. To that end, some inverted *qualia* scenario can be devised (Shoemaker 1982; Block 1990; Byrne 2020) such that the same treatment of the same physico-chemical properties delivers systematically inverted taste experiences in pairs of subjects whose taste *qualia* are inverted. Of course, the success of this strategy is tied to the possibility of adapting inverted *qualia* cases, originally engineered for visual properties such as color, to taste properties.

However, this is not the path I intend to pursue here. So, I will not call into question the (partial) dependence of taste properties on the physico-chemical properties of the ingredients; rather, I will assume it. Instead, I want to raise a different problem— one that I find more interesting, given the purposes of this chapter.[7] For the sake of simplicity, I will initially present it as an objection to weak essentialism. However, it targets moderate essentialism too, as anticipated—I will quickly show how, toward the end of the next subsection. Therefore, it provides us with reasons to drop essentialism as such. In addition, it will pave the way for some more general lessons about recipes.

Against Essentialism

Let us consider the following scenario:

> *The Authentic Margherita.* Nobody knows, but Ciro and Maria are the guardians of the "authentic" recipe of *pizza margherita*, the Authentic Margherita. Contrary to what people believe, the recipe was named after an ancestor of Maria's, Margherita, who invented it in 1800. Maria and Ciro are faithful to the letter of the recipe.

They follow exactly the same procedures and use the same tools and the same oven used by Margherita back in 1800. Moreover, the recipe specifies exactly what ingredients have to be used and where they have to come from. Indeed, over the last two centuries, all the ingredients have been supplied by the same small farm, located right outside Naples. However, the region around Naples has gone through some important climatic and geo-physical changes over the last couple of hundred years. These changes have affected the water, the San Marzano tomatoes, the yeast, the sourdough, etc., thereby leading to some dramatic change in taste. Of course, nobody has noticed this. Yet, if one could compare the taste of the *pizza* made by Margherita in 1800 and the one made now by Maria and Ciro, one would immediately spot the difference in taste.

This case raises the following challenge for weak essentialism. Intuitively, the Authentic Margherita recipe has not changed over time—its taste has changed. This conflicts with the determination claim assumed by weak essentialism, which excludes that the same combination of ingredients and procedures can deliver a different taste. Recall, the determination claim is a crucial part of the view, as it explains what makes a certain gustatory profile the taste *of* a recipe. Dropping it would just be tantamount to dropping the view—or at the very least, it would leave the view incapable of explaining what makes the new taste the taste *of* the same Authentic Margherita recipe.

The weak essentialist will probably push back as follows. Given (Identity), whether or not the recipe remains the same over time depends on whether or not the ingredients that partially constitute its essence remain the same. The intuition that conflicts with weak essentialism assumes that ingredients do not change over time. However, this assumption can be challenged by arguing that, in fact, ingredients do change over time. The weak essentialist might suggest that the changes occurred between 1800 and 2020 in, say, San Marzano tomatoes are such that 1800 San Marzano and 2020 San Marzano are not the same ingredients. If so, then the view is safe and there is no need to drop the determination claim: a difference in ingredients, though combined with the same procedures, suffices to provide an explanation of the changes in taste that is compatible with weak essentialism. The price to be paid, of course, is to bite the bullet and maintain that 1800 Margherita and 2020 Margherita are two different recipes.

As I am going to argue, this is a Pyrrhic victory for weak essentialism. Either (i) it generates a problem that is even bigger than the one it is supposed to solve, or (ii) it does not really solve the initial problem with the determination claim. Therefore, it is not really a way out.

Let us start with the first horn of our dilemma, (i). As we have seen, claiming that in the Authentic Margherita case ingredients change over time presupposes a more fine-grained way of individuating ingredients, according to which micro-level differences count for the identity of the ingredients. The problem with this is the following. For any level of fine-ness of grain of ingredient individuation, we can generate a new version of the Authentic Margherita case that forces the weak essentialist to introduce a new, even more fine-grained distinction in ingredients, and so in recipes, to save the determination claim. For example, we can generate a case that forces the weak essentialist to distinguish between 1950 San Marzano and 2020 San Marzano and then say that 1950 Margherita is not the same recipe as 2020 Margherita. But now, again, another version can be generated that forces the weak essentialist to introduce a further distinction between 1950 San Marzano and 1975 San Marzano, and hence between 1950 Margherita and 1975 Margherita, and so forth and so on. In principle, this can go on until one reaches the point of having one recipe for each existing dish, which would clearly be a bad result. First, it would lead to an over-proliferation of recipes, thereby inflating our ontology for no other reason than just defending weak essentialism. Second, and more importantly, it would undermine the *repeatability* of recipes, thereby making them ultimately collapse into dishes. Losing track of the difference between recipes and dishes is a major problem for a theory of recipes—a definitely bigger one than not explaining the relation between recipes and taste.

This takes us to the second horn of the dilemma, (ii). The only way to block the over-proliferation of recipes and preserve their repeatability is to impose a cutoff, a threshold beyond which micro-level differences are no longer relevant to individuate ingredients. This implies to stop at a certain level of fine-ness of grain. But the weak essentialist cannot really follow this path and save their view. For as we have seen, whatever the level of fine-ness of grain, an appropriate version of the Authentic Margherita case can be generated that challenges the determination claim and makes the initial problem reappear.

The Authentic Margherita case challenges moderate essentialism too. Recall, the latter construes the identity of a recipe not just as determining the taste of a recipe but, more strongly, as partially constituted by it. *A fortiori*, thus, it cannot allow for a scenario in which the recipe stays the same, while its taste changes. So, the moderate essentialist is forced to say that the recipe changes along with taste. However, they need to independently motivate such a counter-intuitive claim—of course, complaining that otherwise moderate essentialism would turn out false does not suffice. It is not clear what the moderate essentialist might say. One natural option would be to make the same move the weak essentialist makes—or even to adopt weak essentialism as a fallback position—and argue that the recipe changes because ingredients change. But, as we have seen, this is not really a way out.

Notice that appealing to a determinate–determinable relation would not help either. It would mean to treat Authentic Margherita as a family of recipes, but this is false by assumption and is anyway quite implausible—at best, Authentic Margherita might be considered as one of the recipes within the *pizza margherita* family. In addition, it would lead to the introduction of a new recipe within the family for any change in taste (or ingredients) across time. As we have seen, any such change can be generated at any point in time and for any level of fine-ness of grain. So, we would still get something very close to the problem raised right above, along with its bad consequences for ontological parsimony and the repeatability of recipes.

What about denying the claim that changes in ingredients deliver changes in taste? This might block the Authentic Margherita case. But, first, the mutual independence of taste and ingredients should be independently motivated. Second, what would be the cost of such a move? It would generate a version of moderate essentialism on which the same combination of ingredients can be paired with different taste experiences in different subjects. In principle, such a view leaves open the possibility that there might be as many recipes as there are subjects. In addition to introducing a too solipsistic criterion for the identity of recipes, this would definitely not solve the ontological parsimony or repeatability issues. (Perhaps, the specific problem would not be *intra*subjective repeatability, but *inter*subjective repeatability.)

Therefore, I conclude, no version of essentialism is satisfying. They all establish a strong relationship between the taste and the identity of a recipe. In so doing, they fail to offer a convincing account.

Lessons and a New Starting Point

In this section, I highlight some general lessons I draw from the discussion on essentialism. Then, on these grounds, I offer a rough sketch of an alternative hypothesis to account for the relation between recipes and taste, thereby setting the agenda for further research.

Lessons

The first lesson is that essentialism should be dropped: the relation between recipes and taste does not fix the identity of a recipe nor does it depend on it. As we have seen, two dishes might taste the same, but that does not make them instances of the same recipe. Conversely, they might taste different and be instances of the same recipe. So, the taste and the identity of a recipe come apart. Clearly, this does not mean to deny that they are somehow associated—of course, they are. The point is to relax such an association and find a different way to look at it, given that our discussion suggests that it is not rooted in the essence of recipes. Plausibly, then, a recipe does not get to be associated with some gustatory profile just by being what it is, but in virtue of something else.

The second lesson is that recipes cannot be too detailed on pain of losing their *repeatability*. They are *elliptic*, as Borghini (2015) correctly points out: they leave out details concerning many aspects of the dishes that count as their instances. As we have seen, too many details about ingredients might make a recipe unrepeatable, insofar as they might be too fine-grained to be replicable across space and time. (Moreover, it is not obvious that *all* those details can even be registered.) So, recipes often gloss over many factors that are instead relevant to taste. A consequence of this is that, contrary to what essentialism assumes, a recipe typically underdetermines its taste: it does not carry enough information to individuate a unique associated gustatory profile.

Connected to this is a third lesson. Their being elliptic is what makes at least some recipes constitutively open to both synchronic and diachronic modification and change, thereby making it possible for the same recipe to variate, evolve, and be innovated. Essentialism cannot accept this—let alone explain it. For it is forced to introduce a new recipe for any significant variation in taste. What we need then is not a theory that denies that the same recipe can have different tastes, but one that embraces this as a fact and provides us with the tools to explain it. This is crucial for us to have a good account of recipes and their relationship with taste.

This invites the following general diagnosis. Insofar as it assumes the priority and the autonomy of recipes, essentialism fails to acknowledge the key point: the elliptic nature of recipes. An alternative account of the relation between recipes and taste should instead start from there.

A New Starting Point: Dishes Come First!

My sketch of a positive view, thus, begins with assuming that recipes are elliptic entities, not only with respect to ingredients and procedures but also with respect to taste—and very much so. That is, the identity of a recipe per se does not include or determine in any way the details about the taste of that recipe. Rather, it is up to the dishes that count as instances of that recipe to fill in the details about taste.

Essentialism is a *recipes-come-first* view. According to it, recipes are prior to dishes. Recipes are the primary bearers of taste and dictate the taste of dishes that count as their instances. This strategy did not prove very satisfying. My proposal, then, is to overturn it by adopting a *dishes-come-first* perspective as a starting point. The general idea is that taste is not something that a recipe possesses autonomously, but by being appropriately related to dishes—namely, by being the recipe of which those dishes are instances. On this perspective, then, dishes are the primary bearers of taste and determine the taste—or the tastes—of a recipe by being its instances.

Unlike essentialism, this strategy does not block in principle the association of the same recipe with more than one type of gustatory profile, insofar as it does not link the taste of a recipe to its identity. On the contrary, recipes are now identified independently of their taste and acquire taste from their instances, which possess it autonomously. This makes variety, innovation, change, and evolution possible. Figure 3.1 sketches the general idea.

We have a set of dishes (D1, D2, …, Dn), each of them having a taste (T1, T2, …, Tn) and being related to the other dishes by some important relation, which constitutes the criterion to determine that D1, D2, …, Dn are instances of the recipe R. By having

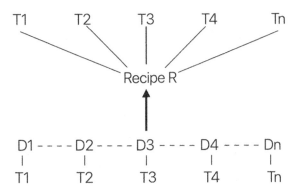

Figure 3.1 Synchronic acquisition of taste by a recipe.

A Philosophy of Recipes

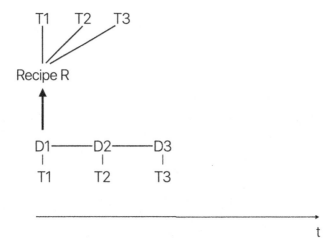

Figure 3.2 Diachronic acquisition of taste by a recipe.

D1, D2, ..., Dn as its instances, R "acquires" all their tastes (T1 ... Tn) as its tastes. Importantly, T1, T2, ..., Tn might be tokens of the same type of gustatory profile, but they do not have to be. If they are not, R acquires different tastes.

Figure 3.1 illustrates the *synchronic* acquisition of taste by a recipe. However, the acquisition of taste(s) by a recipe can be *diachronic* too, as shown in Figure 3.2.

As time (t) passes, more and more dishes, and hence their taste (or tastes), become associated with the same recipe R. Again, T1, T2, ..., Tn do not have to be tokens of the same type. If they are not, R acquires different tastes.

Synchronic and diachronic taste acquisitions are the basis of the innovation, evolution, change, and variation in the taste of one and the same recipe. They provide us with the beginning of a possible explanation of these phenomena.

Open Questions

Far from being conclusive, these remarks are just a first step. So, before concluding, let me quickly illustrate the open questions that must be addressed to consolidate these rough ideas into a fully articulated philosophical view. This sets the agenda for future research. It will also provide the reader with a better idea of the available options and, hence, of the different directions in which a recipes-come-first account can be developed.

First, we need an independent, non-essentialist *criterion* to determine when a dish counts as an instance of a recipe—namely, a criterion (a) other than taste (b) that grounds the identity of a recipe in facts or decisions about dishes. At least two options are available. One might think that there are some mind-independent facts about dishes that carve the culinary space at its joints, as it were, thereby allowing the individuation of different recipes. The idea is that dishes that share some relevant properties (e.g., ingredients and procedures) or have a common origin are instances of the same recipe.

This is a *realist* criterion to individuate recipes and their instances moving from facts about dishes.[8]

Alternatively, one might think that facts about dishes and recipes are not mind-independent but depend, at least partially, on some human *fiat*. The point is not denying that dishes, *qua* material objects, have certain properties. Rather, the thought is that those properties alone do not offer a good enough criterion to determine the recipe a dish is an instance of. That requires something more, namely, human decisions or acts—for example, a declaration of intention of a cook or judgments of authenticity by some experts (Borghini 2015). So, some mind-dependent facts are needed to establish facts about dishes, *qua* dishes, and in particular to determine that a dish is an instance of a recipe. This is a *constructivist* take on individuating recipes and their instances moving from decisions about dishes.

Second, the kind of *priority* that dishes enjoy over recipes has to be specified. This might be *epistemic* or *metaphysical*. In the first case, dishes come first in the sense that they are providers of epistemic access to the taste of a recipe. Our being acquainted with the tastes of the dishes that are instances of a recipe R puts us in the position to tell the taste (or tastes) of R. In the second case, dishes come first in the sense that facts about dishes are more fundamental than, and thus determine, facts about recipes—independently of what we know. So, a recipe R has a taste or a set of tastes in virtue of the fact that the dishes that count as instances of R have a certain taste or set of tastes.

Third, the *acquisition* relation must be better spelled out. The most pressing question is whether this is a *sui generis* relation or can, instead, be cashed out in terms of some more familiar relation, which would be preferable.

The different stances one might take on these three sets of issues, when combined, deliver different views and as many different ways of pursuing and developing a dishes-come-first approach to account for the relation between recipes and taste.

Conclusion

My general aim in this chapter has been to bring to the foreground some general questions concerning the relation between taste and recipes, which has not been the object of scrutiny so far. I have tackled the issue from the angle of the specific question as to whether recipes have their taste essentially, just by being the recipes they are. I offered a negative reply to this question. First, I have reconstructed the view, which I have called essentialism. Then, I have discussed different versions of it and argued that none of them are really satisfying. Hence, I have concluded that taste is not an essential property of a recipe or something that depends on its essence.

What is the relation between recipes and taste then? In the final part of the chapter, I sketched what I take to be the beginning of a reply to this question. My proposal has been to overturn the recipes-come-first perspective presupposed by essentialism in favor of a dishes-come-first one, on which taste properties are primarily properties of dishes that a recipe has only derivatively. This approach looks more promising, especially because it puts us in the position to explain how the same recipe can be associated with different tastes and can change and evolve taste-wise. Finally, I have offered a quick survey of the open questions for the suggested approach that sets the agenda for future research.

One final comment. If my remarks are on the right track, then they might interestingly impinge on the important question concerning the relation between recipes and dishes, at least in the following sense: views that assume that dishes are prior to, or as fundamental as, recipes are better positioned to explain how recipes relate to some types of gustatory profile. This might score a point in favor of those views. However, whether or not this is a decisive point cannot be established here: once again, it is material for future research.[9]

4

Dip It before You Eat It! On Recipes and the Architecture of a Dish

Andrea Borghini and Gabriele Ferretti

Introduction: Dishes and Their Architecture

I am in front of a very elegant dish. It is the first time I am trying it. Nonetheless, I have strong intuitions about how to slice it and that, before savoring it, I would be strongly recommended to dip it in the sauce that the waiter has brought, in a separate bowl, together with the main plate. This seems to be a common situation when we go for novel dishes. Sometimes, the waiter can also suggest how to consume the dish—which utensils we should use, as well as how we should cut it, how we should pair it, or that we should be careful about temperature (e.g., the temporal sequences of flavors), and so on. In short, a great deal of practical knowledge is required by a diner who is attempting to consume a new dish, even a simple dish, such as a bowl of rice, or a simple beverage, such as an espresso.

Though situations like the one just described are common at the table, and our behavior may be taken for granted, a closer look at these scenarios suggests that the complexity of information that diners can elaborate and manage in front of a dish is staggering. This is, after a careful analysis, unsurprising, considering the significance of eating to our evolutionary history and to our lives. In this respect, eating a spoonful of yoghurt or drinking from a cup relies on deep seated cognitive capacities to recognize properties of the surrounding environment—such as that a food is mushy or that a cup has a handle—that guide consumption "performance." Much of food design, in fact, builds upon such capacities (Spence 2017: esp. chs. 3–5).

Our concern in this chapter will be with the role of recipes in delivering the right sort and amount of information for proper preparation of a dish by the cook, leading to proper consumption by the diner. Specifically, we will be concerned with teasing out what sort of practical knowledge is required by the cook to prepare the dish so that it will then *afford* a specific way of consumption to the diner—for example, which tools can a cook employ to *communicate* to an average diner that the item on the plate should be dipped in the sauce?

An important cluster of questions regarding the scenarios we are set to examine concern the role of linguistic communication. To what extent does the transmission of information from the cook to the diner rely on linguistic communication as opposed to other sorts of signs, such as colors, shapes, and utensils? In certain contexts, receiving written or oral linguistic instructions from the cook, the server, or the table companion is necessary to put the diner on the right track for consumption. For instance, this is the case when the server of a fine restaurant lets the diner know that a certain food shall be eaten with hands rather than with silverware. One may be tempted to generalize from cases like these and conclude that linguistic communication always plays a central role in the communication between the cook and the diner.

Linguistic communication, however, can only go so far in guiding a diner. Even by letting a diner know that a dish must be eaten with hands would not instruct the diner about how to handle the food, which parts to consume first, how fast to consume it, how to chew it, and so on. In fact, the list of details that may be necessary to communicate the instructions of how to properly consume a dish to the diner is potentially infinite. Not only does such communication involve motor skills that are best taught by imitation (or what one might call motor transfer by observation) rather than by verbal description, but also it involves some details of the food that are most easily detected through sensory experience rather than through linguistic communication. On top of this, there seem to be some settings where linguistic communication is deemed unnecessary. In ice cream shops, for instance, servers rarely instruct customers on how to proceed in consuming the product—at best, they ask if a spoon or an extra cup could help. Another interesting set of cases regard all those scenarios where linguistic communication is not possible, for example, because the diner and the server do not share a language or because the recipe belongs to a distant past and no reliable authority can instruct a diner on how to specifically consume the food (on this topic, see the chapter by Korsmeyer in this volume). Finally, linguistic communication is sometimes not desirable, for instance, if the cook wants to engage the diner and leave room for different interpretations of the dish.

For these reasons, we shall leave aside an approach to our central issue in terms of linguistic communication. Rather, we shall focus on those characteristics of a dish that can be designed by a cook so that it directly affords, without any verbal aid, certain procedural knowledge to the diner on the basis of her sensory experience and motoric imagination. Linguistic instructions may be reinserted at a later stage of research as a way to enhance the information that a dish directly affords and as a means to construct articulated practices of consumption, such as a guided tasting or a celebratory meal that requires performing specific actions as instructed by some table companions (e.g., making a toast or eating foods in a specific order).

As anticipated, we call "the *architecture* of a dish" the characteristics of a dish that can be designed by a cook so that it directly affords, without any verbal aid, certain procedural knowledge to the diner. The architecture of a dish is not to be confused with its material structure, such as its physical or chemical properties. It is rather fundamentally an experiential notion: it is the ensemble of all those characteristics of a dish that mark and guide our experiences of it, specifically with respect to consumption. As the architecture of a building is not identical to its structure, but rather rests on the ways in which the building enables certain forms of dwelling, the architecture of a dish is not identical to its material composition, but rather rests on the gastronomic experiences it affords, also on the basis of its consumption. As the

Taj Mahal affords certain ways of dwelling to its visitors, similarly, a tube of Pringles affords certain forms of consumption to the consumer. Buildings and foods, thus, when viewed through an architectural lens, convey fundamentally *narrative* frameworks (see Pericoli 2018), with specific perceptual and practical aspects, which enable different forms of agency—dwelling and dining.

Our approach puts together the notion of affordance, related to the possibility of actions detected in the environment, and which is required to read off the architecture of a dish, with the notion of practical knowledge, which is required to reach proper consumption. The link is to some extent intuitive: when I know how to bring about a certain action, the context affords that action and I can spot such an affordance and satisfy it with my practical knowledge. Practical knowledge is in the spotlight of current reflections in philosophy of mind (for a recent review, see Ferretti 2021; Ferretti and Zipoli Caiani, forthcoming). Also, the notion of affordance has been thoroughly researched in the philosophical literature (Zipoli Caiani 2013; Osiurak et al. 2017; Ferretti 2019, 2021).

Thus, while the analysis we offer of the architecture of a dish is a primer, to carry it out we can rely on an established and detailed scholarship on practical knowledge and affordances. We shall begin from the insights coming from these two literatures to propose an account of the practical skills that a cook can rely on in transforming raw materials (i.e., ingredients) into a complex dish, so as to afford a specific consumption performance to the diner.

Next in the chapter, we highlight the core insights arising from the literature on practical knowledge that turn out to be relevant for us to examine the architecture of a dish. Afterwards, we briefly discuss the notion of affordance for the same purpose. Finally, we apply the basic notions from these two literatures to food transformation and consumption, with a specific focus on the role that practical knowledge and affordances play with them.

Our aim is to offer some insights into the nature of recipes and two practical aspects related to them. First, a constitutive aspect of certain recipes is to illustrate to the cook how to transform, in a very specific way, an edible material into a dish, by permitting to understand how to spot the affordances related to preparation and offering the practical knowledge to handle them. Second, in doing so, recipes give a cook the opportunity to flag up to the consumer the correct way to consume the dish in accordance with the recipe, showing the diner the affordances for consumption and the practical knowledge to satisfy them. This twofold use of affordances and practical knowledge within recipes is specifically shaped by the architecture of the dish: not only is it crucial for proper food consumption but, arguably, it is the landmark of a well-executed recipe.

Practical Knowledge

The notion of practical knowledge is in the spotlight of contemporary philosophy of mind and cognitive science (Stanley 2011; Fridland 2016; Ferretti & Zipoli Caiani 2018; Ferretti 2020; Ferretti & Zipoli Caiani, forthcoming). Such a notion was famously proposed by Ryle (1949) when offering the distinction between knowing-*how* (e.g., Lelio *knows-how* to run) and knowing-*that* (e.g., Lelio *knows-that* there is a pillow on the sofa). The distinction is controversial and gave rise to a lively philosophical debate. On the one hand, the so-called *intellectualists* argued that knowing-*how* can be, in principle, reduced to knowing-*that* (see, for example, Stanley 2011). On the other, anti-*intellectualists* argued against such a form of reduction (for a review of the arguments, see Fantl 2016; Ferretti 2020).

One of the most famous *intellectualist* accounts comes from Stanley (2011). In fact, this proposal has been so influential in the literature that most of the attempts to challenge *intellectualism* are, *ipso facto*, a critique of Stanley's view (for a recent review, see Ferretti 2020). The basic idea of intellectualism is that if a subject *knows how* to perform a given action A, then the subject *knows that* a certain way is a way to perform A. The debate is all about whether practical knowledge can be reduced to the possession of the correct propositions concerning ways to realize an action. Whether intellectualism holds true about recipes, or not, is an underexplored question (see the chapter by Borghini in this volume for more details), which has theoretical implications—for instance—on how we frame the identity conditions for recipes, as well as practical implications, for example, on the methods we employ to archive them.

In addition to the intellectualist debate as presented above, the current literature on practical knowledge has discussed at length also the difference between procedural, practical, declarative, and propositional knowledge. The core of this latter debate rests on two main interrogatives. First, what is the relation between know-how (motor, practical knowledge that successfully leads to the motoric performance of a given action) and procedural knowledge (knowledge of the required procedures that lead, step by step, to a given action), and whether the former can be reduced to the latter. Second, how to best characterize the relation between propositional knowledge, concerning knowledge of facts, and declarative knowledge, which permits to verbally articulate the procedures required to perform a given action (see Wallis 2008; Adams 2009; Devitt 2011; Fantl 2016: 3.1; Ferretti 2020: s. 5). A crucial question is, then, what is the relation between these forms of knowledge?

An underlying problem to these debates is the fact that, usually, the motor representations involved in executing an action that forms the basis of know-how have a different format with respect to both the intentions triggering the action and the propositional attitudes accompanying it. In fact, the motor representations are built in a motor format, while the intentions and the propositional attitudes are built in a propositional format. Recently, several accounts have tried to suggest how these two types of representations interlock (Butterfill & Sinigaglia 2014; Mylopoulos & Pacherie 2016; Burnston 2017; Shepherd 2017; Ferretti & Zipoli Caiani 2018, forthcoming; see also Ferretti 2020) by trying to solve the famous problem at the base of such an interlock, the so-called *interface problem* (Butterfill & Sinigaglia 2014).

A shared understanding of (some core aspects of) knowing-how is still looming large and we do not need to delve into the debate in this context. However, the reader may note that the relationships between procedural, declarative, practical, and propositional knowledge are really interesting when it comes to reasoning about how a cook can prepare a dish. That is the reason why we have sketched the main lines of the debate. In this chapter we do not take any position on the debate on the nature of practical knowledge and we assume that it is somehow linked to procedural knowledge. We simply want to rely on these notions, in a very neutral way, and employ them to offer a manifesto of a possible field of research between epistemology, philosophy of mind, perception and action, and philosophy of food.

In this respect, this chapter will rely on these notions related to practical knowledge to understand how the architecture of a dish involves both the practical and procedural knowledge of the cook in preparing a dish, as well as the one of the consumer in properly consuming the dish, with the latter knowledge depending on the former. The architecture of a dish relies on a sort of tacit motor transfer, concerning a motor action related to the act of (proper) consumption, from the cook to the consumer. Indeed, it is crucial for the cook that they can dispose of a practical knowledge (a first-order practical knowledge, one might say) to build a dish, which can directly trigger, in the consumer, the correct procedure, related to a practical knowledge, to perform proper consumption (a second-order practical knowledge, one might say). To be successful, the cook must know how to manipulate raw materials so as to transform mere ingredients into a specific dish, which can then recall a special form of consumption, based on a direct transfer of practical knowledge, to the consumer.

But this is not sufficient. Indeed, in the next section, we argue that mastering the architecture of a dish requires that a cook has the ability to detect appropriate affordances of the raw materials, which make it possible to transform the dish in accordance with the recipe. These materials open up to the cook a range of possible actions to be performed on the raw materials as well as the possibilities of manipulating (this being related to the practical knowledge concerning the recipe) the raw materials as required by the recipe so that the cook can generate a dish with a specific architecture. So, as practical knowledge, also detection of affordances is deeply related at both levels: in generating the architecture of a dish on the part of the cook and in properly consuming the dish on the part of the diner.

Affordances

Objects display geometrical properties (e.g., size, shape, spatial location), which assume a motor significance for an acting subject because they can be thought of as action/motor properties, for they afford to the subject the possibility of motor interaction that can be satisfied with a motor act. For example, the geometrical characteristics of a pencil can be seen as action properties that recall a possible action (grasping), possibly satisfied by a given motor act (a precision grip). These possibilities of action offered by objects are usually called, in the literature, *affordances*.

The notion of *affordance* has been famously developed by J. J. Gibson in his ecological theory of vision. According to Gibson (1979/1986) affordances are possibilities of action visually detected in the environment *directly*—namely, without any representational medium. One of the main tasks of vision is, thus, the detection of affordances (Chemero 2009; Zipoli Caiani 2013; Tillas et al. 2016; De Wit et al. 2017; Osiurak et al. 2017; Sakreida et al. 2017; Ferretti 2016, 2019, 2021; Ferretti & Zipoli

Caiani 2019). Interestingly, they are detected regardless of whether we subsequently actually decide to act on the object. We need to go more slowly through this point.

In this respect, according to the initial insight by Gibson (1979), we do not perceive a set of perceptual features or qualities, but a sort of motor information recalling action performance, namely, affordances. Such a perceptual performance does not require a twofold perceptual process in which the subject's visual system first detects a material object and, only then, attributes to it a motoric significance: affordances are immediately and directly detected by means of a motoric information pick-up directly within the visual stimulus (for an analysis of this Gibsonian claim, see Chemero 2009; Zipoli Caiani 2013; Tillas et al. 2016; Ferretti 2021). This famously suggests, in Gibson's view, that seeing things in the environment means effectively seeing what, in terms of motor behavior, they afford. So, the basic statement of Gibson's ecological theory is that we *see affordances* (e.g., we see a chair affords sitting, a handle affords grasping, and so on).

But the reader should note that affordances have both motor and semantic aspects. The motor aspects relate to the generic possibilities of action recalled by the object: specific geometrical properties will recall in the viewer specific motoric interactions. I can grasp a pen. However, I usually do not kick a pen. The semantic aspects concern the design of the object, which recalls to an agent the proper functional use the object was designed for (Ferretti 2016, 2019, 2021; Sakreida et al. 2017; Zipoli Caiani & Ferretti 2017). This is why, for instance, I usually grasp a pen. Furthermore, on the basis of what I want to do with it (writing vs. placing), I can decide to employ a power grip or a precision grip.

We have so far clarified the notion of practical knowledge, as well as the one of affordances. In what follows, we will use these two notions to characterize the way in which cooks rely on them to build a food architecture to convey to diners the right and specific motor instructions to reach proper consumption performance.

Recipes, Affordances, and Practical Knowledge

We can now employ the concepts and lessons accrued from our selected review of the debates on practical knowledge to further and deepen our theoretical understanding of recipes; in particular, that of the architecture of the dishes that they deliver.

What sort of knowledge do recipes require? It may be useful to begin with the way we represent and share them. Recipes have been archived in many ways. For instance, they can be written down or passed along orally, they may be impressed in individual memory through direct observation, or they can be archived in videos and photographs. Of course, written and oral recipes make use of propositional knowledge, linguistically structured, and with a declarative dimension concerning the procedures that activate some practical motor knowledge. But, also video and photographic demonstrations typically employ verbal shortcuts (e.g., "work the dough steadily for 30 minutes"), which involve a transfer from linguistically structured propositional knowledge to motor knowledge. Interestingly, such a transfer poses a sort of *interface problem of recipes*, connected to the classic problem of establishing a relation between practical and propositional formats and knowledge thereof: in what way are procedural knowledge and practical knowledge, with respect to affordance perception, jointly involved in designing food architectures and ways of consumption?

To address this question, there are crucial aspects related to affordances and practical knowledge worth discussing. Leaving aside the debate concerning the real nature of the relation between procedural, declarative, propositional, and practical knowledge, when it comes to the architecture of a dish, there is something very interesting. Namely, there is a specific relation between what we might call a first- and a second-order practical knowledge, as well as between a first- and a second-order affordance detection. The following three aspects concerning the knowledge required by a cook to master the architecture of a dish let us understand this involvement, concerning the first order of practical knowledge and affordance detection.

First aspect. The cook must possess a specific knowledge that is the knowledge for executing the recipe, which is cashed out in procedural terms. To do so, the cook must be able to transform such a procedural knowledge into practical knowledge that rests upon such a procedure.

Second aspect. The cook must be able to recognize specific affordances in raw materials. This ability rests on the semantic knowledge of the action possibilities needed to transform the raw materials into a proper architecture. Thus, a carrot will afford the cook with the action possibility of peeling it into thin slices, or cutting it into small rounds. A potato would afford the cook with the action possibility of cooking it whole in a pot with water.

Third aspect. The recipe can function as an aid during the first and the second steps, suggesting procedural descriptions of the preparation that will, in turn, lead the cook to spot the affordances offered by the raw materials, focusing on the specific subset of affordances that pertains to the delivery of a certain architecture. Therefore, the recipe illustrates the (first-order) detection of affordances, related to the (first-order) practical knowledge of the procedures, which will lead to the proper realization of the final dish.

Note that these are specific semantic aspects of affordances, as recipes clearly employ not only first-order affordances of the raw materials (a carrot) but also first-order affordances of the tools used in the preparation process (a knife), on the basis of the transformation that the raw materials have to undergo, by means of these tools, for the architecture building. For instance, a recipe would require the cook to hold the rolling pin in a specific way to stretch the dough for some tortellini, and then specify that the cook use their fingers in a specific way to shape them.

In this respect, by looking at the affordances offered by the raw materials, the cook can spot, with their practical knowledge, those affordances which lead to the building of a specific dish. This is a matter of semantic sensitivity to the cultural use of such a dish. By applying their procedural knowledge, the cook can, thus, give rise to a specific architecture of the dish. This is a first-order practical knowledge about affordances in generating a dish.

But then, at the same time, the cook has to be able to generate in the consumer the appropriate trigger of the proper affordances (second-order affordance detection), with the consequent activation of the (second-order) practical knowledge for proper consumption, on the basis of the expected semantic knowledge of affordances of the consumer. In dealing with this aspect, the cook has to master the aspect of the (second-order) affordances of the dish coming from the raw materials. These affordances then relate to the functional way in which the consumer can represent a structured dish, recalling specific affordances demanding a specific procedural knowledge to be practically satisfied. This is, indeed, crucial for the way in which the consumer has to use the dish with respect to the correct consumption the dish has been designed for.

Some foods wear their second-order affordances about consumption on their sleeves. For instance, a bag of freshly made popcorn delivered to the hands of the consumer offers minimal room for equivocation. Analogous considerations apply to bags of chips, salty peanuts, ice-cream cones, pizza slices, or falafels. Other foods, however, raise more difficult cases of communication between the cook and the consumer: consumption is more articulated and so is the range of second-order affordances that the cook may or may not design. By way of illustration, we may consider sushi, a widely discussed case in point also in popular media when it comes to its second-order affordances. Take a sushi roll. On the one hand, a roll may leave "no choice" to consumers, as celebrity chef Noboyuki Matsuhisa also suggested (Barr 2018): each piece should be eaten in one bite. On the other hand, additional directions for consumption are missing and the environmental conditions (e.g., table settings) often trigger undesired ways of consumption. For instance, it is common that a consumer uses a fork to "stab and grab" sushi pieces, thus breaking them apart before they reach the mouth; another common issue is with consumers who give a full immersion to sushi pieces—rather than a subtle dip—into the accompanying sauce. It may be somewhat obvious to note that these communication issues are linked to broader moral considerations, not just of etiquette but also of cultural understanding and respect.

Thus, recipes have a dual nature, so to speak. First of all, they convey the procedural knowledge required by the cook to prepare the raw materials, and to do so they must rely on (first-order) affordances of the raw materials and of the tools employed. Secondly, recipes convey the (first-order) procedural knowledge that aids the cook in spotting such affordances and then in building a specific plate capable of allowing the consumer to spot other second-order affordances—those offered by the architecture, not by the raw materials. Relatedly, those affordances will trigger the consumer to start the second-order procedure concerning appropriate practical consumption, that is, the way in which the recipe suggested to prepare the dish in order for it to be consumed.

The reader might note that, in this perspective, recipes involve a twofold process unfolding in two different moments. First of all, the recipe concerns an appropriate dish preparation: this means that the raw materials, which could be the basis for different recipes, can be used to generate a specific dish, related to (and triggering) appropriate dish consumption. Secondly, such raw materials composing such a specific dish will be consumed, on the basis of how they are organized within the architecture, in a specific manner, among all the possible manners. The two processes link practical knowledge, procedural knowledge, and affordance perception through semantic aspects that involve the cook alone (in the first process) or that go from the cook to the consumer (in the second process).

We can hence distinguish between *dish preparation affordances* and *consumption affordances*. *Dish preparation* affordances are the first-order affordances required to prepare the dish from the raw food; *consumption affordances* are the second-order affordances that pertain to the architecture of the dish. The perspective on the epistemology of recipes that we are introducing here may be used to shed light on and explain apparently heterogeneous aspects of recipes.

First of all, we may rank recipes based on how detailed they are with respect to their *dish preparation* affordances or *consumption* affordances. While, for instance, cooks may need plenty of *dish preparation* affordances to properly prepare meatballs or fries, little *consumption affordances* are provided for their gastronomic appreciation. On the other hand, the preparation of a plate of prosciutto and figs requires minimal instructions and, thus, relies minimally on *dish preparation* affordances; yet, it may call for *consumption affordances* regarding how to consume the figs and how to combine figs and prosciutto.

Secondly, the distinction between *dish preparation* and *consumption affordances* can also serve to frame an old and vexed question concerning an odd epistemic asymmetry between cooks and food critics: why is it that, on average, good food critics need not be skilled cooks? The answer may be hinted at by the very distinction of the two processes that concern recipes: while cooks have to considerably worry about *dish preparation* affordances, food critics tend to worry about *consumption affordances*. By doing so, critics discount a considerable part of the knowledge required by a cook.

A third use of the distinction between *dish preparation* and *consumption* affordances pertains to the different practical abilities and skills that are connected to them. By training to follow recipes, a cook learns how to spot first-order affordances in food to come up with novel recipes by discovering new *dish preparation* affordances as well as by unraveling new practical ways of using them to build novel dish architectures.

These two abilities may be quite different. In fact, we find recipes that may resemble each other in terms of first-order affordances, but not in terms of second-order affordances. For instance, tortilla and lasagna resemble each other in the first-order affordances of corn and wheat flours, but do not resemble each other in the suggested manner of consumption, the first being a finger food while the second typically calling for the use of a utensil.

A more trivial observation worth offering is the following. Consumers, on their part, grow more skilled the more they become familiar with a different array of *consumption affordances*, or lack thereof, and with the consequent practical knowledge fostered by them. By learning how to detect *consumption affordances*, or by learning when a cook may have intentionally omitted them, the consumer knows how to eat a dish and is able to transfer this practical knowledge to novel situations with similar, but different dishes. In the same way that a cook must know how to afford (second order) a dish with a certain experience, the consumer of that dish must possess not only the motor abilities to ingest the food but also the procedural knowledge harbored in the (second-order) affordances of the dish.

Conclusion

In this chapter, we have laid down the foundations for approaching some underexplored epistemological issues related to recipes and the dishes that they deliver. Further discussion, we suggest, should build upon two main pillars.

First, a twofold distinction between the first- and the second-order affordances, or *dish preparation* and *consumption* affordances, that the raw materials (i.e., ingredients) used in a recipe afford to a cook and are detected by the consumer. Such a twofold distinction leads us to consider the twofold nature of practical knowledge when analyzing its mastery on the cook's side, as well as on the consumer's side. Such distinction seems promising not only for framing theoretical approaches to recipes (e.g., to discuss their identity conditions) but also for suggesting how to teach cooking skills, or which information is most important to appropriately record a recipe.

Second, we suggest that future discussion should concentrate on shedding light on what we might consider an interface problem in the philosophy of food, which is parallel to the one in the philosophy of mind and action (Butterfill & Sinigaglia 2014; Ferretti & Zipoli Caiani, forthcoming) and which we might call *the interface problem of recipes*, that is, the problem of explaining in which way procedural and practical knowledge, and propositional and declarative knowledge, with respect to affordance perception, are jointly involved in designing food architectures and ways of consumption.

5

Body, Tool, and Technique: Elements of Work in the Japanese Kitchen

Merry White

There are many ways to eat in Japan, and all of them, from artisanal kaiseki to the best pizza, to the best croissant you've ever had, are Japanese. All partake of certain qualities we might venture to call "Japanese" while all of them speak to the diversity—regional, seasonal, innovative, and personal—that is Japan. These qualities are expressed through the work of food itself, through the values and principles attached to the making, which lie in the meanings of art and craft, but resonate also with the cultural value of ephemerality, and the added enhancements of relationships, between maker and consumer, grower and chef. How information—directions, guidance, models, formulae, and standards—is passed along is rarely signaled in text or standardized routines and does not rely on the "recipe" as is common in Western understandings of culinary communication.

Recipes, as seen in the West—namely, as didactic and precision-quantified—have little reference in the work and work-learning of these foods. Recipes and cookbooks exist of course, and cookbooks (and food programming on television) form a lucrative market. But learning is in the practice, not in the book. Experience, observation, and knowledge of tools are seen as more important guides. Techniques, of course, are to be practiced, repeated to become "second nature" in the body work of cooking, and these are framed by aesthetic, seasonal, and personal qualities that can scarcely be generalized into the kinds of prescriptive principles of order and measurement that shape recipes. One learns to cook by imitation, repetition, and suggestion, and by trial and error; preparations are best learned through observation of a mentor, a chef, a grandmother. As in traditional artisanal crafts in Japan, apprenticeship, however configured in a modern setting, is an honored role or is at least on the path to one. A "recipe," then, is the product, the last stop, the summary of the requirements of creation rather than the starting point. It, like the food itself, is the product of experience, practice, the training of the body, and the uses of tools that coordinate memory, observation, morality, and the senses.

Principles

We might say that cooking adheres to certain cultural scripts—recipes writ large—as art, craft, family narrative, and nutritional work. Work is personal in the body, morally bound by ideas of craft and service, governed by history and place. These parameters are not unique to Japan, but have their own language that positions makers and consumers in a common cultural narrative.

The guiding principles of cooking (aesthetic, nutritional, sensual) in the making and in the appreciating of Japanese food are well described, and often "Orientalized" in the literature on Japanese food. One such is *me de taberu*, or "we eat with our eyes," emphasizing the visual landscape of a dish. Another is "five colors" (white, black, green, red, and yellow) that define a presentation or a meal in both nutritional and aesthetic terms. It is not only about contrast but also represents care: health and beauty are conjoined in visual service. Famously, Japanese food is prepared with an eye to the eye—but also to the ear and to the agents of the other senses—beholding it. The multisensory nature of Japanese food appreciation—attending to these involves another "principle"—includes balance and variety in all the senses: sight, sound, textural qualities, and of course taste and aroma, and the multi-aesthetic sensibility reaches a peak in the tea ceremony meal called *kaiseki*. But it also shows up in the mundane school bento (lunchbox), the *ekiben* or railroad station meal-in-a-box, the convenience store vegetable packet, and on the domestic dining table. Everyone knows and appreciates the importance of shape and the formulae for color, texture, balance that are to entice the eye and then (and thus) the appetite. Children learn this in their mother's lunchboxes and are encouraged by their teachers in their appreciation of the work that went into them. (Notes sent home by teachers to mothers might in fact call out a mother who seems not to have paid enough attention to the eye-catching, child-seductive aspect of lunch preparation.) The particular ways in which the senses are appreciated also rely on cultural knowledge but not always high culture—on an appreciation of literature, of art, capable of recognizing allusions to Basho's poetry or Sesshu's brushstrokes as well as the amusement of a Vienna hotdog cut to resemble a cute octopus. One need not have a classical aesthetic education to appreciate the food, but chefs like Tanigawa of Kyoto's Kichisen restaurant for example, of working-class origin, incorporate such touches in their food, admittedly for an audience that can afford it. A Tokyo neighborhood caterer chided his son for playing mahjong instead of reading art books: "food has to look good to taste good," he remarked. These are cultural norms available across classes in Japan. One person, a designer of food exhibitions in a *depachika* food hall, put aesthetic presentation very high on her list of values, but she saw display as an aspect of service, an aesthetic *omotenashi*, which is a significant "skill" in food preparation.

My own appreciation of such elegant food, however, did not include more than a smattering of recognition of Japanese art and literature. At the beginning food was to be a sidebar to my academic history: after all, food wasn't yet a respected academic topic of research. In 1975, starting my doctoral fieldwork in Japan on institutions and internationalisms, I entered an old and famous cooking school for a year's course. I'd been a professional cook before graduate school so I thought that this would be a leisure activity, relief from the incessant and stressful interviewing of fieldwork. I was so wrong; it was so hard. I learned something about work, and something about myself in the process, but I most definitely did not become proficient in Japanese cooking. I saw that cooks, through experience and constant trials, learned in the tongue, the nose, the fingers, and the eyes—and even in the sounds—what was desirable in food. Though there was indeed a textbook, only the students referred to it and scribbled diligently in their notebooks. The actual performances were not scripted. I became a watchful observer, desperately substituting attention for my lack of linguistic fluency and for my lack of experience in a Japanese kitchen.

I emerged with great respect for those who are fluent in food, including those who work to serve the cook: those who make the tools, weave the baskets, hammer the steel knife blanks, grow the foodstuffs, peel bamboo shoots, and trim the hairs on a *wagyu* cow's chin.

These people are all engaged in what is both art and craft—a distinction by the way NOT relevant in Japan, where artists and craftspeople share the same status, where both the craftsperson (*shokunin*) whose production is of "use" and the artist whose production sits in a museum can become Living National Treasures (*ningen kokuhoo*), an individual certified as "preserver of important intangible cultural properties." Even at lower levels of status and recognition, food makers have the focus, the skills, and the flexibility, all governed by ideas of aesthetics, taste, and service, that make them "artists."

Art however is flexible, adaptable to the available and to the imagination. The lack of scripts, which imply permanence, standardization, or constancy, seems related to the "*mono no aware*" idea that all things are transient, given evidence here in the dominance of seasonality, locality, and the inspiration of the moment. The appearance of the "first" matsutake in the fall demands the simplest preparation: it announces the season. But two weeks later, a dish of matsutake demands creativity and something to surprise the consumer. Menus, dishes, and preparations seem guided by "this time and this time only"—"*ichigo ichie*"—which several chefs mentioned as a principle, in a sense belying the idea of principle itself. Value is embedded in impermanence. The fixed point, the first mover, is the body of the food worker.

Body Work

Much more could be said of the hierarchy of value, its priorities, and its locations in work itself. What food work in Japan illustrates is the complexity and diversity of work itself. The literally visceral nature of food is also engaged with the corporeality of the worker's body. What is most important to the food worker in the experience of work is the body. Body training (like that of martial arts) is often more formal, more codified in cooking schools and their texts than in actual kitchens—for example, as in a text for learning knifework: "in using a knife, the posture of the cook is most important. Lining up the right arm, bending the left arm in a semi-circle, you place one foot behind and to the side of the other, in a 45-degree angle to the counter. This frees up movement allowing for precision of cutting." When I showed this text to a cook, he laughed dismissively. Observing cooks in action, I very rarely saw this particular form, this *kata*, this posture: they were moving too fast, or the counter wasn't the right height, or someone was in their way—or they'd absorbed the lesson of centering and balance at a less than scripted level.

Cooks said their bodies and the biomechanics of labor were the most important aspects and tools in cooking, their skills were second and attributes of the workplace, utensils, and ingredients were third. They said that the physicality of labor demands physical training and that their bodies were their most important tools to maintain. You may remember the scene in the satirical food film by Itami Juzo, *Tampopo*, when Goro, her coach, puts the aspirational ramen chef Tampopo through her paces, literally, as he bikes alongside her while she runs. She must repeatedly lift huge kettles full of water in another strength-building exercise. Any cook will tell you this is scarcely an exaggeration, and physical training does not make a negligible contribution to the work of food. Body work in food is both elemental and stylized—like the gestures of a JR train dispatcher, it is also performance art. The use of the body in coffee preparation can also seem balletic.

What often in the West seems routine can be personal and communicative work in Japan. Noda-san, a "barman" and pourover artist who came out of rock 'n' roll to coffee, engages full body movement and control at the counter of his small basement café in Kyoto—Otafuku—one which is called by café aficionados a "red velvet café"—in his old school pourover method in a Vienna-infused ambience. He has a painstaking performance. He dresses for it as if an actor—in a style of his own like the style of his body movements, dressed in a smart vest over a dress shirt, sporting sideburns and a sharply precise hair cut with cool black aviator glasses. His pour technique has rhythm and symmetry. His action, he says, is part of his intention to make coffee an "encounter"—a "*goen*"—in which he gives not only coffee but also his work in making it to the customer, who is usually sitting at the counter, a mere 12 inches from the action. The pour, performed in a precise balletic sway of his whole upper body, covers the grounds in three separate movements: first to moisten the grounds completely, then to start the spiral-in-spiral-out drip, a continuous motion letting fall a continuous, very narrow drizzle of hot water, leaving a lighter brown pattern over the darker brown first pour. The last will repeat this spiraling leaving a yet lighter foamy trail on the grounds, and never breaking "the wall" or the outer edge of grounds next to the paper filter. He will do this fifty or more times a day. He literally puts his back into it, so to offset the stiffness, he'll do stretches in the tiny kitchen area to one side of the counter.

I encountered this kind of conscious body work in other coffee people—in the owner of Café Sagan whose ramrod straight posture was a matter of honor for him—though he showed me the striking varicose veins in his legs as evidence of his commitment always to be *standing*—an act of *omotenashi,* wholehearted attention to guests—if there was a customer in the shop. Katsuyuki Tanaka's bodywork at Bear Pond in Tokyo's Shimokitazawa is about constantly perfecting the beverage—his work in making the best espresso is in part to personalize the impersonal, industrial-mechanical aspect of espresso-making as he takes apart the La Marzocco espresso machine and steam-cleans the portafilter between each shot, twisting his body around the machine to check the threadings, and reassembling it all before the next shot. He makes the machine, he says, an extension of his arm, allowing espresso to be a "handmade" drink. It is exhausting, and so he limits his production of his prized "angel stain" espresso to about twenty shots a day. Get there after about ten o'clock in the morning, and you'll have to have something else to drink, still good, but lacking the intense body work of the early morning.

Cooks and barmen share the stress of performance whether "on stage" at a café or in a kitchen far away from the customers' view. Tanigawa, the earlier-mentioned *kaiseki* chef in Kyoto, has an important tool in the small storage room next to his kitchen. It is a large professional boxer's punching bag hanging from the ceiling. When the precision and control needed for his fine work becomes stressful, he leaves it to pound the bag, releasing some of the tension before returning to the delicate cuts of fish and vegetables.

Cooks also use martial arts training for balance and strength, using their own weight to stabilize, create pressure, and maintain force—and like Thomas Keller's use of ballet instructors for his team at French Laundry in California, Japanese chefs also emphasize the ways in which bodies in the kitchen must interact, aware of the limited space and risks. Keeping everything in your body tight but supple, one cook said that it takes a lot of energy to be physically alert; he said, I don't eat until the work is done or my body's energy will go to digestion and I might become lethargic. Another worker, whose job was to shred cabbage fine for tonkatsu, worked with repetitive motions, which allow for finer, better work, although others noted that it leads to serious shoulder problems.

Tools

Next to the body, the tools of the cook—the batterie de cuisine—have the most importance for preparers of food. Utensils, tools in the professional kitchen, are not that different from the ordinary tools in the home kitchen—but there is little automation or "appliance" work, less sometimes than in a home kitchen and there are few non-manual tools such as paco jets, butane torches, and immersion blenders at work in a Japanese professional kitchen, and much more hand work. Food workers, in this case people in kitchens rather than in factory production, talked about their relationships with their tools in an intimate way—some said that the relationship between tool, technique, and product created a triangular model with the cook as an intervening variable. The transformation of the ordinary, through the mundane tool doing the work under the worker's control, creating a sense of value and personal satisfaction, completed the triangle. The tool of greatest importance to cooks, after the body, is the knife.

Doi Itsuo is a knife maker in Sakai, a town near Osaka where knife-making is the signature profession—and craft—and art. Doi's father was a legendary blacksmith, recently retired, by whom Doi was trained and for whom he worked for over forty years.

Sakai was a rich merchant city in the fifteenth and sixteenth centuries, well located for trade on water. In the mid-sixteenth century, Portuguese priests and traders visited Sakai and after that Sakai became Japan's leading firearm manufacturing town. Oda Nobunaga seized the town when it refused to give up its autonomy, but it regained its wealth if not its independence under Toyotomi Hideyoshi, a powerful daimyo who is said to have "unified" Japan in the sixteenth century. After the Second World War Sakai became Japan's leading knife-producing city, refining the process of lamination that had been used in swords—and bicycle parts. Family-run workshops specialize in blade-forging, sharpening, handle-making, and other work involved in finishing a knife from blanks to blades, from Doi's forge to another family workshop nearby for honing, thence to a last shop for the addition of a wooden handle and a bolster of bone or horn. To make a single blade the operations usually take at least four days.

There are basically two types of knives: *honyaki* and *kasumi*—the first is forged from a single piece of steel, differentially hardened so that the spine is less hard than the edge, thus the spine is more flexible and the edge more sensitive. Kasumi are the more common now—the *hagane* high carbon steel forms an inner core fused with low carbon steel cladding, or *jigane*, again giving strength and flexibility. With lamination, a knife is capable of very fine honing and thus fine cuts, and this allows for a delicate aesthetic. *Hochonin*, or "knife person," was traditionally synonymous with "head cook"—as cutting was not to be left to less skilled or apprentice cooks. The perfect fish knife, or *yanagi*, in the hand of an impeccable hochonin is able to cut so cleanly through the fish that the KNIFE is reflected in the flesh of the fish—not the fish mirrored in the knife.

There are also regionally specific knives—even for the same use. For example, in western Japan (Kansai), eels (*unagi*) are cut differently from the way they are cut in the Tokyo region (Kanto) and the knives are different too. One cook who grew up in a Kyoto *unagi* shop said she was shocked when she found that Tokyo *unagi* butchering procedures were so different—"isn't it the same fish?" Kansai knives have a rounded profile; Kanto knives are rectangular, squared off. The *usuba* for *katsuramuki* (sheet-cutting) is used differently in Kansai and Kanto. Another knife work regionalism was rather startling: three people mentioned that in Tokyo, the custom is to make the first cut in a fish in its "front," while in Kyoto, the cut is in the rear. A Kyoto-based cook said that it is because, in Tokyo, samurai culture from the Edo period (1600–1868) still has influence and cutting in front is too much like the cut one would make in one's own belly committing *hara-kiri*; he said that for Kyoto people, the aesthetic comes from courtier sensibilities, and the appearance and taste are improved by cutting the belly; they have no samurai sensitivity.

Next to the knife, cooks said the *fukin* (the kitchen cloth) is more important than other tools—that cutting and cleaning were the most important jobs of the cook. Cleaning—which includes everything you do with a fukin, including patting a fish dry or wiping a knife—is a cooking (as well as a moral) act and has techniques and tools of its own—these were regional as well, for instance, the modes of wiping, where you keep the fukin, and the shapes of scrubbing brushes. Fukin themselves can be artisanally made by famous craftspeople, from linen, hemp, and silk.

After knives and fukin, the next most commonly cited tools were *hashi* (chopsticks) and, for the *kaiseki* chefs, *moribashi* (plating chopsticks), for precise positioning of ingredients in the landscape of a dish.

Another story of regionalisms lies in the *tamagoyaki* pan, a rectangular pan, usually tinned copper with a wooden handle used only for making a kind of omelette for sushi or other preparations. Tokyo procedure in making these rolled forms is to pull the cooked egg back from the front of the pan, while, in Kyoto, cooks work from the back of the pan.

Other tools feed other senses, releasing aroma, creating texture, even contributing sound. Graters are prized and expensive if they are hand-cut. These are used for ginger, daikon, wasabi—each purpose-designed. The act of hand grating, like the act of grinding, is said not only to produce a better product but to offer multisensory experiences, both as pleasures of nose and ear, and as indicators of a person's skill.

Suribachi and *surikogi*—ceramic mortar and wooden pestle—especially used in grinding *goma* (sesame seeds) for dressings like *goma-ae*, offer the pay-off of sensual enjoyment and body work: movement, scent, sound. The use of the *sansho* (peppercorn) wood in the pestle adds another flavor, as does the clay of the *suribachi*, or mortar bowl, which eventually is worn down by use, transferring its taste to the food.

The use of an old-fashioned ceramic or cast-iron rice pot, the *kama*, would have to be deliberately chosen, as everyone in domestic and professional kitchens has an electric rice maker in constant use. The "gastronostalgia" for the way things used to taste has led a maker of highly automated "fuzzy-logic" rice cookers to retrofit their rice cookers to refer to pre-industrial tastes—developing an insert—ceramic or cast iron— that will make the perfect, electronically timed rice smell and taste like grandmother's more intuitively timed rice.

Relationships

Imagined or recaptured relationships are aspects of cooking and eating in Japan, as elsewhere—the nostalgia for something lost or from a distant past, an imagined, imbues food with meanings. But contemporary, present relationships also give food meaning. A sushi cook and his fish provider, a chef and his forager, may have relationships several generations deep.

There is often a close relationship between the cook and the maker of culinary tools, to the point where a chef will work with a knife maker to make just the knife needed— for the hand and height and preferences of the user, so the makers of knives are key in the Japanese food world.

Tanigawa Yoshimi, the Michelin-starred chef of Kichisen in Shimogamo, Kyoto, like many, speaks of his food as evidence of durable relationships, like the relationships forged with his knife makers as well as ephemeral iterations of aesthetics. He came to Kyoto at the age of fifteen and was apprenticed to cooks while he studied tea, incense, and poetry. He gathers ingredients from all over the region, some from long-term suppliers and some directly from farmers and foragers: he calls his food "relationship food."

Tokyo chef Zaiyu Hasegawa values above all his relationships "over the counter" with his customers. He performs his "modern" kaiseki meal at Den, it is creative, playful, and seemingly boundary-, recipe-, and rule-free: he says there should be a laugh with every presentation. Sometimes it is a laugh of surprise; his "home cooking to create joy" is nothing anyone's mother—not even his own geisha mother—has made—a salad demanding the simultaneous work of five chefs hovering over a single bowl, topped off with a perfectly posed large black ant, crisp and yuzu-scented, its front leg raised in salute. He refers to the jointly created product as the result of "collective communication." Hasegawa might seem more like Rene Redzepi of Noma, whose Nordic primitivism relies on extreme local foraging, including pine needles and bark. Hasegawa's dessert one night replicated not a beautiful garden at a state of perfection, which might be depicted in the tray-landscape of a traditional kaiseki meal, but the gardener's tools and the glove and dirt involved in actual garden work—edible except for the rabbit-eared cotton glove and "rusty" trowel (the "rust" is *yuzu*-seasoned cocoa). Hasegawa seems borderless, while Tanigawa's skills involve staying within some elegant lines, which delineate imaginative and yet readable seasonality. For both, the inspiration is said to come from pleasing a customer, and each has won two Michelin stars, from pleasing a global audience; Den however has risen to near the top of the "World's Best Restaurant" list, transcending any categorization as "Japanese."

"Reading" Food

In a politely competitive performance of serious chefs held about four years ago, there were allusive rather than explicit dishes prepared, far from belly laughs. Each chef was given an artist-made serving container, dish, or sometimes only a cloth, and asked to prepare a dish for it. The dishes are named rather poetically (and sometimes politically), which emphasizes high consciousness and meaning-heavy intentionality.

One dish—on a folded piece of paper painted in red-earth-tone lacquer—is similar in some ways to Hasegawa's garden evocation. Pieces of tree bark and dry leaves— here not chocolate but actual dry leaves, a Jerusalem artichoke, filled with *uni* and vegetables—are strewn on the paper. Guests dip their fingers in seawater before eating with those briny fingers—themselves participating in the "cooking" by adding a missing taste, like the sansho peppercorn pestle adding taste to the ground *goma*.

The moral component of such elaborately conceived but "simple" evocations contains "*mottainai*" (don't waste). Using elements of nature that might otherwise be thrown away, like dead leaves or the reference to them through edible versions, says "respect nature" by using natural substances rather than by using man-made or industrial components in a meal.

One reference point cooks cited in this "respect nature" trope was called "innovative Satoyama," inspiring poetic nostalgia—foraged, wild, no-waste—in "satoyama" (the areas between mountains and villages).

Food workers in industrial food settings, such as the places where *ekibento* are produced, see themselves as making "real food"—even where one might not imagine it. In the House Foods factory in Shizuoka where prepared foods are produced such as packets of curry roux and stew bases, I observed workers watching chunks of potato, rough chopped, and vaguely trapezoidal pieces of carrot tumble into each other in the gravity-powered high-ceilinged production room. The workers were not consulting computers: the work was eyes-on if not hands-on. One worker explained that they were trained in very sensitive observation, watching the speed, the conjoining of ingredients, the ways in which the foods fell. Paying attention, he said, is their most important skill. He said, "This is real food—it's a real potato, a real carrot." The use of gravity meant that workers did not have to carry anything heavy nor was electrical energy wasted, as production was quite literally top-down, raw materials delivered to the top of the building elevated on the "green" robot trucks to that level, processed through stages as they descended, finally finding each other in small individual portion cooking cups, cooked together as they will be eaten, and sealed in retort pouches at the bottom, to be packaged and loaded in boxes. Retort pouches are hermetically sealed bags of food that can be boiled on a kitchen stove in the bag. These pouches on that day were filled with a cream stew of chicken chunks and vegetables.

What was important to the worker was that it was "real food" and that the company was "green"—using gravity to move the ingredients down the processing flow saved energy and being able to see that the food was recognizably "food" gave pride, and value, to the work and worker. The worker said, "organic and natural" food is beginning to come into production as well, though the premises were far from "nature"— antiseptically white and clean—the workers were in clean jumpsuits, gloves, slippers or slip-covered shoes, and hair nets, and the robot trucks moved materials around the factory campus. One worker called House foods "industrial-artisanal." These sources of value, seen by Western cooks to be indigenously Japanese—fresh, local, and seasonal as well as environmentally sustainable—were expressed in relatively new ideologies— such as "good food," which has permeated other food industries as well, including fast food shops and convenience stores—and, as globalized ideals, are now associated at least aspirationally, with global industrial food.

Invocations

In the work of food, and in the promotion and advertising of commercial food, the word "*kodawari*" is everywhere, even in "industrial-artisanal" food. *Kodawari* means a range of things from "passionate attention to detail" or "uncompromising devotion to a pursuit" to just "handmade with care" to "made by a person with special skills." *Kodawari* has become a "branding" term in Japanese work. Value-adding *kodawari* resides in the person, in the technique, and in the product, and it repeatedly was the storyline of specialty coffee making and also among makers of "*tezukuri*" (handmade) food. The word "*kodawari*" was used by some, such as Hasegawa of Den, with a wry and ironic expression but by others, such as a worker at House Brands, with sincere emphasis. We might see *kodawari* as part of a relationship with a guest, offering the best you can is part of the service in a moral relationship with the guest.

The word "*tezukuri*" ("handmade," "artisanal") adds value, making the hand a better tool than electronic appliances or any mechanical device. Doi Itsuo, the knife crafter in Sakai, said that his father objected to his invention of a pounding device, a simple weighted overhead arm, that could pound a red hot blade with greater force than his own arm, to be used for the first flattening of a blank. This was mechanical, not electrical, and was tied to a foot pedal Doi operated. But it was not his hand alone and only now that his father has retired is Doi comfortable using it, though he draws attention to this as an intergenerational problem.

The importance of service as integral to food work is expressed in *omotenashi* (sensitivity to the needs of others). Like *kodawari* it can be overused but it cannot be overemphasized in these food workers' terms. Beyond the service language of "*Irasshai!*" (welcome!) and the noisy farewells and thank yous, *omotenashi*, or paying anticipatory attention to the guest or customer, is a sense that service is not a second-class skill or an "extra" in the operation of food work. This is borne out in the fact that there is no tipping for service in any Japanese place of business.

Global Japanese

Young chefs are moving out of Japan to many parts of the world to cook. As they and foods designated as "Japanese" move, the question of "authenticity" is often raised. In what lies Japanese identity in food? Locality? Tools? Ingredients? The ethnic identity of the maker? The authority of a chef or of a recipe? A grandmother? The first response might be that—apart from a construction of *washoku* (Japanese cuisine) basically created for the purposes of the UNESCO World Heritage Cuisine designation—there really is no national food in Japan—like that of Italy; it's all regional, seasonal, familial, personal. But there are ideas that become identifiers once Japanese food leaves Japan. Nobu, the famous expat Japanese chef, once said, "With Japanese techniques I can make Japanese food out of ingredients found anywhere in the world." Technique, art, craftsmanship, as well as a few principles of artful simplicity, a priority on taste and quality, service, and the morality of focused labor and not-wasting, might be the answer to what is "authentic." This is not to say that an inside-out sushi roll is "Japanese"—because, well, it isn't—but if it is well made and especially well presented it might be called in Japan an "American roll." One Japanese chef, on including strong-tasting ramps as a seasonal addition to his *kaiseki* menu in New York, said, it wouldn't happen in Japan but this is New York *kaiseki*; and locality and seasonality are more important than "Japanese" accreditation. Sometimes it is foreigners (*gaijin*) who look for orthodoxies in Japanese food rather than Japanese themselves. Recently one writer called Japanese food a "pastiche"—and yes, over many centuries, many new foods have been incorporated and assimilated such as tempura from Portugal, famously, in the sixteenth century, ramen from China, sushi itself from Southeast Asia, and curries by way of England and its South Asia colonies.

Like all food, Japanese food and its makers have been on the move. Japanese chefs now practice, teach, and learn skills everywhere in the world. The best Italian restaurants, a restaurateur in Rome said, have Japanese cooks in the kitchen. Furthermore, Italian foods are interpreted and performed in Tokyo by chefs returning from Italy. The elements, principles, and practices of Japanese food are employed now by non-Japanese chefs in emulation of the foodways they have witnessed in training and observation in Japan. Those principles come down to the words we have used, which are often over-determined, especially by Western observers but sometimes by Japanese "branders" themselves, such as kodawari, tezukuri, mottainai, and omotenashi. Where food is made and by what bodies and tools are guided by simpler, less "principled" forces—gravity, the edge of a knife, practicing a sushi 100 times, paying attention, and noticing a smudge on the lacquer to be removed by the fukin. Framing principles describe but also make abstract and culturally distant the flavors and meaning of food work. Art and craft come down to what you can graciously present to another person. My own tea ceremony teacher in 1976 said to me, when I asked naively how all the balletic, body-focused, and precise movements (in some sense the "recipe") contributed to the tea: "It is all to present the best cup of tea to your guest." It is, after all, the expression of a relationship.

Note

Information in this chapter is derived from field notes during observations in Japan as well as from interviews conducted during the period 1975–2020.

Acknowledgments

Thank you to all the people who helped me learn about foodways and food work in Japan and here in America. I am grateful to you all. Any errors and distortions are my own.

Note: Japanese names are usually family-name first, personal name second, but here I am using the Western name order.

Geoff Lukas
Andrea Borghini
Elizabeth Andoh
Nancy Singleton Hachisu
Zairyu Hasegawa
Seizi Imura
Noriko Nakamura
Shinobu Namae
Noda
Izumi Shibata
Katsuyuki Tanaka
Yoshimi Tanigawa
Keiko Thayer
Adam Simha
Phillip Wolfe

6

On Attunement: Fermentation, Feminist Ethics, and Relationality in Sake-Making Practices

Maya Hey

Introduction: Embodiment Matters

Recipes Are Dialogues with Its Ingredients

Tucked away on the outskirts of eastern Japan sits Terada Honké, one of two natural sake breweries in the nation. Sake is a fermented rice beverage made entirely of rice. "Natural," here, means that laboratory-optimized microbes are not added to the process; instead, the brewery relies on the work of ambient bacteria and yeasts that have inhabited the open-aired brewhouse since the brewery's inception in the 1670s. Like many ferments, sake is made with a starter culture that jumpstarts the process of transforming rice into alcohol. When preparing these starters, Terada Honké uses song to keep the time and mashing rhythm consistent from batch to batch, year to year. Huddling over barrels, the brewers mash rice with wooden poles and do so to the tune of a call-and-response work song with lyrics that give thanks to the rice harvest, the gods for providing abundant blessings, and the well water that springs up in fervor.

This song is more than a procedure to get to the next step; rather, it serves as a crucial component to Terada Honké's sake recipe. Instead of using machines, stopwatches, or even counting, it is in performing the song that an affective, sensory dimension becomes an ingredient to the sake-making process. The song is a gathering, an invitation to come together through rhythm, concord, and the collective well-wishing for good sake. This collection of "ingredients" from which sake emerges includes more than just tangible objects like rice and water; they include invisible entities like microbial life as well as intangible relationships that animate a space. By tuning in to these invisible and intangible ingredients, I contend that fermentation recipes can garner knowledge and know-how about how to live with microbial life. As social theorist Alexis Shotwell acknowledges, "there turn out to be many 'ingredients' in knowledge" (2011: xv).

Recipes are not a static text or guarantors of reproducibility. They are a medium for materially engaging with "ever more corporeal, ever more intimate" relations through food and mediate time, place, ingredients, and people in ways that show "our relationality and our entanglement with nonhuman entities" (Kember & Zylinska

2012: xv). Fermentation, in particular, mediates between microbial bodies, human bodies, and their shared environment, connecting us deeply in meaningful, delicious ways. I approach fermentation recipes as an instance of interspecies communication (Hey 2019). Humans can only encourage or discourage the work of microbes—whose metabolic activity and enzymes transform "ingredients" into ferments—by modulating the ambient environment and tinkering with parameters such as temperature, salinity, and oxygen availability. In other words, human control in these processes is aspirational, never absolute, making the enactment of a fermentation recipe more of a conversation than mere execution. Thus, fermentation is dialogic with microbial life, the ambient environment, and the material affordances of each.

To think of a recipe as mediation emphasizes the processual and contextual nuances of foodmaking as well as foodmakers. A piecemeal approach assumes that the bodies making these recipes are interchangeable and substitutable (purportedly because they "follow" the "same" instructions), making the distinction of the end-products a reflection of the embodied differences of each maker. This places the burden of difference on the bodies who make them, risking reductionist views of embodied difference and essentialist discourses that measure authenticity on the basis of gender, race, or other social categorization.

My argument here is one of holism, moving away from this object-oriented approach to focus on the dynamic process of transformation. I echo Lisa Heldke who notes that food is not objects but "loci of relations" (2012: 70). In handling these loci, foodmaking can be seen as a process that is contingent, emergent, and predicated on intimate relations between interconnected species. I contend that fermentation recipes are one way to practice human and more-than-human entanglements in an ethical manner, tending to the differences and needs of each species without defining the entire relationship by them.

Framing Research Practices and Ethics

My aims are to decenter and mess with some of the major dichotomies that affect our understanding of food, foodmaking, and foodmaking bodies. In recipes, food ingredients tend to be conceptualized as static objects, known through objective measures. Consider the overly quantified ways in which fermentation recipes have been recently recorded, as if insured with consistent outcomes. The masculine ethos of homebrewing and hydration percentages of sourdough epitomize the uncanny imbrication of technology, "bro" culture, and precision fermentation (Evans 2018). But these approaches favor abstractions over feeling one's way through recipes, disembodying the work of fermentation into numbers, isolated variables, and iterative testing.

To be sure, this is not an anti-scientization argument. In fact, I rely on perspectives from feminist technoscience with epistemological frameworks such as situated knowledges that see knowledge production as a socially located process. Situated knowledge counters the myth of some omniscient perspective "up there" as a yardstick for objectivity (what Donna Haraway terms "the God trick") and it presumes that there can be knowing in and through subjective difference that remains true to a particular location or true from the partial perspective of one subject (Haraway 1999). I integrate this perspective with ideas of corporeal epistemologies articulated by new material feminists, who prioritize materialist understandings (and differences) of bodies and embodiment. They lament the postmodern tendency of solely focusing on language and discourse because it has "foreclose[d] attention to lived, material bodies and evolving corporeal practices" (Alaimo & Hekman 2008: 3).

New material feminism argues that material objects and their discussions cannot be separate. By prioritizing this indivisibility, new material feminists "shift the focus from ethical principles to ethical practices" (Alaimo & Hekman 2008: 7). This foregrounding of practices is intentional here, for I ask how can foodmaking (and fermentation, in particular) help us to practice a more ethical way of being and living with others? I do not just mean microbes; I mean other humans as well. Congruent with concerns for health, safety, and sustainability as issues that affect us all, and some more disproportionately, I echo Shotwell's call "to work collectively towards a more collective and relational form of ethics adequate to the global and systemic crises we face" (2016: 132). It matters how we practice being human in the face of ongoing disasters, and these are not exclusively "feminist" concerns.

This chapter draws from data generated during an ethnography conducted at the aforementioned Terada Honké brewery. Over the course of peak brewing season, I engaged with and practiced as an apprentice brewer, working alongside my interlocutors as I conducted fieldwork. I look to Terada Honké not for its singularity but for richness and "fine detail" (Barad 2007: 91) so that I come to know the differences that matter. While there are cautions against tokenizing or exoticizing what is done "over there," situatedness accounts for how this knowledge is socially situated (from my view) and situated in (my) bodies as lived experience. By privileging first-hand experience, I could avoid theorizing purely in the abstract and take seriously the "exceptions that do not fit the theoretical rule" (Pickering 2008: 27).

This ethnography combined different methodological considerations—namely, sensory, multispecies, and feminist methodologies that could "hang together," not as irreconcilable approaches but as a composite for foregrounding materiality and embodied ethics in action (Mol 2016: 242). Together, these approaches enabled me to mobilize the embodied, immersive, and participatory practices of sensory ethnography (Pink 2009, 2012); downplay the role of human agency by practicing the art of noticing other, more-than-human beings in multispecies ethnography (Kirksey & Helmreich 2010; Tsing 2015); and prioritize the building of trust and relations over data collection and knowledge extraction in feminist ethnographies (Skeggs 2001). These modulations were important to consider because fermentation is dynamic and ever-changing without necessarily featuring or serving a human figure, thereby requiring tools that could consider humans not as exceptional but as members of multispecies communities (Rose et al. 2010: 3).

Recipes are more than the sum of their parts because, as I argue below, the process of making it requires a kind of bodily attunement that helps to shift attention away from any one human individual toward a more collective, multispecies ethic. In the first section, I trace the philosophical background of thinking recipes as being embodied. Then, I explain the warrant and mechanism for attunement, a key concept to this chapter. Lastly, I unpack attunement's potential for cultivating a collective ethic.

(Food) Knowledge Is Embodied

Bodies Can Know and Know Differently

This chapter stems from a larger discourse around what a body is in philosophical terms or social phenomena. Several branches of feminist thought converge around the physical realities (or corpo-reality) of a body, how "its very materiality plays an active role in the workings of power" (Barad 2003: 809). Gender, for instance, is thought to be "written" onto the body, where "man […] has *inscribed* her in discourse, but as a lack, as fault or flaw" (Irigaray 1985: 89, emphasis added), evincing how one becomes a woman instead of being born one (de Beauvoir 2011/1949: 301). But being "written onto" does not imply that the body is "merely a passive transmitter of messages" (Coole 2005: 128). On the contrary, bodies participate in discursive formations. For instance, embodied differences such as gender (as well as race and class) do not inhere to the body; rather, bodies are vital to processes of gendering (as well as in race and class formation). Noteworthy here is that the body's materiality is not separate from its discourse, and one does not precede the other. They affect and are affected by each other, recursively. Sharon Krause explains slouching as a concrete example where cause and effect are obsolete; how one carries their body informs and is informed by the body's materiality, always "inscribed with prevailing relations of power" (2011: 305–6). Whether we are conscious of them or not, bodies are active in processes of meaning-making.

New material feminism sees the body as an active participant in knowledge production, not just a vehicle for the mind to drive. Descartes, for example, sees the material self as fundamentally different from the thinking self, such that the needs and desires of the body stand at odds with the reasonable mind (like when overcoming hunger or lust). Phenomenologist Merleau-Ponty argues that mind and body are not split along Cartesian dualisms but are interrelated, as there could be no absolute demarcation between interiority (what happens with the mind) and exteriority (what happens with the body), especially with regard to sensing "the flesh" in the experiential (Merleau-Ponty 1968: 140). Cartesians base their analysis on the presumed universality of the male body, thought to be bound, hard, and rational, compared to the leaky, soft, and affective female body. Building on Merleau-Ponty, feminist thinker Elizabeth Grosz (1994) dismantles some of the philosophical binaries that essentialize female bodies "to reconceive bodies outside the binary oppositions [of] mind/body" (164) because of the longheld assumption that "mind is rendered equivalent to the masculine and body equivalent to the feminine" (14). Grosz reasserts the body as a source for knowledge production as well as a site for contested power relations. Mind and body are incorporated, not one lesser than the other.

Outside of phenomenology, Shotwell applies the Bourdieusian notion of habitus (or, socio-culturally developed habits, skills, dispositions, and perceptions) to the body to understand "the embodied feel" that it can impart as a form of bodily knowing. Shotwell argues that bodily knowledge can be "transmitted implicitly through a pedagogy that encodes practices in the body" (2011: 14). Bodies are not just vessels for information, "not in any way that those meanings can 'wash off' at the end of the day," but perpetually enact identity or group membership that can be learned and taught (14). They are also living, breathing archives capable of imprinting and enacting practices, values, and rituals. In what Heldke calls "mentally manual" activities, our bodies "know" in ways that our minds cannot: "I *know* things literally with my body, that I, 'as' my hands, know when the bread dough is sufficiently kneaded, and I 'as' my nose know when the pie is done" (1992: 218, original emphasis). By thinking about recipes as living information in a body, a recipe becomes transmittable and mediated via embodied knowledge. Thus the enactment of a recipe not only keeps the practical techniques and know-how alive but also ensures a way for the meanings to stay alive. Ingredients may change, swap, or be substituted, but the cultural rationale or social context for a recipe live inside and on bodies.

Embodied Knowledge Is Political

We come to know recipes through embodying them; we communicate and relay them through practice. Whose knowledge and who can know this knowledge are of utmost concerns to feminist thought because of how power operates through gender and knowledge formation. The mediation of embodied knowledge is non-innocent because of how the "gendered power structures of society affect the shape of and possibilities for knowledge production and the exercise of epistemic agency" (Grasswick 2011: xv). Seen through the lens of feminist epistemologies, how we come to know recipes becomes of social, political, and ethical concern.

It matters whose body is embodying, who is making knowledge and how because different bodies are "written onto" differently. One cannot assume a universal body given the differences in flesh and lived experience. So, while discussions about "the body" are important for acknowledging its material dimensions, "the body" cannot be "rendered neuter" in an attempt to maximize applicability (Grosz 1994: 156). Neutralizing bodies erases power, universalizing bodies skews power, and categorizing bodies reinforces dominant powers—such are body politics in action. Thus, the politics of knowledge production sit at the core of feminist epistemologies, namely how can we know in ways that do not reinscribe existing power differentials across the binaries of objective/subjective, male/female, mind/body, and self/other. Binaries themselves are never innocent, they are organized vertically to favor a hierarchical structure (e.g., objective over subjective, self over other) or to hide the interlocking oppressions of each.

Knowledge is shaped differently based on where we each stand in society. Haraway highlights the need to be critical of the affordances unique to each view, arguing that one's "[p]ositioning implies responsibility for our enabling practices. It follows that politics and ethics ground struggles [...] over knowledge projects" (1999: 193). As we participate, emerge from, affect, and are affected by the spaces we occupy, knowledge production must remain committed to an "ethico-onto-epistem-ology—an appreciation of the intertwining of ethics, knowing, and being" (Barad 2007: 185).

Bodies—and their specific affordances—are thus active ingredients in knowledge production. The fact that knowledge is situated (in a body, in a physical place, in a particular social location) demands attention to difference and how those differences come to matter. The resultant embodied knowledge is (1) a politico-ethical matter of who can know, (2) an epistemological matter of how bodies decipher encoded practices, and (3) not universally situated in bodies.

Bodies That Attune

The Sense of Self in Space

With knowledge situated in bodies and these bodies situated in space, how do bodies engage with each other and with the shared environment? How do relations come into being, and how are they sensed?

Proprioception and attunement are frameworks for imagining ourselves as embedded and tethered. Proprioception is a neurokinesthetic phenomenon describing how one perceives their body, or parts of their body, in relation to a given space. It is the sense of self-orientation that, when askew, can produce motion sickness or dizziness when what we see/hear in our eyes/ears does not coincide with how we feel based on proprioception. Astronauts and deep-sea divers are often trained to "override" their proprioceptors to avoid the mixed signals or disorientation that come with zero gravity. While proprioceptors exist in our muscles as a physiological feature of the human body, I mobilize the concept of proprioception to think about attunement, or a way of situating our "sense of self" in relation to a given space.

Attunement extends beyond the physical/corporeal sense-of-self to include tetherings with other bodies in motion. So while proprioception is the ability to orient ourselves in a space, its unit of analysis stays on the level of an individual, and attunement is the ability to notice, listen, and respond to the space *and all that inhabits within it*. The human need not know (or even control) all to which her body is tethered. In fact, it is often the case that humans are oblivious to the larger collection of (f)actors, human and more-than-human. Humans are but a small part of a much greater collective. Consider the brewhouse mentioned at this chapter's opening. The Terada Honké brewery houses more than just the human brewers and includes entire clusters of microbial life, natural materials (e.g., wood, brick), and media (e.g., water as steam or liquid, air as breeze) for each to move through. Attunement allows the human body to sense these forces and connect with them. These relations highlight to whom or what we can respond and inform the ethical potential of thinking beyond the individual.

Attunement at Terada Honké

There are many ingredients to sake-making at Terada Honké. Some are tangible things like rice and water, while others are invisible to the human eye like microbial life. (This can also include invisible forces like electromagnetic frequencies from lightbulbs or soundwaves.) Other intangible ingredients include the relations that make up a commercial enterprise or the interdependencies of a multispecies ecology from which fermentation emerges. To handle these ingredients, the brewers must tune into their senses: their physical senses, their sense of self, and their sense of connection to invisible, intangible relations. It is not enough to rely on quantitative observation; rather, the brewers immerse themselves in, participate with, and attune their bodies to sensory information.

Example 1: Moving Together

Every morning, the entire staff gather at the center of the brewery grounds in preparation for what are called "radio exercises." Like other countries with quasi-nationalized exercise regimens, Japan in the 1920s had instituted a calisthenics program with a warm-up routine guided by radio broadcasters. Recorded onto a cassette tape, the broadcaster's voice instructs each movement over piano accompaniment, counting out the duration of each step. The staff move in unison with each inhale, each stretch, and each bounce, with agility and familiarity. It is what starts the workday and what aligns the entire company to the same beat. Later in the day, when the brewers prepare yeast starters with song, their coordinated movements echo the ease that comes from regularity. The song's fifteen verses, which span twenty-five minutes in its entirety, are fully incorporated into the corps of brewers. The structure of this song is one of call-and-response, with the mashing happening to the beat of the song. Like other historical instances of work songs, the rhythm guides the movement as there would be too much discord and deviation without it. The main singer enumerates the tasks and gratitudes involved in making sake ("*we wash more rice for tomorrow's preparations*" or "*with thanks to the Kozaki shrine/ the water wells up and becomes sake*") and the remaining brewers chime in with agreement ("*Oh yes! Yes!*").

Example 2: Listening Within

This call-and-response structure guides other tasks done by hand. For example, when taking the rice out of the steaming basket, the brewer responsible for digging must call out "*Yo!*" before sending off a bucket of steamed rice because vision inside the brewhouse is obscured with bellows of steam. The brewers receiving the rice must call out "*Sa!*" informing the digger to cue up the next batch. Additionally, the brewers must sense the temperature of the rice with their hands, being careful to turn over "hotspots" that hold onto heat so that the rice releases heat uniformly. In this sense, the brewers listen with their hands *and* listen with their ears to coordinate the meticulous flipping of just-steamed rice. Ultimately the effect of this choreographed effort is that the contents of the entire steaming basket (often amounting to a metric ton of rice) cool evenly even though it is dug up in buckets of ten kilograms at a time. A rhythmic call-and-response ensures consistency in embodied terms in that an individual brewer *responds* to what is seen and sensed with a meaningful *call*. These coordinated tasks require that each being be attuned to one another as well as to their individual selves.

Example 3: Noticing Ambient Cues

As the different kinds of ingredients are combined, they are left to ferment in tanks capable of holding up to 3,600 liters. The contents are stirred frequently to encourage the enzymes and microbes floating amidst the unfiltered sake mixture. It is at this point that the smell and sensation of over-carbonated sake can feel unbearable in close proximity since the carbon dioxide is most concentrated just above the sake's surface. If one hovers their head just over the lip of the tank, the sensation of over-carbonation accosts the nose, similar to the consequences of drinking a soda too quickly. The over-carbonation is actually a sign of poor quality (that is, alcohol is produced faster than the taste compounds that produce depth and complexity of flavor), and this happens as a result of too much ambient warmth over multiple days. Although the brewers measure the temperature of each tank twice a day, the thermometer cannot prove that over-carbonation is happening because these instruments are designed to capture one snapshot in time, not a series of transformations-in-development. Neophyte brewers must therefore hover their heads over the tank to detect it, while veterans notice over-carbonation based on weather patterns, the presence of large bubbles, and previous experience.

These examples demonstrate attunement in action, for each individual must tune into their own bodies as well as that of others to respond meaningfully in sake-making practices. In the first example, the choreographies during singing and calisthenics provide a collective sense of movement in unison, allowing the brewers to move together as one body, *inter-relationally*. In the second, the call-and-response moments of singing and cooling the rice provide an opportunity to use ears, hands, and full body to listen for other members' cues to act. Here, the brewers must process sensory information within one's body *intra-relationally* to cycle through the decoding and encoding that drives the call-and-response. These communication pathways extend beyond human beings, *extra-relationally*, in the last example and include other mediators, agents, and more-than-human (f)actors. As well, the different kinds of attunement seem to be mutually compounding: intra-relationality begets interpersonal relationships of camaraderie, heightened awareness toward extra-relational surroundings makes veteran brewers acutely aware of their bodily senses, and coordinating movement inter-relationally enables the continuity of entire brewing operation.

To summarize the aforementioned examples, the brewhouse contains a collection of individual brewing bodies, with their different corporeal affordances, who embody "recipe know-how" independently and interdependently. Each individual apprehends the "call" from other brewing bodies to produce a "response," which then becomes the next "call" for others to respond to. This back-and-forth co-respondence becomes inscriptions onto brewing bodies in the form of embodied knowledge and eventually develops into technical expertise with iterative practice. But this expertise is not finite or predetermined. Rather, an "expert" brewer is considered one who is capable of responding to as many different "calls" as possible, across multiple individuals, multiple species, and multiple contexts. In other words, sake-making knowledge is not seen as a standalone distinction; it is always in relation with others and with a collective.

Sake-making practices at Terada Honké are not standardized in the sense that brewers aim for predefined markers of "objectively good" sake. The goal of Terada Honké is to make "good" sake with the "good" qualifier used to mean in accordance with nature, in tune with the brewery staff, and in honor of their place-based history—and this often leads to a variable product. While the industry standards do not see variability as a positive asset, Terada Honké views their sake as being true to their operations, consistent with their philosophy of sake-making as a way to practice joy, merriment, and gratitude with oneself and others. These three feelings—joy, merriment, and gratitude—animate the primary "task" for sake-making in which the sake becomes a by-product that keeps the brewery economically viable. In this sense, Terada Honké focuses less on the "what" of sake-making and instead emphasizes the "how" of their sake-making because the latter allows the brewery to practice good relations on collective scales.

This begs the question of where responsibility falls across individuals and collectives. To whom or what should individuals respond? How might one best attune to that call? How do individual responsibilities fit within collectives?

Practicing Attunement to Cultivate Collective Ethics

Recipes for Living Together, Responsibly

Attunement can help us practice collective responsibility because sensing others keeps us receptive to other forms of communication and response. These "responses" may not always be in the form of a song or an audible cue per se; it may be the release of carbon dioxide due to warmer temperatures or even as subtle as "a feeling" in a group or a room.

To heed and respond is an inter-subjective process. We come into being through these response with others, in what Haraway calls a game of "response and respect" where the term *re-spect* evokes the etymology of "looking back with regard" (Haraway 2008: 19). Attentiveness is the mechanism for response and respect, echoing Anna Tsing's call for the arts of noticing in an assemblage (or a collection of agencies). Tsing emphasizes the "patterns" and "rhythms" of these assemblages as a way "to notice the divergent, layered, and conjoined projects that make up worlds" (Tsing 2015: 22). Taken further, this kind of noticing of others (including other species) leads to an expanded understanding of who we ought to include in multispecies ethics: "The cultivation of skills for both paying attention to others and meaningfully responding [...] is concerned with the politics and ethics of how we might come to know others and so (re)craft modes of living and dying on a richly varied yet fundamentally shared world" (van Dooren, Kirksey & Münster 2016: 6). Our responsibility (or, response-ability) in multispecies worlds is both an interpellation and a mandate: we depend on multispecies worlds but may not know how best to respond in them.

It is important to note that these attunements, noticings, and response-abilities are not a checklist to attain some sort of moral advantage. Response is not and cannot be reduced to a calculation, as if executable by command. Like embodied recipes, "there is no formula for response" (Haraway 2008: 77). Rather, the benefit—if it could be called that—to attunement is emergent and comes from many individuals tuning to their senses and their surroundings. Implied in these "surroundings" is an environment that is always shared with other species. In particular, microbial life has been difficult to imagine as an entity worth attuning to or entities with whom we share "surroundings," partly because they are not "big like us" (Hird 2009: 21) or have remained invisible to the unaided eye until "discovered" in the context of disease and decay (Latour 1988). But this does not mean that they are separate from us. Indeed, one need look no further than the phenomenon of antibiotic resistance, a booming probiotics industry, and recent discoveries in microbiome research to see that microbes are inextricably linked to human evolution, physiologies, and industry.

The "surroundings" we share with microbial life are many given their ubiquity; our bodies, our dwellings, and our ecological niches are "ours" as multiple species, shared in instances of perpetual (at times risky) cohabitation. In this sense, attunement runs deeper than the new age penchant for "mindfulness" in that it is corporeal and embodied at the same time that it is deeply philosophical in its decentering of the human form. In other words, it is not enough to "be mindful" of microbes or other brewers to make "good" sake. Getting on well with others is predicated upon being "situate[d] within an ethical horizon" of "'good' relations" within oneself and across species (Zylinska 2014a: 195). These relations come from deep listening and response, as they are practiced while in tune with a shared environment.

Balancing Scales of Individuals and Collectives

Response-ability at scale is difficult to define, even unsolvable, suggesting that we need to remain all the more attuned to the differences within a collective. As Shotwell concedes, there is an ultimate contradiction with moral formation on an individual level that cannot be scalable to a collective because of the presumed substitutability between scalable phenomena (Shotwell 2016: 111). While I see and acknowledge this contradiction as being crucial to opposing homogenization (because, indeed, we are not substitutable), I find opportunities (and perhaps hope) for ethics based on the dynamic understanding of our connectedness *qua* context. Zylinska, for instance, puts forth the notion of minimal ethics (minimal in the sense that it is not being rooted in greater systems) to better articulate dynamic relations between entities at scale. Zylinska argues that individual and collective ethics are not necessarily at odds; instead:

> by speaking of the universal scale we are merely attempting to situate our philosophical endeavors meaningfully and responsibly, without foreclosing them all too early by the kind of thinking that would carve out entities such as "the animal", "the body" and "the gene", and locations such as "the world", "Africa" and "the lab", and then attempt to work out good ways of managing relations between them. (2014b: 25)

Thinking at the universal scale becomes problematic when temporal frames and spatial sites are too overdetermined, too early, in the ethical consideration of how we ought to relate, connect, and tether to these entities. Zylinska quickly follows, "This is not to say that such ethics needs to be *applicable* across all times and locales: it just needs to acknowledge […] *our* specific locatedness in space and time from which we will conduct our enquiry" (2014b: 28, original emphasis). We are unique, just like everybody else. Our individuality is both distinct from others and a common condition we share with others. At the base of these ethical delineations are the imperatives of locating oneself and the attendant relations of a specific time and place. This is consistent with situated knowledges outlined by Haraway, and the understanding that knowledge is specifically oriented to those who produce it: "the joining of partial views and halting voices into a collective subject position that promises […] of views from somewhere" (1999: 196). It is not what the individual considers that should be applied to an ambiguous collective, but how the individual considers their temporality/spatiality to situate their ethics within a collective.

Perhaps the level of reconciliation ought to happen not on the scale of individual versus collective but precisely with what "an individual" entails, given that our bodies have been always nested with many other species ranging from bacterial DNA in our mitochondria to the microbial flora that line our orifices and skin surfaces. Building on the findings of microbiome research, Heldke argues that the relational self is actually a collective self, defined by "the way in which the individual is constituted through relationships with humans and other macrolevel creatures" (2018: 248). This nested and co-constituted way of thinking of "the self" suggests a reframing of how we look at individual scales of ethics. How do we actualize ethics as compound, complex, multispecies creatures? As Haraway contends, "multispecies coflourishing requires simultaneous, contradictory truths" (2008: 105) and "staying with the trouble" (2016). Philosophically engaging with these contradictions (e.g., my innermost 'self' is occupied by non-self, even microbial, species) lays the ethical groundwork for collective thriving by asking us to consider more-than-our-selves: who or what is calling, how ought I respond, and who stands to gain if I act in this way? It is to practice a decentered sense of self.

It is worth noting that Terada Honké believes that the work of the brewers is to be in service of microbes, not the reverse, so that the microorganisms can do the work of brewing. As such, the brewers adopt a mantra of "working from the perspective of microbes." When asked about why he continues working with Terada Honké, one brewer explained that the sake-making process was a proxy for practicing how to be a more attentive, selfless human. Another brewer emphasized that the purpose of Terada Honké was to help people grow through daily practices of support outside of oneself: "It's a kind of training, you know? It's here that I refine who I am."

This sort of self-displacement is neither a means to a collective end nor an act of self-sacrifice. It is an ethico-onto-epistem-ology enacted through sake-making practices that combine knowing and *being well with others* in the co-habitated space of a brewhouse. Put another way, the brewers at Terada Honké do not see their collective as a human-only venture.

Individual and collective tasks are often described at odds with each other as if tension is the only way to describe individualism and collectivism. This binary could stand to be troubled to find nuanced understandings of broader ethics, broadened to include multiple humans, multiple species, and multiple differences. Part of this nuancing is predicated on seeing relations as contingent and emergent, not pre-settled, so that the (f)actors of fermentation are seen as indeterminant and capable of acting if and when the space becomes opportune for action. Rather than presume that individual trajectories are at odds with a collective vision, it may be in our interest to reframe the stakes of interconnectedness and to encourage participation in the form of making spaces conducive for others.

Paramount to Terada Honké's brewing philosophy is to live and let live, to gather through invitation instead of coercion, and to opt for an open and unbound (if slightly unpredictable) process over a sure-fire protocol. This is reflected in their avoidance of chemical sanitizers that would eradicate all microbial life from the brewhouse. It is arguably because of locale, not laboratories, that Terada Honké houses a unique profile of ambient microbes that are kept diverse and alive. At the same time, the seasonal workers and apprentices (such as myself) can alter this microbial profile due to the preexisting microbes that live on our bodily surfaces and inadvertently participate in the brewing process. Rather than curate the ecosystem of microbial life, all species are granted access to the brewhouse, while known threats (e.g., spores) are dealt with deliberately and frequently (e.g., steamed or exposed to the sun's UV rays). These approaches to openness epitomize how Terada Honké begins with the presumption that it is the liveliness and diversity of (microbial) others that determine their recipe's success.

There are no easy answers for making the scalar jump of individual to collective ethics, but it may be prudent for us to think through this stickiness beyond existing examples of intimacy (Berlant 1998), nautical navigation teams (Hutchins 1995), and war conscription (Zohar 1993). Decentering the individual "for" a collective (or, for that matter, decentering the human in favor of other species) is not for the benefit of the latter. While tensions between individuals/collective absolutely exist, it is not necessarily axiomatic that one must wholly give up attention to one to attend to others. Practicing attunement amidst the brewers suggested that cultivating an awareness for oneself and an attentiveness toward others helps to answer the question of how we continue to live-with and be-with one another while holding onto our differences. Difference is not reduced to something dismissible, rather the opposite—being connected to each other in specific ways demands an attention to difference, and it is this specificity that prevents unitary claims about who "we" are or how we "ought" to be. Specificity also pushes against the erasure of relativism that "anything goes." We may not immediately see or easily sense these relations that tether us, but it matters how we are connected and with whom, especially in processes of making and living together.

Conclusion

Recipes are emergent and participatory. They are deeply embodied and greater than the sum of their individual "ingredients." By thinking of recipes this way, bodies emerge as an active carrier and performer of food-knowledge. Crucial to the embodiment and enactment of a recipe is the process of attunement, a way of simultaneously tuning to one's physical senses, the social periphery, and the more-than-human entities that collectively transform foods. Attunement is a corporeal phenomenon as much as it is a philosophical approach to living with and working with others we may not easily see or sense. Attunement means listening with multiple senses. It means comparing and compiling one's sensory stimuli (in an instance of intra-relationality), tuning into each other (inter-relationality), and tuning to the ambient environment (extra-relationality). I have argued that attunement may be one way to imagine and approach cultivating one such collective ethic. Thinking about recipes as an attuned, response-able venture can help us practice collective ethics across species and across difference.

Part Two

Experiencing

Introduction to Part Two: Experiencing

The chapters contained in this second part of the volume are concerned with food consumption and, most often, with aspects connected to tasting experiences.

Taste is a classical topic for philosophical reflection. A widespread tendency is to think that it is more subjective than other varieties of sensory experience, for example, visual experience: taste detects "how things are with us" or "from our point of view," while vision detects "how things are with the world" (Korsmeyer 1999: ch. 1). An illustration may be useful here. Under ordinary circumstances, if a person sees a cat on the mat, that person will thereby form the disposition to believe that the world is a certain way, namely, such that a cat is on the mat. Compare now this with a taste experience. Under ordinary circumstances, if a person drinks a glass of wine that tastes like ripe plum, will that person form the disposition to believe that the world is a certain way, namely, such that the wine tastes like ripe plum? Or will the person be merely disposed to claim that the wine tastes like ripe plum "to them" or "from their point of view"?

There are important lessons to learn from reflecting on the differences between varieties of sensory experiences. For instance, to stay with the thesis that only some of our senses inform us about the way the world is, while others merely tell us about how things are for ourselves, we could ask: is such a thesis justified by what we know of human evolution? How and why would such an asymmetry have formed? Recent work suggests, actually, that smell and taste may be more sophisticated than we used to think (Shepherd 2011; Barwich 2020). Or—to mention another important issue—how did certain human cultures come to form different opinions regarding different varieties of sensory experiences? For example, what is the cultural history of wine tasting? (Shapin 2012, 2016).

But suppose we grant that the subjectivity of taste has been exaggerated. Would this help resolve disagreements about taste, namely the fact that people have very different taste preferences? What is the role that expertise can play in these sorts of disputes? Here, one should bear in mind the distinction between (a) the *descriptive* claim that, for example, a certain wine tastes like ripe plum and (b) the *evaluative* claim that, for instance, one either likes or dislikes the taste of ripe plum. Importantly, taste can be objective in that someone with correctly functioning tasting abilities might be able to experience that the wine tastes like ripe plum while still remaining subjective in the sense that one might either like or dislike the taste of ripe plum (see Todd 2010; Borghini & Piazza 2019; see also the papers collected in Smith 2009 for discussion of these points).

Another important set of questions concerns the range of information that taste can detect, in comparison to other sensory experiences. Vision, for example, can reveal to us not only shapes and colors, but also distance and, through reading, meanings. What about taste? Is it limited to reveal to us that, for example, a certain wine tastes like ripe plum, or can it reveal something more? Taking some form of objectivity of taste as a starting point, the first three chapters by Carolyn Korsmeyer, Patrik Engisch, and Cain Todd move on to inquire about the range of things taste could reveal to us.

Korsmeyer's focus, first, is on a practice at the border of archeology and the culinary sciences that aims to retrieve the taste of past recipes through the retro-engineering on the basis of chemical analysis of ancient food remains. Can we, by means of following such a retro-engineered recipe, produce foodstuff that would allow us to experience how a similar foodstuff tasted a couple of millennia ago? Korsmeyer's answer to that question is cautiously positive, providing we are clear about the questions that can be addressed. While we cannot duplicate ancient taste sensations exactly, we can approach appreciation of older culinary experiences. Moreover, the project of retrieving tastes from the past has other important virtues, including sensitivity to the impending loss of natural flavor sources.

Engisch's chapter also deals with the temporal dimension of recipes, as it studies the normative nature of traditional recipes, namely, recipes that come from the past yet are rooted in the present. In particular, he argues that, under a plausible understanding of them, traditional recipes can—like other traditions—be revealing of past living conditions. Engisch suggests, thus, that the normative properties of traditional recipes can bestow certain representational powers upon the food and the taste experiences associated with them.

Todd's contribution focuses on a specific product—wine—and deals with an original question: under the assumption that wine not only possesses a certain taste but also can be expressive of certain values that we can access through taste (e.g., the artisanal vs. the industrial), what role can recipes play in explaining this expressive power of wine? His answer is mitigated. Even though he denies that the notion of recipe can shed much light on wine and on the helpful notion of wine styles, he nonetheless countenances that one of the main values of wine, authenticity, can be articulated by thinking about the relationship between wine and recipes.

The next two chapters move into different territories. Barbara Haber, first, lends her culinary historian lens to the story of thousands of American civilians, living in the Philippines during the Second World War, that were rounded up by the Japanese and thrown into internment camps where they remained prisoners until the end of the war. Little food was provided to these prisoners and, as conditions of near starvation grew worse, they obsessed more and more about food, dreaming of it at night and fantasizing about it during the day, eventually collecting, creating, and exchanging recipes.

The story told by Haber is of philosophical significance for the question of the nature of recipes insofar as it displays an extended use of recipes, where these don't serve anymore in the preparation of food, but in the guiding of imaginary experiences that function as substitutes for the preparation of food (see Klein [2020: ch. 4] for another recent study on the topic). How exactly can recipes play this role and how exactly can taste be thus imagined? How can imaginary experiences of food be experiences of a kind that can bring comfort and meaning to people who, like these war prisoners, have been deprived of them? This is a clear instance of what we alluded to in the main introduction of this volume as a case where a non-philosopher can shed light on an important topic to be explored further by philosophers of food.

Unlike the former ones, the final chapter by Akiko Frischhut and Giuliano Torrengo tackles a slightly more usual philosophical terrain as it explores the issue of the nature of taste head-on. The authors are concerned with the proper delineation of the boundaries of taste experience, which—they contend—doesn't solely include taste, but also aftertaste. In their contriibution, Frischhut and Torrengo elaborate on the categories of so-called aftersensations, which comprise not only aftertastes but also after-images, such as the image one can sometimes still see for a few seconds after having closed one's eyes. If after-images are universally treated as being figments of the imagination and not appearances of the target of visual experiences, their conclusion is that aftertastes are, just like tastes, *bona fide* appearances of foodstuff. In other words, we cannot only objectively taste foodstuff, but also aftertaste them.

Further Reading

Barwich, A. S. (2020). *Smellosophy: What the Nose Tells the Mind*. Cambridge, MA: Harvard University Press.

Borghini, A. and Piazza, T. (2019). "The Aesthetic Properties of Wine." In: Lars Aagaard-Mogensen and Jane Forsey (eds.). *On Taste: Aesthetic Exchanges*. Newcastle Upon Tyne: Cambridge Scholars Publishing: 101–22.

Kaplan, D. (2020). *Food Philosophy: An Introduction*. New York: Columbia University Press.

Klein, L. F. (2020). *An Archive of Taste: Race and Eating in the Early United States*. Minneapolis: University of Minnesota Press.

Korsmeyer, C. (1999). *Making Sense of Taste*. Ithaca, NY: Cornell University Press.

Mizrahi, V. (2017). "Just a Matter of Taste." In: *Review of Philosophical Psychology*, 8: 411–31.

Richardson, L. (2013). "Flavour, Taste and Smell." In: *Mind & Language*, 28: 322–41.

Shapin, S. (2012). "The Tastes of Wine: Towards a Cultural History." In: *Rivista di Estetica,* 51: 49–94.

Shapin, S. (2016). "A Taste of Science: Making the Subjective Objective in the California Wine World." In: *Social Studies of Science,* 46: 436–60.

Shepherd, G. (2011). *Neurogastronomy: How the Brain Creates Flavor and Why It Matters*. New York: Columbia University Press.

Sibley, F. (2001). "Tastes, Smells, and Aesthetics." In: John Benson, Betty Redfern, and Jeremy Roxbee Cox (eds.). *Approach to Aesthetics: Collected Papers on Philosophical Aesthetics*. Oxford: Clarendon Press: 207–255.

Smith, B. (ed.) (2005). *Questions of Taste: The Philosophy of Wine*. Oxford: Oxford University Press.

Spence, C. (2018). *Gastrophysics*. London: Penguin.

Strohl, Matthew (2019). "On Culinary Authenticity." In: *Journal of Aesthetics and Art Criticism,* 77 (2): 157–67.

Todd, C. (2010). *The Philosophy of Wine*. London: Routledge.

Todd, C. (2018). "Tasting in Time: The Affective and Temporal Dimensions of Flavour Perception." In: *The Monist*, 10: 277–93.

Historical Dishes and the Search for Past Tastes

Carolyn Korsmeyer

In late 2019, Oxford's Ashmolean Museum mounted an exhibit of artifacts excavated from Pompeii, the city famously destroyed in 79 CE when Vesuvius erupted and buried the town and its citizens in ash. Among the relics unearthed were kitchenware and foods, including bread loaves still in their ovens and bottles of the fish sauce called *garum*. In conjunction with the exhibit, chef Heston Blumenthal prepared a feast inspired by the culinary remains of Pompeii. Some dishes were variations on what had been eaten in Roman antiquity, such as pickled mussels in *garum*. Other items added reference to the volcanic destruction itself, such as bread made with heritage flour and charcoal, and a cheesecake with goat curds, figs, grapes, and frozen ash (Sharma 2019). Xa Sturgis, Director of the Ashmolean Museum, said of the event, "In the food-obsessed culture of today, there is scarcely a better topic that can help us make a connection with the people of the ancient world" (Ashmolean 2019).

How does the recreation of historical dishes connect us with peoples of the past? Might eating foods common in antiquity give us a sense of their dining styles, their habits, their preferences—their *tastes*? From one perspective, the effort seems futile. In the words of a historian who has pondered the irretrievability of bygone times, "the past is a foreign country whose features are shaped by today's predilections, its strangeness domesticated by our own preservation of its vestiges" (Lowenthal 1985: xvii). The attempt to understand past times is especially problematic when one tries to imagine the perceptual experiences of people who lived before us. Did the stars look different to people who accepted Ptolemaic astronomy? How did Mozart's music first sound to audiences whose ears were attuned to earlier compositional styles? What did Marco Polo experience when he sampled the cuisine of Kubla Khan? Can we ever recreate historical tastes—or more aptly, the multimodal taste-smell-touch combination that produces gustatory experience?

While the historical record—both written and visual—may inform us about what was eaten long ago, there is a gap between identifying the foods consumed and knowing how they actually tasted to those who ate. Phyllis Pray Bober, on the very last page of her archeology of ancient and medieval gastronomy, remarks that "a major part of any discussion about cookery has scarcely been mentioned. That is: how did it *taste*?" (Bober 1999: 266). She then adds an appendix of recipes garnered from antique sources—all laden with cautions about authenticity and the need for substitutions for the modern kitchen. Pursuing the same question, Jean-François Revel opens his famous book, *Culture and Cuisine*, with this tantalizing remark:

> Even more than the history of various foods, it is the history of *taste* that is the question here. [...] What did a meal, a wine, *taste like* in the third century before or after Christ? And *what sort of taste* did the guests have? What did they like, what was particularly sought after? What sort of wine was in one of the old bottles that Horace took out of his cellar on any and every occasion? [...] And what about the floods of ordinary wine that flowed into the cups of Agathon's guests at Plato's *Symposium*? To readers of the time, reconstructing the exact taste of these things in their minds presented no problem. Gastronomical imagination, in fact, precedes experience itself, accompanies it, and in part substitutes for it. (Revel 1982: 4–5)

Revel reminds us that familiar foods need little description to bring them to mind, but as time goes by, our grasp of earlier allusions to flavors diminishes. If the past is a foreign country, must its tastes remain *terra incognita*? Maybe not.

Resurrecting Recipes and Reviving Tastes

One of the purposes of recipes is to regularize preparation of tasty dishes so that they can be reproduced, spreading gustatory pleasures over generations. In practice, that enterprise has always been rather hit-or-miss, and there are only a few periods of time when recording recipes has been considered important (Colquhoun 2007: 56ff.). A recipe might dictate precise methods of putting together very particular ingredients, or it might more loosely summarize basic know-how. Often that know-how is learned at the elbow of a cook, and over the years such practical knowledge fades away. Anyone who has inherited her great-grandmother's cookbook recognizes that recipes even a few generations old can be challenging to execute with confidence. Moreover, recipes do not always insist that one follow their directions precisely. Sometimes they explicitly permit variations—substitute ingredients, optional additions—not to mention different modes of preparation depending on the cooking tools available. In short, many recipes are inexact and invite a range of adaptations. Within limits, of course, though drawing exact parameters is tricky, especially when exploring the recipes for dishes of earlier times. Assuming one can assemble appropriate ingredients, how confident can we be that today's cookery could produce an "authentic historical taste"—one that contemporary eaters appreciate *and* that more or less "matches" the tastes that were savored centuries before? Pondering bygone tastes and modern tongues opens a host of subsequent questions, both about the similarity of contemporary foodstuffs to older stock and about the reception of ancient dishes today.

Retrieving recipes from long ago can be accomplished in two ways: painstaking recreation of instructions from older cookbooks and from texts such as Apicius (Grainger 2006), and what archeologist Patrick McGovern terms "retroengineering" recipes by means of chemical analyses of residues left at ancient sites (McGovern 2017: 49). The two methods can coordinate nicely, as Blumenthal's Pompeiian feast demonstrates. The second has yielded some remarkably specific information about food and drink from the distant past. By analyzing the contents of vessels from archeological sites, McGovern and his team of chemists have uncovered some astonishing details about what was eaten in antiquity. Their discoveries, on occasion, have also been the basis for recreating ancient meals and for brewing a few early fermented beverages that one might have thought lost forever, the oldest from a 9,000-year-old Chinese site.

Perhaps McGovern's most famous analysis has been the funerary feast of King Midas, ruler of Phrygia in the late eighth century BCE. His mound tomb was discovered in the 1950s in central Turkey, and it was confirmed as the likely resting place of Midas by means of location, inscriptions, and historical records. (It was an earlier Midas who was endowed with the legendary golden touch.) The intact tomb had been buried beneath fifty meters of earth and was in a remarkable state of preservation. The dyes from cloth that once wrapped the king's body still stained the wood beneath his bones, and the residues from the feast that had been buried with him remained in dishes and drinking vessels. These substances in their containers were all carefully sealed and shipped to the University of Pennsylvania's Museum of Archaeology and Anthropology.

At the time of their discovery, little could be made of these residues, but by 1997 the field of molecular archeology had come into being. McGovern and his team analyzed the chemical composition of the feast and identified the ingredients of the meal that had been buried with the king to sustain him in the afterlife (McGovern 2003: ch. 11). The main dish evidently consisted of barbequed lamb or goat. The meat was removed from the bones, chopped, mixed with pulses such as lentils, and flavored with herbs, spices, honey, and olive oil. For drink, the guests imbibed a combination that mingled the ingredients of what we would now separate into wine and beer. Given that there was also honey and barley found in the residue, the drink seems to have been a sort of wine-beer-mead combination. Remarkably, we now know with pretty fair certainty *what was eaten* on one momentous occasion some 2,700 years ago. But can we know *how it tasted*? Despite McGovern's description of a "scrumptious stew for the funerary banquet" (291), we well may wonder whether what was scrumptious then would still be regarded as scrumptious now.

First, let's consider whether the analysis of ancient foodstuffs can be said to yield actual recipes. To be sure, the information provided is incomplete; absent are directions for modes of cooking and—an important gap that McGovern notes—precise proportions of ingredients for blended mixtures such as beverages. Some sound inferences can be made, however: the absence of bones indicates that the meat was removed in preparation, for example. More speculatively, when ingredients are still used in the traditional cooking of a region, current modes of preparation might be illuminating. In any event, retroengineered recipes are only partial. Nonetheless, due caution granted, chemical analysis does give us indispensable information about ingredients, and a set of cooking directions without a list of ingredients is not even a partial recipe. Thus retroengineering supplies the core for recipes that would otherwise remain unknown. Indeed, on several occasions, contemporary cooks have used them as the basis for meals intended to acquaint diners with tastes from the past.

King Midas's funeral feast was recreated in California in early 2001 at Copia: the American Center for Wine, Food and the Arts (now defunct). The foods served there were versions of traditional dishes from the Mediterranean region that were prepared according to the archeological indicators: grape leaves stuffed with mint, raisins, and almonds; lamb and lentil stew seasoned with saffron, cumin, and fennel; and figs poached in Muscat wine infused with anise (Fletcher 2004: 45). The beverage posed a bit of a problem, as its ingredients are now not commonly mingled and required some complex decisions (McGovern 2017: 41–50). McGovern challenged several breweries to come up with something drinkable employing the elements disclosed by the chemical analysis. The winner was Dogfish Head Craft Brewery, which created its *Midas Touch* ale, combining yellow Muscat grapes, toasted barley malt, thyme, honey, and saffron. It was described by one of the guests at the reenacted meal as "a fermented mixture that isn't quite wine or beer or mead, but a wonderful amalgam of them all" (Derven 2001: 5). McGovern himself provides a homebrew recipe for those who dare try to concoct it themselves (McGovern 2017: 50–1). It contains malt, honey, hops, saffron, and grape juice, and aims at a post-fermentation 9 percent alcohol content.

From the accounts recorded by the diners at Copia, we know how the reenacted meal tasted around the turn of our last millennium. But, as Paul Freedman notes, "the preparation of food has involved a craft that, unlike metalwork or glass-making, is by definition ephemeral and so hard to reconstruct" (2007: 9). How confident can we be that the recreated meal truly "matches" the one 2,700 years ago? Can this experience provide an inkling of what it was like to taste the ancient flavors of the original banquet? Before further pursuing a quest for historical tastes, we need to determine just what questions can productively be addressed, beginning with consideration of taste itself.

Entering the Past: Taste and Tasters

The issue of determining what foods tasted like in times now lost to memory actually breaks down into several possible lines of inquiry. When we wonder how an ancient feast would taste, we might mean: "What would their food taste like to me now?" Does this amount to old food on new plates—putting ancient dishes on our modern tables? Or, recalling the opportunism invited by most recipes, would modern versions of ancient dishes provide an adequate answer? Ideally, it seems as if *we* want to re-experience what *they* ate. So are we asking, "What would foods taste like if I were living back then?" This question too is indeterminate. I am a twenty-first-century North American, and if I imagine living back then, should I also try to abandon my own historical position, attempt time travel, as it were? Can we even conceive of such a project without losing track of what "I" refers to? To probe the taste of ancient foods, some stability regarding the taster is a prerequisite.

I proceed on the assumption that when we inquire about tasting the past, we are not proposing to lose consciousness of our own historical position. Not only is that hard even to conceive of clearly, it does not represent a useful goal. To taste the past you need to recognize it as *past*, which requires awareness that one is looking—tasting—in a backward direction from a point in the present. I also assume that our organs of vision, hearing, touch, smell, and taste have not undergone actual physiological change over historical time. Naturally, in the course of an individual lifetime, our sensory capabilities change: vision and hearing may become less acute, for example. But that has always been the case. Therefore, let us grant that the senses have functioned in a stable manner from past to present, a supposition that McGovern also adopts (2017: xxix). Thus, I assume a physiological stability for taste, though a phenomenological flexibility. That is, despite the many individual, cultural, and historical variations that incontestably describe eating—and obviously taste preferences—across the globe, the gustatory senses that register flavor operate in the same basic way.

Stipulating the stability of the organs of sense does not by itself solve a more intransigent puzzle, which arises because one might also think that even if people from different times were presented with the *same food substances*, their *taste experiences* would differ. Taste has long had the reputation of being the most "subjective" of senses, summed up in the old maxim, "There's no disputing about taste." Too much focus on the subjectivity of flavor perception can make the search for historical tastes impossible. According to a common but very limited construal, flavor is just the sensation on the tongue of an individual mouth, private and fleeting. The search for historical flavors would be foreclosed if this were the only meaning attached to the notion of taste.[1]

If we are to make any headway deciding whether past tastes can be retrieved, we need to recognize that the term *taste* points in a double direction, not only to a sensation in the mouth but also to features of the object that trigger that sensation. Analysis of what is meant by "taste" requires some distinctions that tend to merge in discussions of eating experiences. These include subjective elements: (1) flavor sensation (chocolate) and (2) hedonic valence (yum), for tasting something is not the same as enjoying it. Regarding the substance in question, taste might refer to (3) the descriptive character of a substance (the taste of fancy Belgian chocolates or of drugstore candy bars) and (4) micro-features that arouse flavor sensations (the chemical make-up of cocoa, sugar, and other ingredients). A cheap candy bar that has sat on the shelf for months does not taste quite the same as a fresh truffle from a high-end chocolate manufacturer, but few consumers would have difficulty recognizing both as having the taste *of chocolate*— shared recognition being separable from shared preference. As a starting point, let us grant that we automatically employ flexible gauges of similarity when identifying the objects of gustatory experiences. Loosening the standards for "tasting the same" will help considerably in the quest for historical tastes.

How loose can those standards be before sameness disappears? Variations on this question include sameness of the object of taste (identifying the type of object, detecting its particular flavor properties) and sameness of response (of flavor sensations in the mouth, of pleasure). Gustatory enjoyment adds an especially tricky element. McGovern describes Midas's feast of lamb stew as "scrumptious," but suppose contemporary eaters were to find it unpleasant? A number of ancient foods have rather bad reputations:

> Wines sweetened with sugar and spices were greatly esteemed in ancient Greece and medieval Europe, but now, with few exceptions, are regarded as dubious Christmas novelties at best. The Roman Empire's attachment to fish sauce is often thought of as alien and unimaginable, and it certainly differs from European preferences of recent centuries. [...] Cuisine changes faster than most people think. (Freedman 2007: 8)

When two people sample the same food, but one likes it and the other does not, are their taste sensations the same and their preferences different, or does the difference in preference indicate that the sensations of flavor differ as well? (Again, the term "taste" here refers to the multimodal experience of eating and drinking, not merely to the response of tongue receptors.)

Philosopher Barry C. Smith distinguishes between what he labels *tastes*—referring to the sensible properties of food and drink—and *tastings*—referring to the flavor experiences of people as they eat and drink. He also separates tastes from hedonic responses—whether or not we enjoy what we experience. He draws attention to the phenomenon of acquired taste, which refers to shifts of appreciation when a substance once disliked (such as whiskey or coffee or mushrooms) becomes familiar enough that one can discern and enjoy flavors that earlier were rejected or perhaps not even noticed. In the case of mushrooms it might be a sort of earthy quality that one learns to savor; in the case of whiskey it might be coming to appreciate the strong peat flavor of Scotch distilled in the western regions of the country. The fact that one's taste can adjust to enjoy flavors of prior dislike, and to detect subtleties in food and drink that were previously overlooked, supports the distinction between subjective response and the flavor properties inhering in food and drink.

> Tasting is a subjective experience (as in seeing or hearing), but what we taste (or see or hear), i.e. what we experience, is separate from the experience itself. What we perceive better or worse are the tastes a food or a wine has. And while liking may be a part of, or an accompaniment to, my experience of tasting, it is not part of a food or liquid's taste. Likes and dislikes may vary between individuals but the tastes we like or dislike need not. (Smith 2017: 251)

Smith's distinctions are useful in pursuing whether historical tastes can be recreated. If taste sensation is distinguishable from its hedonic valence, it is possible to share tastes but simply differ in what one makes of them. Suppose we can discover exactly what was eaten at some meal in the distant past, including its specific ingredients in their proper proportions and preparation. Then we might be able to concoct a very similar meal and sample it. Whether or not we enjoyed the fare would be incidental to the fact that we actually did taste it. I think it is a fairly safe conclusion that the Californians and the Phrygians would identify their tastes similarly as *of* lamb and lentils, Muscat grapes, honey, and so forth. So we have a minimal foundation for sharing tastes: they are recognized as *of* the same things. Granted, it is very minimal so far and not much of a triumph in the quest for past tastes. But, as with settling the stability of the human taster, it is a step in the right direction.

Gastronomical Imagination: Habits and Expectations

What about more subtle aspects of flavors and the enjoyment or dislike those substances evoke? This question returns us to recipes and their relationship to the tastes they are designed to produce. The molecular analysis that yields retroengineered recipes provides increasingly fine-tuned information about the ingredients of ancient food and drink, although modes of preparation require educated guesses. Even when there are ancient texts to serve as guides, formulating full recipes requires the skills of archeologist, historian, linguist, and cook. And because the goal is to recommend dishes for us today, some adjustments to accommodate contemporary sensibilities are sometimes advisable. To that end, recipes designed to recreate ancient dishes often aim at achieving similar tastes and dining experiences, but with the aid of substitute ingredients.

With dishes for which there is ample historical evidence, appropriate ingredients are not impossible to find, although they can be prohibitively difficult to obtain. Bober substituted a sheep's stomach in a recipe that called for the womb of an unfarrowed sow, for instance. What is more, aversion to certain substances can be so profound that it inhibits eating altogether. When Bober found her diners so repulsed by eating bulls' eyes ("I tried this *once* with the eyes of a calf," she reports, "not a success"), she substituted small onions for eyeballs. Even more dramatically: "My experience with stuffing a 102-pound wild boar with great strings of Italian sausage [imitating intestines] taught me that people's sensitivities do not condone such realism" (294). Substituting a palatable item for one that revolts present-day eaters reminds us that sophisticated gustatory enjoyment can skirt the boundaries of disgust (Korsmeyer 2011: ch. 3). When disgust cannot be overcome, there is little point in urging one's guests to savor the taste of the repulsive item on their plates.

Other substitutions aim at recreating an ancient taste with a contemporary substance that has a similar flavor but a different cultural and historical provenance.[2] As mentioned earlier, the infamous Roman fish sauces such as *garum* and *liquamen* have long been regarded as just too nasty for the modern palate. Both Bober and Sally Grainger disagree. Grainger, who has adapted dozens of recipes from Apicius for the modern kitchen, spends some time discussing how to concoct these sauces, starting with raw fish, layering it with salt, and letting it age for several months. While this process can be accomplished, both she and Bober agree that one can take a shortcut and adjust several of the widely available Asian fish sauces to make something that has an equivalent taste. Grainger remarks that a contemporary Italian product made according to ancient directives "resembles many of the Thai fish sauces familiar today and could not be distinguished from them in blind tastings" (2006: 28).

These substitutions try to reproduce ancient tastes by using ingredients with similar chemical properties that derive from entirely different cultural traditions, subtly complicating what it means to experience the *taste of* something. Is tasting *garum* the same thing as tasting Thai sauce; tasting *liquamen* the same as tasting *Nuoc mam*? (Bober 1999: 299). With this particular taste, the answer might be a hesitant yes, for the sauces are made similarly; indeed, fermented fish sauces appear to have been developed independently in Europe and Asia (Kurlansky 2002: 71). In many cases, however, I am inclined to say that substitutes *resemble* older tastes, but are not really the taste *of* the relevant historical substances. This may sound like hair-splitting, but recalling the double direction of taste—to the subjective experience of the taster and to the object that produces that taste—it is clear that there are further questions to be addressed: Do recipes prescribe ingredients of the things we eat, or just the kind of taste that they have? Does finding historical tastes require that one eat the same things that people used to? Or is it sufficient to experience similar tastes from different things? While not commonly pressing questions, this line of inquiry is pertinent to the recreation of the tastes of historical foods, for dishes are more than things with flavors; they are also particular substances assembled in particular ways, and sometimes for particular occasions. Recipes are rarely so strict as to prohibit opportunistic ingredients, but substitutions might make it a bit too easy to believe one is recreating dishes from the past.

While there are some places on earth where food preparation seems not to have changed for centuries, they are few and dwindling. We know that fruits and vegetables sold today represent but a fraction of those that were once available, and that global market regulations are restricting products that have been made for centuries. Some things that we know used to be eaten are now completely unavailable, such as extinct game birds and plant varieties. If those had distinctive flavors, they are gone from memory. These changes may be more significant than we realize when we try to recreate old recipes, as we don't know what we have lost.

Kevin Begos has spent many years studying ancient wines, seeking out places where methods of fermentation have changed little over centuries and where grape vines used for wine have grown for generations. He speaks eloquently of the flavors that nature holds waiting for us, out there in the world to be rediscovered, retrieved, and savored again today. Chemical analysis of ancient residues, he argues, tantalizingly opens up "an ancient repository of flavors and aromas" (Begos 2018: 207). He pleads for the retention of grape stock that was used to make wine historically, but which is now being crowded out of existence by standardization of production, reducing the variety of wines once enjoyed. "Each had a special flavor profile. Losing one could mean losing certain tastes forever" (9). Taking this observation seriously would require resistance of substitute ingredients for old recipes, suggesting that the epistemic quest for acquaintance with past tastes requires a stricter gauge. To have the same taste one needs the same old substance in the wine.

But there is a counter-consideration to ponder: after centuries of hybridization and refinement, it may be the case that the stuff that enters our food and drink is often *better* than what people used to put up with. Furthermore, our sensibilities have developed accordingly. For most people, taste preferences are calibrated to contemporary food and drink, and reverting to older substances (when possible) would not improve appreciation. Among the many things that frame our tastes, both artistic and gustatory, is familiarity of style and presentation, a point that can be pursued with a comparison between tasting foods of the past and listening to music of the past.

Food and Music

Food and music present some interesting similarities (Monroe 2007). Music can be scored, rather like food if you think of dishes with recipes (whether passed down in a written tradition or retroengineered). Musical performance takes place over time, as eating does, and in a sense it disappears when the performance is over. Performances can differ and hence do not produce the exact same sonic pattern each time, especially if they are played on a shift of instruments. What is more, music provides us with the notion of variations on a theme. The facility with which we can recognize a theme repeated in different parts of a composition is somewhat comparable to recognizing different versions of the same basic dish.

There is a particular debate among music historians that pertains especially to the quest for past tastes, and that concerns the notion of authenticity, especially regarding substitutability of instruments to play compositions from an earlier time (Kivy 1995). Devotees of early music are divided over whether such pieces are better played on period instruments (say, a harpsichord or crumhorn) or on their modern descendants (piano or oboe). To put just one element of a multifaceted debate in a nutshell, those who argue on behalf of early instruments claim that only with them can one hear an authentic performance of the same music that was composed centuries before. Perhaps those instruments should even be tuned to the way they were originally played and not adjusted to contemporary temperaments.

A highly authentic performance is likely to be one in which instruments contemporary to the period of composition (or replicas of such instruments) are used in its performance, in which the score is interpreted in the light of stylistic practices and performance conventions of the time when the work was composed, in which ensembles of the same size and disposition as accord with the composer's specification are employed, and so forth. (Davies 2008: 60)

The opposing position argues that our current instruments are better (more stable in tuning, for instance) and—especially—that our ears are not attuned to the older styles. One music theorist regards historical authenticity as both unattainable and not worth seeking. Among other difficulties is the fact that our expectations for music have changed radically, as for instance with the perception of consonance and dissonance.

Some intervals which are now heard as consonant were in the past heard as dissonant. [...] Medieval listeners hearing [...] a composition which contained a third would hear the interval as dissonant [...] Modern listeners hearing the same medieval composition will hear the thirds as consonant. The same piece will sound quite different to modern and medieval ears, even under ideal conditions. (Young 2008: 76)

These claims refer both to the objects producing the music (instruments) and to its reception—how it is "heard." Even if contemporary appreciative listeners hear a harpsichord piece played without amplification in a wood-paneled room, they will not hear it as it was first heard centuries ago. A veridical performance may produce musical sounds that replicate the tones and frequencies of those played centuries ago, but repositioning the ears of the listeners to hear it as it once was heard is a more daunting task. Similarly, producing and preparing ancient foods, even if they were chemically identical, will not suffice to transform utterly the sensibilities of those who eat. (Recall Revel's comment: "Gastronomical imagination, in fact, precedes experience itself, accompanies it, and in part substitutes for it.") In short, while we may come to know and even to like foods prepared from ancient recipes and even to appreciate the cultural environments that surrounded eating in the past, we will never fully enter that world. "We will have to make do with simple approximations and accept that our desire to know is destined to remain superficial, even if it is intellectually prudent and informed. This is like traveling in foreign countries and trying to understand cultures alien to our own, but being unable to *feel* them" (Montanari 2015: 15). Nonetheless, I would argue that the impossibility of *fully* participating in a very old gastronomic culture does not foreclose the possibility of *approaching* the tastes of bygone times.

The comparison between appreciating ancient foods and hearing old music parallels two ways to pursue the retrieval of historical taste experiences. One accommodates current preferences and takes advantage of the opportunism of recipes to use substitute ingredients and methods of preparation. This option recognizes that taste preferences for food change just as taste for styles of music, and appropriate substitutions of ingredients and flavor profiles maximize enjoyment for the contemporary palette. The other path—which I am inclined to endorse—is stricter and pursues earlier flavors by seeking the exact same edible substances, or as close as we can get with the ingredients that are still available, regardless of how difficult they may be to enjoy. The latter may not always yield immediate appreciative pleasure, for some flavors will be startling or obnoxious to contemporary eaters.

One may object that the attempt to be very exact about what used to be eaten imposes standards on recipes that are out of character with their flexible nature. What is more, it runs the risk of sacrificing *appreciation of tastes* to approach (with undue fanaticism) what we take to be accuracy of the *objects of taste*. In other words, we achieve precision only at the expense of pleasure. In response, I would point out that our senses and sensibilities are flexible, trainable, and generous. Just as our ears can adjust to enjoy harpsichords as well as pianos, so our tongues can adjust to unfamiliar spices and modes of preparation. The more Renaissance music we hear, the less alien it sounds; the more our spice range expands, the more readily do we enter a meal prepared within a spice-heavy culture. While we are unlikely to get terribly familiar with dishes from antiquity, the fact that we could do so given the opportunity needs to be taken into account when we think of tasting the past. I surmise that were we able to sample the very substances eaten at Midas's feast, we could eventually accommodate our preferences to appreciate them. In theory, that is. If things they ate are lost to us, our approximation may fall very short indeed. To be sure, the epistemic goal of discovering how things tasted in the past can only be approached; for the reasons adduced above, it is unlikely to be completely attained. However, that approach is likely to come far closer to the experiences of peoples of the past if what was once eaten can still be found.

This reason weighs heavily in favor of the stricter construal of the reclamation of historical dishes and their tastes, for gastronomical imagination is stymied if there are no flavors left in nature that are available to tease it into action. Unlike harpsichords and crumhorns, which can be dusted off and used again, or else precisely replicated, ancient ingredients with all their flavor potential may disappear forever—indeed, many already have. Even if tasting the past does not require exact sameness of sensory experience, the success of recreating ancient recipes is more than a little dependent on whether our contemporary foodstuffs come close to matching the ingredients of original dishes.

All of which should remind us that the project of retrieving historical tastes is more than a curiosity. The recovery of historical recipes not only expands our tasting worlds, it suggests an urgent directive: insure that ancient ingredients do not disappear from the earth. Tasting the past does not erase awareness of our own situation in time; any more than listening to sixteenth-century music cancels our twenty-first-century sensibilities. Both, however, do expand our sensory worlds, enliven our sensibilities, and deepen our understanding of the varieties of culture and ways of life that have been produced through the ages. Considering tastes of the past should prompt some timely awareness of the inadvertent losses that occur when we hurry carelessly into the future.[3]

Recipes, Tradition, and Representation

Patrik Engisch

Introduction

What is the nature of our relation to food, broadly conceived to encompass different things like recipes and dishes, namely, anything that can be eaten or drunk? Even though our primary relation to food is a matter of calorie assimilation, this cannot be the whole story. Besides, our relation to food also gives rise to complex sensory experiences. But is that it? Does the conjunction of these two models exhaust the nature of our relation to food? Arguably, there is more to it.

Indeed, beyond mere sensory experiences, our relation to food also bears on issues as diverse as cultural identity, our relation to the environment (Engisch 2020), the embodiment of values (Engisch, forthcoming)—and, as I shall argue in this chapter, our relation to the past. Arguably, if we are to make sense of these issues, a more complex model of our relation to food will be required—what we might call a "cognitive model." This chapter tries to make a case for the development of such a model, and for the role that the notion of recipe should play in it.

Crucial for such a cognitive model is the question of whether food, broadly conceived, can be representational. That is, whether food can, like things such as language and pictures, say something about something else. In this chapter, I argue for a positive, though somewhat restricted, answer to the question of the representational character of food, broadly conceived. More precisely, I argue that recipes of a certain kind (traditional ones), their instances (traditional dishes), and experiences of their consumption can be said to represent past living conditions.

The chapter is structured as follows. First, I clarify my use of the notion of representation. Second, I sketch the logical space of the question of whether food can be representational. Third and fourth, I outline my conceptions of, respectively, recipes and traditions. Fifth, and finally, I put these elements together and argue for the representational status of traditional recipes and dishes as well as their corresponding culinary experiences.

Representation

This first section comes with the modest aim to introduce the philosophical notion of representation I will be using. As such, it is mostly intended for readers unfamiliar with philosophical work about representation. However, as one can hardly say anything philosophically uncontroversial about this topic, more seasoned readers might also profit from coming to know which notion of representation I will rely on.

I begin with the following basic claim. Philosophers traditionally understand reality as in some way or other possessing what they call a *predicative structure*. In other words, they understand the world as being composed of objects bearing properties. The computer in front of me, the tree I see outside of the window, the coffee cup on my desk are all objects, and they all bear properties. For instance, my coffee cup is white, made of ceramic, and possesses a certain shape.

In this metaphysical picture, properties play a crucial role: they determine what, and how, an object is, and by turning our attention to them, by simple processes like perception, or by more complex ones such as scientific experiment or philosophical reflection, we can come to know what, and how, an object is. Of course, such a picture raises many questions. What are objects? What are properties? What is the relation, if any, that obtains between the former and the latter? These are fundamental philosophical questions, but here is not the place to address them. I merely want to use this picture of reality as an entry route into the nature of representation and will leave these questions untouched.[1]

Of interest for the topic of representation is now the following fact: not every property an object can bear merely tells us what, and how, that object is. Besides, some objects possess special properties in virtue of which they can tell us what, and how, some *other* objects are. My coffee cup possesses a certain shape and my map of Milan as well. However, the latter can also tell me that the Duomo lies south of the Central Station. That is, my map of Milan possesses special properties such that it can tell me what, and how, some other object is: of Milan, that it is a rather large city where the Duomo lies south of Central Station. These special properties are called *representational properties* and the objects that bear them are called *representations*.

But what are representational properties? Philosophers have attempted to answer this question in many ways. Here, I shall endorse the following standard one. For an object to bear representational properties is for it to have what philosophers call a *content*, namely, some semantically evaluable information as to how the world is. A map of Milan, therefore, possesses representational properties because it possesses a content that encodes information about Milan's geography.

But how can having a content be a way to cash out the idea of a representation telling us something about something else? The central idea is that representations can be semantically evaluated, namely, they can be evaluated as true or false, correct or incorrect, veridical or non-veridical. They can be evaluated as such because they have a content, encoded information of the form "The Duomo is located south of the Central Station." In virtue of this fact, we can also say that they are about something: what they are representing is what makes, or would make, their content true or false, correct or incorrect, veridical or non-veridical.

The class of representations is heterogeneous, as many different kinds of objects can possess representational properties. Philosophers disagree about the extension of this class. Still, most agree on the following list: natural language sentences (e.g., "The Duomo is located south of the Central Station"), maps (e.g., a map of the city of

Milan), pictures (e.g., a photograph of the Duomo), drawing and paintings (an etching of the Duomo), thoughts (e.g., my judgment that the Duomo is located south of the Central Station), and perceptual experiences (e.g., my perceptual experience that the façade of the Duomo is triangular shaped).

However, it is important to note that not all these representations possess their representational properties in the same way. In particular, philosophers distinguish between two sub-kinds of representations:

a) representations that possess representational properties because of the kind of things they are; and
b) representations that possess representational properties because these have been imposed on them.

My perceptual experience of my coffee cup on my desk is an instance of the first kind of representation. Indeed, that my experience does possess the representational property of thus representing the world stems out of its very nature as a perceptual experience and has not been imposed on it by anything. The sentence "The Duomo is located south of the Central Station," on the other hand, is an instance of the second kind of representation. There is nothing in the nature of ink marks on a piece of paper that accounts for them being able to represent the fact that Duomo is located south of the Central Station. Rather, that this sentence is a representation is the result of us having imposed conventionally the property of representing something on this string of letters.

Time to sum up. First, representations are objects that possess special properties, representational ones, that allow them to tell us how and what other objects are. Second, representational properties are to be conceived as the property of having a certain content that represents the world as being a certain way by laying out a condition that must be met for the representation to represent the world as it is. Third, some representations have content in virtue of the kind of things they are while some representations have content as a result of a process of imposition.[2]

Food and Representation

In the previous section, I introduced a certain notion of representation. In this section, I shall now turn to a follow-up question: can food, broadly conceived, be representational? In light of the threefold distinction between recipes, dishes, and food experiences, raising this issue amounts to asking three separate questions:

a) Can recipes possess representational properties?
b) Can dishes, like a *finocchiona* or a bottle of wine, possess representational properties?
c) Can food experiences, like smelling and tasting a *finocchiona*, possess representational properties?

Importantly, each of these questions can take two readings, a weak and a strong one, depending on the kind of things that can be candidates for being represented by, respectively, recipes, dishes, and food experiences. According to the weak reading, the questions target the issue of whether recipes, dishes, and food experiences can represent properties and elements of *food itself*, such as ingredients, dishes, and their respective olfactory and gustatory properties. According to the strong reading, the questions target the issue of whether recipes, dishes, and food experiences can represent properties and elements, which stand *beyond* ingredients, dishes, and olfactory and gustatory properties. We can then break down a)–c) in six different questions:

a-weak)   Can recipes possess representational properties that target food elements and properties such as ingredients, culinary instructions, and dishes?

a-strong)   Can recipes possess representational properties that target things beyond ingredients, culinary instructions, and dishes?

b-weak)   Can dishes possess representational properties that target olfactory and gustatory properties of food items?

b-strong)   Can dishes possess representational properties that target things beyond olfactory and gustatory properties of food items?

c-weak)   Can food experiences possess representational properties that target olfactory and gustatory properties of food items?

c-strong)   Can food experiences possess representational properties that target things beyond olfactory and gustatory properties of food items?

An important point concerning these six questions is that if a-weak) is trivial—language can represent and recipes are pieces of language that represent ingredients and culinary procedures—the five remaining questions are all philosophically substantial. In this section, I shall discuss briefly b-weak) and c-weak) while dealing with b-strong) and c-strong) in the remainder of the chapter.

There is a rather easy answer to b-weak). Dangling from a market stand are a series of salamis, each of a different sort. A customer points at one of them. In response, the butcher plunges in a bucket and hands the customer a sausage. What has happened? The customer pointed to a particular sausage and received another one in return. Did the butcher make a mistake? Of course not! The dangling sausage was there to perform a specific task: to represent a type of salami of which it is a token. This is a standard case of what Nelson Goodman calls "exemplification" (Goodman 1976), where one object serves the function of exemplifying properties of a certain kind of things, and this is a clear case of a dish possessing representational properties.

That being said, one might still be willing to distinguish between a) something *serving as* a representation and b) something *being* a representation, and point to the fact that salamis, at best, can serve as, but not be, representations. This is a serious objection. What should we make of it? The distinction between serving as a representation and being one is bound to be slightly messy. Still, the following is definitely on the right track: things that merely serve as representations have representational properties only momentarily, in a specific context, while things that are representations possess their representational properties in a more stable way, namely, across times and contexts. A *finocchiona* dangling from a butcher's stand functions as a representation for a short time and in a specific context, but things aren't so with, for example, the word "dog." Note that the problem is not that these things possess their representational properties differently: both possess them only extrinsically, as both possess representational properties as a matter of imposition. The matter is rather that things that are, and don't merely serve as, representations possess their representational properties, whether intrinsic or extrinsic, in a way that is designed to overcome the passage of time and the changing of contexts. To sum up, if a positive answer to b-weak) can be easily provided, it must nonetheless be qualified: dishes can easily serve as, but not be, representations. (I shall come back to this issue and formulate a stronger answer in the fifth section of this chapter.)

Moving to c-weak, perhaps more surprising is the fact philosophers are often worried about treating olfactory and gustatory experiences as representational on a par with, for example, visual experiences. To put things in very rough terms, olfaction and gustation seem to provide us with experiences that are more subjective and more ephemeral than visual ones, and this threatens their representational credentials. To wit, do olfactory properties seem to you to inhere in objects like visual properties? Or can you re-identify a same smell in the way you can re-identify a same chair? From this, philosophers have concluded that in comparison with visual experiences, olfactory and gustatory ones seem representationally impoverished—that is, if they turn out to be representational *at all* and not things like mere sensations.[3]

This issue has exercised many philosophers. However, one may wonder whether the issue of the representational nature of olfactory and gustatory experiences, in particular as they arise in the context of the appreciation of food, has been well posed. Indeed, holding a *finocchiona* under our nose feels much more like getting acquainted in a multi-modal way with a single object that possesses properties of different kinds than being acquainted, in different modalities, with different objects bearing different kinds of properties, for example, one object that we see and a numerically distinct object that we smell. In other words, it seems that the issue is not whether olfaction and gustation are like vision but, instead, how these modalities team up to provide us with multi-modal access to multi-modal objects. This issue, however, is massively underdeveloped in contemporary philosophy of perception. One can only hope that recent development in multisensory philosophy of perception will pave the way for an approach to olfactory experiences that will both be able to recognizethe difference between, for example, olfactory and visual experiences, and yet be able to account for the fact that, for instance, olfactory experiences can be instances of attribution of olfactory properties to everyday objects (see Todd 2018a; O'Callaghan 2019; Engisch n.d.).

To sum up, a positive answer to a-weak) is trivial, a positive answer to b-weak) is easy to provide but must be qualified, and a positive answer to c-weak) is very much an open philosophical issue, up to the point that the very way to understand c-weak) remains to be determined. I will now turn my attention to the strong readings of the above questions. However, as we will see later, once certain elements are in place, I shall also be able to strengthen some answers to the weak readings.

What Is a Recipe?

The first step in my argument in favor of the strong readings is to set up a specific— though, hopefully, acceptable—conception of recipes. First, let me clear some initial fog by distinguishing between a recipe and a dish. I will assume that a dish is what is to be found on your plate: a concrete, edible item. A recipe is what is being represented in your exemplar of Yottam Ottolenghi's last cookbook: an abstract, non-edible entity (see Borghini 2015). These two things, however, can stand in an important relation. If not all dishes need a recipe (one might, for better or worse, proceed to cook some ingredients in a random way) and if some recipes, like some buildings, exist merely on paper, dishes are often instances, or concretizations, of recipes.

With this initial distinction in place, I want to make explicit three desiderata a theory of recipes should meet before unfolding my sketch of an account of their nature. The first is obvious: a theory of recipes should be answerable to our culinary practices. But what do we mean by "our culinary practices"? On the one hand, we can conceive of them narrowly, as what is merely happening in the kitchen. However, this would be missing a lot of what is of interest about recipes. As noticed by Janet Floyd and Laurel Forster,

> Recipes surround us: in cookery books and magazines, in newspaper and television programmes, in films and novels, we seem continually to read about, observe and be encouraged to absorb ourselves in the preparation and serving of food. (Floyd & Forster 2010: 1)

In other words, recipes, and discourse about recipes, are not confined to the kitchen. This ubiquity, I contend, should be considered an integral factor of our culinary practices. As such, it should be expected from a philosophical theory of recipes that what it has to say be poised to bear on such a broad conception of our culinary practices. In other words, it should be able to explain not only what recipes are, and how they feature in kitchen work, but also to shed light on why recipes occupy such a central place in our lives.

A second desideratum is that a philosophical theory of recipes should be able to say something explanatory about the fact that recipes come in kind, and that different kinds of recipes turn out to have different properties. For instance, not all recipes can reasonably be tempered with or adapted without risking criticism. A chef recipe like Massimo Bottura's *Five Ages of Parmigiano Reggiano* (Bottura 2014: 32), for instance, is not likely to survive changes and adaptations, or at least not without having to face negative evaluation, as it seems that qualitative similarity is an important element in judging whether a dish is, or isn't, an instance of a chef recipe. On the other hand, it is much less plausible that mere routine recipes come with such a high requirement of qualitative similarity. In other words, it seems that different kinds of recipes come with different properties and different norms, and an adequate theory of recipes should not only be able to register this fact but also to explain it.

A third, and final, desideratum is that one should take into account that *some* recipes are social and cultural artifacts, endowed with corresponding normativity. By this I mean that realizing a recipe cannot in all cases merely be seen as a realization of one's own intentions or goals. Rather, pretty much like playing a Beethoven sonata, in which case one is bending one's musical intentions to Beethoven's, and in which case one subjects the realization of one's musical intentions to independent musical standards, in some cases at least, realizing a recipe can be matter of subjecting the realization of one's culinary intentions to independent culinary standards. A theory of recipes should make room for these elements as well.

Admittedly, these are rather broad desiderata and it might well be that different theories of recipes might be able to meet them. However, in what comes next, I provide a sketch of what is, I hope, a not too complex and somewhat flexible account of recipes. It contains only three clauses, two obvious ones and a third more controversial one.

The first clause says that a recipe requires a list of ingredients. This list generally covers two parameters, ingredient and quantity, but it might also contain more, or less, parameters. Some further ones might pertain to geographical or agricultural (e.g., organic vs. non-organic) properties of ingredients. All parameters can be more or less specific: some recipes are painted with rather broad brushes while some others are crafted with excruciating details.

The second clause says that a recipe requires a specification of a combinatorial procedure that takes ingredients as input and delivers an instance of the recipe—a dish—as an output. This combinatorial procedure generally covers several parameters that pertain to processes such as washing, peeling, cutting, preparing, and plating ingredients. It can also be more or less specific. Some combinatorial procedures might contain few parameters, others might contain a lot; also some procedures, or elements of them, might be very precisely described and others only hinted at. Finally, a procedure might completely ignore, or on the contrary constrain, the kind of tools to be used for the realization of the procedure.

Once these two clauses are in place, a temptation might arise. Why not stop here? Couldn't we explain what makes two recipes fall into different kinds merely by virtue of, say, the specificity of their list of ingredients and of their combinatorial procedure? Is the difference between a convenience recipe for scrambled eggs and Bottura's *Five Ages of Parmigiano Reggiano* simply not to be found in the fact that the former is much less specific than the latter? This proposal initially rings plausible, but stopping here, I contend, would be a philosophical mistake. Indeed, one might well make a very specific list of ingredients and accompany it with a very precise combinatorial procedure, and one might still wonder why one should abide, if at all, by the recipe and its specificity.

The issue that arises here is that recipes seem to be endowed with some kind of normative force: not only do recipes describe causal paths, but they also come with the claim that we should—have a reason to—follow it. Here comes my third clause. Recipes are not merely descriptive entities. That is, they don't merely describe what happens if we combine some set ingredients in a set way. In addition, a recipe always comes with a certain normative force that tells us that we *should* combine some set ingredients in a set way.

This third point is, in itself, rather innocuous. The real issue arises when one tries to dig into the source of this normative force. At this point, the following minimal answer could be attempted. Recipes describe causal paths that tell us what happens if we combine some set ingredients in a set way. Granted that we can identify our goals and aims with the output of this path, we can explain why recipes have a certain normative force in terms of their having a guiding, and not mere causal, role in the realization of our goals and aims. In other words, what we need to add to the picture is the fact that recipes can be instruments of our instrumental rationality, namely, the kind of rationality at play when we are trying to realize our goals and aims, and thus be endowed with a corresponding normative force.

This answer is rather minimal as it grounds the normative force of recipes in a rather deflationist way: recipes are normative entities only in the sense that we, as culinary agents, have goals and aims, and that recipes can, *ceteris paribus*, be conducive to their realization. Accordingly, the normativity with which recipes are endowed is purely extrinsic: it is a property they inherit from us, not a property they come with and that can exercise normative force on us independently of our goals and aims.

Such an answer goes in the right direction and is probably sufficient to explain the normative force of most recipes. Overall, however, it turns out to be insufficient as, for at least some recipes, the kind of normative force they possess cannot be reduced to instrumental rationality. Indeed, why, independently of one's own goals and aims, can someone cooking *bucatini all'amatriciana* with regular bacon instead of *guanciale* be said to produce a dish that might legitimately be said to be sub-optimal? Or why, independently of one's own goals and aims, can someone realizing Bottura's *Five Ages of Parmiggiano Reggiano* with *Grana Padano* instead of *Parmiggiano Reggiano* be said to be somewhat missing the point?[4]

The idea here is that some recipes are not merely guides to the implementation of our goals and aims but, rather, norms that guide the implementation of certain values we have reasons to pursue independently of our own goals and aims. In the case of *bucatini all'amatriciana*, one may of course argue that *guanciale*, being stronger in taste than *pancetta*, is necessary to the taste profile of the dish, and that we thereby have an independent reason—a gustatory value—to use *guanciale*. The problem is that this wouldn't yet explain why one should aim for that taste profile and why the use of *guanciale* should be aimed for reasons that don't rely on one's idiosyncratic taste preferences. A stronger reason could be the following. Being an icon of *cucina povera*, it is significant that *bucatini all'amatriciana* uses *guanciale* instead of *pancetta*, as the former is a lower cut than the latter. Within the proper way of preparing *bucatini all'amatriciana* is thereby embodied a certain approach to food preparation and meat consumption, where everything must be used, and everything, even the lower parts, must be magnified. These are strong values of decency and sustainability, and the standard recipe for *bucatini all'amatriciana* embodies them, quite independently of our goals and aims. Insofar as one recognizes that these are values to be pursued, then one possesses, quite independently of one's own goals and aims, a reason to follow the standard recipe for *bucatini all'amatriciana* and, in such a case, the recipe serves as a norm that aims at implementing these values.

The case is probably the strongest with chef recipes, such as Massimo Bottura's *Five Ages of Parmigiano Reggiano*. Such recipes have two particular features. First, they are individuated with reference to a specific individual: we speak of the recipe *of* a particular individual, for example, Massimo Bottura. As such, the recipe is endowed with a particular aim: embodying the culinary perspective of this individual. This perspective, moreover, aims at realizing particular, usually quite refined, culinary values such as balance, texture, technical mastery, or even more cognitive things like surprise (see, e.g., Engisch 2020). Accordingly, the normative force of such recipes is rather strong and independent of one's own goals and aims. In other words, such a recipe prescribes you to cook in a certain way in light of the realization of a specific culinary value and, accordingly, tempering with the list of ingredients or the combinatorial procedure might legitimately give way to criticism. "That's not the recipe!" is the adequate answer to someone attempting to produce an instance of Bottura's iconic dish while substituting *parmigiano reggiano* with *grana* or, God forbid, *pecorino*.

Of course, all this doesn't mean that what we might call *culinary reasons*, that is, reasons to follow certain recipes in a rather strict way, are indefeasible. Culinary reasons, if there are such things, are definitely not categorical reasons. It also doesn't mean that substituting an ingredient in a recipe where one should refrain to do so always is a ground for criticism, as sometimes such substitutions turn out to be necessary: for instance, maybe *guanciale*, contrary to *pancetta*, is not available in one's area. But all this is compatible with considering that there is more to the normative nature of a recipe than mere instrumental rationality.

Recognizing the normative nature of recipes turns out to be very helpful. Not only does it shed light on the fact that recipes come in kind, it also allows us to explain why recipes that fall into different kinds have different properties and come with different norms. In addition, it can allow us to meet the above first desideratum of a theory of recipes. Indeed, if recipes are norms, and since these norms aim at the realization of values—whether strictly culinary, such as gustatory values, or broader, such as ethical, moral, and political ones—this explains, at least in part, their cultural resonance (see Engisch, forthcoming). In other words, it is at least because people are generally interested by things like pleasure, health, sophistication, or social justice, and because recipes can offer guidance in the way to realize these values, that they are such ubiquitous items in human culture.[5]

What Is a Tradition?

Having put in place a certain conception of recipes, the second step in my argument in favor of a positive answer to the strong readings of the above questions a)–c) will be to offer a certain conception of traditions. This, however, raises a principled question. Indeed, beyond the fact that traditions are cultural practices that must somehow be iterated, there is very little consensus about their nature.[6] How, then, should we proceed? I have opted for the following methodology. Starting from the just given rough characterization of traditions, I have attempted to list down further conditions, selected through reflection on paradigmatic cases, that a cultural practice must meet to count as a tradition.

Such a methodology faces two main dangers: first, ending up with conditions that turn out too broad and capture more cultural practices than just traditions; second, ending up with a list of conditions that turn out too strict and capture only some of the practices that deserve to be called "traditions." I don't take these two pitfalls to be equally problematic. The first is a genuine one: it would indeed be problematic to aim at capturing something about traditions and, instead, to end up saying something about a much broader category. The second one, however, is much less to be feared. One shouldn't have too much hope in coming up with a neat, well-formed concept of tradition. Due to its intrinsic complexity and fuzzy borders, it is much more likely that *tradition* turns out to be a cluster concept, according to which many different practices might be deemed traditions without, thereby, all of them sharing a unique nature. In that respect, zooming in on a particular area of the cluster and revealing properties that might not fit all practices within that cluster are not such a big deal as long as the properties revealed seem to be constitutive of what makes a practice, or a series of practices, a tradition. I am confident that the upcoming account doesn't fall prey to the first problem, and I also contend that it manages to navigate the second one, but I am happy to leave the matter open for the reader to decide.

As mentioned above, a tradition is

a) a cultural practice that must be iterated.

To this, let me add five things:

b) it must be reasonably widespread within a community;
c) it must not only be iterated but also be such that it is in its nature to be iterated;
d) it must have the function to pass along some value to a group or community;
e) it does so in close relation with a location or environment; and, finally,
f) the way it can realize this function is by means of generating, at different times, different tokens of a same type of experience, which thereby end up constituting a shared repertoire of experiences—the experience of being, and having been, part of the tradition.

Let me highlight here that this is a purely functional account of traditions. It specifies some background conditions, a function, and some special means to realize it. As such, it doesn't come up with—and certainly doesn't intend to support—the conservative claim that there is something intrinsically valuable about traditions. Rather, on this conception, the value of a tradition, if any, is a function of the value(s) it serves to promote.

It will be helpful to illustrate this characterization of traditions by means of two examples, one failing and one meeting it. Take, first, the practice of brushing one's teeth. This is a reasonably widespread and iterated practice; it is also one whose very nature it is to be iterated. Brushing one's teeth is not a mere habit, but a practice with a certain function, to protect one's teeth from cavities and related dental issues, and this effect can be achieved only by conceiving the brushing of one's teeth as to be performed at regular intervals, and by abiding to this requirement. Teeth brushing, however, is not a tradition. If it can be said to serve the function of passing along values on a group or community (dental health and hygiene), it doesn't entertain any close relation with a specific environment. In fact, the latter would even be detrimental to its function, as the practice of teeth-brushing aims at being valid in any environment.

Compare now brushing one's teeth with the practice, still very much alive in some parts of Switzerland and nearby Alpine countries, of the *Désalpe* (in French), *Poya* (in local Franco-Provencal dialect), or *Alpabzug* (in German), namely, the guiding down into their primary homes in the valleys of animals (principally cows, but also sheep and goats) that spent the whole summer in mountainous terrains, escaping the heat and looking for pasture to graze. The richly decorated, bell-carrying animals, accompanied by properly dressed farmers and helpers, progress for several kilometers, surrounded by large crowds of onlookers, as they pass through countryside and villages before reaching their winter quarters.[7]

In the above-proposed sense, this counts as a tradition. Certainly, this practice is iterated, is so by nature, and also serves the function of passing along values to a community. We can mention here not only a sense of identity but also a celebration of small-scale agriculture and its strong relation to the environment and to climate. As suggested, this practice can have this function because it allows a community to share, through memory, different yearly tokens of the same type of experience, the experience of the *Désalpe* or *Alpabzug*.

I will now put this account of traditions in place together with my account of recipes in the next section and defend my answers to the strong readings of the questions a)–c).

Traditional Recipes and Representation

It is time now to move, finally, to the question of the relation between traditional recipes and representation. My main thesis is the following: traditional recipes, their instances, and experiences of their consumption can be said to represent past living conditions. As such, we can give a positive answer to the above a-strong), b-strong), and c-strong). My argument for this thesis goes as follows:

1. At least some recipes are endowed with normative power and provide us with culinary reasons that are independent of our aims and goals.
2. Some of the recipes endowed with such normative power are such that there are specific, normative relations between their instances, such as normative relations of culinary similarity of some degree.
3. Consequently, for some recipes at least, there is a way their instances should be.
4. In the specific case of a traditional recipe, the way its instances should be correspond to the way the recipe and its instances were at some point in the past, namely at the point in time where the recipe acquired its traditional status.
5. Consequently, traditional recipes, their successful instances as well as culinary experiences of their consumption can be said to be representations, in a proper culinary mode, of past living conditions.

Let me now discuss in more details some of these premises, starting with 3). As we saw in the third section of this chapter, some recipes are such that any principled relation between their different tokens is very relaxed. On the contrary, some other recipes prescribe additional, stricter, normative relations between their tokens, such as relations of culinary similarity, from the requirement of there being some similarity to the extreme of qualitative identity. Convenience recipes are instances of the former type, while chef recipes are instances of the latter.

Indeed, the relation between several tokens of a convenience recipe is essentially causal. That is, all these tokens stand in a same causal chain of culinary achievements, but there is no reason to assume that two tokens of such a causal chain, an early and a late one, should stand in a relation of culinary resemblance.[8] Note that the point is not that this cannot be the case. Rather, the point is that there is no principled reason to assume that it should be so. Compare now this with the case of chef recipes. Such recipes have a very different aim: realizing the once and for all determined intention of a chef. As such, the relation between different tokens of a chef recipe, even if they stand very far apart in a chain of successive realizations, isn't merely causal. Besides, it is also required that they should stand in a rather strong relation of culinary similarity. Of course, this normative requirement of similarity might fail to be met and, hence, there is no guarantee that any attempted token of a chef recipe resembles previous instances of the recipe. But since such recipes come with a strong normative force, we can distinguish between successful and unsuccessful instances of such recipes, and some criticism of unsuccessful realizations of such recipes might therefore be justified.

Already at this point, we can discern the representational power of some recipes and of dishes and culinary experiences mediated by such recipes. Indeed, in the second section of this chapter, I discussed the possibility for dishes to possess representational properties and ended up concluding that dishes, like a salami, could at best serve as, and not be, representations. Our having pointed out the strong normative nature of chef recipes allows us to do better. Indeed, their strong normative nature makes it such that there is a way they should be. Accordingly, any successful instance of a chef recipe can be said to represent past instances of it. Indeed, instances of such recipes are not only causally, but also normatively, related to each other. That is, for each instance of a chef recipe, there is a way it should be, and it can then be evaluated as being a more or less accurate representation of earlier successful instances and of the chef's culinary intention that they embody. In other words, it has content of a sort that has been imposed on them by culinary intentions in a rather stable way. Of course, there is no guarantee that an instance of a recipe does represent earlier instances, as something could have gone wrong in its elaboration. But this is a familiar feat of representations: they can succeed or fail to represent what they should represent, depending on whether their content is satisfied by the world. My final answer to b-weak) is then stronger than the one sketched above in the second section of this chapter.

Moving from recipes and dishes to experiences thereof, we can say the following. We can discern a stable representational relation between present and past experiences of certain dishes, namely those which are instances of recipes that impose normative relation of gustatory similarity between their instances. That is, tasting Bottura's *Fives Ages of Parmigiano Reggiano* doesn't only tell about your present food experiences, it also tells about past instances of similar experiences, granted that you are now enjoying a successful instance of the recipe. Here again, this can allow us to consider a positive answer to c-weak), though in a way different than sketched above in the second section of this chapter.

But I think we can go further and allow another kind of recipe further representational power. This brings us to premise 4). Like chef recipes, traditional recipes come with a rather strong kind of normativity that they inherit from their being instances of traditions. As such, it is part of their function to produce tokens of dishes that are normatively related to each other: each of them should resemble each other and fit an experiential template specified by the recipe.

Such a claim must face the problem of explaining how a traditional recipe can be endowed with such normativity. In the case of chef recipes, an explanation of this fact is rather straightforward: it is because such recipes are representations of the culinary intentions of a specific individual that enters in the individuation conditions of the recipe. But such an answer is implausible in the case of traditional recipes, as their individuation conditions don't plausibly rely on specific individuals.

That being said, it seems that if the exact same explanation cannot be applied to traditional recipes, another one in a similar vein can be attempted. Namely, traditional recipes are individuated not with respect to a specific individual, but with respect to a community. If individuals can have intentions as individuals, communities can also have intentions as communities, either as the sum of the intentions of their individuals or in a stronger sense. Accordingly, it seems plausible that we can individuate a traditional recipe in part by referring to the intentions of the community to which it is attached and that such a communal intention aims, among other things, at the continued iteration of the tradition in its set form.

However, this only pushes the problem one step further. What is the set form of a traditional recipe and how does it come about? The problem with these questions is that they are largely empirical ones and, as such, fall beyond the scope of philosophical analysis. Let me, however, add the following minimal considerations. First, it is unlikely that there is only one way through which a recipe can acquire its traditional status. In some cases, this might occur by decree, as when a more or less institutional entity issues an official version of a recipe. Much more likely is the fact that a certain recipe acquires its traditional status progressively and in a rather decentralized manner, as it starts to play a certain function in a community. Second, let me concede that the acquisition of the status of tradition doesn't prevent a recipe from undergoing changes. But let me flag that such changes won't have the status of changes occurring in the case of a simple convenience recipe. On the contrary, they are likely to cause uproar, negotiation, and to leave traces in the history and historiography of a recipe.

As a result, then, let me venture the following broad account of the acquisition of the status of tradition by a recipe. The basic change a recipe is undergoing when it becomes a traditional one, whatever the way it becomes one, is one of losing its autonomy. That is, it becomes such that changes in its ingredients or combinatorial procedure become subject to strong prescriptive norms inherited from the intentions of a community. Importantly, if there is no discrete point in time at which a recipe acquires such a status, there is nonetheless, for any traditional recipe, a moment in the past at which its status as a traditional recipe has been consolidated.

This brings us now to 5), my final conclusion: traditional recipes, their instances, as well as food experiences that result from their consumption are, if meeting their success conditions, representations of the past. Namely, they can be representations of past living conditions at the time, or shortly before, the recipe lost its autonomy and acquired its status as a traditional recipe. The recipes themselves represent these past living conditions symbolically, namely, through the use of linguistic symbols. Dishes that are instances of traditional recipes, on the other hand, represent these past living conditions non-symbolically: as a set of categorical and dispositional properties the latter of which, when triggered, can allow us, literally, to smell and taste paste living conditions. In other words, traditional recipes, their instances, and experiences thereof can put us in a position to say things such as: "Life in the past, or at least its culinary aspects, used to be like this."

This is a rather strong thesis, of course, and for it to have any plausibility at all it must be added that the semantic evaluation that pertains to traditional recipes, their instances and experiences thereof is unlikely to be truth. Indeed, truth is an either/or fact of the matter: a proposition is either true or false, and the content of traditional recipes, their instances, and culinary experiences that result from their consumption are unlikely to be like that. Truth, however, is not the only semantic standard around. Perceptual states, for instance, are said to have accuracy or correctness conditions, and such kind of semantic evaluation allows for evaluation in terms of degrees (see, e.g., Crane 2014).

Take, for instance, the case of looking at a white cube while wearing red glasses. The resulting visual experience will be as of seeing a red cube at a certain distance, and the experience will be fully accurate or correct just in case one is indeed seeing a red cube at that distance. Since the cube is white, and not red, the present visual experience isn't fully accurate or correct. But it isn't also completely mistaken; there might be no red cube at a certain distance, but there is still *a* cube at a certain distance. In other words, such a visual experience got some things correct about the world. We might then say that this visual experience fails to be fully accurate or correct, but that it is nonetheless partially so.

As I conceive of the matter, the correct semantic standard to evaluate the representational powers of traditional recipes, their instances, and experiences thereof is not truth, but accuracy or correctness. In that sense, a traditional recipe, its instances, and culinary experiences thereof might be said to represent past living conditions, with either complete or, what is more likely, partial accuracy or correctness. Indeed, maybe the exact right sort of tomato isn't available anymore, or one will cook with electricity instead of fire, or who knows what. Yet maybe the instance of the recipe will be successful enough for it, and the culinary experience that results from its consumption, to give us a glimpse—or more—of past living conditions.

Conclusion

This chapter started with the following question: What is the nature of our relation to food? I have argued that this relation can, in some cases at least, be a cognitive one—and pretty strongly so, as some food items can serve as *bona fide* representations of past living conditions. A key step in my argument is played by a conception of recipes as norms. It is because at least some dishes come into existence as instances of recipes, and because at least some recipes come with some kind of normativity that is not purely instrumental, that traditional recipes, their instances, and culinary experiences thereof can be said to be representations of the past. Indeed, there is a way these recipes, their instances, and culinary experiences thereof should be: as they were when the recipe gained its traditional status. When instances of such recipes meet their success conditions, they can be said to represent, more or less accurately, past living conditions in a distinctively culinary way.[9]

Authenticity, Style, and Recipe in Wine

Cain Todd

Introduction

In this chapter I want to explore the question of whether thinking about wine in terms of recipes can illuminate the values that wine is often supposed to manifest. I will argue that the notion of a recipe does not, by itself, do much to illuminate the nature of wine since in general wines lack the functional connection to recipes that food has. For any particular wine, it is just not the case that it can be readily replicated by anyone other than the maker/producer of that wine. This is partly for practical reasons, as is evident from the fact that there simply do not exist, for instance, wine recipe books in the way that such books for food are innumerable. These practical reasons arise from the determinate nature of the product itself. More specifically, insofar as they are to be imagined—since they are not generally written down—the relation between wines and recipes is largely uninformative, since they necessarily under-specify too much to be practically replicable. Wine recipes are, as we shall see, too *elliptic.* In particular, the idea of a recipe does little to help us understand what differentiates certain *styles* of wine from others.

It is, I will argue, more helpful to think of wine in terms of style, because this allows us to get to grips with some of the values that are peculiar to wine, including the expression of terroir, as well as with some of the norms governing the evaluation and demarcation of wine. What constitutes style is difficult to articulate with any precision; yet, I will suggest that one of the main values associated with style, namely, authenticity, can be articulated by thinking about the relationship between wine and recipes. As such, I do not wish to make the contrast between the notions of style and recipe, as applied to wine, overly stark and I will suggest that style in wine can be thought of as a modification of wine recipes.

Recipes

What is a recipe? Basically, it is a program—or the description of a process—for producing a product. This product can be referred to as a dish. I will follow Borghini here in thinking of a dish very broadly: "anything that is ready for someone to be eaten up" (2015: 722) or drunk counts as a dish. So, dishes are not just the result of a cooking process, they also include "simple" products such as cheese or chocolate or wine. The distinction between recipe and dish is formulated by Borghini in the following way: a slice of pizza can be thought of as *that* concrete object that is *now* in my kitchen (dish), or as the array of the *repeatable aspects* whose repetition would deliver a slice of *pizza* of the same sort (recipe).

A bottle of wine, then, can on Borghini's view be considered either as a dish or as a recipe. I will remain neutral on the question of the type/token distinction, but for my purposes here it will be easier to think of a wine recipe as the description of the process that results in the stuff in the bottle, and hence to think of a particular bottle of wine as a dish.[1]

Prosaically, a recipe is a program consisting of (a) a list of ingredients and (b) a set of instructions for how to combine them, where (a) and (b) can be specified in more or less detail. For example, the list of ingredients will usually specify type and quantity, and the instructions for combining them will specify, also in more or less detail, the ways in which the ingredients should be treated and any further processes involved in this, including the kinds of implements required.

An important feature of recipes, according to Borghini (2015), is that they are *elliptic*: they leave out details concerning many aspects of the ingredients, processes, and dishes they result in. This is partly for practical reasons, since it would be too difficult or even impossible to specify, on the one hand, every single aspect of every action or ingredient required to make a dish and, on the other hand, all of the properties of the resulting dish, including olfactory and gustatory properties. Partly, however, it is due to the fact that, as Bordini (in this volume) notes, too many details about ingredients—even assuming they could all be articulated or specified—might make a recipe unrepeatable, insofar as they might be too fine-grained to be replicable across space and time.

Bordini discusses two interesting consequences of this. First, a recipe typically underdetermines its taste: "It does not carry enough information to individuate a unique associated gustatory profile." Second, their being elliptic is what makes at least some recipes "constitutively open to both synchronic and diachronic modification and change, thereby making it possible for the same recipe to variate, evolve, and be innovated."

It is useful also to bear in mind a distinction Engisch (in this volume) makes between what he calls "routine" recipes and "chef" recipes. The former type allows some adaptation and might include generic recipes such as *Pizza Margherita* or *Sole meunière*. As an example of a chef's recipe, Engisch gives Massimo Bottura's *Five Ages of Parmigiano Reggiano* (Bottura 2014: 32) which, to be successfully replicated, requires a high degree of qualitative similarity. Roughly, then, it seems that we might say that routine recipes, since they are less fine-grained in their specifications, can be characterized as generally more, and chef's recipes as generally less, *elliptic*. Clearly this is a rather indeterminate boundary, however, and as we shall see below, being more or less "elliptic" does not map neatly onto the routine/chef's distinction. It is also important to note that the routine/chef distinction does not neatly correspond to a simple/complex distinction. Some simple recipes, requiring few ingredients and processes, may nevertheless specify these to a high degree of detail and will to that extent be less elliptical than a prima facie more complex recipe that leaves out enough detail such that, to some degree, it underspecifies its own processes, ingredients, or dishes.

How important is it that a recipe is replicable? On the face of it, it might seem more important that a routine recipe is easily replicated than is a chef's, where "easily" here means something like: "can in principle be followed by anyone with sufficient skill and the right ingredients and implements." At least, easily replicated by anyone other than the chef, for a chef's recipe might be easily replicable by, and yet only replicable by the very chef who invented it, in terms of—at the upper limit of what is conceivable—the possibly unique ingredients or processes or skills to which only that chef has access. However, the notion of replicability is in fact differently applied to each type of recipe. A chef's recipe, on Engisch's view, requires qualitative similarity, whereas a routine recipe does not. This issue of replicability, and of what kind, is important for understanding wine's value and I will return to it below.

Engisch notes also that recipes are not just descriptions but seem to be endowed with some kind of normative force that tells us that we *should* combine some set ingredients in a set way (Engisch in this volume). Although he doesn't himself put it quite like this, I will contend that this normative force can be understood in terms of the realization of certain values. For example, one should follow this Pizza Margherita recipe because it offers a distinctive taste: either a generic Pizza Margherita taste, or the Pizza Margherita taste distinctive to this particular variant. Here we have a straightforward gustatory value, by which I will simply mean a sensory appreciation of a dish's textures and flavors.

However, there are also non-gustatory values that may give a recipe normative force. In addition to simply tasting good, a recipe can be traditional or authentic, creative or experimental, hearty or healthy, heavy or light, warming or refreshing, organic, ethical, sustainable, vegan-friendly, biodynamic, and so on (see Engisch in this volume and Engisch 2020). Insofar as we do value these things, we have a reason to follow the recipe and/or to consume the dish. It is an open question as to whether such values can become gustatory values if they appropriately influence the sensory appreciation of a dish.

Wines as Recipes

How do these observations apply to thinking of wine as a recipe, and to explaining the fact that there are no wine recipes that exist in a way corresponding to the nature and ubiquity of food recipes? The first thing to note is that it will depend, among other things, on what *types*—or more specifically, what level of generality—we focus on. Corresponding to a routine recipe like that of pizza may be something like French white wine, or corresponding to Pizza Margherita, for example, a narrower category like that of "Bordeaux." The equivalent of a chef's recipe may straddle a spectrum from a wine made by a big industrial producer—for example, Jacobs Creek (JC) Shiraz—to a large Champagne house, to a small *domaine* in Burgundy.

If we can pursue this parallel—and whether it can remain a moot question, as we shall see—it seems that the narrower the wine category the less elliptic the recipe ought to become, because the ingredients and/or processes will become more and more fine-grained. But is the recipe for an industrially produced wine like JC Shiraz less fine-grained, more elliptic than, say, the 2014 Bonnes-Mares produced by Domaine Francois Berthaud? At the level of description, arguably not. The JC Shiraz needs, *qua* industrial wine, a high level of replicability so that the kinds of consumers who buy it can learn to trust its uniform gustatory profile. As such, one can expect the recipe for producing it to be very specific. In contrast, the gustatory profile of this Bonne-Mares will be subject to the climatic contingencies of terroir and the values or disvalues conferred by vintage. These cannot be easily distilled into a useful recipe, since the only way they can be referred to is demonstratively. One must use *these* grapes from just *this* vineyard, the assumption being that these products are simply unique. This in a nutshell is what the controversial concept of terroir amounts to.

I will come back to this, but the point for now is simply that the notion of fine-grainedness underpinning ellipticality can be understood not just as referring to the descriptions, but in terms of the nature of the ingredients of the recipe. The replicability of a recipe will depend on the degree and type of fine-grainedness involved. Thus, a very specific chef's recipe may be more elliptic than a routine recipe, in terms of being a broad rather than fine-grained description, precisely because of the fine-grained nature of the ingredients. To borrow a phrase from Engisch, in the case of chefs' recipes, detailedness comes with artisanality, but in the case of industrial recipes, it comes with industriality.

Nonetheless, in another way, the Bonnes-Mares will be fine-grained at the level of specified detail, for two main constraints on replicability at this very refined level of winemaking will be the *varying* expression of grape + terroir according to vintage, and the particular individual "house style," namely, the particular style the winemaker wishes to achieve. It is an extremely difficult question to determine what exactly style in wine is, and we will return to it below. In any case, to achieve a certain style, one must assume that the specification of processes for using the ingredients will be very fine-grained. Indeed, these processes in the case of wine arguably begin well before the grapes are picked, and so the recipe for making such a wine will have to include a description of more or less everything involved in growing the grape themselves.

Interestingly, therefore, in the case of the Bonne-Mares, what counts as replicable will likely be quite different from what counts as replicable for a JC Shiraz, particularly because the ingredients of the former themselves may be prone to certain acceptable variations: indeed not just acceptable, but even valuable, within the limits imposed by the overall style of the wine. Thus, the fact that the Bonne-Mares recipe may be more rather than less elliptic might seem to count in favor of its lesser degree of replicability. But the point I am making is rather different: its replicability will be determined by stylistic constraints that have built into them a certain valuable flexibility, rather than the fine-grained specificity of ingredients and processes. This point will become clearer below.

Another wine type it is worth thinking about in this light is natural wine. On the one hand, given the relative lack of intervention by their winemakers, the recipes for natural wine will look quite sparse and very elliptic, even in terms of their processes. Yet if, for example, a detailed and comprehensive list of biodynamic principles is used to produce a certain wine, then at least before the grapes are crushed the recipe may consist of a very fine-grained description indeed; and yet, not so fine-grained as to be impractical. To take an example, Caroline Henry writes of the grower's champagne produced by Franck and Isabelle Pascal in Baslieux-sous-Chatillon:

> The terroir is mixture of silty limestone and clay interspersed with pierre meulière, silex, marl [...] the subsoil is wet chalk. The soil is ploughed completely from the beginning of spring till flowering; afterwards the grass and natural plants are allowed to grow back. Franck uses most of the biodynamic preparations, herbal teas and fermented plant extracts as well as selection of homeopathic treatments to reduce the doses of copper and sulphur he uses [...] the soil is exclusively ploughed by horse. Franck and Isabelle pick their grapes at optimum ripeness so no additives are needed. Once pressed the juice is allowed to settle before being racked into tank and barrel where the first fermentation is allowed to start spontaneously. The malolactic fermentation occurs naturally in spring [...] the wines are bottled without fining, filtering or added sulphites, in accordance with the cycles of the moon. (Henry 2016: 230–1)

It has to be borne in mind here, however, that unlike chef's recipes there may, in the production of a wine, be very little actually written down in the form of instructions. Indeed, as I have already noted, there is nothing obviously in the world of wine that really corresponds closely to the functional role that recipes play in the world of food. This is not surprising, since after all people generally do not make their own wine. It is also in part due to the fact that the producer will rely on well-practiced know-how, but also, more importantly, because room must always be allowed for a certain level of "on-the-spot" adjustment and improvisation depending on all the variables involved in the complex process of making wine. Given the ever-changing nature of the ingredients undergoing the constant processes involved in making wine, wine recipes, if they were to be written down, would look quite different from many food recipes. For one thing, they might contain many more conditional statements, depending, for example, on how the grapes were ripening, or how the fermentation was developing.[2]

Most importantly, as we are about to see, whether the terroir is being expressed adequately, whether the wine is balanced, or whether the style is being accurately produced are all delicate issues of judgment that no recipe can succeed in specifying. One way of thinking about this is the following, which is far too blunt to be correct but may nevertheless be a helpful starting point: whereas food dishes and chef's recipes require as a success condition that the resulting dish taste a certain way, wine recipes don't merely vastly underdetermine their tastes, but style is not something that can be reduced to taste. It is worth contrasting this notion of style with what we might term a "chef's style," in the world of food. Although a chef's dish may exemplify her style, the explicit intention need not be to aim for this exemplification. Wine seems, prima facie, like it might be different in this respect—the stylistic aim must be more or less explicit to control every stage of the varying process of production in accordance with the overarching goal.[3]

Before returning to these issues in the next section, we can sum up the discussion hitherto in the following way: it does not seem as though there is just one way in which the relationship between wines and recipes can be conceived. We can distinguish various ways in which wine recipes and ingredients can be more or less fine-grained, and it is not straightforward to determine how this relates to the ellipticality of wine recipes, or to the question of style governing the production of a wine. Indeed, it is not yet clear how much is to be gained by thinking of wines in terms of recipes, since given the general lack of such recipes their ellipticality is itself a matter of guesswork. To get a better grasp of the links between wine as a dish and wine as a recipe, we need to look more closely at the roles of terroir, grape, and style in winemaking and how they give rise to certain distinctive values.

Style, Terroir, Taste

What exactly is style in wine? Here is a description of Chateau Margaux:

> The style of wine produced by Chateau Margaux at its best, blends elegance, purity of fruit, harmony and finesse. If wines were actors, perhaps it could be described as having the charm, style, finesse and elegance of Cary Grant. This suave wine is not light. It is rich, full bodied and offers cassis, truffle and haunting scents of violets.[4]

Style here consists of a list of attributes typical of this particular wine, among which we find basic descriptive terms, evaluative terms, and metaphors. Of course, these attributes clearly do not suffice to differentiate Chateau Margaux from other wines, so the style is not reducible to them. The question is, whether any such list could differentiate it successfully in this way. Arguably, not, simply because the purportedly unique individuality of such a wine itself precludes descriptions that could be applied anywhere else. As such, there must necessarily be a level of indescribability that applies in such cases. This in turn is a symptom of the role of terroir and taste in the production of such wines. Terroir also does not seem to be the kind of thing that can simply be captured in terms of bio-geo-physical descriptions; rather, its manifestation in the wine must be (literally) a matter of taste.[5]

As such, if style is in part a product of terroir, style must be detected first hand, by being directly perceptually acquainted with a glass of Chateau Margaux, and perhaps also with certain background cognitive elements playing an influencing role, such as: some expertise with wines of this kind, certain expectations concerning them, perhaps a background knowledge of intention and production methods, and so on (see Todd 2010). So, the reason why style is to some extent indefinable, or at least is such that it cannot be fully articulated in a recipe, is because it necessarily incorporates the *haecceity* of the wine where a large part of this is the expression of *terroir*.

What can we say about more "routine" wines? It is difficult to say to what extent such wines aim for or achieve a style. Insofar as they do, the "style" might be so generic that it cannot and is not supposed to individuate this particular wine from other similar wines. So, the "style" of JC Shiraz, for example, can be described like this:

> A medium bodied **Shiraz** with good mid-palate sweetness, vibrant fruit and soft velvety tannins. This wine is a great example of the approachable style of **Jacob's Creek** classic wines.

The style is "approachable," which might apply to any routine wine the very aim of which is ease of drinking. It is not really an individual style that such a wine is aiming at. At best, it will offer some expression of the grape variety and will be more or less well made, in the sense that it is without obvious faults or exaggerations and will therefore be easy to drink for most consumers.[6] A nice way of putting this is to borrow from Engisch (personal communication) the idea that some wines have a "wine-to-consumer" direction of fit, where the wine must fit the consumer, and some wines have a "consumer-to-wine" direction of fit, where the consumer must fit the wine. Industrial wines would be of the former kind, where we do produce a product which fits a pre determined palate.

These different kinds of "style" clearly bear different relations to replicability. The JC Shiraz style is simple and generic enough that it can be relatively easily replicated, its recipe, such as there is one, just fine-grained enough to guarantee consistency of product, and elliptic only to the degree that acknowledges the superfluousness of any more fine-grained detail of ingredient or process. Overall, for such wines, style is not much more than taste. Indeed, one might suggest that this notion of style is rather deflationary and is perhaps better thought of under the notion of "type" or "category." So, the "style" of such an industrial wine may be best captured under the label "table wine," for example. Clearly, this notion or type of "style" differs markedly from that arising from a concentration on the individuality of a particular wine and its terroir, which is my main concern here, but just where the hazy boundary between the two lines lies will have to await discussion another day.

It may help to compare this with the case of a small Domaine using just one grape variety to produce just one type of wine, where the climatic conditions are relatively stable, and where the intention may be simply to produce the most fruit-driven wines that it can. The wines produced should be drunk when young, and they will conform to a style that may be quite easily replicable year-on-year, at least by the makers of this wine. Insofar as this wine is supposed to be an expression of terroir, its relationship to its recipe may not differ markedly from a more routine corporate wine. Its style too will be largely determined by taste, but the style will at least be dependent upon capturing the individuality of the terroir in a way that justifies talking about such a wine in terms of style rather than just in terms of some generic category in which it fits.

In contrast, the style of very fine wines bears a more complicated relationship to taste, since it will adhere much more closely to important variations of intention and terroir. So, for example, a complex wine like Chateau Margaux, involving a blend of different grapes, a large terroir subject to varying climatic conditions, and made with the sophisticated intention to manifest multiple qualities—for example, elegance, tight structure, floral, and tertiary aromas—may not only be less easy to replicate more or less exactly year-on-year, but may make a virtue of the fact that the Margaux style will be recognized *through* significant variations in these other qualities: that is, through different vintages. The style, one might say, will be in this way *less* closely connected to or determined by the particular taste of the wine dishes than is the case for industrial wines, as we saw above.[7]

This will simply be a function of the fact that different vintages can result in different qualities or different emphases. The expression of terroir is subject to different climatic conditions, year-on-year. This is what makes it possible, for such wines, to express a unique terroir, and hence to have a consistency of style, even where the taste of the wine may differ even quite a lot between vintages. The hallmark of excellence here is therefore to aim for as much consistency as possible, in terms of style and quality, despite adverse conditions, while nevertheless allowing for the manifestation of different virtues corresponding to different vintages. Some might be more robust, others more delicate, some better drunk young, others left to age, and so on.

Of course, beyond a certain limit on the variation of taste, the wine may not preserve the style that was intended. A bad vintage might result in a wine that is no longer recognizably Margaux. Indeed, to be frank, even below this limit it is a little bit mysterious how a unique style can be guaranteed to be preserved despite some significant changes in the taste of the wine. One might, not implausibly, direct some skepticism at claims that, for example, the Chateau Margaux can be recognized at a blind tasting and distinguished from its close neighbor of the same vintage simply by its taste or style. After all, many top Bordeaux producers aim for the same qualities as Margaux: complexity, aging potential, elegance, structure, violets, and so on.

Nonetheless, if we're not guessing during a blind tasting, the intentions and virtues underpinning a particular style can obviously enhance our appreciation of that wine and in some broad sense perceptually acquaint us with that style, and its variations when drinking it. In other words, we can try to taste the style through drinking it, in something like the way we can detect a musical theme through its variations, or hear a sonata as Brahmsian in style. The Gestalt-like experience is difficult to articulate, and remains semi-mysterious, but is not less real for all that.

The recipe for Chateaux Margaux, then, would ideally include detailed descriptions of its terroir, and all of the further descriptions of ingredients and processes would be given in terms of their role in achieving the overall goal, that of the house style, in a way that is commensurate with the expression of terroir and the variables of the vintage. Any such recipe, however, would necessarily underdetermine the taste of the wine dishes—particularly so in light of the changes that occur after bottling and the variation in tastes depending on when they are drunk—and might be more or less elliptic depending on how many aspects of the grapes and terroir could be and were required to be manipulated to achieve the intended style. This might require in certain cases a great deal of fine-grained instruction concerning the interventions required to preserve style and manifest terroir in adverse conditions.

In sum, then, if we are to imagine the formulation of a recipe for something like Chateau Margaux, no matter how fine-grained its descriptions might be, the fine-grained nature of the wine's terroir and tastes, and the necessary limitations on our ability to fully articulate in words the house's style entail that any such recipe will be in this respect elliptic to a large degree and will vastly underdetermine the taste of any particular bottle of wine.[8] This does not entail that winemakers do not follow recipes, and style can perhaps be best conceived as a modifier of recipes. But it does suggest, I think, that at least for certain wines the notion of style plays a more central role than that of recipes in thinking about their nature and value. In particular, I will now argue that the inherent ellipticality of wine recipes, such as they are, allows us to understand how and to what extent authenticity can become a seminal value as a function of style.[9]

Authenticity

One of the consequences of our discussion so far is that it might seem to enable us to rank wines as more or less creative. In his discussion of what makes a recipe or dish creative, Engisch (2020) discusses the case of Rene Redzepi, head chef and founder of the acclaimed restaurant Noma, who claims that all ingredients have the same worth. Although it is not the only way of being creative, Redzepi's particular creativity consists in being heavily constrained by territory, with all ingredients limited to a relatively small area. This constraint, according to Engisch, enables a "thorough exploration of the culinary richness of an area via innovative transformations of basic ingredients" (2020: 71).

Some winemakers are clearly experimental, trying out new grape varieties in new territories, and the natural wine movement in particular might seem to embody this kind of creativity, taking risks with conditions and with unusual tastes that test the palates of seasoned drinkers. The constraint on winemaking provided by an adherence to the notion and expression of terroir seems at first glance to play a similar role to the geography of Noma, enabling or motivating a thorough exploration of the richness of the land and its grapes.

Yet, although winemaking involves the radical transformation of a basic ingredient, by the standards of winemaking as such there is no radical innovation involved here. Does creativity come in via the way in which variation may be managed with respect to vintages in a way that allows a consistent style to be manifest? It is doubtful that this meets the standard of innovative transformation. Indeed, if we consider some of the aspects of wine discussed above, it becomes evident that the notion of authenticity plays a greater role in wine recipes and wine styles than that of creativity. Indeed, authenticity seems to be at odds with creativity; rather, authenticity in winemaking requires skill and embodies the virtue of craftsmanship. It is artisanal, rather than artistic. In this way wine contrasts with many food recipes, where ellipticality may be of service in the pursuit and manifestation of authenticity, but where the possibility of creativity plays, or can play, a greater role.

The notion of authenticity is deeply vague. I think, however, we can make a few basic distinctions. The first concerns authenticity as applied to an object:

> *Nominal authenticity*: the correct identification of the origins, authorship, or provenance of an object, ensuring, as the term implies, that an object of aesthetic experience is properly named.

Expressive authenticity: having to do with an object's character as a true
expression of an individual's or a society's values and beliefs.

The second concerns the difference between attributing authenticity to an object and
to an attitude:

Object: continuous with tradition/apt or accurate manifestation or expression of
the source/the thing itself. This is not the same as nominal authenticity since it
can refer to expressive properties, for example, terroir.
Attitude/method: being faithful to the original source. This notion is linked to
intention.

So, in these terms, one can follow recipes faithfully, and hence authentically, and a
recipe can be more or less authentic, namely, accurate. Something (e.g., dish, wine) can
be more or less authentically (*attitude*) authentic (*object*).

An important question is whether authenticity is intrinsically valuable, where this
means something like valuing the original thing for being just that (original) thing,
valuing the (continuity of the) tradition for its own sake, or valuing the attitude/method
(of production) for its own sake. In this light, one might doubt that it is authenticity
as such that is valued. Rather, it's either the properties of the object or tradition that
are valuable, or alternatively, the value of the attitude/method of production because
it allows access to *the* real thing. Thus, authenticity might only be derivatively or
instrumentally valuable because what it gives access to is (intrinsically) valuable.

In this way, one of the functions of authenticity is to preserve valuable flavors as well
as to ensure that they can be recreated. One problem with this is that the authentic might
come apart from the tasty: something could be authentically disgusting. Moreover, if
you could just create ex nihilo the thing that tastes good, what would authenticity's
value amount to? So, as far as recipes go, it is not obvious yet that authenticity is
intrinsically good. What is intrinsically good is the taste/flavor. Insofar as recipes have
taste/flavor as their primary function, their authenticity is instrumental value at best.

Yet recipes, and wines, can be vehicles for expressing certain attitudes and values
that are not just tastes. Or rather, we can broaden the notion of "taste" to reflect the fact
that flavor experiences may be directly influenced by various non-sensory, cognitive
elements such as beliefs and expectations (see n. 5). They can be bearers of significant
cultural values, such as the expression of terroir. I would like to claim that some forms
of expressive authenticity plausibly can be intrinsically valuable. Wines are valued
for their expressiveness, for their personality, and (more controversially) for their
embodiment of *terroir*. We have already seen some examples of this earlier, but here
is another:

The domaine makes a point of picking its Montrachet as late as possible, often
well after all the other producers have completed their harvest. Co-owner Aubert
de Villaine has noticed across the years that grapes in Le Montrachet retain their
acidity even if left late on the vine. This late picking results in extraordinary
opulence and an almost monolithic intensity that speak more of the producer than

the vineyard. But after time in the glass, the incredible character of the vineyard starts to show. (Beckett 2008: 347)

The expression of *terroir* and personality is thus in part the result of the intentional act of the winemaker. To the extent that a winemaker's intentions are successfully realized, they are identifiable *in* the wine the more complex, expressive, original, true to *terroir* the wine is, the greater the achievement it represents. This is so even where the winemaker's explicit intentions are to let the winemaking process be as natural as possible, for it is human guidance that selects and allows this process to succeed:

Not only did the wine with our guidance and care make itself, but you could find distinctive character in the wines that you hadn't created by blending or adding or subtracting, but that actually came from a piece of ground. So it struck me that if you were really talking about wine as a natural product, as something authentic, then you should be seeking out those parcels, those pieces of land, where there was individuality of character and real quality in the grapes themselves. You would tend the vineyard and guide the transformation in the cellar, but the wine would reflect nature and the natural process. (Jefford & Draper 2005: 201–2)

Partly connected with the expression of *terroir*, the most complex and sophisticated wines are held to express individuality and uniqueness, and they are often described as having "personality" or "character," and being expressive of, among other things, certain human-like character traits.

For example, wines can be "joyful," "refined," "friendly," "attractive." Wines that do not bow to the pressures of commercialization are described as "authentic" or "sincere," and wines that "try" and "fail" to be something that they are not can be "pretentious," "dishonest," or "commercial."

Wines are made in certain ways, embodying certain decisions, and these can be detected as expressive properties in the wine itself. Wines can be expressive of certain attitudes and views concerning, for example: civilized life, sophistication, simplicity, the rustic/rural vs. the urbane/urban, elegance, authenticity, variety, subtlety, and so on. Calling a wine "elegant" or "rustic" may refer not just to the intrinsic properties of the wine that it exemplifies but also to an array of attitudes to life and the world that have allowed it to come to be made in just this way.

So, describing a wine as authentic in one way can be to say that it is a "true" expression of terroir. In another way, it could also refer to the fact that it is made authentically (attitude/method) to arrive at this goal. Arguably, both types can be intrinsically valued and valuable. Thus, wines can express authenticity authentically, just as they can be authentically authentic, rather than accidentally or fraudulently so. Where they do so, this quality is intrinsically valuable in the sense that it is not just an instrumental way of getting to flavor properties. Indeed, arguably flavor is as much a way of experiencing authenticity as authenticity is a way of getting at flavors. One can only tell that a wine is true to terroir by tasting it.

Of course, then, industrial wines can also be authentic. They are established with some aim in mind, and with constraints governing their production, which serve, for example, to embody the taste of shiraz grapes made in this way. Yet, this kind of authenticity is not itself valuable; it is valuable only insofar as it results in a reliable and consistent product. Such wines, we might say, are authentic, but their style—such as they have a style—is not one of authenticity, it is perhaps in terms of authenticity then that we might draw the distinction mentioned earlier between style and category.

If authenticity rather than creativity is one of the hallmarks of wine's value, constrained by terroir and style and manifested only fully in the taste of the dish rather than the specifications of the recipe itself, this should be clearly reflected in the way we interpret a wine's recipe. I think that wines that have an individual style are usefully thought of as falling under what Engisch (in this volume) calls the category of "traditional recipe." Among other things, they belong to a cultural practice that functions to pass along some value to the consumer and perhaps wider community in virtue of being in close relation with a location or environment. The way a wine does this is:

> by means of generating, at different times, different tokens of a same type of experience, which thereby end up constituting a shared repertoire of experiences— the experience of being, and having been, part of the tradition. (Engisch in this volume: 120)

With qualifications on the extent to which we can expect such wine recipes to be iterated, given vintage variability and stylistic consistency, this is one way of understanding the value of a wine recipe as a bearer of and communication of authenticity.

Writing Cookbooks behind Barbed Wire

Barbara Haber

> We simply do not know the uses of food, and our ignorance is explosively dangerous. It is more convenient for us to take a veterinary surgeon's view of food as animal feed, to think of it as mere bodily input, than to recognize its great symbolic force.
>
> —Mary Douglas, *Food Is Not Feed*

As Mary Douglas affirms, the study of food encompasses much more than understanding its nutritional value. Its constant presence in the lives of all people and under differing circumstances makes possible the use of food to interpret human thoughts and behavior at any time. The wartime experience of captured American civilians in the Philippines during the Second World War is a moment in history that illustrates the profound symbolic connection between food and, in this case, the yearnings of a distressed population. Memories, dreams, and fantasies about food allowed for an escape from harsh reality.

Suddenly thrown into prison camps and facing starvation, internees not only talked about food but were driven to create personal cookbooks even though they lacked ingredients and decent cooking facilities, and many had no cooking skills at all. Nevertheless, they feverishly wrote down recipes for longed-for dishes that evoked happier times. Food was a stand-in for normalcy when eating a hamburger or a slice of apple pie was unremarkable. Their selected recipes were aligned with identity, revealing regional favorites, connections to family, and flights of the imagination. When a recipe for lemon chicken calls for chicken, lemons, a cup of stock and a pound of butter, we realize a prisoner's craving for flavor and protein topped off by an abundance of silky fat, and we have a better understanding of the privations of prison life.

Within weeks of attacking Pearl Harbor, the Japanese invaded the Philippines and set out to defeat and incarcerate their enemies. Diaries and memoirs describe the privations suffered by imprisoned civilians as well as the military—their frustrations and fears, and certainly their hunger as they endured captivity. Less familiar testimonies of the war are the cookbooks or accounts of them that were produced by starving prisoners. They demonstrate that something as mundane as recipes can serve as evidence of how captives struggled not only to survive but to preserve their identities as human beings. These cookbooks reveal what food means to people beyond mere sustenance, how it defines who we are and where we came from, even though the foods we know best and favor the most are only a memory.

Though countless descriptions exist, the cookbooks from civilian camps have not survived because after liberation people saw their behavior in writing recipes using imaginary ingredients as a form of temporary insanity. So they threw their collections away. One internee said:

> Reading cookbooks and such old magazines as were available and copying recipes became a real hobby that amounted to almost a mania with many of the women. We would spend hours looking at pictures of food and talking to one another about them, and copying out recipes, or gleaning from other women their choice recipes that they could recall from memory. We let our minds daydream and our mouths drool as we anticipated the days of tomorrow when we would each have her own kitchen and could cook all those lovely foods. No one could have convinced us then that this obsession to cook and eat would soon vanish after we were liberated. We had yet to learn that once one's body is satisfied with the necessities of life, the subject of food, instead of dominating all one's waking hours and disturbing one's sleep, automatically slips into its rightful place in the scheme of life. (Ogle 1958: 215)

Thousands of American civilians living in the Philippines at the start of the Second World War remained in the internment camps for more than three years, some dying from diseases brought on by poor nutrition, and the rest doing their best to survive by the creative use of available resources. They were there at this precarious time because some had been living in the Philippines since the Spanish-American War when America had taken over the country. Others had come as missionaries, and many more were there because they had left Depression-ravaged America for such good jobs as managing gold mines or sugar plantations, or representing American corporations in Asia. For these expatriates, the Philippines offered not only well-paid employment, but adventure and a privileged lifestyle with comfortable homes staffed with servants who did the cleaning, child care, laundering, gardening, and cooking. Instead of reacting appropriately to the impending war by leaving, civilians were in a state of denial, much like people living near a fault line who blot out thoughts of a possible earthquake. And so, they stayed. One internee said:

> When talk of war became louder in 1940 and 1941, they couldn't tear themselves away from the Philippines—not so soon after finding peace in their lives. War was theoretical. Their private peace was too precious to risk. That is how we came to be caught in a war. (Maynard 2001: 11)

Civilians were shocked to find themselves imprisoned, for they had expected only to be registered and then allowed to return to their homes. Just before her capture, Elizabeth Vaughan started a letter to her husband who had gone off on a business trip, was caught and imprisoned by the Japanese, and later died in a camp. In writing this, Vaughan had no idea that she and her two babies would be interned, and that she would never again see her husband.

> Jim, remember how you wanted a potato ricer for the kitchen, for every time we had mashed potatoes, the cook, Consuela, left lumps in them? So I ordered a ricer from Sears-Roebuck to please you [...] The ricer arrived a few days before you left for Manila—in the rush of things, I didn't tell you [...] [when] the war came, Consuela rushed off without a word, the potatoes were exhausted, so here I am, with a shining new ricer all the way from the States to please a husband and a cook, and now there is no husband, no cook and no potatoes. (Vaughan 1985: 22)

Among the solid citizens in Manila's Santo Tomas, a university campus that was converted into the largest of the civilian prison camps, were refugees from Shanghai. Their evacuating ships were diverted to Manila because of dangerous sea mines, and their passengers included a colorful mélange of athletes, entertainers, crooks, gamblers, and prostitutes. They had been living in Shanghai because it was an open city attracting characters of various and often dubious backgrounds. These outliers sometimes clashed with other internees, but not always. One of the entertainers, Dave Harvey McTurk, was a professional comedian who became the camp's beloved master of ceremonies, making up songs that parodied camp miseries—lousy meals, ubiquitous bedbugs, and the rampant rumors that had become a persistent part of camp culture, what some called "latrine news." Most often, rumors were about the state of the war, offering false claims about imminent rescue. In fact, the war in Europe was a priority for American leadership and full attention to the war in the Pacific came later.

A common saying in the camps was "If you want privacy, close your eyes." Mingling among the camp's solid citizens were social deviants, causing one female internee to remark that every room had at least one kleptomaniac, drug addict, or prostitute and that "it was a bit of a shock to learn that the quiet, curly-haired girl in our room, so wholesome in her appearance, with a sprinkling of little freckles across her pretty nose, was the manager and part-owner of the most notorious houses of prostitution in Manila" (Whitfield 1999: 82–3).

Interned families had to cope with such ordinary life occurrences as pregnancies and births, the supervision of young children, dealing with adolescents, and maintaining cordial relationships with spouses and other adults. But now they were living in a community of strangers that had been forced upon them. Coping with scarce food supplies was made even worse by the internees' lack of cooking skills and little knowledge of local ingredients. They had been eating familiar American foods including products shipped in from the mainland, such as canned hams and assorted canned vegetables and fruits. Elizabeth Vaughan listed and complained about unappealing local foods:

> Poto—rice flour cakes, small puffy, snow white, gelatinous-like In texture.
> Tinola—fish head soup, fish-eyes glaring from pot, one head with each serving, Ghastly and nauseating to think of eating head and wide-open eyes, but favorite dish of Filipinos, often served in camp.

cincomas—tasteless, turnip-like white root, eaten boiled or sliced and fried and
called in camp "Dutch fried potatoes."
Patola—a stringy okra-like vegetable sliced and boiled in coconut milk. (Vaughan
1985: 153)

Calamitous overcrowding was an affliction to be endured. To eliminate procreation,
men and women were housed separately and children stayed with their mothers
in rooms that were randomly assembled, with everyone sleeping in cots jammed
together with little space for personal belongings. Early on, when ingredients were
still available, internees found ways to produce food within these crowded conditions.
Natalie Crouter, an inexperienced cook who was interned along with her husband and
two children, got hold of a cookie recipe and proceeded to mix up the batter on the
surface of her cot. "June and I mixed the Ice Box Cookie recipe. Jerry says he peeked in
the window and nearly died laughing at us on the bed with tray, flour sugar tins, paper
sacks and bottles." Natalie later referred to these treats as "Bed Cookies" (Stark Family
Papers, Harvard University, Schlesinger Library, folder 2100).

Recipes using native ingredients as substitutes for unobtainable favorites were
posted on the camp bulletin board at Santo Tomas. Such tips were enthusiastically
tried by internees.

Someone discovered [...] that a type of hot bread could be made from sour mush
and soda, which required no eggs and only half the flour called for in the original
recipe. In chop suey we found that we could substitute for water chestnuts a root
vegetable called cincamas [...] which tasted approximately like an apple crossed
with a raw turnip. We learned to bake in banana leaves, to rub our skillets with salt
to save shortening, and to reboil leftover beans that were on the verge of souring.
(Van Sickle 2007: 249)

Internees at Santo Tomas had access to a wood-burning stove whose surface was
always crowded with competing pans of food. A startling scream once came from a
woman who shouted, "I didn't think one woman would do such a thing to another
woman. I never heard of anyone being so cruel! Women don't do things like that to
another woman!" (Whitfield 1999: 216–17). Her anguished accusations were not about
a stolen husband or a harmed child, but about a collapsed pan of rising bread dough
that had been shoved to a dangerously hot place on the stove. The outburst was aimed
at a scrawny woman who had moved the pan, not deliberately, but only as an attempt
to find a little space to bake a pan of ersatz muffins made with cassava flour instead of
wheat and with chunks of dried coconut instead of blueberries.

Using cassava flour was popular, but results could be disastrous. One man,
excited to be making biscuits with it, invited friends to partake of his treats, only
to discover that no one could bite into them because they were denser than hockey
pucks. Disappointed but amused, the group decided that it would be their patriotic
duty to send the biscuits to General MacArthur to use as a secret weapon against the
Japanese.

Internees spoke of using cold cream to sauté foods when normal cooking oils had run out. Natalie Crouter called it "the ultimate low in cooking grease [because] its scent detracted from the dish" (Stark Family Papers, Harvard University, Schlesinger Library, folder 720).

People get resourceful when they are hungry and thirsty, especially for alcoholic drinks. A friend of Natalie's, having read about old women in South America making beer by chewing cassava—the enzymes in saliva being the active agent—did that very thing, adding water, and winding up with an active brew. Her only problem was that she couldn't tell her husband how she made it (Stark Family Papers, Harvard University, Schlesinger Library, folder 460).

Since the Japanese supplied little food, internees were left on their own to secure what they needed. Early on, when the Japanese allowed it, servants were delivering money, food, and clothing to those lucky enough to have such contacts. Others had to find creative ways to be fed. One woman with cooking skills prepared meals for a man who was so mechanically handy that he could barter his skills for ingredients his lady friend would then prepare. One of the prostitutes traded her services for a ham sandwich, which she generously shared with a sick and hungry friend. As the war dragged on, food supplies diminished and internees became increasingly obsessed with food. Their worries were existential—keeping children alive and staying alive themselves. The vastly substandard diet in the camps led to deficiency diseases, and as their conditions of near-starvation grew worse, prisoners obsessed more and more about food, dreaming of it at night and fantasizing about it during the day.

> Starving prisoners were always digging into their memories for food stories to tell. Bedtime stories for children were not from the Brothers Grimm or Hans Christian Anderson but were promises of chocolate cake and ice cream sundaes children would receive after the war. One man, Whitey Smith, an ex-boxer turned drummer and an evacuee from Shanghai, describes a conversation he and others had with a fellow prisoner. They had been sitting around, telling stories about food when one fellow talked about the time he saw in a bakery window "a great big thick cherry pie [...] with cherry juice seeping through in big sweet drops" which he bought and then, he explained, had eaten three quarters of it, and threw the rest away. Smith says, "He was lucky to get away from us alive. We hardly spoke to him for the rest of the internment, because every time we saw him we thought of that cherry pie—not the part he ate but the part he threw away." (Smith 1961: 172)

While random and ceaseless conversations about food dominated the camps, the meticulous documentation of recipes, what most described as a mania, gave internees a mission. Generally idle, they were now putting pencil to paper and creating documents that could be compared and argued about. With no ingredients available, they nevertheless concocted cookbooks filled with their favorite dishes from their pre war lives, creating menus and exchanging recipes, and arguing over whose dish was the best. One heated discussion was only resolved by the intervention of a trained dietitian. People latched onto and passed around the few available cookbooks and women's magazines in search of appealing recipes. Some internees saw this behavior as crazed. Tressa R. Cates, a civilian nurse who was interned in Manila, had a disapproving response:

> A peculiar though understandable mania had seized the camp. Men, women, and children copied recipes from morning until night. These recipe addicts copied and exchanged recipes with others addicted with the same mania. They dug up old magazines and gazed longingly at colored pictures of temptingly arranged and prepared food. What made the mania so pathetic and futile was that they copied and concentrated on recipes that called for hard-to-obtain ingredients even in a normal world. It stimulated their desire for food, and it used up energy that they could ill afford. It seemed like the cruelest form of torture. (Cates 1981: 233–4)

Grace C. Nash, a professional violinist and a mother of two who gave birth to a third son while interned, at first believed that everyone around her was crazy:

> A mild form of insanity had settled over ninety percent of the camp—the frenzied copying of recipes. I knew that such fanaticism happened to explorers, isolated without sufficient food reserves, but I was determined not to give in to it. Children from ten years old to feeble, aged men who had never cooked in their lives, were now engaged in recipes! Exchanging, copying, talking recipes filled their waking hours—but not their stomachs! (Nash 1984: 208)

But Nash soon gave in and joined the frenzy:

> Recipes, recipes, dreams of food, hallucinations of malted milks, sirloin steaks, Irish potatoes, paraded through my mind. Grabbing a pencil stub and [a] worn notebook, I wrote in feverish speed, gathering recipes from other internees to copy in my book. My mouth watered as I scribbled down the ingredients, imagining the supreme joy of eating the whole recipe myself. (Nash 1984: 208)

Although this behavior could be interpreted as a form of masochism, it seems more likely that these deprived people were trying to reassure themselves by looking to the past for the simple pleasures that would be theirs again when life returned to normal. To them, food was not just sustenance but a profound symbol for what had gone wrong in a world gone mad that would be put right when pre war life returned. By writing down recipes, these hungry and dislocated people were giving a structure to their dreams with painstaking accuracy when describing dishes they planned to cook in the future. One woman told another that she had written down luncheon menus for an entire year without a single duplication. Grace Nash relates that an elderly gentleman, who probably had never cooked in his life, brought her two typewritten recipes— salmon casserole and a special salad. "It sounds wonderful, Grace," he said. "Thought you might like to try them when we get out" (Nash 1984: 208).

Young, single, and exceedingly devout, Judy Hyland, a missionary from Minnesota, prayed regularly and was dismayed to find that the craving for food interfered with her spiritual life. "How many times at night I would begin to pray—only to waken in the morning realizing that my mind had drifted off into a fantasy of bacon and eggs and pancakes" (Hyland 1984: 77). Not lacking a sense of humor, Hyland describes the time when she and a friend were praying together but remembered that the Philippine peanut harvest was about to begin. As Hyland tells us, her friend said:

> Let's ask God for peanuts. We began to voice the prayer that some of those peanuts would come our way. The thought was all right, but when we heard the words, they seemed ridiculous. We began to laugh, the heartiest laugh we had enjoyed in weeks. Here we were, two single missionaries, in the middle of a global war, when generals and admirals were calling on the Almighty for guidance and victory, and we were saying, "Please God, you know how hungry we are. Give us some peanuts, please." (Hyland 1984: 77)

In her account of the cookbook mania, Hyland makes the point that such "gourmet" dishes as Lobster Thermidor were of little interest. Instead, people longed for the simple, everyday foods they remembered and used to take for granted such as ham and cheese sandwiches, fried eggs, or doughnuts and coffee. That's what made the saliva run. A father said, "My dream is to sit down to a plate of six eggs." His son commented, "My dream is to have one egg today and to know there will be one egg tomorrow and one the next day" (Hyland 1984: 77).

It is regrettable that the cookbooks so reverently maintained before liberation were immediately discarded when the internees had access to real food. Their books would have provided insights into what exactly people longed for and the regional differences in what they craved. Along with other sources, they would have given evidence for what people living at that time and in that place had endured.

But a wartime cookbook has survived and was published in 1946. *Recipes Out of Bilibid* is a collection gathered by an American prisoner of war who was confined to Bilibid, a notoriously cruel POW camp in Manila. Before the war, Bilibid was an old Spanish prison for criminals but was used by the Japanese after the fall of Manila to imprison their military enemies. The book compiled there has survived because Dorothy Wagner, the aunt of the man who collected the recipes, understood their significance.

Her nephew, Colonel Halstead C. Fowler, was the young man Wagner watched in 1941 as he boarded a ship for Manila. He was a well-tailored West Point graduate carrying a vast amount of luggage including a case of champagne meant to ward off seasickness. Forty months later, she saw him return from the Philippines wearing borrowed clothes and carrying a bag that contained little more than a small bundle of envelopes containing recipes. Fowler had miraculously survived the Bataan Death March and more than three years inside Bilibid prison, but came back emaciated with three bullets still lodged in his body and his vision severely impaired from the effects of beri-beri. So moved was his aunt by his clutch of recipes that she decided to turn them into a professionally published book, instinctively understanding the value of such a relic of the war. In compiling the cookbook, she was able to visualize not only the suffering of her nephew and his comrades but also how much reflections about food mattered to these abused prisoners.

> No matter how the conversation began it always turned to food, the food the prisoners had once relished and were determined to enjoy again. For they talked in the future tense, harking back to the past only to make concrete their plans when they should finally be rescued. They gave reality to their dreams by dwelling not on the flavors or sentimental recollections of feasts, but on a painstaking accuracy in describing the constituents of the dishes they remembered and longed for and resolutely purposed to enjoy again. (Fowler 1946: viii)

The cookbook is brief—only seventy-seven pages—and the recipes lack the precision we have come to expect from modern cookbooks, the size of baking pans, oven temperature, and yield. They are presented in random order so that a recipe for ginger snaps is plunked down between fish chowder and "hamburger mixture." But the value of all the recipes is that they give meaning to remembered dishes, and sometimes in head notes, some facts about the men who contributed them.

The book is organized by national group, with American recipes dominating the collection. Information about contributors includes their nationality, rank, combat history, and what lay ahead for them. Some were rescued, but some died in prison, and others died on the Oryoku Maru, the infamous hell ship that was bombed at sea in December of 1944. The Japanese had pulled prisoners out of Bilibid, stuffed them into the hold of this unmarked cargo ship, and were attempting to transport them to Japan to work as slave laborers. Most were killed when American planes, whose pilots never realized who was aboard that ship, went ahead and sank it.

A few of the contributors had been mess sergeants, ships' cooks, or chefs before the war, but many were ordinary men who relied on childhood memories of favorite dishes, so recipes disclose varying levels of sophistication. For instance, the first recipe in the book is for baked beans and has just three ingredients—one can of baked beans, one can of kidney beans, and a bottle of pickled onions. The next, bouillabaisse has eighteen ingredients and was contributed by the son of a chef who worked at the Hotel Chamberlin in Hampton Beach, Virginia, which at the time had a famous restaurant.

One dish, lemon chicken, was provided by an unidentified American sailor and reads like a fantasy because it calls for a full pound of butter. He said that it had been passed down from a distant relative whose mother had served in the kitchens of the Emperor Franz Joseph. The recipe contains small chickens, lemons, a cup of stock and melted butter. The chickens are sautéed, then placed in a casserole with sliced lemons. Melted butter is poured over them and the dish is baked for forty minutes. So much butter suggests the craving for fat that comes up again and again in prison camp memoirs.

Regional cooking is reflected in some of the American recipes. Several were attributed to a couple of men with Pennsylvania Dutch heritage—Buckwheat Cake Batter, Spiced Corn Beef, Hamhocks with Sauerkraut, Hasenpfeffer, and dill pickles.

The pickle recipe is interesting because it does not include vinegar or hot peppers, but instead resembles what was produced in the kegs of kosher delis on the Lower East Side of New York.

Pack cucumbers in a keg, with a layer of dill between each layer of cucumbers. Cover with a 40 percent solution of salt (strong enough to float an egg). Add garlic and whole black pepper, one clove of garlic and half a teaspoon of pepper for each layer of cucumbers. Let the mixture stand for 2 or 3 weeks. (Fowler 1946: 10)

A recipe for "Old Army Mincemeat" has about 100 pounds of ingredients, enough to feed an entire platoon. It is attributed to Major "Pappy" Archer whose background makes clear that he had served in the military way before the conflict with Japan. He fought in the Spanish-American War; as a member of "Reilly's Battery" in the Boxer Campaign; in Mexico in 1911; throughout the First World War; and finally on Bataan (Fowler 1946: 15). While we may never know how he came up with that huge recipe for mincemeat, what we do know is that American prisoners in both the civilian and prison camps were people of unexpected and varied backgrounds.

In a recipe for "Mushroom Noodles," the head note reads, "This recipe is unidentified, but the use of canned soup marks it as of American origin" (Fowler 1946: 16). It is so wonderfully of its time when casseroles using condensed soups were the rage.

1 package wide noodles
4 cloves garlic   1 can mushroom creamed soup
1 cup cream or chicken stock   ½ lb. fresh mushrooms (or 1 small can)
1 tablespoon flour
1 large handful parsley
Boil the noodles in as large a pot as the kitchen affords in salted water for 10 minutes. Drain into a collander [sic] and pour cold water through the noodles. Place in a greased casserole. Grind the garlic [beans} and chop the parsley into the garlic, chopping it very fine. Fry the parsley in butter or oil; add flour, then the can of soup, then the mushrooms (including the liquor if canned mushrooms are used): and lastly the cream or stock. Season well with pepper and salt, and pour the sauce over the noodles, mixing it thoroughly. Cover, and bake in a slow oven (not over 300 degrees) for at least an hour. When ready to serve, sift grated Parmesan cheese over the dish.

Another recipe in *Bilibid* that takes us much farther back into American history is for Stone Fence, an alcoholic beverage containing rum, sweet cider, and apple jack. The recipe is attributed to Captain Danny Barry who was from the apple-growing state of New York. Although still made and served today, Barry's version is more closely linked to its origin in American colonial history, and said to be the drink of choice for Vermont's Ethan Allen and the Green Mountain Boys who led the assault on the British-controlled Fort Ticonderoga in 1775. Modern recipes for the drink sometimes use rye, bourbon, or brandy instead of rum, but what is interesting is that this drink described in a rare Second World War cookbook leads back to the origins of the United States.

Stone Fence

6 apples	3 tablespoons butter
½ cup strained honey	1 cup sweet cider
½ cup rum	½ cup apple jack

Core the apples and place in a baking dish, preferably earthenware. Heat the cider, add the butter and honey; when well blended, remove from stove and add the rum and apple jackPour the syrup over the apples, cover the dish tightly, and bake in a moderate oven till the apples are soft (about 40 minutes). Cool and serve. (Fowler 1946: 20)

The last recipe in the American section in *Bilibid is* for another alcoholic cocktail, White Cargo, still being made today. It calls for a pint of vanilla ice cream and a half pint of gin that are shaken together in a cocktail shaker. It is attributed to Major Frank Lightfoot described as being "endlessly helpful to his fellows on the Death March [and] In prison [...] talked so enthusiastically of the ice-cream, chocolate, and eggs he had enjoyed in Indiana." Sadly, Major Lightfoot was one of the victims who died on the December 13th Hell ship.

The British dishes in the cookbook were contributed by men who arrived from Singapore in August 1944. They had been imprisoned on the Malay Peninsula since 1942, and from there were sent to Bilibid. Confined to a different part of the prison from the Americans, their recipes had been smuggled to Fowler, and contributors were not known, but recipes are decidedly British. They include such classics as Yorkshire Pudding, Scotch Eggs, and Toad-in-the-Hole, a dish that comes down from the eighteenth century. Based on Yorkshire Pudding, it includes leftover bits of meat, what the head note describes as "the tag-ends of the Sunday joint" and calls it a dish elevated from a sad leftover "to one that can command enthusiasm in its own right, for it transforms the remnants of a roast or bits of pork in the ice-box from remainders to advance notice of a genuine feast." This description suggests that Dorothy Wagner threw herself into her role as the compiler of these recipes by doing a little research.

Yeoman Yorkshire Pudding
1 egg
¾ cup of flour
1 cup milk
1 teaspoon salt

The pudding should be prepared as soon as the roast is placed in the oven, for the secret of success lies in permitting the batter to stand, covered and brooding, for an hour or more, the longer the better. Sift the flour and salt into a deep bowl, making a well into which the unbeaten egg is dropped. Add 4 tablespoons of the milk, and with a wooden spoon stir the egg and milk gently into the flour, so that the wall of flour gradually yields and droops into the liquid. When the mixture reaches the consistency of boiled custard add more milk till ¾ of the cup is used. Then beat with purpose and resolution, using a mixmaster if one is available. When the mixture is bland and smooth, add the final ¼ cup of milk and resume beating till the batter bubbles. Then cover and set aside. (Fowler 1946: 27–8)

To cook the dish, a pan lavishly coated with fat is set in the oven and when sizzling hot the batter is poured in and cooked at 450 degrees. After twenty-five minutes the pudding should be browned and crisp around the edges and ready to eat. In the case of Toad-in-the-Hole, bits of meat are dropped into the hot pan before the pudding batter is poured in.

It takes little imagination to understand the appeal of this recipe to starving British prisoners, for it contains several kinds of fat and is a dish that brought comfort from early days in the nursery to the present.

The remaining few recipes in *Bilibid* are for international dishes. For instance, there are Chinese recipes that came from a chef who had worked in a Manila club. He huddled near an American fellow captive, and the two whispered about food since their hunger was what they most had in common (Fowler 1946: 33).

His recipes include such familiar dishes as Egg Foo Yung, Chinese shrimp, sweet-pungent fish, and sweet-sour pork.

Filipino dishes using various forms of coconut are attributed to American as well as Filipino officers, reflecting the American colonial presence in the Philippines.

Some of the remaining international recipes are from captured allied seamen and include a French recipe for Baba au Rhum, a Dutch seaman's description of a Rijstafel with a list of twenty-seven side dishes, and a recipe for Norwegian Lut Fisk. The few Italian dishes come not from Italian nationals but from Americans, for as Wagner tells us, "there were a good many prisoners [...] of Italian descent [...] many of them sharing the same preferences but disagreeing volubly as to the method of preparation" (Fowler 1946: 47). We are told that only the six recipes men agreed upon were included—two using anchovies, bologna, a meat pie, stuffing for shoulder of lamb, and a holiday cake.

All of the recipes in *Bilibid* bear witness to the dislocation and suffering brought on by a war that affected people throughout the world. They offer historic information about foods and provide what may be the only written information we have about the contributors.

But much more is known about one of them, Commander Thomas H. Hayes, an American medical officer from Tidewater, Virginia, who left behind a memoir. His scraps of paper written while imprisoned were turned into a book published in 1987 as *Bilibid Diary: The Secret Notebooks of Commander Thomas Hayes POW, the Philippines, 1942–45*. In the Bilibid cookbook, Hayes contributed a recipe for fish chowder, and in his memoir a touching recipe for ersatz coffee, which he describes as "made from banana skins. We bake the skins very dry, then crumble them in boiling water. The resulting drink is dark and sweet, not bad to taste, but it's not coffee and has no kick to it" (Hayes 1987: 110).

Hayes was a man with strong opinions who set unobtainable standards for himself, and felt increasingly helpless to alleviate suffering. His book affirms that by May of 1944, malnutrition, sickness, and overwork had killed hundreds in Bilibid and almost terminally demoralized the men who were left alive to care for the survivors. Hayes believed that if he and his fellow medical officers made it through the war and went back to America, their return would be regarded as an unwanted intrusion.

> I'm convinced that life at home has now gone on too long without us. We will never fit in again. Adjustments have undoubtedly been made and our loved ones have detoured their lives around the missing. We would be an ill-fitting part in the smooth running machinery of their daily routine. At times it seems silly for us to suddenly barge in and disrupt lives that have become used to being without us. Wade talks of going to Shanghai. I'm thinking of Singapore. Cecil says that Australia is in his future. (Hayes 1987: 197)

Irreparably damaged by imprisonment and lacking essential supplies—he was surrounded by men he could not save—Hayes was brought down by the loss of his identity as a protector and provider. His despair indicates that imprisoned men generally suffered more psychological pain than women because of their loss of status. Sadly, Hayes would never be tested on his response to liberation for he died at sea on the catastrophic late 1944 Hell ship.

His low morale and pessimism differ from positive post war expectations expressed by other prisoners, especially those in the less brutal civilian camps. Many fantasized about a future dominated by food—opening restaurants and catering businesses, or buying farms to raise their own crops; however, such dreams, like the cookbooks they discarded, did not seem to survive the war. The immediate need to earn a living took over.

But fantasies about food had sustained people, and prisoner cookbooks reveal that recipes have the power of imagination to bring us from despair to a happier time and place. They illustrate that food is indeed more than just feed, as Mary Douglas decreed. Its universality gives it the scope and power to symbolize all manner of human experience. For wartime prisoners, it symbolized what used to be taken for granted—home, loved ones, community, freedom from fear, and uncertainty. It illustrates that when all vestiges of peacetime life are stripped away, the memory of food served in better times remains imperishable and reconnects both soldiers and civilians to their basic identity as humans.

A Puzzle about Aftertaste

Akiko Frischhut and Giuliano Torrengo

Introduction

Imagine yourself on a warm summer evening on a terrace, enjoying a perfectly cooled artisanal Riesling. Its crisp tartness develops slowly into a satisfyingly complex citrus aroma that stays with you for moments after you have swallowed it. The stock that has been lovingly simmering for hours on the stove is unctuously savory due to its rich umami aftertaste. I love this chocolate because it has such an elegant, slightly bitter aftertaste. The milk, tasting good at first, develops a thoroughly unpleasant sour aftertaste, which unmistakably tells me that it has gone bad. Foods and drinks do not only have flavors and tastes, they also have aftertastes. We take aftertaste experiences seriously: we often identify or evaluate our food and drink by their aftertastes, and we detect important properties through aftertastes. Even recipes can be framed as to track a certain aftertaste. This can be explicit, as in the case of recipes of herbal liquors or infusions, or more indirectly, as in the case of the stock in our opening example.

But what are aftertastes? A first answer comes from considering the temporal features of what happens when we experience flavor. Gustatory experiences unfold over time. As Cain Todd puts it, "the perception of flavour is distinctive amongst our sensory experiences [...] in being experienced essentially temporally" (2018b: 278).[1] Every gustatory experience is a temporally extended experience with successive phases. The "primary taste" occurs immediately when the food is put into the mouth.[2] It lasts until the food is swallowed. The "aftertaste" occurs after the food is swallowed.[3]

In psychology, aftertastes are seen as belonging to the same category as afterimages. Vision scientist Richard Gregory, for example, defines an afterimage as "an image seen immediately after the intense stimulation of the eye by light has ceased" (1987: 13), whereas psychologists Neely and Borg characterize aftertaste as "the stimulus intensity perceived in the moments immediately following removal of the stimulus (to differentiate with adaptation, in which the stimulus is constantly present)" (1999: 21). Similarly, the *Oxford Dictionary of Psychology* explains aftertastes as "a sensation of taste or flavour that lingers after a sapid (tastable) food or drink has been in the mouth." No surprise then that the same work of reference groups afterimages and aftertastes into the same category of "aftersensations." Here is the *Oxford Dictionary of Psychology*'s definition.

> AFTERSENSATION: Any sensation persisting after the cessation of the stimulus, especially an afterimage or an aftertaste.[1]

Philosophers have, at least to our knowledge, hitherto completely ignored the phenomenon of aftertaste. Afterimages, on the other hand, have been subject to a great many heated debates. One reason for this disparity may be grounded in a general interest bias toward visual experience. Another, admittedly more speculative reason, could be that philosophers have simply followed psychologists in grouping aftertastes in the same category as afterimages and have since not deemed them unique enough to motivate any interesting reflection. We will, hopefully, remedy this pitiful situation with this chapter.

The debates about afterimages mainly turn on the question of whether or not afterimages reveal the existence of visual sensations, although how that is understood exactly depends on the understanding of the term "visual sensation" and is "a theme with many variations" (cf. Phillips 2012: 421). One such more recent variation is the debate about pure representationalism and the idea that the phenomenal character of experience is exhaustively characterized by its representational content. One side sees the occurrence of afterimages as evidence that the view is false; the other tries to deflate that point. "Sensationalists" argue that afterimages are intrinsic, non-perceptual features of visual experience of which we are directly aware, and thus a strong counter-example to pure representationalism.[5] "Purists" about perceptual experience attempt to deny this in various ways.[6]

The most interesting aspect to us, however, lies in the fact that both sides deny afterimages any (or at least any valuable) epistemic import. For sensationalists, afterimages are "mere sensations," which, by their very nature, cannot give us information about the external world. For purists, afterimages present us with public objects, but even if they disagree among themselves on what they present us with exactly (material objects or light phenomena), they all concur on them being illusory and hence void of epistemic value. This general view of aftersensations as epistemically insignificant experiences creates a puzzle when applied to aftertaste, which can be summarized in three individually plausible, but jointly incompatible claims.

1. Aftertastes and afterimages are in the same psychological category of aftersensations.
2. Aftersensations are of no or little epistemic value.
3. Aftertastes are epistemically reliable; hence they often have epistemic value.

In what follows, we will focus on this previously unnoticed puzzle. In the section "The Epistemic Unreliability of Aftersensations" we present the received view according to which aftertastes are aftersensations, and aftersensations lack systematic epistemic significance. In the section "The Epistemic Reliability of Aftertaste," we defend the commonsensical view that aftertastes have epistemically significance, and we point out several differences between afterimages and aftertastes. In the section "Against the

Received View: Aftertaste Are Exceptions," we explore a way to solve the puzzle based on denying that *all* aftersensations lack epistemic value, by providing an explanation of the phenomenology of aftertaste that accounts for their apparent epistemic reliability. Ultimately, we reject the solution since it overgeneralizes. In the section "Against the Received View: Aftertastes Are Not Aftersensations," we offer an explanation of the epistemic significance of aftertaste that motivates a more radical reconceptualization of them. In the "Conclusions," we provide some final thoughts.

The Epistemic Unreliability of Aftersensations

As we have already pointed out, the received view in psychology and philosophy is that aftertastes bear enough similarities with afterimages to be considered of the same basic category of aftersensation. If aftersensations are epistemically unreliable and aftertastes are epistemically reliable, though, either aftertastes are an exception to the unreliability of aftersensations or are not aftersensations after all. Either way, the received view should be revised deeply.

To understand in what sense aftersensations are epistemically unreliable, let us begin by contrasting aftersensations with *primary perceptual experiences*, by which we mean experiences like the one you have when looking at your screen or tasting an overly spicy sauce. What is it for a primary perceptual experience to be epistemically reliable? "Epistemically reliable" is meant here in the minimal and hopefully relatively innocent sense that, when epistemically reliable, then perceptual experiences are truth conducive, if only in the minimal sense that they do not gravely deceive us. Of course, "not gravely" is once more a phrase that is pleading for sharper delineation, but for current purposes let us just say the following. When I have an epistemically reliable visual experience as of a cup on my desk, then there is a cup on my desk—unless I have been badly deceived either by my visual system (e.g., I am hallucinating because of a drug) or by the external conditions (e.g., the light hits the surface of the desk in such a way that it looks like there is a cup over there). We can usually trust the reliability of the information delivered to us by our senses because it is simply the function of our perceptual organs to provide us with information about the environment we are in.[7]

Standard cases of primary perceptual experience are characterized by certain conditions conducive, or at least not obstructive, to this process. These conditions include, for example, that you are awake and not dreaming, that you are a healthy enough human being with eyes, a nose, and so on, functioning the way they should, that there is nothing in your surroundings that hinders you in having these experiences, and so forth. They are also characterized by a straightforward causal process, which relates your experience to whatever in the world it is an experience about.

Contrast this with aftersensations. Unlike primary perceptual experiences, aftersensations are not considered to be epistemically reliable sources of information about the world. We will come back to the fact that in general aftersensations do not *seem* to be reliable in the next section; here we consider the reasons why they may indeed not *be* reliable. The root of the epistemic inequality lies, *ceteris paribus*, in the different causal processes involved in the generation of primary perceptual experiences and aftersensations. For primary perceptual experiences that causal process can be schematically illustrated as one that leads, in two steps, to a *primary percept*, as follows:

THE CAUSAL PATH TO PRIMARY PERCEPTS
Distal stimulus (DS) → proximal stimulus (PS)
PS + internal processing (IP) → primary percept (PP)

The distal stimulus can be considered the "topic" of my experience, namely, the physical object that my experience is of or about. The distal stimulus directly causes the proximal stimulus, namely, whatever excites the perceptual organs (photons, chemical molecules, etc.). The proximal stimulus, together with some internal processing, then directly causes the primary percept. The distal stimulus is constitutively responsible for the quality of the proximal stimulus. In other words, the proximal stimulus retains some crucial information of the object perceived. Similarly, the proximal stimulus is constitutively responsible for (the quality of) the primary percept. Thus, the primary percept inherits core features from the proximal stimulus, and indirectly from the distal stimulus, the physical object I am having an experience of. Given the right background conditions, we have what we may call good cases of primary percepts. A good case is roughly one where the system is in its normal conditions, and the causal chain is "untampered" by external interfering factors, which guarantees that information about the perceived object is preserved and which, in turn, makes the primary percept epistemically reliable.

Let us contrast this with aftersensations.[8] Here, the causal chain can be illustrated as follows:

THE CAUSAL PATH TO AFTERSENSATIONS
DS → PS
PS + IP → PP
PP + internal processing (IP') → aftersensation (AS)

The aftersensation is directly caused by the primary percept and a second, further internal processing (IP') and indirectly caused by the distal stimulus and the proximal stimulus. Where and why do we lose the epistemic reliability when we move from primary percept to aftersensations? The relevant difference might lie within the natures and roles of internal processes IP and IP'.

IP is merely facilitating or realizing the qualitative outcome that is (to the largest extent) determined by the proximal stimulus. In contrast, IP' is together with the primary percept *constitutively responsible* for (the quality of) the aftersensation. IP' is an emancipated contributor to producing the aftersensation powerful enough to determine the character of the aftersensation. IP, on the other hand, plays a merely supportive role. In consequence, the character of the aftersensation may differ so much from the object it is an afterimage of that it ceases to be an accurate representation of it. This would certainly fit in the case of afterimages. Try, for example, to fix your gaze on a vividly colored image. When you then look at a white screen, you will observe a persistent afterimage with colors complementary to those of the original image. The colors of the afterimage are complementary due to adaptation of the retina cells. The image is persistent due to the processing that occurs at the level of the retina cells. All these are internal processes that contribute to the qualities of the ensuing aftersensation, which differ drastically from the original image. Here is another way to put it. Primary percepts are direct experiences of the world.[9] Aftersensations, on the other hand, are experiences only indirectly connected to the world since by AFTERSENSATION, they occur once the proximal stimulation has ceased. In a sense, when they happen, the contribution of the world to our experience does not matter anymore. It might seem the same with aftertaste. At least in certain circumstances, the quality we are aware of in an aftertaste experience differs radically from the quality we are aware of in the corresponding primary taste experience. For instance, a gentian liqueur may have an intense chamomile aftertaste that was not at all present in the primary taste phase of the gustatory experience, or a carelessly prepared avocado soup can quickly turn the eater's experience from one of a smooth buttery flavor to one of pungent bitterness after swallowing.

Notice that the epistemic insignificance of aftersensation does not mean that they cannot tell us anything interesting about how our perceptual systems work. To the contrary, psychologists study them precisely because they are by-products of perception, and thus their study is useful to retrieve information about the physiological, cognitive, and neural mechanisms underlying perception. But as by-products they do not share the epistemic profile of primary perceptual processes.

The Epistemic Reliability of Aftertastes

The previous causal considerations speak in favor of the thesis that aftersensations are epistemically unreliable. The very phenomenology of certain aftersensations suggests the same. Afterimages are a case at issue. If I close my eyes now, or quickly turn to look at the wall, say, I have an afterimage of the screen I have been looking at. Yet I am not inclined to regard this image as a perceptual encounter with my surroundings. In other words, afterimages lack what others have called "phenomenal objectivity" (Masrour 2013: 116): they seem to present us neither with features that are independent of our own mind nor with ways the objects of the world appear to us.

Why do we not regard afterimages as having objective import? People have made various features of afterimages responsible. Whereas ordinary experiences are usually of a familiar, stable world, afterimages are "typically feeble and fleeting" (Phillips 2012: 442). Afterimages do not seem to possess spatial locations independently from us and do not meet certain expectations implicit in ordinary perceptual experience, for example, like the expectation that objects look bigger the closer we get (cf. Masrour 2013). And Ned Block adds that "afterimages [...] don't look as if they are really objects or as if they are really red. They look [...] illusory" (1996: 32).

All these features do plausibly reduce the phenomenal objectivity of afterimages. Those doubts about the phenomenal objectivity of afterimages are generally taken in support of the view that there is no objectivity in the information afterimages provide us, full stop. After*tastes* have *some* phenomenal features that point in the direction of a reduced phenomenal objectivity. For example, one might think that there is some sense in which aftertastes do not seem to possess spatial locations independently from us. Tastes are bound to their bearers; the taste of the truffle is where the truffle is, a point that is made blatantly obvious by the fact that we have to literally touch it with our tongue to perceive its taste. And even flavor, which includes smell, is at least dependent on the presence of some chemical molecules.[10] Instead, the aftertaste is supposed to occur (roughly) in the mouth of the taster, once all of the food is removed. Remember that aftertaste occurs "after the stimuli have been 'removed'" (Neely & Borg 1999) and "after the cessation of the stimulus" (Colman 2000: 42). It is in that sense one might argue that the spatial location of aftertaste seems not entirely independent of the taster. One might even argue that there is some implicit expectation about gustatory perception to the effect that our taste sensation disappears or at least fades away, but certainly doesn't change after the food has been swallowed.

However, for the most part the phenomenology of aftertaste seems to be radically different from that of afterimages. This is witnessed in the way we treat aftertaste in ordinary social interactions: we value a wine for its aftertaste, we prefer a chocolate over another for the aftertaste it leaves in our mouth, and more generally we attribute properties to foods and drinks on the ground of aftertaste experiences. Contrariwise, we attribute shapes and colors on the ground of visual experiences, but we do *not* attribute those properties to objects on the ground of afterimage experiences—unless the circumstances are highly deceptive. For instance, in certain artificially reproduced circumstances an afterimage can be so vivid that we can mistake the experience we are having for an ordinary visual experience (cf. Phillips 2012).

Still, it is a fact that we do not rely as much on afterimages as we do on aftertastes when we want to gather information about our environment. One part of the explanation could be that aftertastes are just more persistent; they last longer and tend not to be as fleeting as afterimages. Indeed, we ordinarily experience much more afterimages than we realize, but since afterimages are usually very brief, we tend not to notice them; therefore it is not surprising that they do not carry much information. It is enough to hold your sight fixed for a few seconds on an object, and when you move it, a short-lived afterimage will be easily created, for instance if your gaze moves to a white wall right after. But this cannot be the entire explanation.

Firstly, it is possible to induce very persistent afterimages, hence the ephemerality of afterimages is not a constitutive feature of them. A flash right in our eyes produces a persistent afterimage, and the pictures and instructions that we find in psychology handbooks all lead to vivid experiences (if not, something went wrong and you have to repeat the "experiment").

Secondly, afterimages entertain a different counterfactual relation with their source, that is, the distal stimulus at the origin of their causal chain, than aftertastes. Experiencing a mouthwatering stew would be less informative in terms of the stew's flavor, if the experience did not include the delicious umami aftertaste. We would say to know less of the stew if, for instance, through some artificial inducement, our experience was suppressed before developing the aftertaste. A visual experience of a cup without an afterimage, on the other hand, could hardly be described as informatively diminished. No information would be lost if the experience was phenomenologically suppressed in the right moment. The epistemic import of an afterimage is at best redundant (as in the case of a brief retention of an object's image right after we have moved our sight away from it), potentially misleading (for instance about the position and the color of the distal stimulus, as shown in many handbook experiments), and at hindrance for further visual inspection of the object (if the afterimage is persistent). In other words, even if we speak in terms both of an afterimage *of the screen* and an aftertaste *of the stew*, the "of" plays a different role in each case. An afterimage of the screen does not seem to reveal anything *new* about the screen but that it has produced an afterimage experience—or if it does so, it does in a misleading way (by representing a position and a color that the screen doesn't have). Contrariwise, the stew's umami aftertaste tells us something new *about the stew*, something we did not have access to before we had the aftertaste experience: the stew that *was* in my mouth *now* tastes umami (and this also happens when the aftertaste quality is very similar to the quality of the primary taste—in that case we will say of the stew that it *still* tastes umami in the aftertaste).

Those considerations about the phenomenological difference between afterimages and aftertastes lead us to think that there is a presumption of epistemic reliability concerning the latter. Such a presumption should be taken seriously, unless we have independent reason to believe that we are systematically mistaken.

Against the Received View: Aftertastes Are Exceptions

In "The Epistemic Reliability of Aftertastes" we saw that the physiological processes leading to an aftersensation *constitutively* involve a second internal processing IP', which occurs after the experience of the primary percept, and this fact is taken to be responsible for the general "epistemic remoteness" of aftersensations. However, the presence of IP' does not motivate per se a complete segregation of the aftersensation from the world, nor does the lack of phenomenal objectivity. The complaint, for example, that "after-images are not seen as material objects any more than, say, a ringing in one's ear is heard as a real noise" (Boghossian & Velleman 1989: 86–7) is clearly without base when we are to judge whether the experience in question is perceptual or not. As Ian Phillips points out about afterimages, we can very well be perceptually presented with non-material objects, rainbows, shadows, reflections, and the like, which are real at least in the sense of publicly accessible. This should be even more obvious for other sense modalities, for example, in olfaction.

Of course it is true that aftersensations often *mis*represent many features of the distal stimulus (its position, whether it is moving and in which direction, its color, the dimension, etc.), but the mistakes are systematic and can be reproduced in different subjects by exposing them to analogous conditions. Hence the link with the stimulus is in some sense stable, IP' notwithstanding, and their being generally illusory is after all a matter of degree. Although most aftersensations are in general on the "illusion" end of the spectrum, aftertastes may be exceptional in being mostly on the "veridical" side.

A phenomenal feature that seems to support the veridicality of aftertastes is the role of the "specious present" in their temporal structure. As we pointed out at the outset, gustatory experiences are temporally extended experiences, which have phases. More precisely, they are *phenomenally unified* experiences, that is, experiences whose phases pass one into another in a continuous manner. From a subjective point of view, they are experiences of the food that we ingest. Unless something triggers unusual attentive activity (more on this below), the primary taste phase (PT) "moves into," as it were, the aftertaste phase (AT).

An obvious way to spell out the structure of this phenomenal diachronic unity is in terms of the specious present. A specious present is an interval t_0-t_n during which anything that is experienced is both experienced as occurring over t_0-t_n and apprehended all at once. We can say that what is represented in the specious present is *phenomenally present*, even if not all of its parts are presented as temporally present.[11] A gustatory experience is phenomenally unified in virtue of being constituted by a series of (possibly overlapping) specious presents.[12] Crucially, at least one specious present contains both primary taste phases and aftertaste phases (Figure 11.1).

Although the swallowing of the food is the dividing moment, the experience is phenomenally unified, and this explains why we tend to consider all its parts as reliably providing information about the food. In the primary taste phase of the experience we are presented directly with the food. The activity of the receptors (both the taste bud and the smell receptors cells)[13] together with the internal processing presents to us how the food that *is in our mouth* tastes *now*. In the aftertaste phase the experience is less directly linked to the gustabile, but from the subjective point of view it is an evolution of the previous phases rather than a new sensation that is only accidentally linked to the primal taste. Hence, even if the receptors are not directly involved in interactions with the food when we have the aftertaste experience, we can say that their activity, together with IP', the secondary internal processing, presents us with how the food that *was in our mouth* tastes *now*.

If this description captures the phenomenology correctly, then aftertastes are not experiences of *pure gustabilia*, as for the sensationalist afterimages are experiences of pure visibilia. In an aftertaste phase the food or drink itself appears to us in a certain way, which may be (and usually is) different from the way it appeared to us in the primary taste phase. This is why it is perfectly natural to say that the stew (say) tasted bland at first but then revealed its blasting umami side, even when we are only talking about experiencing one single mouthful rather than a number of spoonful.

Notice that for the experience to appear epistemically as one, temporally extended, complex experience of the very same food item, it is crucial that the transition from the

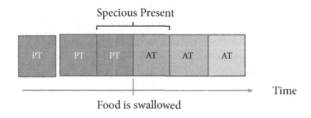

Figure 11.1 Primary taste and aftertaste in the specious present.

primary taste phase to the aftertaste phase is part of the overall phenomenology, if not the full focus of attention. We have to be phenomenally aware of the food changing from tasting such-and-such to tasting thus-and-thus (or keeping on having that such-and-such taste). If for some reason we do not attend *at all* to this transition, then it is not clear that the aftertaste experience would still qualify as an awareness of the way the food that I had in my mouth tastes now. In that case, the aftertaste may even appear, akin to an afterimage, "not real," as pure sensation. Imagine yourself happily diminishing an enticing little sandwich when suddenly the piercing, demanding squeak of a hungry guinea pig distracts you and captures all your attention. After you regain your attention for what you were doing, you might "find yourself" with a weird taste in your mouth. It is slightly sour and almost minty, but very different from the taste you experienced when you were chewing the sandwich. Where does it come from? You can of course *infer* that it is an aftertaste of the sandwich filling by excluding other sources (I am not sick. I have not ingested taste-altering drugs. I am not hallucinating), and you can confirm this hypothesis by enjoying (or undergoing, at any rate) another aftertaste experience with the next bite. But without awareness of the continuity, something (the "after" in "aftertaste" one is tempted to say) is missing.

There are two problems for this solution to the puzzle. The first problem is that an appeal to the phenomenologically unifying role of the specious present structure of gustatory experiences can only explain why we take aftertaste experiences as reliable indicators of qualities of the food, rather than as purely sensorial epilogues or "codas" to the way food has appeared to us in primary taste. But, as we have pointed out already, there are good reasons to think that aftertaste *is* actually reliable; it does reveal to us properties of food (such as its dangerousness in the case of certain unpleasant aftertastes) that are independent from its being experienced, and an appeal to the phenomenology is at best a very partial explanation of this. If something seems epistemically reliable that may be a prima facie evidence that it is reliable, but it cannot be the end of the story.

Now, maybe we could be content with this account nonetheless. The "exceptionality" of aftertastes as aftersensations could entirely reside in their having an appearance of epistemic reliability—regardless of the fact that there may also be independent reasons to take them as actually reliable with respect to certain objective properties of the food. After all, afterimages do not seem to share this phenomenal trait or at least not to the same extent. Maybe Philipps or some other purists are right and afterimages are not pure sensations either, but there are still many more "phenomenal defeaters" in the case of afterimages, features that make us subjectively doubt the epistemic reliability of afterimages, than in the case of aftertaste. Moreover, there is no doubt that afterimages are for the most part illusory, and unless in very unfavorable circumstances, we do not tend to take them as otherwise.

Unfortunately this will not do. If we are content with explaining the phenomenal difference between aftertastes (experienced as representations of public features or objects out there) on the one side, and afterimages on the other side (at least not obviously experienced as public features or objects), then an appeal to the specious present is of no use because it overgeneralizes. There is no reason why the transition from primary visual percept (let's call it the *primary image*) to an afterimage could not also occur within one phenomenally unified specious present episode. To the contrary, it does so occur normally. If aftertastes seem epistemically reliable due to the phenomenal diachronic unity of our temporally extended experiences, then the same should hold true, at least to some degree, for afterimages. Of course we might appeal here to the plethora of phenomenal defeaters we find for afterimage but not for aftertaste experiences—the ephemerality, the lack of kinetic independence, the lack of size constancy, and so forth (cf. Phillips 2012). Still, if phenomenal diachronic unity was the core reason for the epistemic reliability of aftertaste, even if just subjectively, one would expect the same criterion to carry more weight for the subjective reliability of afterimages too.

But it clearly does not. We do not have any tendency at all to construe an afterimage as a way the distal stimulus *that was seen* is experienced *now*. An afterimage of a flash in our eyes is not a way the flash that almost blinded us looks now. An afterimage of the US flag in complementary colors that I see on a white page is not the way the picture of the flag initially perceived (in its usual colors) looks *now*. Even when we clearly recognize the similarity with the original image (it has the same shape and flutters a bit on the right), afterimages simply do not seem to present us with further, initially somehow "hidden" properties of the original object perceived. Notice that purists do not have to deny this. Even if afterimages are illusory presentations of material objects, they do not need to be presentations of the very same "object source" (that is the external stimulus that originates the corresponding primary image).[14]

Again the Received View: Aftertastes Are Not Aftersensations

If aftertaste experiences are different from afterimage experiences because they seem, and are, (more) epistemically reliable, then maybe the difference between the two is deeper, and we should not put them in the same basic category. Afterimages are aftersensations; they are experiential "spandrels" with little epistemic significance, whereas aftertastes are experiences that, even if they too depend on a primary percept (in the way illustrated by THE CAUSAL PATH TO AFTERSENSATIONS above), reliably add information about source objects.

It is hard to deny that there are situations in which aftertastes reliably signal an objectively obtaining state of affairs, independently of how objective that signaling seems to us. An unpleasant aftertaste in milk is usually a sign of its dangerousness for our health, and even if (some of us) may appreciate a bitter aftertaste in craft beer and coffee, bitterness as it is revealed in aftertaste (and sometimes only in aftertaste) can be a sign of a poisonous element. But for an experience being a dependable signal of some mind-independent state of affairs is for it to be reliable; hence—given that revising the idea that aftersensations in general are not reliable seems explanatorily costly, as we have seen—the more radical solution is the only way to go. Aftertastes are not aftersensations; they simply have a feature in common with aftersensations (they, too, appear after the stimulus has ceased).

Now, aftersensations are not always epistemically idle. Suppose that, by misfortune (or sheer stupidity), one takes an afterimage to veridically represent the object of one's primary experience, and as a result misjudges many of that object's properties. We can still think of unusual scenarios in which the information we get from the afterimage is useful, and it is so in virtue of its connection with the object source.

For instance, imagine someone who has the misfortune to be kidnapped. Locked in a bare room they have but a few moments to orientate themselves and memorize the layout of their confinement. Before all too long, they are blindfolded and, to add insult to injury, injected with some substance that is supposed to erase their entire short-term memory. It fails. Instead, it only erases from memory their most recent perceptual experiences. It seems to us that it would be worse for that person if the drug had worked properly—and not only for the obvious reason that it would have caused greater damage to them. For suppose that our poor kidnapping victim has no (perceptual) memory of the room they have just seen but still a vibrant afterimage of the visual experience; they may, from that afterimage, understand the shape and the relative position of the window and even of the glaring metal door and use that information to navigate their escape.

However, the lack of systematicity in the way afterimages can usefully be exploited by an embodied cognitive system is a likely signal of the fact that they play a very different role than aftertastes. To illustrate this point, it may be helpful to refer to a contrast Louise Richardson draws between experiencing odors on the one hand and experiencing rainbows on the other. According to Richardson,

> [t]he visual system is not tuned to the presence of rainbows as the olfactory system is tuned to the presence of odours. Rainbows are perceived merely as a side effect of a system devoted to the direct perception of ordinary objects. (Richardson 2018: 22)

In our comparison, odors are likened with aftertastes and rainbows with afterimages. Employing Richardson's point further, we might say that our cognitive systems are tuned to the presence of aftertastes because aftertastes are instrumentally valuable in providing us with further information about their sources. The reason why this is so may be evolutionary (bitterness in nature may be a symptom of poisonousness, and it is advantageous that an animal has a surplus of resources to detect it). Afterimages, on the other hand, are merely "a side effect of a system devoted to the direct perception of ordinary objects" (Richardson 2018: 22), in other words, an evolutionary spandrel.

The difference in the role of afterimages and of aftertastes for the subject is plausibly reflected by some physiological difference between the IP's (the internal processing constitutively responsible for the quality of the aftersensation) in the two cases. We will not go too much further at this point since we are rapidly moving into empirical terrain. However, looking at some evidence from empirical research, the hypothesis that a difference in IP'-afterimage and IP'-aftertaste explains the epistemic disparity seems not outlandish. Phillips, for example, drawing on various empirical findings,[15] writes:

> There is now substantial evidence that afterimages cannot solely be accounted for as photochemical process [...]. Rather, at least under certain experimental conditions, neural adaptation in the retina forms an essential process. (Phillips 2012: 421)

Now consider the following quote by psychologists Naim and colleagues about aftertastes:

> In the context of aftertaste, *the combination of both receptor-dependent and receptor-independent processes* have been proposed to explain the signal transduction mechanisms for foods with distinct aftertastes, particularly those that are bitter. [...] The receptor-independent process involves the diffusion of bitter, amphiphilic chemicals like quinine across the taste receptor cell membranes, which activate both the taste receptors on the cell surface, as well as the signaling pathway proteins in the intracellular space. *Intracellular signaling may be slower than taste cell receptor* activation [...]. *This delayed activation of intracellular signaling proteins in response to the bitter compounds,* in addition to the extracellular receptor signaling *is proposed to be related to the lingering aftertaste* associated with bitter foods. (Naim et al. 2002: 2–17, our emphasis)

In both cases, there is talk about receptor-independent processes (in the first quote these would be the processes other than the photochemical ones). For aftertaste, however, this process is described as a delay in the activation of certain signaling proteins. It seems to us that a delayed processing of a stimulus is still a processing of that stimulus. Although this process is in some sense more remotely connected to the distal stimulus than the process that generates the primary taste, it can still reliably connect with the source object. The idea here is that IP'-aftertastes are processes that are intrinsically reliable with respect to certain aspects of the stimulus—for instance its bitterness. At any rate, if IP'-afterimages do not have the same intrinsic characteristics, and are thus less able to reliably track features of the external stimulus, then they are mere "echos"—possibly distorted ones—of the original experience and should fall in a different category than the one in which we put aftertastes.

Our second suggestion as to why aftertastes are epistemically more reliable than afterimages, and thus should not be classified as belonging to the same category, is probably in equal parts more important and more daring than our first suggestion. We propose that aftertastes are epistemically more reliable than afterimages because they are, to a large extent, constituted by another genuine perceptual sense, namely the sense of "retronasal smell." Smell, as psychologist Paul Rozin phrased it, "is not a single sense but rather a dual sense, comprising orthonasal (breathing in) and retronasal (breathing out) senses" (cited in Shepherd 2012: 17). Retronasal smell is nowadays recognized as the most important component for our awareness of flavor. Neuroscientist Gordon M. Shepherd, for example, argues that

> [a]s delivered by the retronasal route, smell dominates flavor. We often characterize our food in terms of how it "tastes," but the sense of taste as properly defined consists of sensitivity only to sweet, salt, sour, bitter, and umami. What we call the taste of our food beyond these simple sensations should be called flavor and is mostly due to retronasal smell. (Shepherd 2012: 2–3)

Here is how Shepherd describes the physiological processes involved in retronasal smell (Figure 11.2 below):

> The retronasal route to the smell organ begins with the food or drink that comes into the mouth. There the food is moved about by the tongue as it is chewed (masticated). [...] At the same time, the taste is sampled by the taste buds on the tongue and the back of the mouth and into the pharynx. **When the chewer exhales, air is forced from the lungs up through the open epiglottis into the nasopharynx at the back of the mouth. There the air absorbs odors from the food** that coats the walls and back of the tongue and that have volatilized from the warm, moist, masticated mass. **Because the mouth is closed, the odor-laden air is pushed into the back of the nasal chamber and out through the nostrils, sending eddy currents within the nasal chamber up to the olfactory sensory neurons to stimulate them.** (Shepherd 2012: 26, our intonation)

Then, particularly relevant to us,

> [f]inally, the motor control of **swallowing takes over, and the (food) goes down to our stomachs (followed by our breathing out for a last enjoyment through retronasal smell).** (Shepherd 2012: 186, our intonation)

> The arrows show the pathways in humans for sniffing smells by the orthonasal route and for sensing smells from the mouth by the retronasal route. (Shepherd 2012: 25)

While retronasal smell is crucial to the primary flavor experience, we argue here that it plays an even more decisive role for aftertastes. More precisely, we are arguing that the impingement of the olfactory system by volatile aroma molecules through

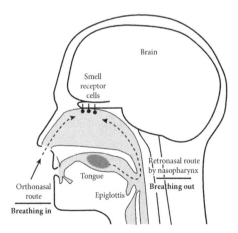

Figure 11.2 Pathways of orthonasal and retronasal smells.

retronasal smell is a (temporally) second genuine perceptual input that carries additional first-hand information about the eaten food. In other words, the quality of aftertaste is constitutively determined by *two different proximal stimuli*: indirectly, via the primary taste, by the molecules in the saliva that excite the taste buds and directly by the molecules that pass through the retro-pharynx to excite the olfactory nerves. Aftertaste, thus, seems to be a more complex phenomenon than aftersensation; its causal path is "richer." The second input provides a distinguishing contribution to IP' and thus to the qualitative profile of the aftertaste experience. We can schematize this idea as follows:

THE CAUSAL PATH TO AFTERTASTE
DS → PS
PS + IP → PP
PP + secondary input from retro-smell (RS) + IP' → AT

By swallowing the food the air is pushed in the nasopharynx, and thus aftertaste inevitably includes retronasal smell. Given that retronasal smell is part of the IP' that leads to the aftertaste experience, the contribution of the second perceptual input RS is *constitutive* of the experience. Now, if retronasal smell is a means to an epistemically direct contact with the object source (the food), then it should be no surprise that the aftertaste experience is after all a *reliable* source of information about the food that is the topic of the gustatory experience as a whole. While aftersensations such as afterimages are constituted by an IP' that does not benefit from a further channel of information from the external stimulus, since it is entirely triggered by the first elaboration of the stimulus, aftertaste depends also on a second input from the food, namely the molecules that impinge on the olfactory receptors through the retronasal route.

Recall that we started this chapter with some definitions of aftertaste as given by prominent psychology references. These quotes define aftertastes as sensations "persisting after the cessation of the stimulus." This might seem problematic in the context of our proposal since we are arguing that there is a stimulus that is directly responsible for the quality of the aftertaste. Rest assured, though, it is not our intention to boldly dismiss definitions built on decades of solid empirical work. But our argument is in fact compatible with such definitions: while there is some stimulus present and involved in the generation of the aftertaste, the *taste* stimuli, the molecules that excite the *taste buds*, have indeed ceased once the food is swallowed (at least we can assume that there are cases where there may really be no such stimuli left but aftertaste still occurs).

This explains also why aftertastes are, more often than not, qualitatively different from primary tastes. The perception of retronasal smell is usually mingled with taste and touch. As Shepherd (2012: 117) observes, "retronasal smell is never sensed by itself, but always together with virtually every other sense in the mouth." Never, except in aftertaste when all the food has been swallowed. So where flavor is a combinatory experience of taste, touch, orthonasal, and retronasal, aftertaste is a comparably impoverished experience, which has as direct perceptual input merely the retronasal aspects left.

Why then, one might ask, would aftertaste be labeled as a kind of taste at all? Flavor, Shepherd writes, and we might extend this to explicitly include aftertaste, is "not [...] recognized by us as coming from the nose. Rather it is perceived as coming from the mouth" (2012: 30). And Charles Spence confirms that we are, most of the time, ignorant of how much information that we think we taste with the tongue comes in via the retronasal route. This is due to a phenomenon called "oral referral": the phenomenon that food aromas are experienced as if coming from the mouth (cf. Spence 2017: 51). If that is true for primary tastes, then there is no obvious reason why the same phenomenon should not also be responsible for experiencing after*tastes* as tastes rather than smells. We can now see, moreover, why aftertastes might have been lumped together with afterimages into the category of aftersensations in the first place. Our experience of aftertaste as taste rather than smell has made us focus more on the fact that there are no stimuli anymore to excite the taste buds when aftertaste occurs than on the fact that there are nevertheless still olfactory stimuli present, which are also responsible for creating the sensation. In the end, the problem might be one of mouth over nose bias.

Conclusion

While afterimages are connected to their distal stimulus only as by-products of the perceptual process, and have a somewhat eerie appearance, aftertastes have the mark of phenomenal objectivity and provide us with valuable information about the food that was just in our mouth. We have given an account of this difference, which has led us to reject the received view according to which aftertastes and afterimages belong to the same category of aftersensations. Epistemically, metaphysically, and physiologically, aftertastes have a distinct profile and a distinct function from afterimages. Theoretical and empirical investigation should take such differences seriously; otherwise we risk underestimating the role of aftertaste in gustatory experience.

Part Three

Valuing

Introduction to Part Three: Valuing

This last part of the volume focuses on the axiological and normative dimensions of recipes, namely, the ways they can be valuable and subject to norms. The terms "axiological" and "normative" should be understood broadly here, as pertaining to norms and values of different kinds, both theoretical and practical, or as pertaining to different domains, such as ethics, law, social norms, or even philosophy itself.

A value, according to a standard philosophical account, is a feature of something that can serve as a reason for its appraisal, whether positive or negative. Standard examples include moral goodness, beauty, friendliness, practicality, and so on. Philosophers, however, standardly distinguish between two kinds of values: intrinsic and instrumental ones. A value of something is intrinsic if it provides a reason to appraise the thing in and of itself; a value of something is instrumental if it provides a reason to appraise thing not in and of itself, but as an instrument for something else. The beauty of a landscape is a recurring trope of intrinsic value; namely, the beauty is a feature of the landscape that gives us a reason to appraise it in and of itself, regardless of the consequences of our action (or even despite the consequences). That a stick is long enough to fetch apples on a tree is an instrumental value of it: it is a feature of the stick that gives us a reason to appraise it not in and of itself, but merely as an instrument to fetch apples.

What about norms? Establishing and following norms allows us to realize certain values and to eschew the realizations of others. There are also different kinds of norms. Some norms encapsulate duties, namely, what one ought or ought not to do, such as "You must not steal" or "You must help people in need." Some norms, on the other hand, seem to impose weaker demands on us, recommending rather than demanding us to do or not to do something—for example, "You should drink with moderation" or "You shouldn't talk too much about yourself."

The chapters in this third part address some of the values, intrinsic and instrumental, and some of the norms, strong or weak, that pertain to recipes.

The first contribution in this section by Lisa Heldke considers the theoretical value of recipes, specifically, the value of modeling our understanding of theories on the model of our understanding of recipes. Heldke's contribution is a classic in the literature on the philosophy of food and takes place in the following context.

An important dichotomy in philosophy is between what philosophers refer to as realist and antirealist conceptions of a certain domain such as morality, aesthetics, mathematics, or even reality itself as a whole. To be a realist about some domain is to countenance the thesis that elements of that domain exist and that, in some cases at least, we can get objective knowledge of them. To be an antirealist about some domain, on the other hand, is to claim that elements of that domain don't exist and that, therefore, there is nothing there for us to have objective knowledge of. In the domain of mathematics, for instance, to be a realist is to claim that mathematical objects (e.g., numbers, functions, or theorems) exist and that we can come to know them, while to be an antirealist is to claim that, at best, mathematics turns out to be a kind of shadow shed on the world by our own making.

According to Heldke, philosophy could learn something from recipes insofar as conceiving of theories as recipes rather than as models of reality that can either fit the world or mimic such a fitting could help philosophers to steer a middle course between realism and antirealism. If this is correct, then recipes could have genuine theoretical value of an instrumental kind; namely, they could be valuable instruments in our quest for knowledge.

In the next chapter, Rafi Grosglik and David Kyle move on to some of the social values and norms that govern our appreciation of star chefs and their recipes. In particular, they focus on the celebrated culinary show *Chef's Table* and on the social construction of the star chef as a genius that produces magical foodstuff. As they see the matter, *Chef's Table* constructs different narratives of chefs as geniuses, though all are characterized by their possessing a kind of special quality that escapes codification, justifies their high praise, and sets them apart from the rest of us.

Within that framework, chefs are presented as pertaining to the re-enchantment of the mundaneness, where food would serve as a way out of our overly planned lives. However, Grosglik and Kyle argue that framing this re-enchanting power of food in terms of genius amounts to a mere form of escapism and cannot really achieve what it pretends, as *Chef's Table* is precisely not a standard cooking show with instructional value. Viewers are rather stuck in a narrative of talentism that reinforces the social norm that one must be a genius to run the show and to be in a unique position to accumulate value. As such, *Chef's Table* is just another story of another elite, the culinary one, occupying a privileged position in the late capitalist society. In sum, if recipes and food are to have any kind of social value, it is doubtful whether the norm of viewing the chef as a genius as promoted by *Chef's Table* can really help us implement it.

The social value of recipes and food is explored from a very different perspective, and with very different conclusions, in the chapter by Joanna Forman. She explores the different avenues through which recipes and food can serve as a positive force in the mediation of human relationships, from private to institutional settings, as well as the way they can serve as a force of social change.

Here, two aspects can be distinguished. On the one hand, there is the issue of recipes and foodstuffs having, in some cases at least, some kind of intrinsic cultural or social value. In such a case, food is not merely the currency of a social exchange, but its very object, just as any other cultural artifact could be. On the other hand, there is the issue of recipes and foodstuffs having, in some cases at least, instrumental cultural or social value. Here, several cases must be distinguished from each other.

First, there is the fact that food sells and that many nations or regions of the world have engaged in forms of gastronomical geographical branding, where food and the people that prepare it serve as informal ambassadors. In such a case, food serves as an instrument of cultural and economic promotion and sees its instrumental value indexed to that function. Second, there is the fact that food is an effective social lubricant that allows exchanges in a positive environment, an instrumental value that can be deployed in a more or less formal environment, from private gatherings to diplomatic events. Third and finally, there are the diverse ways in which food can leverage social changes. Indeed, the ubiquity, diversity, and value-laden nature of food make it a powerful instrument for social change. It is this last aspect, what is commonly referred to as social-gastronomy, that Forman takes as her main focus.

The next chapter by Enrico Bonadio and Natalie Weissenberger moves on from social norms and values to legal ones. Indeed, recipes not only have culinary value proper but also possess creative and economic values, and such values can be protected by the law through intellectual property rights. This is already the case, to some extent, with respect to geographical indications. In their contribution, however, Bonadio and Weissenberger expand the analysis to other kinds of subject matter and inquire into the possibility for restaurant recipes and food presentations to benefit from such legal protection.

They show that the debate over the opportunity to enforce intellectual protection of food creations is still very much open. This raises interesting philosophical questions. A central one awaiting development is the following: Which values should a recipe bear so that it can be elected to the rank of candidate for intellectual protection? Are some kind of intrinsic values necessary or should mere instrumental values be sufficient? Can there be a trade-off between different kinds of values a recipe can possess that could explain the need to either protect, or fail to protect, it?

The next chapter by Anne Barnhill and Matteo Bonotti takes us into more familiar philosophical terrain, namely, moral values and norms, and in particular the ones that govern the modifications of recipes. Some recipes come in a set form and their having this form can be legitimately invested with value—whether cultural, financial, or a combination of both—by individuals and communities. However, for different kinds of reasons such recipes can also undergo changes. Some of these changes are harmless, but some others can be impactful. When is such disruption unproblematic and when does it legitimately result in an action that might be deemed morally bad?

A prominent example discussed by Barnhill and Bonotti is the one of cultural appropriation. Take the case of a restaurant serving an exotic cuisine with no relation whatsoever with the cultural background undergirding it. Is such a practice ever acceptable, with or without alterations of the original recipes? Another important example is the one of a state recommending changes to recipes for public health reasons. When a certain recipe is culturally particularly significant for a community as, for example, in the case of soul food for African Americans, is a state ever justified to attempt to curb citizens' dietary choices?

The final contribution within this third part, by Benjamin Wurgaft, deals with recipes and meat consumption—a well-known *locus* for discussing moral values and norms when it comes to food. Wurgaft's chapter focuses on a specific issue: the prospects of cultured meat (see Wurgaft 2019 for an overview of the topic) and the specific moral framing that it is receiving.

As Wurgaft points out, an important fact about moral issues generally, and issues about meat consumption in particular, is that one cannot really do moral theorizing in the absence of a certain moral framework, namely, a framework that provides us with a conception of what makes a certain action morally acceptable or unacceptable, as well as a conception of the intrinsic and relative strength of moral norms. An influential, albeit much-debated, moral framework is utilitarianism, according to which a moral action is one that maximizes pleasure and minimizes pain, and according to which moral considerations are absolute. From this starting point, a question quickly arises: whose pleasure should be maximized and whose pain minimized? In what ways can a global utilitarian calculus take into account the perspectives of nonhuman agents such as animals, plants, or ecosystems?

Wurgaft discusses the general utilitarian framing that is most often invoked to promote cultured meat. Its supporters argue that cultured meat will help us to eliminate the environmental damages and the animal cruelties entrenched with large-scale animal farming. However, Wurgaft argues, the utilitarian moral framing of the issue obscures valuable philosophical questions that meat raises, about the differences between human and nonhuman animals, and about human nature as well.

Further Reading

Adams, M. (2018). "The Aesthetic Value of Local Food." In: *The Monist*, 101 (3): 324–39.

Borghini, A. (2014). "Authenticity in Food." In: P. M. Thompson and D. M. Kaplan (eds.), *Encyclopedia of Food and Agricultural Ethics*. Berlin: Springer: 180–5.

Bramble, B. and Fischer, B. (2015). *The Moral Complexities of Eating Meat*. New York: Oxford University Press.

Chignell, A., Cuneo, T., and Halteman, M. C. (eds.) (2015). *Philosophy Comes to Dinner: Arguments About the Ethics of Eating*. New York: Routledge.

Engisch, P. (2020). "Recipes and Culinary Creativity: The Noma Legacy." In: *Humana. Mente,* 13 (38): 61–82.

Kaplan, D. (2020). *Food Philosophy: An Introduction*. New York: Columbia University Press.

Ravasio, Matteo (2018). "Food Landscapes: An Object-Centered Model of Food Appreciation." In: *The Monist*, 101 (3): 309–23.

Singer, P. (2009). *Animal Liberation*. Updated Edition. New York: Harper.

Todd, C. (2010). *The Philosophy of Wine*. London: Routledge.

Wurgaft, B. (2019). *Meat Planet: Artificial Flesh and the Future of Food*. Los Angeles: University of California Press.

Recipes for Theory Making*

Lisa Maree Heldke

Could it ever make sense to think of cooking as a form of inquiry? Could thinking about cooking ever illuminate our thinking about philosophy? This paper is my attempt to show why "yes" is the appropriate answer to both these questions. Through an exploration of cooking—an exploration that focuses on the nature of recipes and recipe use—I'll develop my claim that cooking is a form of inquiry that is anti-essentialist, that successfully merges the theoretical and the practical, and that promotes a self-reflective and interactive model of an inquiry relationship.

My account of cooking grows out of a particular epistemological tradition, a tradition I label the Coresponsible Option. Members of this tradition are attempting to develop epistemological frameworks or attitudes that avoid the dichotomies of realism/antirealism and foundationalism/relativism. I contend that these dichotomies are not exhaustive and that it is in fact important for feminists to find ways around them—to construct alternative attitudes in which to engage in epistemology. Before I turn to my account of cooking, I'll sketch out this epistemological tradition.

Why Should Feminists Worry about Foundationalism and Relativism?

Philosophers working in a variety of traditions are trying to develop positions that avoid the sharp, pointy rocks of absolutism, realism, and foundationalism without falling into the murky swamps of relativism. Theorists engaged in these sorts of projects attempt (implicitly or explicitly) to undermine, dismantle, begin before, or otherwise avoid the metaphysical question, "Is there something Out There that exists, unchanging and independent of us, or are we the creators of all that there is?" and the related epistemological question, "How can we ground our knowledge of the world—or *can* we?"

Sandra Harding, one important figure in the movement I'm describing/constructing, asks, "[D]o we—should we—still believe that our representations can in principle reflect one uniquely accurate image of a world which is ready-made and out

* From *Hypatia* 3 (2):15–29, 1988. Reprinted with the permission of the author.

there for the reflecting? Should we really think a feminist philosophy or science can be the mirror of nature any more than non-feminist ones can?" (1985: 16). Philosophical claims are not "'approximations to the truth' which can be woven into a seamless web of representation of the world 'out there', but permanently partial instigators of rupture" (1985: 17–18). Philosophy is valuable not because it can uncover the Real, but because it can create alternate ways to think about whatever reality it is we've inherited/discovered/created.

Richard Bernstein, a theorist engaged in a related project, calls his an attempt to move "beyond objectivism and relativism." He suggests that we have to stop treating the epistemological terrain as necessarily bifurcated—as if there were a fundamental opposition between "the basic conviction that there is or must be some permanent, ahistorical matrix or framework to which we can ultimately appeal in determining the nature of rationality, knowledge, truth, reality, goodness, or rightness," and the view "that all such conceptions [taken to be fundamental] must be understood as relative to a specific conceptual scheme, theoretical framework, paradigm, form of life, society, or culture" (1983: 8). This opposition—accompanied, as it is, by the assumption that its two alternatives constitute our only available options—rests upon what Bernstein calls the "Cartesian Anxiety" (1983: 16), the conviction that either there is a firm foundation for our knowledge, or we are condemned to swirl endlessly in the morass of intellectual and moral indecision.

The assumption that our epistemological options are limited to two is unwarranted. Furthermore, neither option—neither foundationalism nor relativism—is particularly useful or desirable in its own right. My assessment of these options arises out of certain feminist concerns and aspirations; it is my contention that the epistemological "attitudes" that are foundationalism and relativism hobble efforts to inquire into, and theorize about, our experiences. In order to be able to do the kinds of inquiry I want to do, I feel the need to be free of the constraints these two attitudes place upon me.

Let me explain. I am interested in developing ways to do feminist inquiry that are respectful and illuminating of the differences in women's lives—that embody a respect for difference. At the same time, I do not want to interpret respect for difference as a blanket sanction of all and any differences. Specifically, I do not translate "respect for difference" into a demand that we respect or accept misogynist, racist, classist, or otherwise oppressive views, simply because they are different from ours, or a demand that we always "resist the temptation" to try to convince others of our views. I think foundationalism and relativism are inadequate frameworks for doing this kind of inquiry.

Foundationalism treats difference as a "stage" or "phase" we pass through on our way to constructing adequate theory. Difference, for the foundationalist, reflects an inadequacy, a failure or incompleteness in our theorizing; if we had developed an adequate set of theories about subject X, the need for—and perhaps the possibility of—different approaches would be eliminated. On the other hand, relativism allows for and even encourages difference but disables us from criticizing the theories of others for being incomplete, uninclusive, or otherwise inadequate. The relativist is left to say, "[D]ifferent is different; it's neither better nor worse."

In contrast, I would like to construct epistemologies that are respectful and representative of the differences in women's experiences without being glib, unreflective, or uncritical about those differences—that is, without defining all differences as necessarily good and desirable or declaring a moratorium on convincing and persuading. In order to carry out this project, I find it necessary to develop attitudes toward inquiry that will allow such epistemologies to exist. That is, I want to develop epistemological options that are neither absolutist nor relativist.

My own approach to/avoidance of absolutism and relativism I label the "Coresponsible Option." The term "coresponsible" embodies the atmosphere of cooperation and interaction, which characterizes inquiry activity.[1] Whether we acknowledge it or not, we enter into relationships when we engage in inquiry; relationships with other inquirers, and also with the things into which we inquire—the things labeled "objects" on a traditional account. The model of inquiry I'm suggesting rejects the strict subject/object dichotomy with its emphasis on hierarchy and separation. In its place, I suggest we think of inquiry as a communal activity, that we emphasize the relationships that obtain between inquirers and inquired. In the words of John Dewey, inquiry is "the correspondence of two people [or things] who 'correspond' in order to modify one's own ideas, intents and acts" (1958: 283).

I label my approach an "option" to suggest that what I offer here is simply one way to think about the world and about inquiry, not *the* way. This is not simply a modest claim about the fallibility of my thought; it is an assertion of my view of the status of theories in general. They are tools we may choose to use, outlooks we may elect to assume. Some are more useful than others; none are universally reliable.

Why Should Philosophers Worry about Cooking?

I situate my examination of cooking within this context—a context in which the issue is not "Do we cast our lots with absolutism or with relativism?" but rather "How can we avoid both of these headaches?" I want to ask a question about inquiry and theorizing: If I do choose to resist the temptation to enter the absolutism/relativism debates, in what *spirit* might I set out to inquire and to develop theories? And how might I explain and be doing theory?

(An aside. I speak here only partly facetiously of the "temptation" to enter these, for I have found them extremely seductive, for reasons I can't quite diagnose. Choosing to throw them over has proven difficult psychologically—and *persevering* in avoiding them sometimes even more so. Part of the difficulty for me stems from the fact that I just don't have good ways to talk that are both nonfoundationalist and nonrelativist. Furthermore, even when I *find* the ways, I always want to *use* them. There's something extremely comforting about believing that my alternatives are cut-and-dried, limited to two. This paper is my attempt to develop some useful and *attractive* ways to think about inquiry and theorizing, which break the seductive hold of this dichotomy.)

I'm motivated to ask questions about the "spirit" in which to inquire, and to develop and promote theories, because doing theory is an activity whose legitimacy cannot be regarded as unimpeachable, once I reject the absolutist/relativist dichotomy. As I see it, I can no longer justify my theory-production-and-sale on "objectivist" grounds—that is, by asserting that "our" task as theory makers is to formulate true, faithful-to-Reality theories, which we then press upon "the public," on the assumption that they will of course want to adopt these truest-to-date theories (because true theories are epistemologically and morally superior to less true ones). By the same token, I cannot be satisfied with a relativist shrug of the shoulders, and the assertion that, of course, we don't really have any "independent" reasons to promote or defend one theory over another, although, given our tradition, we'll of course prefer one over the other and will be motivated to share that theory with others, the way we share a favorite story.

If I am going to do philosophy, I want to do it, think about it, and describe it in ways that are neither foundationalist nor relativist. This paper explores one possible way, a way entered through the kitchen.

Cooking is an activity that is somewhat foreign to the Western epistemological tradition, especially in the twentieth century, in which discussions of theory have come to be framed almost exclusively in terms of scientific models. I'm not a scientist, but I am a cook, and my familiarity with cooking methods and language allows me to speak with more knowledge and flexibility about this activity than about science.

That's one reason I've chosen to talk about cooking. Another reason is this: the activities that fall under the category of "cooking" manifest qualities that I want manifested in my philosophizing.

Simply put, I think cooking is a kind of inquiry. I take my cue here in part from John Dewey, who defines inquiry as "the controlled or directed transformation of an indeterminate situation into one that is so determinate in its constituent distinctions and relations as to convert the elements of the original situation into a unified whole" (1938: 104–5). Such a definition certainly encompasses cooking. Furthermore, I follow Dewey in eschewing the strict dichotomy between theory—the "knowledge gaining" activity—and practice—the "getting-things-done" activity. These are not two separate domains of human life, but two interrelated, interdependent domains. The difference is one of degree, not kind: "One is the pushing, slam-bang act-first-and-think-afterwards mode, to which events may yield as they give way to any strong force. The other mode is wary, observant, sensitive to slight hints and intimations" (1958: 314). For Dewey, the paradigm example of a discipline that had "completely surrendered the separation of knowing and doing" was science (1929: 79). I don't think this claim can still be made about the sciences, if indeed it ever could. For, whatever it may be that scientists do, the way in which most philosophers talk about science renders it a most abstract and theoretical activity, one in which "practice" is assigned a decidedly inferior role.

Cooking doesn't suffer from this problem—at least certain kinds of cooking don't.[2] In it, the theoretical and the practical work together in an activity that genuinely does justice to Dewey's definition of inquiry. I want to speak in praise of the practical. Cooking is a vehicle that allows me to do so.

I must stress here that I'm not using cooking and recipes simply as analogies to, or metaphors for, philosophical or scientific inquiry and theory. Certainly my account of recipes can be regarded as a metaphor. But it is something more and other than that. It is a philosophical investigation of the nature of cooking—cooking being an activity that has yet to be so investigated. I am considering cooking *qua* inquiry, if you will.

This suggests yet another reason I've chosen to discuss cooking. It has never really been the subject of philosophical consideration (Plato's discussion of pastry cooking notwithstanding). This is at least partly due to the fact that cooking is a "woman's activity," like child rearing. Traditionally, Western philosophers have regarded such women's activities to be philosophically irrelevant; they have defined them out of existence, rendered them invisible, and described them through their silence. They have done so by constructing categories that consider and account for only (certain) men's activities. Activities like cooking and child rearing turn out to look trivial on traditional philosophical accounts because they don't fit into any philosophical categories. In exploring cooking, I want to begin to remove this curse of irrelevance under which it has lain and to begin to illuminate its philosophical significance.

Even as my account is a philosophical investigation of cooking, it is also my intention that it enhances and expands the ways in which we do philosophical theory. To be succinct: I am using the tools and language of philosophy to investigate a particular set of human practices. In turn, I intend for my investigation of those practices to have an impact upon philosophy.

My exploration of cooking tends to focus on the construction and use of recipes. I'll look at five aspects of recipes and recipe-cook relationships and shall show how each aspect can illuminate our thinking about theorizing. First, I briefly explore some of the ways cooks create recipes. I then consider the forms or systems under which people collect them. Next, I turn to the focus of my account: an explanation of how cooking, because of the relationships that obtain between cook, recipe, and ingredients, escapes both absolutism and relativism. In relation to this, I consider the issue of flexibility: how do I-the-cook determine how flexible a recipe is? I conclude with a discussion of flops in the kitchen.

Anti-essentialism in the Kitchen: Creating Recipes

Cooks create new recipes and experiment with old familiar ones for all sorts of reasons— to enter contests, to use up a bit of leftover something, to experiment with tastes, to secure their job, to play. It's important, I think, to recognize that there is *no one* reason people experiment in the kitchen. I may be faced with economic necessity—I have only cornmeal and a little dried-up cheese in the house, and no money for groceries. I may be feeling playful—I have an afternoon free, a full cupboard, and the urge to make something gorgeous and delicious. Or I may have a set of job demands to meet—I have sixty people to serve on a limited budget and am required to meet certain stipulated dietary requirement.[3] Furthermore, any two people respond to a particular demand in different ways; a fun, exciting challenge to you may be a tedious exercise in battling miserliness to me.

Perhaps you might argue that, although I might be motivated—or compelled—to come up with a new recipe for a variety of context-dependent reasons, this does not deny that there is still a general, overarching, *aim* in experimenting in the kitchen, namely to produce some *food*. But in fact this is not always the case. Sometimes food is a sort of accidental byproduct of the experiment, second in importance to some other aim. Sometimes, for example, the experimenter herself may never actually *make* the food for which she's created a recipe; I've heard of cases in which people won contests with recipes they've never tried. And even in the many cases where creating some food is the aim, a variety of not-necessarily-related things may count as fulfilling that aim. Making a special surprise dish for someone's birthday is quite a different thing from making a filling food that can be prepared in ten minutes and will serve 100.

I stress the fact that cooks create recipes for a variety of reasons, because I think this observation is helpful for thinking about epistemological inquiry and theorizing. It seems to me that there isn't one central reason, or type of reason, people come up with new theories or modify existing ones. My sense is that theories, like recipes, are most usefully regarded as tools we use to do things. The range of things that we may do with them is at least as broad as the range of things one may do with recipes. I may develop a theory to help myself tolerate a situation in which I find myself, or to explain to myself and others a set of experiences I've had. I may take up and modify a theory in order to help me develop a relationship with another person or persons. I may create a theory in order to have something to write about in a paper for a class.

Granting my claim that people create theories for many reasons, you might still want to ask me, is a theory like a recipe in that, when it *is* implemented, a "product" results? In thinking about theories in relation to recipes, I was initially quite troubled by this question. I couldn't seem to come up with something that was the *theory* equivalent of *food*—that all theories *produced* when they were implemented. I toyed with the suggestion that all theory aims at improving our ability to get on in the world or at establishing relationships in the world. But this seemed obviously false. It may be regarded as a good "product" of theory, but surely not the only good product, and definitely not the only product. But then I flipped the problem over; I realized that what I had taken to be an obvious general fact about the creation of recipes—namely that their creators are all *ultimately* interested in making food in some unambiguously essential sense of the word—is simply not a fact and that, as I said above, food doesn't always even result when someone creates a recipe.

My conclusion from all of this is that perhaps we might want to say that the "product" of theorizing is some sort of relationship or practice in the world, but that such a claim has no more value as an essentialist claim about theorizing than the claim that the "product" of creating a recipe is food.[4]

Some people "never use a recipe," by which they mean that they never look at a cookbook and perhaps never do the same thing twice, while other people religiously follow a recipe no matter what they're cooking and how often they've made it. The way you treat written recipes often reflects your degree of skill and confidence as a cook, your spirit of adventure, your knack for imagining what foods might taste good together. Blending flavors in creative and artful ways requires you to be sensitive to those flavors, to know which ones "like" each other and which ones don't. It also requires a spirit of adventure, the derring-do to mix together two ingredients that normally aren't thought to go together. And it requires the expertise to know when enough is enough: when a rule cannot be broken or bent, or when adding another ingredient will upset the balance of flavors you've constructed.

The level of cooking at which dramatic-and-daring experimentation goes on is a level perhaps few of us reach. In order to be good at it, you must understand the foods with which you're experimenting; you need to know what temperatures they can withstand, how they react with other foods, how much of them is needed to produce a particular result. This kind of knowledge is difficult and time-consuming to obtain. It's also extremely rewarding and useful, for it allows you to create wonderful foods, and it enables you to be flexible in the face of a nearly-empty refrigerator.

So it is with theorizing. It's relatively easy to take up a theory, whole-cloth, and use it. But to do so is to run the heavy risk of being irrelevant, harmful, or destructive. To do useful theory, I think it is necessary to explore and experiment, to know extremely well the things with which you're inquiring. It's necessary in inquiry in a way that it may not be in cooking, for whereas in cooking a failure to experiment leaves you with a boring diet, in theorizing, it makes you into an arrogant, unperceptive inquirer.

A Browser's Guide to Recipe Collections

Recipes get collected into all sorts of books and files, organized under myriad systems and anti-systems, by people with any number of motives for collecting them, profit or personal use. Go to any large best-seller bookstore, and you'll find at least three rows of cookbooks. There are general cookbooks that will instruct you in the rudiments of preparing anything from a boiled egg to a roasted armadillo (Rombauer & Rombauer 1977: 516). Then there are cookbooks devoted to recipes for a single kind of food or for food of a single ethnicity. Others feature recipes for special diets—low sodium, gluten-free, sugar-free, vegetarian. There are cookbooks put out by civic organizations and churches, containing their members' favorite recipes. And then there are the recipe files, recipe drawers, recipe boxes of individual cooks. These, if they are organized, are done so on the basis of the particular idiosyncrasies of that cook and the eaters for whom they normally cook. (My mom has separate bundles of recipes, housed in plastic strawberry boxes, for recipes containing either rhubarb or dried apricots, two of my family's favorite foods.)

Most recipe collectors have stacks of recipes—in cookbooks, copied out of magazines, clipped out of newspapers—that they've never tried. Collecting and exchanging recipes, and imagining what they might be like if I made them, is an activity that takes up as much of my time as cooking does.

I think of philosophical theorizing as collecting, trading, developing, using, adapting, and discarding recipes/theories. I collect ideas from various sources. Some of them I try—and some of these I keep and modify for use again. Others I talk and think about, the way I talk about what a recipe might taste like and how long it might take to prepare. They don't become a part of my theoretical/practical life but hover in the wings, waiting for a situation in which they might be useful.

Sometimes, when I'm thinking about theorizing, I see myself as trying to write an epistemological cookbook—not *the* epistemological cookbook, mind you, but a largish volume that attempts to provide ways to think about a wide variety of issues.

In developing and passing out epistemological cookbooks, I include recipes on which I'd stake my reputation—I'm not going to abdicate responsibility in the event of their failure but will try to discover why it occurred and to think of ways to fix it. Nonetheless, some of them might fail.

I connect the recipes in my cookbook in a systematic way, but I don't pretend that they are the only sorts of recipes one would ever need, or that this system is the only system under which they could be organized. There are at least as many varieties of philosophical systems as there are cookbook organizing schemes. And, as with cookbooks, it would be misguided to believe that one system only is sufficient or useful or reliable—that only one system could or should be used to organize theories.

You could use my epistemological cookbook exclusively—many cooks swear that all they need is a copy of Julia Child—but I would advise against such exclusivity. Better that my recipes be used as part of a larger collection or that certain of them be selected and modified for use in your cookbook. They are my recipes, filled with the idiosyncrasies of my life. I cannot imagine that they would prove universally useful to anyone else. (They aren't even that for me.)

Out of the Frying Pan *and* the Fire: Avoiding Absolutism and Relativism

A recipe is a description or explanation of how to do something—specifically, how to prepare a particular kind of food. As such, it does not present itself as *the* way to make that food—the opinion of some cooks notwithstanding—nor does it suggest that this food is the food to eat—the opinion of some eaters notwithstanding. Consider theorizing in this light: imagine developing and exchanging theories the way you create a recipe and share it with a friend. What would such theorizing be like?

On the "recipe plan" of theory/recipe development and exchange I, as theorizer, do not (generally) assert that the project I take up must be taken up by others. On a "recipe plan" I-the-theorist don't set an absolutist agenda of things that you-the-other-theorist must work on. Rather, I present issues that I find important and suggest reasons that you may also. Likewise, I cannot assert that anyone who does choose to take up this project must approach it using the same methods I use. All I can do is offer my approach, explaining why I found it useful.

I think of pieces of philosophical theory created on the recipe plan as if/then statements: If you find this project compelling, then you might find this approach useful. "Do you like asparagus? It's really inexpensive right now. You might like to try the recipe I have for asparagus soup."

This way of thinking about theorizing, and about how to offer theories to others, is not absolutist. But, while it avoids absolutism, doesn't it send me sliding into relativism? Nothing I've said so far seems to *prevent* it. After all, if anyone is free to select problems "at random," and if no one must proceed in any particular way using any particular strategy, then haven't I simply asserted (in the now-famous words of an infamous philosopher of science) that anything goes? I think this is not the case. Let me explain why.

Recipes allow cooks to vary their preparation techniques and to fiddle with the ingredient list. Some recipes permit considerably more fiddling than others, but virtually all of them have their breaking point. I can make equally wonderful chocolate chip cookies either by dumping all the ingredients in a bowl at the same time and stirring them together, or by first mixing butter and sugar together, and then adding eggs one at a time. Chocolate chip cookie dough is extremely resilient; when I mix the ingredients for it, almost anything *can* go and they'll still turn out. If I attempted the same sort of radical variation in technique when I was making puff pastry, I'd probably produce all sorts of interesting food products, but only some of them would resemble puff pastry.

Similarly, some recipes allow me to substitute, to add or delete items, while others "demand" rigid adherence to their ingredient list. You can toss in anything from nuts to cheese to herbs when making bread, but if you're making Scotch shortbread, you dare not change a single ingredient. (If you add raisins to shortbread, one cookbook warns, you may make something delicious. But it won't be shortbread.) I should point out here that many kinds of reasons may fuel a demand for adherence to a recipe. The example I've given is of a case in which the "historical integrity" of the product rests on the integrity of the ingredient list. In other cases, changing an ingredient might not only destroy the integrity, it might actually render the product inedible.

Here, then, is the basis for my assertion that the recipe plan is not relativist: once you decide to make a certain food—take on a certain philosophical problem—some methods of proceeding will be closed to you, because of the nature of the project. The number and nature of those limitations will vary according to the project you've chosen, but almost any project will have its limits. Similarly, the ingredients (aspects of the world) you select will be restricted because of the project you've chosen—again, in degrees that vary with the project. In other words, while it may be true that there is no cherry pie that is more cherry pie than any other, it is also true that certain things just aren't cherry pies; recipes are not infinitely flexible.

I'd also suggest that the recipe plan avoids relativism at an earlier stage: my initial *choice* of recipes is not simply the result of personal whim combined with tradition. Certainly these factors come into play; I choose to make certain foods because I grew up eating them, and I'm very fond of them. But other concerns influence my choice as well; health/nutrition and environmental concerns restrict the range of foods I prepare. These concerns may well transcend the narrow limits of gastronomy and enter the realm of morality; my decision about the foods I eat is shaped by my concern for the environment and my concern about the labor and investment practices of the companies that produce my food. None of these concerns binds me, but once I choose (or am enjoined) to pay attention to them, my subsequent food choices are affected. If I decide to become a vegetarian, I will have to give up the chicken I now eat.

In describing recipes as non-relativist, I've been drawing a picture of nested concerns-and-suggestions; I've suggested that selecting a particular moral stance might restrict the recipes I use, while selecting a particular recipe might restrict the ingredients and methods I use to execute it. At no level have I labeled something as "imperative," because in the strongest sense of that word, *nothing* is imperative. There are some rules that we might call absolute—such as the rule that you boil all water that comes from an untested source or the rule that you do not pour boiling water on yeast—but if you look back a step, you find that even these imperatives rest upon choices, choices so universally made in favor of one alternative rather than another that we almost stop thinking of them as choices. The demand that you boil water assumes that you are interested in preserving your life—that you don't want to get parasites or any of the other things you can get from water these days. And the demand that you do not pour boiling water on yeast assumes that you want the yeast to live—that the reason you're using yeast in the first place is that you want your bread to rise.

Me and My Recipe: Understanding the Relationship

I've described recipes as flexible to varying degrees. One question that arises from this kind of description is, when faced with a new recipe, how do I go about determining how flexible it is? How do I determine what I can and can't do to it? Learning the limits on a recipe is part of what is involved in learning to be a cook. It's a *self-reflective* process, because in order for me to determine the spirit in which I should receive a set of instructions, I must know what kind of an operator I am—how I tend to work with ingredients and so on. Ultimately, I must determine how I and the recipe work together—how I am to interpret the instructions given by the writer of the recipe.

Let me be more specific. In assessing the flexibility of a recipe/theory, it's often important to consider its source—the person or institution from whom I received the recipe. Why have they given the instructions the way they have? Is it really necessary that I do step B before proceeding to step C? If my mom gave me a recipe, she's no doubt stripped the instructions to the bare minimum, even leaving out steps she knows I'll know to do. On the other hand, if I use a recipe from the 4-H cookbook that I got when I was nine, I know that I can eliminate about half the steps immediately ("Ask your mother if you can use the oven").

On a related note, the tone in which a rule is issued need not be the tone in which you receive it. Sometimes the recipe writer tells you it's absolutely necessary to use this particular ingredient or method. The experienced cook will realize that this is the preference of the author speaking or a marketing ploy being used by the Kraft corporation to get you to use Parkay margarine. The more I know about the recipe giver, the more able I'll be to assess the relevance of their instructions for me.

Pie crust makers are notorious for issuing *commands* when they give out recipes: they insist that only shortening X will produce a light, flaky piecrust. Sometimes shortening X is lard, sometimes it's Crisco, and sometimes it's Another Vegetable Shortening. Having made a lot of piecrusts in the last ten years, I can say quite confidently that it doesn't matter one whit what you use. Unless you're motivated by additional dietary concerns, lard and vegetable shortening work equally well. But recognizing this fact— and recognizing that what looked like imperatives were actually personal preferences— was something I was able to do only when I had enough experience to formulate my own judgment.

This propensity to command that you often find in recipe givers suggests that it's important to learn how to assess the motives of the recipe giver. In my Kraft example, it's obvious that the giver has something to gain by issuing a rule as if it were a command; they'll sell more Parkay margarine. In other instances, it may not be so obvious why someone tells you to do something a specific way—but it's important to try to figure out. (There's an old joke about a family in which two generations of women cut the end of their roasts before roasting them "because Mom did it that way." And why did the original Mom do it that way? Because her roasting pan was too small.)

In general, when I receive a recipe, the more I know about the recipe giver, the better the position I'll be in to assess the relevance *for me* of their instructions. And, when I'm in the position of giving out recipes, the more I take into account my recipient, the more I attempt to give information that is sensitive to their level of experience, the better off my recipient will be.

Let me reiterate this point specifically in terms of theories. In interpreting the theories of others, it is vitally important that I understand the motives driving those "others." How is it that they have come to pay attention to this issue? What do they stand to gain from issuing that rule as an absolute demand? Why do they leave out entirely any discussion of that concern in their theory? Developing such an understanding is important, and it can be very difficult. Sometimes it may well be that the person who created the theory wishes to conceal certain ulterior motives from me-the-recipient. Examples of this phenomenon include political theories through which those in positions of power mystify those whom they oppress in order to ensure the continuance of their power.

In cases where such willful concealment is being employed, no easy access to the theorist's motives is available. But, although that theorist may not volunteer information about their motives, it may be possible to get that information through other means. In such a situation, I would suggest that it is of particular importance to investigate the other's motives, for it is precisely in such situations where ignorance can leave you disempowered.[5]

When Recipes Fail (or When We Do)

Recipes are usually tested by someone—your grandmother or the Betty Crocker test kitchen worker—and the tester often offers some sort of promise that the recipe will work for you. (This promise varies considerably in formality—and effusiveness—depending upon its source.) Despite this promise, the recipe may not work, for all sorts of reasons. Perhaps the food turns out just as the recipe "intended" it to, but you find out that in fact you don't like tripe. Or perhaps you live in a place where climatic or other conditions cause different dietary concerns to come into play, and this food doesn't fill the requirements.

On the other hand, maybe the recipe really doesn't turn out as it was intended to, because you haven't established a working relationship with the recipe; as I've suggested, learning how to read a recipe involves learning what kind of relationship obtains between you-the-cook and this recipe (and its author). In instances where the recipe doesn't work, perhaps you've used techniques or ingredients or are working under conditions (like high altitude) that differ from those used by the recipe creator in ways that this recipe can't tolerate. So the recipe/cook team fails. Or it succeeds in a totally unexpected way (lousy popovers, but great edible tennis balls.)

This kind of failure may be overcome by *thoughtful practice*; by following the recipe more literally, perhaps, and introducing variations only when you've achieved the results you desire; by asking the recipe creator for a more detailed explanation of how to do whatever it is they're telling you to do; or by asking someone else for suggestions about how they would proceed.

The recipe-cook team might also fail because of a poorly tested recipe or a recipe that leaves out an ingredient or instruction. In such cases, fixing the problem might be extremely difficult, especially if you cannot consult the person who wrote the recipe but are left to unravel the problem on your own. And again, the recipe creator might intentionally leave something out, or might deliberately obscure the instructions, in order to guarantee your failure and ensure the "superiority" of their cooking skills.

To describe these *recipe* failures in *theory* terms, I'd suggest that it won't do to treat theorizing as an activity in which I, the disinterested, semi-omniscient theory creator, unveil a set of universally applicable laws about a bunch of mute, lifeless Stuff of the Universe. Nor is it useful to think that I, the theory recipient, can simply take up someone else's theory as is, follow its unambiguous, universally applicable instructions, and unproblematically apply it to the "same" phenomena they were exploring.

With respect to the former assertion, that theorizing is not the one-sided activity of a detached subject, think about making bread. The dough responds to your warm hands' kneading action, and you learn to respond to it, to know when you've kneaded it long enough and when to add more flour. It's an activity that depends upon a connection between bread maker and bread dough. This relationship takes time to develop; the first time you make bread, it may well turn out dry or holey because you haven't yet figured out how to read the messages the dough is giving. Reciprocal responses characterize things that exist in relation to each other, that can affect and be affected by each other. When I use a recipe, I enter into a kind of relation with the ingredients. I do not assume complete separateness from them, nor total power over them.

I think the same claim can be made, to some degree, about any kind of inquiry-activity. It's most obviously true of theorizing with ("about") other people. And, although it is yet to be shown, I'm willing to believe that the same will be true of even the hardest of "hard sciences."[6]

With respect to the latter assertion about the way to approach someone else's theory, I'm suggesting that it is useful to ask the giver about the conditions that prompted the development of a particular theory. Trying to see how their experiences relate to mine, how they challenge and conflict with mine, and how their theory fits with or contrasts to mine enables me to create useful, successful, helpful theories. At the center of this activity stands always a relation between me and the other theorizer. The more developed this relation, the better equipped am I to modify and implement their theory.

What I've given in this paper is, I suggest, a little methodological cookbook. In it, I've offered a collection of some ways to go about doing philosophical theory. I offer them as tested products and as parts of an integrated system. Further tests may prove them wrong or unhelpful or misleading, and I may have to throw out some recipes. But I issue them in good, provisionally foundational faith.

13

The Recipes of Genius on *Chef's Table*

Rafi Grosglik and David Kyle

Talent hits a target no one else can hit;
Genius hits a target no one else can see.
—Arthur Schopenhauer ([1819]1958)

Introduction

Although recipes for food preparation—the forms according to which dishes should be prepared—are the main means of communication about food in contemporary culture, they seem somewhat incongruous with the Zeitgeist of "creative economies" and the genius creators said to be at the center of them for the first two decades of the twenty-first century. In the realm of restaurant and professional kitchens, recipes, as such, are largely absent from the overt discourse of culinary creativity and from the public performance of elite and celebrity chefs (Leschziner 2015). An example of a discourse that praises the avoidance of using recipes can be seen in the first episode of the Netflix series *Chef's Table France*, when Anthony Beldroega, the Sous Chef of the three-star Michelin Parisian restaurant *L'Arpège*, says: "At *L'Arpège* we worked instinctively [...]. Nothing is written in recipes [...] this is the magic of *L'Arpège*." Alain Passard, a French chef and the owner of *L'Arpège*, asserts that no recipes are required. "At *L'Arpège* there aren't any kitchen notebooks. I've never written down a recipe. We don't record anything. We don't write anything down." However, this does not mean that there is no use of formulas in elite cuisine.

One can think of a recipe as "a code" or an "algorithm" within which a certain composition of ingredients, techniques for changing the molecular structure of those ingredients, and methods of serving them operate as the basis for different versions of a particular dish. Philosopher Andrea Borghini (2015) differentiates between the notions "recipe" and "dish"—which are often used interchangeably. According to him, a dish is the *stuff* (or matter), and a recipe is the *idea* (or the mind beyond matter) that "comprise the repeatable aspects of a dish whose replication would deliver a dish of the same sort" (Borghini 2015: 722). This chapter explores our beliefs in the amalgam of *talent creativity, artistic formation, spiritual inspiration, leadership, and scientific precision* seemingly required for making complex dishes in the absence of recipes in the discourse of the elite culinary field. Following Borghini's distinction between "recipe" and "dish," we argue that the culinary discourse that evolves around elite cuisines, and the celebration of their creativity, is based on an implicit discourse revealing the recipes for the making of creator personas, the geniuses who eschew recipes or perhaps invent entirely new ones for others to emulate. *Chef's Table* (CT) is an award-winning Netflix series that provides a quintessential example of how creative chefs—who seemingly work without recipes—invoke prior "recipes" (or cultural scripts) of genius in Western cultural history. We use CT as a case study of how recipes of creative geniuses infuse the presentation of elements in the kitchen and beyond that serve to enchant rather than explain why recipes are anathema to nearly every chef portrayed.

First aired in 2015, CT documents the lives and creative methods of elite chefs. The show (including *Chef's Table Pastry* and *Chef's Table France*) was nominated seven times for the Emmy Award, twice in the category of Outstanding Documentary or Nonfiction Series. The sweeping cinematography and epic soundtrack of the show are considered by many to be as awe-inspiring as the beautiful novel dishes and strong personalities of the depicted chefs. Plated dishes are lovingly ogled by the camera in eye-popping close-ups at the climax of each episode. According to the overt message of the show, these dishes, in all their innovative glory, are the products of highly *imaginative* thinking at the hands of the most *creative* chefs on the planet. Viewers are invited to be awestruck by this imaginative process, which is clearly not about improving the cooking skills of its vast global audience.

CT does not fit entirely within recent or past food-television programing. This is not a cooking show in which one can find a hint of "try this at home," nor a reality-TV cooking program that focuses on culinary talent in the making. These genres entertain because we can imagine ourselves as viewers in the shoes of the protagonists finding and developing the talent and technique to work and excel in both domestic and professional kitchens. We, along with them, learn how to cook and how to be a cook. However, the viewers of CT are led to believe that they are *not* like the protagonist chefs and probably never will be—for they participate in something magical, supernatural, and ultimately unexplainable. Thus, it is not surprising that dishes seen in CT such as "Camouflage; Black Truffle Explosion," "Birth," "Textures of Wild Berries, Lemon Curd & Spruce Cake," "Swan Liver & Fermented Baked Milk," or "Sea Tastes" are not accompanied by recipes. We, the viewers, are not permitted to aspire to prepare these enchanted dishes, only to gaze upon them. It's an inspiration to worship the magic, but not a calling to "try it at home." Hence, one will not find in CT even a hint of instructions on how to grow, buy, prepare the ingredients (many of which are extremely rare) or cooking principles, nor any clear "recipe telling" (Matwick & Matwick 2014) or televised cooking demonstrations. The show explicitly asserts that the chefs profiled represent a creative talent *beyond* the majority of us. The nature of this extreme "culinary talent" presented as culinary *genius*, and its ability to invoke "awe," is the subject of this chapter. As we discuss below, the hallmark of "the genius" is the inability to explain what they do through any conventional known process, or recipe, primarily because there is often no evidence of one in the normal sense, something "geniuses" themselves often assert.

Drawing on content analysis, we interpreted the spoken dialogues and the visual aspects of all thirty-four episodes comprising the show. We aim to understand and explain how the experience of watching the spectacular dishes, images, and narratives of the protagonist chefs in the show resonates with the sociological structure of contemporary creative meritocratic capitalism (Littler 2018). Put differently, we would like to understand how CT puts into form the inarticulate social experience ("structure of feeling," to use the terminology of Raymond Williams [1973]) of faith in creativity, and the fascination of *the most* creative, *the most* talented—the genius of any social field. For that purpose, we conducted a thematically open coding process (Strauss & Corbin 1997) in which all elements in the episodes—televised techniques, soundtrack, cooking procedures, narratives, and biographical information of the participants— were analyzed. We transcribed in detail the content of each episode as well as closely read the language and discursive strategies used by the participants of the show. With this corpus in hand, we then interrogated our categorized notes and brought them to bear on our argument on how "culinary creative talents" and the creative process (creativity) are depicted. During this process, we began tracing the ways in which traits of "culinary genius" were associated with the narratives, scenes, and even music from beginning to end. Of particular interest were the ways in which the protagonist chefs reflexively describe themselves in retrospective vignettes and statements chosen by the producers. We then identified the major cultural themes that inform the show: (1) the interrelated depictions of dishes, cooking processes (creativities), and exceptional talents; (2) a depiction of chef biographies as a series of milestone revelations of challenges and realization of their exceptional talents, even genius; and (3) the use of food and cooking to present a manifestation of the archetypical genius or "recipes for genius."

We begin our analysis with a review of the historical meanings and roles of genius and how its evolution as an idea tracks the four distinct "recipes of genius" organizing our findings below.

Genius and Its Variations

The "mystique of genius," namely the idea of the existence of innate and distinct individual qualities and a ranking of "brains," is a centuries-old belief (McMahon 2013). The worship of genius in the twenty-first century pales in comparison to past hero worship, but nevertheless continues to signal many of the same features of past geniuses lodged in the (Western) cultural psyche. Sociologist Andreas Reckwitz (2017) points out that "genius" (or "creative stars") are those able to present aesthetic novelty and distinguish themselves from "ordinary" individuals. Contemporary "creative stars," according to him, masterfully perform and operate according to the cultural imperative of creative aestheticization. Another fork in the road in the late 1700s was the opposite: the social construction of the creative genius as master of the imagination without following any aesthetic codes, roles, or recipes.

As cultural logic developed over centuries with layers of meanings taken on or discarded in every era, there is no singular model (or recipe) for genius. The notion of "the genius" includes a repertoire of types fitting the notion "creative imagination," which emerged from its religious foundations and later became central to secular cultural political life (Engell 1981). This ideology of genius as master of imagination and innovation can be viewed in CT as constructed into four "recipes of genius" (or ideal types in the Weberian sense) and implied by the protagonist chefs: *the saint, the inspired artist, the executive officer,* and *the scientific industrialist.*

Each of these archetypes of genius contains similes originating in successive eras of the social history of the genius construct. The "recipe" of the saint genius chef draws from the traits of what scholar Alon Goshen-Gottstein calls "religious genius," referring to the ability of certain people to bring about new understanding of reality through religious traditions. Religious geniuses are those who are grounded in awareness of a broader existential dimension, have deep understanding of "the secrets of the cosmos" (nature, God, and the spiritual life), and lead processes of personal and social transformations (Goshen-Gottstein 2017: 12–13). The second "recipe" of culinary genius that we identified in CT is related to the "artistic genius," in the Kantian sense. According to this archetype, the artistic genius is a highly gifted individual whose work may exert influence upon "lesser artists" (Murray 2007). Another element of the artistic genius as an icon of Romanticism is related to a deep appreciation for nature and the ideology that artist geniuses "[unite] transcendental philosophy with a philosophy of nature," as indicated in the work of philosopher Friedrich Schelling (Engell 1981: 301). The other two dominant archetypes of culinary genius are less overtly spiritual—these are fully secular saints with nonetheless unexplainable superhuman powers: the "executive officer," who is endowed with leadership abilities of military acumen and the bureaucratic management of people, and the "scientific industrialist" who represents the "marriage of business and genius" (McMahon 2013: 200). The latter is embodied in the mystique of people such as Henry Ford and Thomas Edison, and the former is grounded in the romantic similes of the genius as an oracle of his people with Napoleon as the iconic figure (McMahon 2013).

The following sections describe these four "recipes of genius" as presented and embodied in the chefs profiled in CT, followed by a discussion section offering the cultural and political meanings of the new emergence of a discourse on genius within the realm of gastronomy and beyond.

The Saint Genius

The quintessential representation of the genius as a saint—namely a creator of "spiritual dishes" (who is also "an instrument" of the Creator her-/himself)—can be seen in the depiction of the Buddhist nun Jeong Kwan. Kwan is portrayed as a talented cook who, unlike all the other protagonist chefs in the show, does not own a restaurant and has never had formal culinary training.

When she was seventeen, she joined the Jogye Order of Korean Buddhism and resided in Baegyangsa Temple, where she discovered her calling of spreading dharma (cosmic law and order and the Buddhist "right way of living") through cooking. According to the narrative of the episode, Kwan refers to food in traditional-collective meanings, as materials that are based on philosophy, cooking methods, and even ingredients literally created generations ago: "Soy beans, salt and water, [should be kept together] in harmony, through time […]. They are heirlooms […]. By making soy sauce, I am reliving the wisdom of my ancestors." However, the narrative of the episode asserts that we should not be fooled by this traditional ethos—Kwan should be considered a first-rate creative chef. As celebrity French chef Éric Ripert says in the episode: "Jeong Kwan is very spontaneous in her cooking. At the same time, she keeps a certain tradition, but she breaks a lot of rules." Though Ripert's presumed assumption is that the culinary creativity of a genius chef could be expressed by "tradition" or by "breaking the rules" (in the modern Western sense), Kwan doesn't view herself, or her actions, primarily as either one of these: "It's been almost half a century since I entered this way. I did it in pursuit of enlightenment. I am not a chef. I am a monk," she says. "Just as water springs from a fountain, creativity springs from every moment."

Kwan's products—her dishes and recipes—are not only an outcome of creative assemblages of a data set of culinary information, but they are the product of wisdom and self-introspection, of a deep insight into spiritual reality. In her words: "If you look into yourself, you see past, present, and future. You see that time revolves endlessly […]. You must be able to freely move in and out of your mind […]. There is no way you can't open up your creativity." Theologist Alon Goshen-Gottstein argues that the knowledge of those he named religious geniuses is different in its essence from the (secular and scientific) ego-bound knowledge. The knowledge of religious geniuses—and therefore also their talents and skills—are always "grounded in humility, in the transcendence of the self" (Goshen-Gottstein 2017: 14). The portrayal of Kwan echoes this commentary several times in the episode. She says: "creativity and ego cannot go together […] You must not be your own obstacle. You must not be owned by the environment you are in. You must own the environment, the phenomenal world around you. […] There is no ego to speak of. That is my belief."

Throughout several episodes of CT, this essence of the genius saint "who owns the environment" is signified and invoked through images and utterances related to nature. In the episode on Kwan it is expressed by a depiction of her alleged intimate connections to nature; her own entity is part of nature itself, sublimated to "the *whole*" (whatever that is for her).

While Kwan represents the ideal type of the genius saint (namely a member of a religious order), other chefs are portrayed in similar but more covert ways as *secular* saints, the very definition of genius historically (McMahon 2013). For example, the episode on Slovenian chef Ana Roš evokes a "flavor" that ranges from magical-fantasyland-wizardry to spiritual sainthood without the trappings of religiosity.

Slovenia itself is perceived as having a kind of fairyland mystique, although what it lacks, according to the episode, is a culinary reputation. Roš, the chef and the co-owner of Hiša Franko (a restaurant in Kobarid, Slovenia, which is on the list of the World's 50 Best Restaurants), managed to do the impossible: she put Slovenian cuisine on the world's gastronomy map. "Slovenia is a very little-known country," says Alexander Lobrano, a writer in *Saveur* magazine on the background of captivating shots of fields, rivers, and mountains with breathtaking wide-angle shots. The point is clear: the producers of the episode aim to portray Roš's restaurant as nestled in a sort of Shangri-la and to describe Roš herself as a culinary prodigy who works nothing short of a miracle. "What you get here," says Lobrano referring to Roš's restaurant, "is the thrill of going somewhere completely unexpected that you can't imagine." He also says: "Her genius in the kitchen is that she knows exactly how to take all these different Slovenian traditions, and she tweaks them to make them modern. There's a Wizard of Oz quality [in Hiša Franko]." Later in the episode he continues: "[Roš] has this particular genius with the unexpected. She'll have these totally off-the-wall combinations of things." As he speaks, the viewers are exposed to close-up shots of Roš's hands preparing one of her dishes named "Squid with Lamb Sweetbreads, Black Garlic and Cave Cheese." "Everything [in this dish] is accentuated," he says. "One thing blends into another, and you're almost at a loss as to how to explain how has this happened [...]. Where does that genius come from?"

The narrative of fantasyland, as well as the framing of the restaurant and the dishes as miraculous, serve more than a stage within which Roš performs as both the wise Wizard of OZ and the wide-eyed Alice (from Alice in Wonderland). It is a setting that symbolizes the mysterious and mythical place from which genius-saints come. These depictions suggest that Roš is actually channeling nature—the nature of Slovenia, which is already framed as magical.

In reflecting on both of these episodes, what connects Kwan and Roš is the way we, the viewers, are led to believe that they represent a category of chef with an ability to conjure up a supernatural reality, which is not clouded by institutions, greed, mediocrity, irrationality, mundane ugliness, or stress, through a strong belief in an inner ability to communicate with nature.

The Inspired Artist Genius

While the previous "recipe of genius" emphasized an otherworldly source of creativity with an equally otherworldly goal of salvation, the artist genius recipe is a subtle but critical variation: it retains much of the same elements of divinity, but without the overt reference to God or any religious milieu. Instead, a central theme in this archetype is *freedom* and the Romantic movement's construction of "the artists" as those who are freely and passionately pursing their dreams, a pursuit that is often depicted as "divine inspiration" or "their genius" (Pearsall 1925: 95–114).

Massimo Bottura is a renowned Italian chef who runs Osteria Francescana, a three-Michelin-star restaurant located in Modena, Italy. The episode on Bottura portrays him as the quintessential artist genius acclaimed for his freedom and ability to interpret traditional recipes and use traditional ingredients "in a way that no one else does." Bottura's personal story is narrated as one of an exceptional talent with an inborn hereditary quality, though, like many geniuses, unrecognized for many years. Leaving university before graduating, his culinary training with acclaimed French chef Alain Ducasse profoundly shaped his artistic "break-from-tradition" approach, a fact that made him feel like an outcast, as many considered him a "traitor" in the Italian culture of culinary conservatism. When he opened his own restaurant in his hometown of Modena, the local people were unimpressed. Eventually, he prevailed in becoming recognized as one of the most creative chefs in the world of elite fine dining.

Indeed, much of the episode is a sketch of Bottura through the eyes of Lara Gilmore, Bottura's spouse and business partner. We learn from her two important things about him, resonant with the features of the artist genius. First, no one can really understand his ideas. Even she, working and living with him every day, cannot fully understand him or "catch him," to use her words. "Massimo is someone you kind of have to chase. He's always ten steps ahead of you. He's running down the street, and you're in his shadow." Second, we learn from her that he chafes at anything that compromises his freedom—tradition, rules, and recipes. As such, the episode on Bottura is a celebration of unfettered freedom, even from the most basic social and culinary norms of Italian cuisine.

Bottura's ability to impose his taste and meanings is demonstrated in two long vignettes meant to convey his creative artistic genius; one involves an objet d'art of pigeon poop, and the other a lemon tart accidentally dropped on the kitchen floor. With regard to the former, Lara recalls:

> We were at the Venice Biennial [...] where you have all these great Italian artists. [We saw] these taxidermy stuffed pigeons, and Massimo says, "What are these pigeons doing here?" [...] And the closer we looked, you could see that he had also painted them, literally, pooping on the walls and on some of the other artists' artwork. Massimo was like, "That is genius! That guy is amazing! Those pigeons, that's like me. I'm trying to change the Italian cuisine, but the only way I'm going to get noticed is if I kind of go up in the rafters and look from above and, in a way, deface the generation that came before me. I'm gonna be that pigeon."

Indeed, Bottura is portrayed throughout the episode as free to fly above "the realm" of traditional Italian cuisine, free as a bird. "This artwork," says Lara, "somehow kind of made its way through the back door into the kitchen and really had a great influence on the way he thought through the recipes."

A second story that illustrates this highly subjective artistic framing: the story of how a dish entitled "Oops! I Dropped the Lemon Tart" became a menu item. With an orchestral swell in the background and a visual of Bottura and his sous-chef Taka Kondo working frantically, he describes what he did after Taka dropped one of the only two lemon tarts left, leaving half of it on the counter: "Taka want[ed] to kill himself [and] I said: 'Taka, stop, stop. Look through my fingers.'" As he tells this story, he waves his hands in the air, forming a square shape with his fingers, representing a picture frame.

> That is beautiful [Bottura told Taka]. Let's rebuild [the dish] as [if] it is a broken stuff. At first, he [Taka] didn't understand, but he trusts me so much and he said: "okay, let's try." So, we get the lemon sabayon [custard] and we spread it on the plate [...]. That was the moment in which we create "Oops! I Dropped the Lemon Tart."

Later in the episode, Lara sums up his genius as a form of artistic freedom, seemingly without regard to existing structures or measures: "Everything that comes to his mind gets thrown out there on the table immediately. There's no editing [...]. If I don't write down, take note, decode what the recipe is about, and find a way to make that accessible to other people, nobody's going to."

The episode on Virgilio Martínez, a celebrity chef and rising star in Peruvian gastronomy, represents another variation of the artist genius. Martínez is depicted in CT as a genius artist with a mysterious supernatural ability to intuit and interpret Peru's enormous biodiversity and varied culinary practices of the equally varied Indigenous cultures in distinct locales—from the Pacific coast up the volcanic Andes and back down to the Amazonian basin. His dishes are attempts to artistically translate bounded ecosystems onto the plate, as if they were beautiful, edible mini-terrariums.

In the episode, we see him hiking on mountain cliffs, kneeling on the banks of rivers, strolling along the pacific coast, or walking in a rainforest, but always engaged in what looks like a communing with nature with hardly a word spoken. He is seen, however, talking with Indigenous guides who pass on their "native knowledge of unknown plants [to him, to his diners, and presumably, to CT viewers]." This results in a dizzying array of elements, including pieces of bark from wild trees, scarce herbs, delicate mushrooms, craggy barnacles, roots, and rare fruits that he then artfully arranges back in his kitchen.

Martínez, who grew up in Lima in a sheltered upper-class family in one of the most unequal countries in the Americas, rarely experienced first-hand, like most of his wealthy patrons, the wealth of Peru's natural and cultural diversity. But when he began to venture out to discover this wealth, he realized that the Indigenous people he encountered were experiencing "the world in different levels and altitudes," contrary to "most people [who] see the world in horizontal way," to use his words. Later in the episode he says: "At Central [the name of his restaurant, located in Lima], we want to show you Peru in a vertical way." His genius, we learn, is to take the diner on a culinary journey that both brings Peru's verticality to life on the plate and simultaneously creates the illusion that he has also flattened the Peruvian class structure. Every dish is named by altitude and climate. Dishes such as "Altitude 860M | High Jungle," "Altitude 210M | Tambopata Jungle" or "Altitude 2190M | Solar Mucilage" (as written in his restaurant's menu and in the episode) reimagine and culturally launder a Peru nearly devoid of the social and class stratifications. Thus, his unbound creative imagination and his artistic reinterpretation of Peruvian nature and society transcend the concept of Peruvian cuisine (as well as the concept of cuisine in general).

The Executive-Officer Genius

The third archetype of a genius presented in CT conveys the traits of a leader—another important element in the historical definition of genius (McMahon 2013). In this "recipe for genius" we identified two variations: first, the charismatic genius military leader (Weber 1964: 361); and second, a genius leader with a more entrepreneurial facet (see, for example, Isaacson 2011).

The first version involves, as the name implies, the near supernatural power of geniuses to think strategically and creatively while bending the social institution to their will. This involves techniques of control over workers, the implementation of military organization and hierarchies in "bureaucratic vision," and "systematic" modes of production in business corporations (Shenhav 1999). Since the emergence of French gastronomy in the latter decades of the nineteenth century, the concept of the "head chef" (*chef de cuisine*) as the leader and the manager of modern kitchens has been established in public discourse and popular culture. Other common connotations include coach, maestro, and military-general (Fine 1996: 89–92; Fantasia 2018: 31).

In several episodes of the show—especially when male chefs are profiled—genius is associated with Napoleonic acumen in control in the midst of a battlefield, no less than by culinary skills or creative dishes and recipes. These commander geniuses are known for serving "masculine dishes," namely dishes that are constructed as a "declaration of ego," as observed by food writer Charlotte Druckman (2010). Tim Raue, considered to be "the best chef in Berlin," is portrayed as the quintessential commander genius in which his ego, and his alone, is the alpha and omega of the dining experience. In the episode he mentions that he realized that the meaning of "egocentric" is "you build your own universe in which you are the center point." In this regard, he says: "I'm egocentric and I'm proud of it," echoing one of the hallmarks of genius as the overwhelming desire and ability to create a world of their own and inhabit it (Robinson 2011).

Raue grew up in one of the poorest parts of Berlin; he had several abusive experiences and a life of juvenile delinquency. One step away from a life of prison, as he tells it, cooking school provided his way out with no particular calling. But there he discovered his cooking talent. The narrative of the episode suggests that he has a talent for cooking, indeed, but a genius for bending others to his will. His talent and creativity were forged in the ring with attributes to a life of contests and conflicts: aggressiveness, survival, ambition, and control. As presented in the episode, he is a fighter who constantly struggles to be at the top of any social hierarchy he inhabits. And to lead.

Much like entering the officer ranks, he became a "head chef" at the age of twenty-three, giving him an early "taste for power" and highlighting everything he's accomplished since. In one of the sequences of the episode he is seen entering his cavernous kitchen with dozens of staff at attention shouting "good morning Chef" in unison. He has clearly reached the highest echelons as a culinary commander. If this point was not already clear, by the end of the episode, Raue speaks in a way that Napoleon would appreciate: "I was the one who was standing in the front, announcing the orders, telling the others what to do and when to do it. I was the toughest, I was the strongest, I was leading the pack."

Another example of an executive-officer culinary genius, especially in its more entrepreneurial mode, is seen in the episode on Alex Atala, one of the most famous Brazilian chefs. Much more than his cooking techniques, dishes, or recipes, it seems as if the producers of this episode try to stun the viewers with the myriad of entrepreneurial initiatives in which Atala takes part. Besides being an acclaimed chef of a world-renowned fine-dining restaurant, he runs ATA—a venture he founded, which promotes food diversity and sourcing ingredients from local farmers. He also runs projects promoting the use of insects as gastronomic ingredients, he initiated and manages the production and marketing processes of Baniwa (a spice made from special peppers harvested by Indigenous people in the Amazon rainforest), and—if that were not enough—he directs projects dealing with marketing sustainable meat, local vanilla, and honey from native bees.

Just like other CT protagonists, he is outdoors much of the time. The viewers see him cruising in a motorboat one second, then jetting to a business enterprise, and in between—spearfishing, scuba diving, practicing martial arts, cutting his way through an Amazonian forest, slaughtering a wild duck, logging like a lumberjack, all the while making offhand comments about their possible culinary uses. While other protagonist chefs refer to the wilderness for inspiration and ingredients, we see Atala as dominating nature and his social world. The main theme here is distinctly one of raw power and charisma symbolizing rugged self-sufficiency and command.

Similar to other protagonist chefs in the show, the narrative of Atala's personal and professional story is told as a "walk through the valley of the shadow of death," a long struggle that turned to success (see also Ulver & Klasson 2018). In this case, Atala's success is the result of his decision, after years of working without appreciation for his special talent, to focus on Brazilian culinary traditions. At some point in his career he decided to "go to the forest, deep in the sea to understand the ingredient[s] better." The viewers are led to believe that his courage, adventurousness, determination, and self-resiliency are the traits that helped him create extraordinary dishes and recipes such as "Pirarucu [Amazonian river fish] with Manioc Flour [cassava flour], Tucupi [a sauce extracted from wild manioc root in Brazil's Amazon jungle, which is toxic before it is boiled] and Tapioca" or "The Amazonic Ant—Golden Amazonian Ants over a Coconut Meringue." These dishes convey similes of both Brazilian locale and culinary genius. But they can also be seen as representing existing inequalities between Atala—the genius chef who is capable of "translating" and "commodifying" Amazonian fauna, flora, and culture—and the Indigenous people and local food purveyors he employs in his ventures, those who would not have been able to distribute their foods without him paving their way to the global gastronomic world. As such, though his depiction in CT can be seen as purely colonial, it seems that the producers of the episode aim to portray Atala as both an entrepreneurial genius and a culinary leader.

The Industrial-Scientist Culinary Genius

Another "recipe for genius" presented in CT refers to the era in which the supernatural miracle-working powers of religious saints were transposed to the new democracies in the United States and Europe in the late eighteenth century, as part of the Protestant Reformation and the Industrial Revolution. Throughout the industrial age that followed (1760–1975), human activity was characterized by efforts to control nature in order to transform it into capital and the transformation of labor energy into matter and consumable goods (Marx [1867] 2000; Mintz 1996: 67–83). Industrial capitalism was also based on technological and bureaucratic efficiency (instrumental rationalization, according to the terminology of Max Weber), corporate rationalization (such as

Taylorism, "scientific management"), the mechanical organization of manufacturing standardized goods along a moving assembly line (Fordism), and the standardized organization of consumption. Within this emergence of universal standards of capital and labor, self-sufficiency shrank and artisanal production was replaced by heavy industry (Moulier-Boutang 2011: 101). Within the proliferation of industrial restaurant chains (especially "fast food" chains [Ritzer 1993]), the talent of artisans and small-scale food manufacturers began to be reevaluated and appreciated among affluent consumers (Paxson 2013). The episode on Nancy Silverton refers to these issues and epitomizes what we call the recipe of the industrial genius.

Although Silverton initiated, owned, and operated a mass-production bakery and owns an upscale Italian restaurant chain, a pizzeria, and a gelato and sorbetto company, she is portrayed in CT as a master artisan. She is depicted as having an extremely detail-oriented approach to baking and cooking. As seen in the episode, the most important "ingredients" in this "recipe of genius" are obsessiveness and passion.

The episode tells the story of a chef whose "claim to fame" is not for an artistic culinary style, but rather for casual dining. Chef Mario Batali, who serves as a culinary authority in the episode, describes her cooking style as: "different from a lot of the fancy Michelin star kind of chefs [...]. She does not need tricks [...] What does she do? Pizza, pasta and salad!" Later in the episode he says: "Why would anybody spend this much time making something like this, when all they do in Italy is put salt, yeast and water with some olive oil in the flour and just mix it all up? [...] Her pizza dough is almost anti-Italian. [...] Her recipe is incomprehensibly long. It's inefficiently long. It's ineffectively long."

At a superficial level, her genius is portrayed as the ability to create "simple-but-perfect" dishes. Her obsessiveness is depicted as an admired virtue, an unusual asset that results in a "creative-perfection" with overtones of scientific management. Notions such as "patience," "perfection," "keen to detail," and, of course, "obsession" are uttered repeatedly by her and other participants in the episode. Jonathan Gold, the late *Los Angeles Times* food critics, says: "When Nancy grabs hold of a problem, she does not let it go until it's solved [...] I suppose if it were under different circumstances, you'd call it OCD." Chef Mario Batali joins Gold's remarks: "Her obsession is her mantra. But she works so much on something. By repetition, a thousand and a thousand and a thousand and a thousand times over again. That level is very craftsmanship, not necessarily artistic."

Silverton's relationship to "perfection" is fundamentally different, we are led to believe, from the average talented artisan. The themes of perfection and obsession are articulated as less about hard work and more about the genius tortured by her own eternally receding creative horizons—even for a pizza. As Batali says in his blunt and infamous rhetoric: "It's a sickness. It's a twisted, inside-her-mind, Los-Angeleno-crazy-person thing. But the result is perfect." Later in the episode she describes the challenges of "governing" and "controlling" natural ingredients (yeasts, water, salt, flour, and the like) molding them into novel inventions that have no resting point or stasis. "[As a baker,] you're always looking at all of the nuances that make your perfect loaf," she says. "When you're depending upon something that's alive it can't be completely controlled," she says, echoing a modern-industrial concern of controlling nature.

Another example of the industrial genius, especially in its more scientific mode, is the episode on Albert Adrià—a Spanish chef who is described in CT as an idiosyncratic individual genius. Adrià began his career as the head pastry chef of El Bulli, the original mecca of molecular gastronomy and the "modernist cuisine movement" founded by his brother, the renowned chef Ferran Adrià (Opazo 2016; Borkenhagen 2017). Adrià's culinary philosophy is based on what he calls "culinary magic." At *Tickets*, his restaurant in Barcelona, he tries to convey the aesthetics and experience of "magic" in a way that seems to be more the magic of science.

In the episode, we see diners with expressions of childlike surprise when confronted with dishes such as "Green Almond Ice Cream with Olive Oil" or a "Rose with Lychee and Raspberry Sphere and Rose Water Gelatin." We are led to believe that these culinary creations are the outcome of a scientific-technologically innovative process that is based on Adrià's genius, who is himself portrayed as a sort of "mad scientist": wearing thick glasses, he sits in front of a desk in a dark room that looks more like a laboratory than a successful restaurant kitchen, sketching drawings, charts, and graphs with great concentration. The precise attention to detail combined with the curiosity of a scientist and the vision of a research and development manager is conveyed in every vignette, for example, a close-up shot of a pinkish piece of meat coated with golden crust. Adrià instructs his team: "We need to slice it thinner. It should be fried. Fry, then chill it." The camera then cuts to him and his team looking intently at a bowl from which liquid nitrogen smoke emerges. The table is packed with measuring instruments, bottles, and aluminum containers. Adrià sprinkles phosphorous green-colored crumbs on a dumpling that he pulls out of the bowl of liquid nitrogen, while explaining: "It will be crispy, like this."

At the end of the episode, Matt Goulding, one of the culinary authorities in the episode, says: "What does a person like Albert do after he's reached the top of his craft? What is his future? I have no idea. But I know, for Albert—the sky is the limit." For the industrial genius, drawing on the research of actual scientists and other technologists, his ability to invent is limited only by the edge of scientific knowledge.

Discussion

Foods and recipes—especially those that are embedded with high aesthetic and creative values, such as the dishes depicted in CT—are often seen as miraculous artifacts that can re-enchant (Weber [1905] 1958: 221) the mundaneness and mediocracy of our overly planned lives, which often feels like a dull recipe. But the narratives of the culinary genius who creates these dishes resonate with the prevalent ideology of meritocracy (i.e., the belief in existing opportunities of social mobility through talent and effort [Littler 2018; Markovits 2019]); within a contemporary ethos of innovation for profit; and combined with an ethics and aesthetics of creativity, thus valuing the disruption of culinary traditions and the rejection of recipes. The genius chefs—whether they are portrayed as saints, inspired artists, executive officers, or industrial-scientific genius—are not merely better producers and performers in the kitchen, but have, rather, a "je ne sais quoi" innate attribute or power for unlocking the magic of nature, science, technology, and capitalist markets.

Thus, CT can be read as a culinary manifesto for "talentism"—the social construct of talent as a dominant form in contemporary culture. Talentism, according to sociologist David Kyle, can be seen as a fitting label for the reductionist social Darwinist ideology of belief in the innate abilities of highly talented "creators" as our natural betters, and a near total inability to see inherited privilege and luck as anything but individual prowess (Kyle, in preparation). In this context, the genius of CT is on ideological point: creative talent is a kind of democratic universal of all normal human brains (regardless of race or gender), while relentlessly fostering and justifying the resurrection of our beliefs in a cadre of supernatural humans at the top of a Jeffersonian "aristocracy of talent and virtue" (Cappon 1988).

Talentism, valuing "golden brains" as much or more than gold bullion in winners-take-all meritocratic fields, conveniently revives the genius discourse without the authoritarian and racist connections it once held. CT celebrates the highest ideals of creativity and talent reduced to stories of individual geniuses who are able to produce genius foods and genius recipes. The culinary talented-as-genius retains much of the mystery of the genius, while not entirely inhabiting a separate sphere from the talented. Thus, a subtle message of the show is that hard work, talent, and even skills dearly acquired don't of themselves justify the highest rewards in a given field of cultural and economic production—genius does, if only you had the recipe.

14

Food Presentations and Recipes: Is There a Space for Copyright and Other Intellectual Property Rights?

Enrico Bonadio and Natalie Weissenberger

Introduction

Copyright law aims to protect creativity, thereby incentivizing artists and creators to produce works without fear of their efforts being exploited by free-riders. This is the utilitarian and incentive-focused function of intellectual property (IP) rights, based on the belief that creators need the lure of strong monopolistic rights to come up with new creations, as without such prospect "the Progress of Science and Useful Arts" would not be promoted (as stressed in Art. I, § 8, of the US Constitution). An overprotection of such rights, however, may have just the opposite effect. If creators become too trepidatious in their creative pursuits for fear of infringing others' IP rights, this may result in a "chilling effect" on creativity. Thus, a correct balance must be struck between protecting creators' work on the one hand, while also maintaining a culture of free artistic inspiration on the other. The food sector discussed here provides an interesting case study where such a balance seems to be needed.

This chapter discusses the potential for protecting culinary creations through copyright and other IP rights, predominantly under US law. It is important to keep in mind that culinary creations involve various elements—the recipe per se, the expression of the recipe in textual or other form, the process of preparing the dish, and the presentation, or "plating," of the dish. Accordingly, a distinction is to be made between rights applicable to food presentation on the one hand and to recipes on the other. The former will be discussed in the first section of the chapter, while recipes will be analyzed in the second section. In the third section, different views of industry insiders and legal scholars and experts regarding the desirability of such protection will be highlighted. Finally, the last section will expand on whether food presentations and recipes may be protected by alternative IP rights, including patents, designs, confidential information, and trade dress. A short conclusion will then end the chapter.

Food Presentations

While it has long been common to draw inspiration from, and even entirely copy, culinary creations produced by highly qualified chefs with little interest in legal suits, recent cases and disputes have given rise to the question of whether the plating of dishes might satisfy the criteria for obtaining copyright, thereby granting chefs protection over their food presentation. Food plating is not mentioned in copyright statutes as protectable subject matter. This is also due to the fact that the creativity present in the culinary world today was not previously foreseen, especially at the time copyright laws in several countries of the world were introduced. Nevertheless, the culinary world has advanced to such an extent that today it would be difficult not to recognize the creative efforts of chefs as artists and their creations as works of art. However, there has yet to be a decision in any major jurisdiction where a court has found food presentations to be protectable by copyright as artworks. Indeed, in the Age of the Internet, where information and imagery are more accessible than ever, the phenomenon of food plagiarism has, according to some commentators, become the "hottest food trend of the past five years" (Ramanathan 2016).

In this section, we will address such issues, in particular focusing on whether these works may be considered within the copyrightable subject matter, and satisfy the originality and fixation requirements necessary to obtain copyright protection. Aspects of "functionality" of food presentations will also be dealt with. In the interest of cohesion, we will mainly focus on the US scenario. The US Copyright Act provides that a work is subject to copyright if the relevant subject matter is an original work of authorship, fixed in a tangible medium, and contains artistic aspects separable from its utilitarian functions. Each of these criteria will be evaluated below in determining whether food presentations may be considered copyrightable works.

(i) Subject Matter

The first question to be addressed is under which subject matter food presentations would fall. A likely candidate appears to be the category of artistic works, in particular sculptural creations. Though a plate of food may not be the first thing to come to mind when one imagines a sculptural work, certain food presentations very well fit the definition. In fact, there are many examples of sculptural artists using food as their material of choice. Moreover, some scholars have noted that food presentations are perfectly comparable to more "traditional" forms of sculptural works, which use materials such as wood, metal, or stone (Smith 2014: 5). It is unlikely that if certain food presentations were made of such "traditional" materials, there would be any question as to their copyrightability. Thus, the mere fact that chefs make use of less conventional materials in their creations should not stand as an obstacle to protecting these works. Indeed, the US copyright statute does not pose a problem to such categorization, as it provides an open-ended list of copyrightable works, thus allowing for the possibility of protecting previously unthought-of works. This provision is also in line with the international copyright regime governed by the Berne Convention for the Protection of Literary and Artistic Works of 1886, which provides a non-exhaustive list of works subject to copyright.

It may therefore be argued that in the absence of clear requirements in terms of the materials to be used in creating a sculptural work, the same protection that applies to traditional sculptures may equally apply to those made, for example, of salmon roe and sweet red onion crème fraiche, topped with salmon tartare resembling ice-cream cones, as if these appetizers were made with old-style materials, such as marble, wood, or stone (Smith 2014: 6–7).

(ii) Originality

As mentioned above, only original works of authorship may be copyrightable under US law, as is the case in most jurisdictions. The originality criteria in the culinary realm may pose some obstacles. This is first and foremost because most chefs often draw inspiration from their colleagues' creations and from dishes they have previously come across. In other words, as noted by Smith (2018: 128), cooks expand their knowledge through a "sharing and borrowing" approach. Indeed, cooking is generally viewed as a derivative form of art and chefs are often deemed to work in an open-source model (Cunningham 2009: 23). This model entails that chefs' ideas, besides deriving from fellow chefs and creators, often originate from the predecessors that have passed along their knowledge, thus creating a culinary tradition shaped by multiple generations. Moreover, as described by Buccafusco (2007: 1151–2), there is a unique factor, which is specific to the culinary world, referred to as the "hospitality gene." This entails a certain "culture of hospitality" meaning that chefs usually view food as something to be shared and possibly used as inspiration. These features may make it more difficult for many plating arrangements to meet the originality criteria set forth by copyright laws.

The above objection, however, seems rather weak. It may indeed be counter-argued that several traditional artistic movements are and have been based on the practice of borrowing images and details from other artists (as well as from popular culture). Pop art for example has challenged the traditional concept of fine art by incorporating elements from the news, celebrities, and advertising world, where material is often taken from its initial context and transposed into a completely opposite artistic location. And what about "appropriation art" (let's think about Picasso, Georges Braques, and Marcel Duchamp), which is based precisely on the use and arrangement of preexisting objects or images?

A further potential obstacle to meeting the originality requirement is that elements of food presentations are often common and therefore not protectable. The case of *Kim Seng Co v J & A Importers Inc.* (C.D. Cal 2011) exemplifies this point. The issue here was whether a "bowl-of-food" containing rice sticks, egg rolls, and grilled meat was original enough to attract copyright. The plaintiff, Kim Seng Company, alleged that the defendant J&A Importers, Inc. had infringed the copyright on their "bowl of food sculpture" by using the exact image on their packaging. The court, however, was of the opinion that the bowl of Asian food was comprised of unprotectable common elements and that the dish thus lacked originality.

What the court stressed in *Kim Seng Co v J & A Importers Inc.*, though, may not be applicable for the less common, more extravagant culinary creations, which combine colors, textures, and placement in such a way as to create a truly artistic and extravagant work. As most fine-diners or self-proclaimed foodies know, creativity is often present in food creations, perhaps even more so than in certain photographs, sculptures, and paintings. Take, for example, some intricately and thoughtfully designed dishes such as the "Oysters and Pearls" and "Salmon Cornet," considered the signature dishes of late chef Thomas Keller of the French Laundry, or the "Orkney Scallop, Hazelnut, Clementine and Manjimup Truffle" served at the Clove Club in London's Shoreditch district, or even the "Almond's Nougat" desert dish, served at Quique Dacosta in Spain and described as "pure poetry." The latter examples could hardly be compared to the plating presentation in *Kim Seng Co v J & A Importers Inc.* in terms of plating creativity.

After all, originality in food presentations may come in many forms. It may result from multiple elements being selected and arranged in a way that brings about an innovative and original visual (food) work that has never been seen before. Examples of such arrangements abound in the modern gastronomy scene. Modern chefs create their plates by combining, elaborating, and twisting already known components and ingredients. It may then be argued that although the individual elements of such dishes are not copyrightable in and of themselves, because they are arranged together in a particularly original way, such elements can embody a high degree of creative selection thereby qualifying as original (artistic) works.

(iii) Fixation

The requirement of fixation may also initially seem problematic given the inherently non-permanent nature of food. This requirement entails that a work be fixed in a tangible medium of expression for long enough to be accessible to the senses, that is, to permit it to be perceived and reproduced. A chef's creation must therefore qualify as a "fixed" work in a tangible medium in order to attract copyright.

In the previously discussed *Kim Seng Co* case, the court found that the culinary creation was perishable and therefore not fixed, hence not eligible for copyright protection. In arriving to this conclusion, the court cited previous case law from the US Seventh Circuit's *Kelley v Chicago Park District* case (7th Cir. February 15, 2011), which revolved around the question of whether an artistically conceived garden could be considered copyrightable. The court in *Kim Seng* noted:

> Like a garden, which is "inherently changeable," a bowl of perishable food will, by its terms, ultimately perish. Indeed, if the fact that the Wildflower Works garden reviving itself each year was not sufficient to establish its fixed nature, a bowl of food which, once it spoils is gone forever, cannot be considered "fixed" for the purposes of § 101.

This, then, seems to negate the possibility of food presentation being subject to copyright. However, looking more closely at the *Kelley* case relied upon by the court, it is notable that the Seventh Circuit court in that case expressly stated that physical impermanence does not necessarily conflict with the fixation requirement under the US Copyright Act. Indeed, in *Kelley* the court recognized that "no medium of expression lasts forever." Thus, what is likely of greater importance, as the court also recognized in *Kim Seng*, is the underlying purpose of the requirement, which is to "ease problems of proof of creation and infringement."

Indeed, food dishes are (for the most part) destined to vanish as they are designed and intended to be eaten. However, as has been highlighted, fixation does not equate to permanence and there exists a plethora of examples outside of the culinary context that confirm this. One may recall the famous *My Bed* exhibition by artist Tracey Emin, which was displayed at the Tate Britain in London in 1999 and was a finalist for the prestigious Turner Prize. Inspired by a difficult time in the artist's life, the work consisted of an unmade, disheveled bed surrounded by various items varying from bottles of Absolut Vodka to house slippers. The work was of an inherently impermanent nature—each time the piece was exhibited in a new location, it needed to be taken apart and reassembled, thereby changing its composition. It was also easy for passers-by to touch and change the bed if they so wished (as happened in 1999 by two performance artists who believed the piece could be improved by jumping on the bed). Nevertheless, despite the work not being appreciated by all, no critic ever doubted its qualification as a work of art, despite its lack of physical permanence. Hence, if we accept that fixation requires permanence, we would arrive at an absurd result, namely to consider many artistic works that are movable and impermanent, such as Tracey Emin's *My Bed*, as unprotectable artistic works.

Issues of fixation have also arisen in the European context in relation to the taste of a particular cheese. In the *Levola* case the Court of Justice of the European Union (CJEU) held that said taste cannot be protected by copyright because it is not identifiable with sufficient precision and objectivity. The court did not explicitly mention the fixation requirement, but such a finding may inevitably be interpreted as introducing a harmonized de facto fixation condition (Sganga 2019). In doing so, the court followed the opinion of the Advocate General Melchior Whatelet that—after arguing that originality is necessary but not sufficient for copyright protection—noted the fact that tastes are ephemeral, volatile, and unstable prevents them from being precisely and objectively identified and thus considered copyrightable works. In particular, the CJEU held that "unlike, for example, a literary, pictorial, cinematographic or musical work, which is a precise and objective expression, the taste of a food product will be identified essentially on the basis of taste sensations and experiences, which are subjective and variable." The court also noted that the only categories of works included in the definition of the Berne Convention ("every production in the literary, scientific and artistic domain") are those that can be perceived through sight or hearing, but not other senses such as taste, smell, or tactile sense. In addition, it stressed that—given the difficulty of capturing the evanescent and fleeting character of taste as well as its very subjective experience—a defined and neutral identification of a taste is almost impossible.

The above case, however, cannot be relied on to affirm that food presentations cannot satisfy the fixation requirement. The two subject matters—the taste of food and its artistic layout once it is cooked and presented on a dish—differ significantly. The latter indeed may easily be identified with precision and objectivity by a large number of people in the same way a sculpture is appreciated in a museum, gallery, or public square.

(iv) Functionality and Separability

Works that have prominent functional features may be considered uncopyrightable in several jurisdictions (in the United States this is known as the "useful article" doctrine).

The requirement that works must not conform to technical necessities is in some way related to originality. Indeed, any work whose relevant aspects are dictated by functional necessity may at the same time lack originality. Where the work also meets the requirements for patent protection, this exception serves the important policy role of keeping patent and copyright regimes separate by preventing creators and innovators from relying on copyright to obtain a "backdoor patent" on a functional article that cannot be patented or whose patent protection has expired (as iterated in the US Case *Smith & Hawken, Ltd. v Gardendance, Inc.* N.D. Cal. 2005).

Yet, where artistic features are incorporated into a functional product (e.g., a garment or a decorative chair), these features are still eligible for protection in many countries subject to various conditions: in several jurisdictions—including the United States—such artistic features are protectable provided that they are separable from the underlying product. In essence, this doctrine entails that for a creative work that also has some utilitarian function to attract copyright, it must be conceptually separable from the product in which it is incorporated.

When it comes to food presentations, there is no doubt that the food as presented on a plate is "useful" in the sense that it provides nutritional value to the persons who consume it. Thus, the relevant issue here is whether the dish stimulates in the mind of the consumer a concept separate from this nutritional value (Smith 2014: 7). As consumers of fine (or even not-so-fine) cuisine will know, the experience of enjoying a dish may go well beyond simply obtaining the nutritional value therein. The growing haute cuisine industry, as well as the great success of culinary television shows such as *Master Chef*, and the pervasive social media "foodie" culture pay testament to consumers' desire for beautifully presented culinary creations and the increasing emphasis placed on the plating of food rather than the food in and of itself. Thus, it may well be argued that most dishes and their visual appearance may also be determined by creative expressions independent of their functional influences and thereby possibly attract copyright.

The above may be particularly relevant in the United States, especially after the Supreme Court ruling in *Star Athletica v Varsity Brands* (580 U.S. 2017), which held that the pictorial and graphic features of cheerleaders' uniforms could be applied to other medium and therefore could be protected by copyright: as has been correctly noted, in light of such decisions also culinary presentations that contain artistic qualities independent of any functionality might now receive the same protection (Smith 2018: 142).

Recipes

Recipes, as defined by the *Oxford English Dictionary*, are "a set of instructions for preparing a particular dish, including a list of ingredient required." The question of whether recipes should be legally protected has been described as "one of the most significant issues facing the global culinary community today" (*Sydney Morning Herald* 2006). Given the seemingly ever-growing culinary industry in the form of entertainment culinary shows, food blogs, and the omnipresence of social media "foodie" culture, the question of protecting recipes is increasingly relevant.

Yet there are several obstacles to such protection being granted, including statutory omissions, the seemingly hostile attitude of the courts, and reservations on the part of the culinary industry itself. This section will begin by providing an overview of how recipes are currently protected through various guidelines and social norms in the industry. Next, the discussion turns to the position of the courts to date in regard to copyright protection of recipes.

(i) Protection of Recipes via Social Norms

Certain guidelines and self-enforced norms already exist within the culinary industry with cooks that are found to be copying other chefs' recipes being exposed to negative gossip regarding the imitation within their community. Take, for example, the case of (in)famous Melbourne-based chef Robin Wickens who in 2005 was named one of Australia's most talented young chefs. Wickens became known for his uber-creative culinary creations such as his pickled cucumber-dried mango concoction or his smoked yoghurt. The problem with these creative works, however, was that they were not his own, but rather they had been copied from recipes developed at various American restaurants (from their plating down to the accompanying silverware). Wickens was exposed for his "recipe plagiarism" by the online culinary forum eGullet after publishing photographs of the creations on his restaurant's website.

To address such problems, the International Association of Culinary Professionals issued ethical guidelines requiring members to pledge to not knowingly use any recipe or intellectual property of another for their own financial or professional advantage. However, given the industry's tradition of borrowing ideas and gaining inspiration from others' culinary creations, the guidelines also provide for such exceptions of acceptable use of others' work, provided there is recognition for the original creator. Similarly, the Food Blog Alliance has provided guidance in navigating the realm of the "social rules" that apply to food bloggers. These guidelines focus primarily on attribution to the original creator by providing words such as "adapted from" or "inspired by." As we have seen, scholars have also made this point, referring to the unique social norms and principles, which pervade the culinary industry such as the long-standing "sharing and borrowing" approach and the "culture of hospitality"— even described (as mentioned above) as an innate "hospitality gene"—as widely accepted among chefs.

Nevertheless, as will be seen in the following discussion, the problem of recipes plagiarism persists and may begin bothering an increasing number of chefs and recipe creators, especially given the current boom of Internet recipe sources, which may exacerbate the issue. Moreover, chefs are more likely to abide by social norms such as refraining from copying one another if they are confident that their fellow chefs will reciprocate. Thus, if the chain of trust is broken in the culinary industry, the problem of recipe plagiarism is likely to be self-perpetuating (Di Stefano, King & Verona 2013).

(ii) Case Law

This section will provide a brief overview of the position of the US courts toward protecting recipes under copyright law. It should firstly be noted that the scant number of cases dealing with this issue coupled with the emphasis placed on case-specificity in each of those disputes should warn against drawing too general conclusions from the decisions. Nevertheless, tracing the changing attitude of the courts over the years does provide an illustrative picture of the complexity of bringing recipes under the domain of copyright. As of yet, there has been no case providing a definitive answer to the question of whether recipes may be subject to copyright. Should that be the case, the category of protectable outputs that would best accommodate such creations would certainly be that of literary works.

The earliest case law dealing with the question of protection for recipes seemed hopeful for the prospect of bringing recipes under the purview of copyright, though later judgments have taken a decisively more hostile stance toward such an idea. The first decision can be traced back to 1884 in *Belford, Clarke & Co v Scribner*. In that case the plaintiff contested that over 170 recipes from his cookbook had been copied "verbatim et literatim." The lower court sided with Belford finding that the language and subject matter of the defendant's book were the same as the plaintiff's in "every substantial sense" and thus constituted an infringement of the plaintiff's copyright. The ruling was subsequently upheld by the district court as well as the US Supreme Court.

The decision in the 1924 *Fargo Mercantile Co v Richter Co* case was similar. It involved a bottle label, which featured a series of new and original recipes. The Eighth Circuit court there distinguished between the emblem and advertising aspect of the label on the one hand and the recipes printed on the label on the other hand and found that the recipes on the label were protected by copyright. The reasoning of the court was that the recipes constituted more than "mere advertisement" and were "original compositions serving the useful purpose of advancing the culinary art." Moreover, the court stated that "[i]f printed on a single sheet, or as a booklet, [the] recipes could undoubtedly be copyright."

Such US case law, however, did not last, especially following the publication of Melville Nimmer's influential treatise *Nimmer on Copyright* in 1963. In his work, Nimmer maintained that recipes should not be subject to copyright because of (1) their functional character and lack of originality and (2) the fact that they describe a process or procedure, which is notoriously excluded from copyright law. US courts began following this approach starting with *Publications Int'l Ltd v Meredith Corp* (7th Cir. 1996). The case involved a book published by Meredith Corp. entitled *Discover Dannon-50 Fabulous Recipes with Yogurt*, which, as the name suggests, consisted of fifty recipes making use of Dannon yogurt. Meredith had already secured the copyright in the compilation of recipes as a collective work but argued that Publications International Ltd had infringed its copyright in the individual recipes by copying and using them in various publications. While the district court found the recipes to be protected by copyright and issued an injunction, the appeal court took the opposite stance: it recognized that the recipes of the plaintiff and those of the defendant were substantially the same, humorously noting that "it doesn't take Julia Child or Jeff Smith to figure out that the PIL [Publications International Limited] recipes will produce substantially the same final products." Yet the court concluded that the plaintiff's recipes could not attract copyright as "[t]he identification of ingredients necessary for the preparation of each dish is a statement of facts" and the recipes in question did not "contain even a bare modicum of the creative expression" as is required for copyright protection. The court, in fact, defined a recipe as "a set of instructions for making something [...] a formula for cooking or preparing something to be eaten or drunk: a list of ingredients and a statement of the procedure to be followed in making an item of food or drink [...] a method of procedure for doing or attaining something." However, the court also noted that such a "mere listing of facts" stood in contrast to recipes that might "spice up the functional directives by weaving in creative narrative." This "spice," according to the deciding court, might come in the form of authors "lac[ing] their directions for producing dishes with musings about the spiritual nature of cooking or reminiscences they associate with the wafting odors of certain dishes in various stages of preparation." The Court of Appeal therefore did not definitively close the door on copyrightability of recipes; it indeed left open the question of whether and to what extent a recipe laced with particularly creative language may be protected.

A subsequent case, *Lambing v Godiva Chocolatier*, also followed the approach adopted in *Publications Int'l Ltd*. The dispute focused on a claim of copyright infringement brought by the plaintiff Lambing against famous chocolatier Godiva for copying both recipe and design of its distinctive chocolate truffle named "David's Trinidad." The Sixth Circuit court rejected the claim noting that "[t]he identification of ingredients necessary for the preparation of food is a statement of facts" and lacks the "expressive element deserving copyright [...] Thus, recipes are functional directions for achieving a result and are excluded from copyright protection."

The above approach seems to be accepted by the US Copyright Office, whose regulations codified in the Code of Federal Regulations (CFR) state that "mere listing[s] of ingredients or contents" are among the materials not subject to copyright protection. Yet a more recent case—*Barbour v Head* (S.D. Tex. 2001)—appears more open to granting recipe copyright. The case involved the Texas-themed cookbook *Cowboy Chow*, which, along with a selection of classic Texan recipes, also contained "ideas, historical information, and other cowboy fun." The plaintiff Barbour had acquired copyright for the cookbook at the time of publishing in 1988 and subsequently entered a publishing agreement with the fellow Plaintiff Cookbook Resources. The two plaintiffs sued the defendants James Head and Penfield Press arguing that they had published recipes from the *Cowboy Chow* cookbook in an online magazine and a cookbook, respectively. The defendants raised similar objections as those raised in *Publications International* reminding that recipes are "[m]ere listings of ingredients" by citing a letter from the Register of Copyrights. The District Court of Southern Texas noted that the letter cited is not an authoritative source, and moreover, that the way in which the defendants quoted the document misconstrued its meaning by "conveniently omitting" the second half of the quote which reads, "However, where a recipe or formula is accompanied by substantial literary expression in the form of an explanation or directions [...] there may be a basis for copyright protection." The court went on to find that the recipes in question were "more than mechanical listings of ingredients and cooking directions" and thus may be "sufficiently expressive to exceed the boundaries of mere fact." On that basis, the court refused the defendant's motion for summary judgment, which was based largely on the claim that recipes were not subject to copyright.

What emerges from the above case law is a scant and somewhat muddled picture of the copyrightability of recipes. Although early case law did not hesitate in answering the question in the affirmative, later courts appear to have rethought the matter. The publication of the multivolume treatise *Nimmer on Copyright* also undoubtedly swayed the courts in this regard. However, the most recent *Barbour* decision may be viewed as an indication of the tides turning once again as the court seems at least more receptive to the idea of individual recipes meriting copyright, albeit under limited circumstances.

Similar to the United States, case law regarding questions of recipe copyright in certain civil law jurisdictions is sparse and somewhat contrasting. In France, for example, a court affirmed that recipes are merely "sets of instructions or methods of assembling ingredients—they are know-how (savoir faire) and therefore lack the originality required for copyright protection" (Germain 2019: 11). On the contrary, in Italy a court found that copyright is available for recipes, holding that their language and text (as well as the selection process and research underpinning them) show the creative nature of the chef's personal contribution and that such contribution is not limited to a mechanical list of known elements (Milan Court, No 9763/2013).

The Growing Debate on the Desirability of Copyright for Culinary Works

As we have seen, a precise answer to the question whether culinary works can be protected by copyright has not yet been given with courts producing conflicting decisions. Disagreement also remains among industry insiders and legal scholars and experts. As shown above, although norms of attribution have long formed part of the culinary culture and chefs have prided themselves on their "hospitality gene," there is an increasing recognition that the modern high-stakes, competitive restaurant industry, which places great emphasis on innovation, will require more than merely trust among chefs. Among those in favor of allowing food creativity to enjoy copyright protection is former lawyer and founder of the aforementioned culinary forum eGullet, Steven Shaw. Recognizing that allowing such creations to be copyrightable would require the law to carve out a huge number of dishes in the common domain, recipes that are truly novel—he stressed—should be protected as this would spur creativity in an important (nowadays profit-driven) sector. In Shaw's words "if there's money to be made from new kinds of soup, then more chefs will make soup" (Cunningham 2009: 36).

Yet, despite the growing sense of need for food creativity to be afforded the same level of protection as other works, other commentators maintain that this is either not realistically feasible due to the unique character of the work or not practically desirable due—as previously mentioned—to the deeply ingrained culture of sharing and borrowing in the industry. Indeed, chefs recognize that, to be successful, they should create a welcoming and hospitable environment in their restaurants. The education most chefs receive involves much sharing of their work as their future careers will require them to do the same. This culture of sharing and of hospitality somewhat clashes with the idea of exclusive ownership. A further concern is the potential rise in cost of dining out due to the legal fees of monitoring and enforcing copyright as chefs may pass onto restaurants' clients part of these costs, which runs the risk of rendering the restaurant experience too exclusive (Cunningham 2009: 22). To support this critical stance toward granting copyright protection to culinary creations, some have pointed to an in-field study of French chefs' attitudes, which found an overriding social norm of attribution to be part of the community, namely that in the culinary sector "respect trumps legal notions of property" (Fauchart & von Hippel 2006: 4576). It has been noted, however, that such a culture is rather fragile and works best in a small community, where a "name-and-shame" system serves as an adequate deterrent (Straus 2012: 187). This, of course, is in contrast with the vast and continuously growing restaurant business.

Still, several scholars and chefs still point to the fact that culinary creativity is very much alive despite the lack of legal protection and the high risk of imitation. The culinary industry has indeed been compared to the fashion industry, a field of creativity that lives in the so-called IP "negative space" or an area of "low IP-equilibrium"—a space in which innovation thrives despite lack of IP protection (Buccafusco 2007: 1122). Some commentators even believe that allowing copyright for food creations would in fact have the opposite effect than intended. This is because—the argument goes—the high costs in terms of time and money as well as the added fear of potential legal repercussions for copyright infringement would deter rather than incentivize chefs from creating new presentations and recipes, thereby producing a "chilling effect on innovation and ingenuity in the food sector" (Goldman 2013: 182). It has equally been argued that introducing an IP culture into the culinary context would bring an air of suspicion to chefs' kitchens and build walls to keep others out—going against the "sharing and borrowing" culture discussed above.

Ultimately, the question remains open: would copyright incentivize chefs to create even more, with the security and financial motivation it brings? Or, would it hinder the considerable culinary creativity chefs and consumers alike have become accustomed to over the years? Though commentators have argued either way, the fact remains that no one can definitively predict how future case law on these very issues will develop, but the growing problem of presentations and recipes plagiarism witnessed in recent years points to the fact that something, somehow, may soon change. Should culinary creativity eventually enter into the copyright realm, what would be desirable—we believe—is to push for a so-called thin copyright, namely a kind of protection only against virtually identical copying of the presentations and recipe, thereby allowing other chefs to take inspiration from and adapt them. This outcome may turn out to constitute the balance necessary to incentivize and protect food creators without producing a "chilling" effect on the industry and chefs' propensity to adapt and reinterpret food created by other cooks.

Possible Alternatives to Copyright Protection of Culinary Works

This section considers some alternative means to protecting culinary creations. Patent protection, trade secrets, as well as trademark and trade dress regimes are considered.

(i) Patents and Designs

While copyright protection is intended to protect the creative expression of an idea, patents aim to protect innovative technology and functionalities, including in the context of manufacturing processes. Patents have also been granted in relation to food. For example, the late molecular gastronomist chef Homaru Cantu obtained several patents, most famously for his inventive creation of producing chemical inks that, when printed on edible paper, taste of the food item printed thereon (Buccafusco 2007: 1132). However, the majority of chefs who do not employ such technologically advanced techniques may find the patent route overly cumbersome, both in terms of threshold for obtaining such protection and the high costs associated with filing and prosecuting the patent application.

Another possibility may be seeking protection of food presentations through design registration. There are various examples of this, especially in the field of pre-cooked and packaged food, including the US design patent for the Kellogg's waffle shape and for the popular Viennetta cake produced by Unilever (Ciani 2015: 23). What about Europe? The broad definition afforded to the term "design"—especially in the EU context—may prove useful. Indeed, the EU Design Directive and Regulation define designs as "the appearance of the whole or a part of a product resulting from the features of, in particular, the lines, contours, colours, shape, texture and/or materials of the product itself and/or its ornamentation." Such a broad definition seems capable of including, at least in theory, particularly eye-catching food dishes. Nonetheless, obtaining design protection is not without its obstacles. Under EU law, for example, chefs would still need to meet the requirement of new and individual character for their culinary creations, which especially given the aforementioned culture of "sharing and borrowing" in the industry and community, may prove difficult. This route may also have the drawback of only offering protection for the look of a product rather than the recipe itself (Janssens 2013: 18). Moreover, the costs in terms of both money and time for design registration would make it more economically feasible for large companies, such as Kellogg's or Unilever, to make use of this means rather than individual chefs or non-franchise restaurants.

(ii) Trade Secret and Confidentiality

A more often-used method of protecting recipes is through trade secrets. Trade secret is intended to protect "information, including a formula, pattern, compilation, program device, method technique or process," which "derives independent economic value, actual or potential, from not being generally known" and is "subject of efforts that are reasonable under the circumstances to maintain secrecy" (Cunningham 2009: 23).

In other words, to be considered a trade secret, a method, process, or formula such as that found in recipes must be of independent economic value and there must be some means put in place by the creator or proprietor to protect it.

Many well-known food companies use trade secrets to protect their special recipes or formulas. Some famous examples are the age-old and still unknown Coca-Cola recipe, the secret "Original Recipe" for KFC's chicken, and the "special sauce" in McDonald's Big Mac. Of course, use of trade secret protection is not limited to large food companies; there are also many cases involving smaller establishment restaurants claiming trade secret infringement by ex-chefs and employees. In fact, such protection may be most useful for smaller-scale restaurants and individual chefs as the barriers to obtaining protection are relatively low, especially when compared to other forms of protection such as patents, as discussed above. However, trade secret protection grants limited legal recourse once the secret becomes known, unless this is due to improper misappropriation, which may be fairly difficult to prove (Goldman 2013: 184). A specific downside of relying too heavily on trade secret protection is the growing potential of reverse engineering of recipes, especially given new advancements in technology, which may assist in deciphering the exact ingredients and proportions used.

A further layer of protection of trade secrets is through so-called nondisclosure agreements (NDAs), which seem to be used for culinary creations currently. In essence, an NDA is a contractual tool, which ensures confidentiality of certain information between two or more parties and is legally binding and enforceable between them. The aforementioned molecular gastronomist Homaru Cantu, for example, required all employees and all visitors to his kitchen to sign NDAs before entering (Cunningham 2009: 50). This method of protection is also supported by the International Association of Culinary Professionals ethical code ("IACP Code"), which states that restaurants and their chefs should provide a written contract stipulating employees' responsibilities upon their departure, especially in regard to their "use of proprietary information."

NDAs may therefore serve the useful purpose of better protecting secret recipes. However, the high turn-over rate and the practice of partaking in frequent internships and traineeships by chefs may make enforcement more difficult in practice. Moreover, requiring all kitchen guests, whether visiting chefs or members of the media, to sign an NDA before entering may have the effect of creating an air of secrecy, thereby running counter to the aforementioned "hospitality gene" many chefs pride themselves in.

(iii) Trade Dress

While trade secrets and NDAs may prove useful for chefs seeking to protect their recipes, in the US trade dress protection may be a viable route for protecting the plating of certain dishes (we have seen above that the eye-catching and ornamental elements of food presentations may also be protected by design rights). Trade dress, a subset of trademark law, is intended to protect the "overall image of a product" when it functions as a brand signifier. In contrast to other IP rights, trademark (and hence trade dress) does not explicitly aim at encouraging creativity through monetary incentives, but instead grew out of a need to protect brand owners, aid consumers in identifying brands, and product presentations as well as ensure a certain quality standard. A classic example of trademark registration for a shape is the Coca-Cola bottle. The distinctive silhouette serves the useful purpose of helping consumers identify the brand and thereby the source, even in the absence of the textual brand name.

In general, to obtain trade dress protection, the mark must be used in commerce, it must not be purely functional, it must be distinctive, and consumers must recognize and associate the mark with a particular source of goods or services. Straus (2012: 242) argues that trade dress, as an underdeveloped area of law and one with an historically generous interpretation, may prove the perfect solution for protection of culinary creations. She maintains that plating of dishes could come under one of three categories of trade dress: (1) plating as product packaging, deeming food as a product and the unique plating as its packaging (though this may give rise to issues when the plating itself is edible); (2) plating as "*tertium quid*" meaning that the plating of the food would form part of a separate category, similar to restaurant décor, as it forms part of the restaurant experience but is not the main product nor, strictly speaking, its packaging; or, (3) signature dishes as service marks. Where the dish is inherently distinctive and serves as a source indicator for a restaurant, as Thomas Keller's aforementioned Salmon Cornets do, for example, this may well fall under the category of a service mark.

Hopeful as this may seem initially, problems may arise with regard to enforcement of trade dress protection. This is because proving trade dress infringement requires that the plaintiff prove the defendant's use of his or her mark causes, or is likely to cause, confusion to customers as to the source of the product. This may be difficult to prove for plating of food since, unlike the well-known shape of a Coca-Cola bottle, restaurants' food plating styles are not usually ubiquitously known and customers are therefore unlikely to believe that copying a restaurant's dish is somehow associated with the original, though this will, of course, depend on a variety of factors and ultimately be case-specific (Straus 2012: 242). Moreover, the scope of protection would be quite narrow if a chef sought protection only for a signature dish. Otherwise, obtaining protection for each and every dish on a menu, granted the above-mentioned requirements are fulfilled, would be overly cumbersome and not be very accommodative to changing menus and dishes. Nevertheless, Straus rightly points out that trademark law is an area with an expansionary history (in contrast to copyright) and therefore may prove the most hopeful frontier for protection of unique dishes (Straus 2012: 248–52).

Conclusion

This chapter has given an overview of the current state of IP protection (or lack thereof) for culinary works in the form of food presentations as well as recipes and has ventured into the area of the future of such protection. As has been shown, the opinions of judges, industry insiders, scholars, and experts very much differ as to the appropriate way forward for ensuring chefs' efforts are not unduly exploited. While some maintain that chefs, like any other type of creator, deserve the financial incentives and legal protection offered through copyright (or other IP rights), others are hesitant to disturb the "low-IP equilibrium" the culinary world is believed to currently inhabit.

As a simple Internet search or a flick through foodie magazines also reveals, the issue of whether copyright (or other proprietary rights) should be available for culinary creativity is clearly of increasing concern to many chefs, restauranteurs, and IP practitioners alike and is unlikely to disappear anytime soon. Though the "sharing/ borrowing" and "hospitality gene" arguments are certainly appealing and may well explain the history of the culinary world, as the industry develops and competitiveness between cooks and restaurants continues to rise, it is understandable and somewhat inevitable that some chefs may find attractive the prospect of protecting their creative efforts in the kitchen through IP rights. It is therefore likely that in the coming years we will see increasingly more cases of chefs claiming such rights in their creations, whether through copyright or other means, and this may eventually compel courts to pronounce themselves on the matter more regularly and possibly more consistently. If and when this does happen, what will be of paramount importance is to strike an adequate balance between protection and deterrence so as to not produce a negative "chilling effect" on industry creativity. This might be done, for example, through granting a "thin" copyright protection for recipes and sculptural food presentations while also maintaining a large enough public domain, thereby allowing for inspiration but not blatant appropriation.

15

The Ethical Dimensions of Recipe Modification

Anne Barnhill and Matteo Bonotti

Introduction

In the emerging literature on the philosophy of food, little if any attention has been paid to the issue of recipes (for an exception, see Borghini 2015). Yet recipes are central to individuals' and groups' culinary habits. While people sometimes eat raw ingredients, they more often tend to combine them into more complex food products. This normally requires recipes, which are "key tools in any culinary culture, instructing diners on how to prepare ingredients in a safe, nutritious, pleasing fashion" (Borghini 2015: 720). More specifically, "a recipe [...] comprises the array of repeatable aspects of a dish whose replication would deliver a dish of the same sort" (Borghini 2015: 722). A dish, instead, is "a specific concoction of (typically perishable) edible stuff, such as those specific actions that led to this slice of pizza sitting on my kitchen counter" (Borghini 2015: 721–2).

In this chapter, we do not focus on recipes per se but rather on the modification of recipes. More specifically, we examine four examples to establish in what sense recipes can be modified, why they are modified, why they are still called the same (modified) recipe, and what ethical issues this modification raises. Our goal, therefore, is not to defend a particular normative stance but rather to provide a map of key ethical issues surrounding the modification of recipes that can be used in further work on this topic.

Our first example is that of a kosher restaurant in Rome that offers kosher carbonara pasta (see www.bellacarne.it/en/blog-en/carbonara-without-any-pork-delicious/, accessed October 16, 2020). Carbonara as traditionally cooked in Rome is made with pork pig cheek and pecorino cheese. Being kosher, this restaurant could not use pork, and they could not mix meat and cheese in the same recipe, as this would violate kosher requirements. Therefore the restaurant developed a kosher version of carbonara: they used beef instead of pork, and they used kosher cheese made from vegetable curds.

Another example of recipe modification—or in this case, of *non*-modification—concerns a traditional pie and mash shop in London (Ranta 2018). This pie shop was located in a gentrifying neighborhood. New residents increasingly visited the shop asking if they sold vegetarian or vegan pies. They wanted to eat pie but, as vegetarians or vegans, not the traditional meat pie. The owner refused to accommodate their requests. He was quoted as saying: "It's like some kind of bad joke—we're a traditional pie and mash shop, of course we don't sell vegan pies" (Ranta 2018). That pie shop eventually went out of business. In contrast, those pie shops that were willing to accommodate customers' changing eating preferences were more successful (Ranta 2018).

A third example comes from Oberlin College in Ohio in the United States, where a student cafeteria served a dish labeled "Banh Mi" (Friedersdorf 2015). But, as a student newspaper reported, "[t]he traditional Banh Mi Vietnamese sandwich that Stevenson Dining Hall promised turned out to be a cheap imitation of the East Asian dish. Instead of a crispy baguette with grilled pork, pate, pickled vegetables and fresh herbs, the sandwich used ciabatta bread, pulled pork and coleslaw" (Tran 2015). Students objected to the sandwich as an instance of "cultural appropriation" (Tran 2015). In this example, concerns about authenticity are connected with concerns about cultural appropriation: the dining service is charged with appropriating the recipe and presenting an inauthentic version of it.

A fourth kind of recipe modification is the promotion of healthier version of traditional or "ethnic" cuisines to encourage healthier eating. For example, the United States National Institutes of Health created and promoted a recipe book with variants on Soul Food items (National Heart, Lung and Blood Institute [NHLBI] n.d.-a, n.d.-b). Soul Food is a cuisine that originated in the American South and was developed by enslaved Africans and is linked to African American identity. Soul Food classics include many dishes that are fried, high in fat, and high in salt. This recipe book includes "heart healthy" versions of Soul Food classics and "shows how to prepare dishes in ways that help protect you and your family from heart disease and stroke [...] [which are] the first and the third leading cause of death for African Americans" (NHLBI n.d.-a). The recipes include lower fat macaroni and cheese made with low-fat cheese, a recipe for fish stew instead of deep-fried fish, okra sautéed in oil with spices instead of deep-fried okra, and green beans made with herbs but no salt. In this example, the healthier versions of recipes are framed both as healthier and as ways to "honor your African American culinary heritage" (NHLBI n.d.-b).

As we will discuss in this chapter, these modifications raise ethical issues connected to authenticity and cultural appropriation, which we discuss in the section "Cultural Appropriation and Inauthenticity," and issues connected to legitimacy and public justification, which we discuss in the section "Legitimacy and Public Justification." Along with considering the normative issues inherent in modifying recipes, we can step back and consider some of the broader social phenomena that the recipes modifications are part of and consider the normative issues therein. In the section "Recipe Modification in a Broader Context: Gentrification, Promotion of Plant-Based Diets, and Social Justice," we consider two such broader social phenomena— gentrification and the promotion of plant-based diets. But let us consider first why recipes may be modified and why there may be a desire to still call them the same (modified) recipes, rather than labeling them with a new name.

Why Modify Recipes, and Why Consider Them Modifications of the Same Recipes, Rather Than Entirely New Recipes?

Given that the modification of recipes might be problematic or raise eyebrows, why even do it? Our four examples show multiple reasons why recipes are modified.

In the fourth example, the clear intention behind creating and promoting modified versions of familiar and preferred recipes is to improve the health of the people who use these recipes. In the first example, carbonara was modified to a kosher version to accommodate religious dietary requirements and to allow people who also want to comply with kosher rules to eat carbonara. Similarly, some London pie shops started serving vegan and vegetarian pies to accommodate people with those dietary preferences. These pie shops presumably have a profit motive—they are catering to changing local tastes to become more profitable, or to remain profitable and stay in business, as the neighborhood changes and the preferences of potential customers change. Finally, in the third example from Oberlin College, why did the dining service not just serve a sandwich that is closer to the traditional Banh Mi? We do not know their specific reasons and can only speculate. One possible reason is that they might have wanted to accommodate local tastes: perhaps many of the college kids eating at this cafeteria will like this sandwich better than a traditional Banh Mi. Or perhaps the ingredients used in the sandwich were easier to source, or cheaper, than the ingredients in a traditional Banh Mi.

But even once we have considered the reasons why people might want to modify the recipes of familiar dishes, another question presents itself: why continue to call the modified recipe the same recipe rather than a new recipe? Why consider the new recipe to be carbonara or Banh Mi? Why not just give it a new name and present it as a new recipe? Once again, reflecting on the cases above suggests a few potential reasons.

Consider first the case of kosher carbonara. Why might the restaurant want to draw the connection between what they are serving and the familiar recipe carbonara, rather than creating a brand new recipe with a new name? Here we think that a number of answers are available. First, considering the modified recipe to still be carbonara makes it socially legible and familiar to customers. Carbonara is a familiar recipe, especially in Rome, and customers might just feel more comfort and more enjoyment from eating it. They might have positive associations with carbonara that they bring to the recipe if it is called carbonara.

Furthermore, considering a modification to be the same recipe can allow people to express multiple identities at once and thus is more inclusive. Eating a dish based on a familiar recipe that is connected with a particular social identity may be a way to express that identity and feel included in that social group, in the same way in which a multicultural conception of (the same) citizenship may be more inclusive toward members of ethnic and cultural minorities than a monocultural one, thus guaranteeing unity in diversity (e.g., Kymlicka 1995).

For example, people who comply with kosher dietary rules may not want to simply create new recipes but prefer to be included in the Roman culinary culture, of which carbonara is a key element, and to be allowed to develop modifications of that recipe without being asked to give the modified recipe a different name. In this case, being able to call the food item "carbonara" means being accepted into a certain tradition in your own terms. In this way, modifying a recipe and having it count as the same recipe can allow people to express multiple identities—for example, offering kosher carbonara allows someone to express both Roman and Jewish identities. These kinds of social accommodations reduce the tensions between identities, reduce the trade-offs that people must make, and allow people to express their multiple identities more fully, which has value for them as individuals and for the communities they are part of. However, when these accommodations involve the watering down of a cultural product, we might ask whether they are the right response. Do they strike the right balance between inclusivity and accommodation of diversity, on the one hand, and protection of cultural products on the other hand?

Consider next the vegan and vegetarian variants of traditional meat pies. In such a case, why market the vegan pie as a variant of the traditional kind rather than just marketing it as a new kind of pie? As with the kosher carbonara case, presumably presenting the vegan pie as a variant of the traditional pie makes it more familiar and/or allows the customer in some way to have a better experience of eating it. It also allows those who are vegetarian or vegan to live according to their dietary preferences (and the moral values that underlie them) while also embracing an additional identity associated with the traditional pie, for example, "Londoner" or "English."

Consider next the example from Oberlin College. If the sandwich served is not a close replication of a Banh Mi, why even call it "Banh Mi"? Why not just consider it to be a different sandwich (perhaps one loosely inspired by a Banh Mi) and give it a different name? Notice that this case is relevantly different than serving a modified (kosher) version of carbonara in Rome or modified (vegan) version of traditional pies in London; those are both examples of offering a modified version of a locally traditional or locally significant food item to accommodate locals who have specific dietary restrictions. The Oberlin College case, instead, is an instance of serving a dish based on a recipe from one cuisine, namely, Vietnamese, in a different cultural context, namely, a college campus in the United States, which is a multicultural context but also one with a culturally dominant group (i.e., white Americans). We can only speculate on why this sandwich is still referred to as a "Banh Mi." Perhaps Banh Mi is a familiar sandwich—familiar even to non-Vietnamese students on campus—and marketing the sandwich as a "Banh Mi" is once again an effort to make it more socially legible and familiar to students. Or perhaps there is a different marketing purpose: perhaps calling the sandwich Banh Mi gives eaters the impression that they are experiencing another culinary culture, and this is appealing to them. In this case, it is not the recipe's familiarity but rather its otherness that renders it appealing. Or perhaps offering a "Banh Mi" is meant to be part of a process of educating students to culinary diversity and culinary toleration. Understood in this way, the choice to call the modified recipe with the same name may not be consumer-driven but rather part of the college's broader commitment to multicultural education. But if students are educated to a *fake* culinary diversity, then arguably this will not achieve its purpose.

Consider next the example of healthier variants of Soul Food classics and other cuisines. Why are the promoters of healthy diets proposing healthier variants of Soul Food recipes rather than just recommending different, new, healthy dishes based on new recipes? Once again, familiarity and social legibility may be reasons: the target population of the public health intervention may be more likely to try dishes and recipes they are more familiar with. Eating a more familiar dish might also give them more comfort and enjoyment. It is also possible (though we can only speculate) that these public health interventions are based upon research about which recipes the target populations like most; if a government is trying to persuade people to eat more healthfully, providing them with healthier versions of recipes they already like will make it more likely that they will use the modified recipes. Furthermore, this will reduce the costs to them (gustatory, social, and cultural) of eating more healthfully, which also seems a desirable goal.

Perhaps, also, these efforts specifically intend to promote health in a more inclusive way: rather than advocating one mode of healthy eating, which might be most legible to dominant cultural groups (e.g., white Americans), they are trying to promote multiple modes of healthy eating that appeal to different groups. If health authorities presented all populations with a unitary model of healthy eating, that model of healthy eating might or might not be culturally resonant with them. Promoting healthier versions of cuisines that are already culturally resonant is a way of being inclusive and recognizing distinct cultural identities. A less positive interpretation—and possibility—is that these public health efforts simply intend to leverage racial-ethnic identities to promote health, without careful consideration of whether or not this waters down cultural products or is otherwise problematic.

Cultural Appropriation and Inauthenticity

In the previous section we considered the reasons why recipes might have been modified in the four examples examined and, more importantly, why these continued to be called versions of the same recipes rather than new recipes. In this and the following section we examine instead the potential ethical issues arising from the modification of recipes.

We start from the issue of cultural appropriation and inauthenticity, which was central to the case of the "Banh Mi" sandwich at Oberlin College—the latter was accused by a student of having "a history of blurring the line between culinary diversity and cultural appropriation by modifying the recipes without respect for certain Asian countries' cuisines" (Tran 2015). We see here that concerns about authenticity are connected with concerns about cultural appropriation: the dining service is charged with appropriating the recipe and presenting an inauthentic version of it.

Concerns with authenticity also appeared in the vegan pie example. Recall that the owner of the traditional pie shop expressed the following view: "It's like some kind of bad joke—we're a traditional pie and mash shop, of course we don't sell vegan pies." Perhaps the pie shop owner here is expressing an objection to an inaccurate or inauthentic version of a traditional recipe being presented *as a traditional recipe*. In other words, presumably there is no objection to calling a vegan pie a "pie." A pie with vegan filling is still a pie, and it would be bizarre not to call it a pie. The objection must therefore concern calling (and selling) a vegan pie as a "traditional" pie. Let's unpack and assess these concerns about authenticity and cultural appropriation and consider what kinds of specific ethical concerns they might register.

According to philosopher Lee McBride, the core claim behind charges of cultural appropriation is that "one group has misappropriated, usurped, or stolen another group's cultural product(s)" (McBride 2018: 338). For example, when it comes to food, "[s]ome have taken offense at the British appropriation of Chicken Tikka Masala as its national dish. Others claim that Americans have appropriated, distorted, and bastardized various Asian foods" (McBride 2018: 338). Thus "cultural appropriation" denotes *use* of cultural products by outsiders but also often connotes *misuse* of these cultural products.

Charges of cultural appropriation may register concern with various ways in which recipes are used and treated. First of all, there may be "a distorting or watering-down" (McBride 2018: 339) of a recipe, or an inauthentic version of it may be presented. We see this kind of concern in the Banh Mi example: students objected that the version of the Banh Mi offered in the college cafeteria was not an accurate representation of Banh Mi. We also see this kind of concern in the London pie shop example— according to the pie shop owner who refused to accommodate vegetarian and vegan customer's requests, selling a vegetarian or vegan pie as a "traditional" pie distorted and misrepresented the original traditional recipe.

Charges of cultural appropriation, however, do not always register concerns with inauthenticity per se. Instead, other types of ethical issues may be at stake. One concerns situations when someone from an "out-group" is using a recipe without *crediting* the group whose recipe it is. The other arises when someone from an "out-group" is profiting from a recipe without *compensating* the group whose recipe it is. Both instances of misuse (which we could call "substantial misuse") can be compatible with preparing the dish based on the "authentic" version of the recipe (therefore avoiding what we could call "formal misuse").

We can find both charges in another recent example that achieved notoriety on social media and in the popular media: two white American women went to Oaxaca, Mexico, watched Oaxacan women making tortillas, and obtained some information from them about their recipes. Then they returned home to Portland, Oregon, where they opened a successful burrito cart using the information they had learnt. When their backstory became public, they were accused of cultural appropriation, of stealing intellectual property, and of profiting off the labor of people of color without compensating them (Bamman 2017). The tortilla making expertise of Oaxacan women was used to make profit, without properly crediting or compensating those women.

While charges of cultural appropriation and inauthenticity highlight serious ethical issues concerning the modification of recipes, some commentators and scholars take a critical eye to them (McBride 2018). Cuisines are continually changing, and we cannot pin down what *the* authentic version of a recipe is. In response, though, one might argue that while it is true that recipes are constantly changing, and cultural innovation and evolution is constantly happening, there might be a morally relevant difference between members of a cultural group modifying a recipe as part of a normal process of cultural evolution and members of out-groups modifying a recipe to suit their tastes or ends.

This brings us to the root normative claim often underlying charges of cultural appropriation: recipes, foods, and cuisines are in some sense "owned" by certain cultural groups (McBride 2018: 339). More modestly, we might say that cultural groups have a set of normative and epistemic entitlements vis-à-vis the recipes and cuisines that members of out-groups do not have. These entitlements might include having the authority to say what counts as a modification of the recipe; having a moral entitlement to modify the recipe whereas others do not; having a moral entitlement to control how the recipe or cuisine is used; and having a moral entitlement to profit from the use of the recipe or cuisine.

But should the normative claim that cultural groups have ownership of foods be accepted? McBride, for one, rejects it. He points out that cuisines and recipes have been produced by culinary change, and this culinary change is the result of cultural exchange (McBride 2018: 339). Indeed, what are now considered traditional English meat pies are the products of immigration and cultural exchange between Dutch, Irish, and Italian traders and immigrants in London (Ranta 2018). McBride does acknowledge that cultural appropriation can be problematic when groups' contribution to cultural products is not recognized (McBride 2018: 341). However, in this case the remedy is to recognize groups' contributions to cultural products, not to assign them proprietary ownership of cultural products, including recipes.

Applying this critical perspective to the Banh Mi case, one might argue that there is no single authentic version of a Banh Mi, and thus the charge that Oberlin College served an inauthentic rendering of a Banh Mi does not hold water. But does this latter conclusion really follow? Even if there is no single authentic version of a recipe, there could still be versions of the recipe that are inauthentic—versions that use the wrong ingredients or are just too different from what is generally considered a Banh Mi. But if one concludes that cultural groups do not "own" recipes or cuisines, where does this leave one with the Banh Mi example? Does this mean that any use or modification of recipes is acceptable? Not necessarily. Even if cultural groups do not "own" recipes or cuisines, and thus no one else can credibly be accused of misappropriating them, there can still be other ethical problems with how recipes and cuisines are seen and used. For example, recipes and cuisines can have significance and meaning to cultural groups and for this reason should be treated with sufficient respect.

For instance, philosopher Lisa Heldke, in her book *Exotic Appetites*, argues that we often display a disrespectful or "glib" attitude toward other groups' cuisines and see it as unproblematic to try, use, and modify others' cuisines as we see fit (Heldke 2003: 46). But, Heldke argues, food is central to culture, and we should treat food accordingly as an aspect of culture deserving of respect. We should recognize that cuisines can be harmed and that harming a cuisine can harm a culture. This seems to impose significant moral constraints upon the way people approach other cuisines and recipes, beyond the demand to avoid formal and substantial misuse. It is also worth noting that if one accepts Heldke's concern that modifying cuisines harms those cuisines and the related cultures, this harm cannot be avoided by simply renaming the recipes that one borrows and modifies. Insofar as the newly renamed recipe is strongly influenced by the old one, and builds on it, and could influence how the old recipe is understood, these concerns would remain.

Legitimacy and Public Justification

A second ethical concern that emerges from the analysis of the modification of recipes is related to the issue of legitimacy and public justification. Unlike the issue of cultural appropriation, which normally concerns the relationship between citizens and groups within society, the problem of legitimacy and public justification concerns the relationship between citizens and their state. More specifically, it concerns the question of whether a government's political rules can be rightfully imposed upon its citizens. This ethical issue is therefore relevant to the fourth case examined here, namely, the modification of Soul Food recipes by the US National Institutes of Health (NIH). The NIH is a governmental body, being part of the United States Department of Health and Human Services. Therefore its actions and decisions ought to be politically legitimate. But what does this imply?

One of the most influential conceptions of political legitimacy in political philosophy, and the one that we embrace, grounds legitimacy in public justification. More specifically, political rules are legitimate if they are publicly justified to those who are subject to them, and this justification should appeal to reasons that all citizens could accept at some level of generality (Rawls 2005).

How is the idea of public reason, then, related to the modification of recipes by the NIH? To be able to answer this question, we need to understand first what it means for reasons to be public and therefore suitable for public justification. While some argue that public reasons must be shared among citizens, this is a very demanding requirement. It is more plausible to claim that reasons are public if they are grounded in some underlying basic values and principles that all citizens share (e.g., see Vallier 2014). Sharing these basic values and principles is consistent with holding different reasons for or against a policy, as when two fellow citizens both recognize non-discrimination and religious freedom as fundamental values in their (liberal democratic) society but still disagree on the question whether the Catholic Church should be allowed to exclude women from priesthood (Quong 2011).

What shared basic values and principles underline the NIH's modification of Soul Food recipes? While we cannot discern the actual motivations of those who designed the policy, we can at least identify some plausible candidates.

First of all, the recipe modification central to the policy intervention clearly aims to promote health. The promotion of health can be considered a shared value in liberal democratic societies. More precisely, promoting health, rather than being an end in itself, can help realize certain liberal political values that we can consider shared in a liberal society, for example, "equality of opportunity" and "social equality" (e.g. racial equity) (Rawls 2005: 224). The connection between health and equality of opportunity is well established in the literature, especially in the work of Norman

Daniels (Daniels 2007). Promoting health, and in particular the health of racial/ethnic groups already experiencing higher rates of illness, is a way to promote racial equity. It therefore seems that by modifying Soul Food recipes in a healthier direction the NIH acted in a way that was publicly justified and therefore politically legitimate.

But things are not as simple as they appear. Even if we accept that promoting health helps realize certain valuable shared goals such as equality of opportunity and reducing health inequalities between racial/ethnic groups, this may be in tension with the realization of other shared values or shared goals. These may include, for example, other dimensions of racial equity. If efforts to modify recipes are experienced as, or are, disrespectful toward shared cultural products, then these efforts may undermine racial equity in one respect even while promoting health equity across racial/ethnic groups. Healthy eating efforts could also undermine the realization of other shared values. For example, efforts to encourage healthier diets could undermine gender equality if the burden of enacting them (i.e., making healthier meals) falls disproportionately on women. If those designing recipe modification efforts or other healthy eating efforts do not consider these kinds of moral tensions, these efforts risk being unreasonable and therefore publicly unjustified. As Quong points out, an argument advanced in public justification "must represent a plausible [i.e., reasonable] balance of political values. An argument, even if based on a political and free-standing value, fails to be a reasonable public justification if it does not plausibly address other political values that may be at stake" (Quong 2011: 207).

Recipe Modification in a Broader Context: Gentrification, Promotion of Plant-Based Diets, and Social Justice

Along with considering the normative issues (such as cultural appropriation and political legitimacy) at play in the modification of recipes, we can step back and examine some of the broader social phenomena that the modifications of recipes are part of as well as consider the normative issues therein. Consider again the case of vegan pies being offered in a gentrifying London neighborhood. This example points to two broader social phenomena, which we will consider in turn: gentrification and promotion of plant-based diets.

Gentrification

The London pie shop example occurred in a gentrifying neighborhood. Gentrification can be defined as

> a transformative process driven by the influx of middle-class people into formerly lower-class areas, which consists in a change of the spatial appearance and social composition of urban spaces and which can yield implications for both residents and those who engage in economic or social practices in those spaces that range

from the mere transformation of neighborhoods to the expulsion of those who reside or work there.

(Huber & Wolkenstein 2018: 381)

Gentrification is both a widely tolerated phenomenon and one that is widely seen as problematic, though few philosophers have attempted to explain the respects in which gentrification is problematic (Kohn 2016; Huber & Wolkenstein 2018).

According to Huber and Wolkenstein's (2018) insightful account, what renders gentrification unjust is the fact that it undermines people's ability to pursue "located life plans," namely, "plans, projects, and relationships […] [that] are in numerous ways intertwined with certain spatial arrangements, in particular with one's location of dwelling" (Huber & Wolkenstein 2018: 382). Pursuing one's life plans in a certain place has various benefits, including aesthetic pleasure, familiarity, community, and support networks (Kohn 2016: 99). Since most of their life plans are located, "[i]ndividuals […] have a strong interest in the continued use of, and secure access to, a place of residence, and indeed, places in which their economic or social life is situated […] given that this is a necessary background condition for the pursuit of virtually any conception of the good" (Huber & Wolkenstein 2018: 383). They argue that this interest should be protected by granting individuals "occupancy rights," "i.e. rights to continuously occupy the place in which their social, cultural, and economic practices are anchored" (Huber & Wolkenstein 2018: 379). This will require such anti-gentrification measures as rent stabilization regulations and zoning laws, which help prevent or delay residents' displacement or the need for them to change their life plans (Huber & Wolkenstein 2018: 387).

The threat that gentrification poses to people's located enjoyment of their life plans points to a key problem in the background of the London vegan pie example. On the one hand, food is often one of the key drivers of gentrification (Cohen 2018). When new supermarkets, restaurants, cafes, and other types of food outlets appear in a neighborhood, this may attract new people to it. On the other hand, the changes brought by gentrifiers also constitute a potential threat to the located life plans of existing residents. These include both consumers and sellers of traditional meat pies. In other words, a key issue here is that the demand for vegan and vegetarian pies is driven by an unjust process that has two consequences.

First, it displaces existing residents, especially low-income ones, who are no longer able to afford living in the neighborhhood. This will prevent them from continuing to access the traditional food establishments that they leave behind them, such as traditional pie shops. Even if they manage to find new pie shops in their new neighborhhood, this may not be sufficient for them to replace their lost food-related located life plans. Not everything that is part of food-related life plans can be transplanted elsewhere. The specific shops and networks of people that define a certain life plan (e.g., eating traditional pies in a London neighborhood) often form an interconnected package that gentrification may dissolve.

Second, and as a consequence of the previous process, food sellers, such as the traditional pie shop owner, will also be under a significant pressure. As their traditional clientele moves out of their neighborhood, they will face a shift in demand from meat pies to vegan and vegetarian pies. To the extent that this change is driven by an unjust gentrification process, it is also itself unjust.

This, however, may not be the whole story. Gentrification has not only losers but also winners. More specifically, local restaurants and food establishments that adapt to new residents' tastes may flourish as a result. Furthermore, gentrifiers themselves can pursue their food-related life plans in their new neighborhood if the latter changes to adapt to their preferences, and such life plans may with time become located there. Crucially, in the London pie shop case (and in similar cases) this change may contribute to more environmentally friendly and animal welfare-friendly diets. These benefits cannot be discounted when morally assessing the modification of recipes resulting from gentrification. In sum, the process of gentrification involves a complex moral landscape that forces us to consider and weigh the interests of the various actors involved. Slowing down gentrification, as its critics argue, may promote some of these interests but not others. Furthermore, if we consider the promotion of more environmentally friendly and animal welfare-friendly diets (especially the former, which may be less controversial) beneficial not only for gentrifiers but for the whole society (including those who are displaced by gentrification), then it becomes even less clear whether gentrification processes that promote such dietary patterns, and which may put food establishments under a strong pressure to modify their recipes, are to be challenged. Yet this points to a further issue: the shift to plant-based diets may involve various forms of social exclusion that cannot be neglected. We examine this problem in the next section.

Promotion of Plant-Based Diets

We cannot know the motives of the pie shop patrons who requested vegetarian and vegan pies in this particular gentrifying London neighborhood. However, increasing interest in vegan and vegetarian food is part of a broader social movement to shift dietary patterns toward plant-based diets for ethical reasons, including both environmental and animal welfare reasons. A chorus of scientific experts have called for significant shifts toward plant-based diets in high-income countries, given the high environmental burden—greenhouse gas emissions, other forms of pollution, and land use—associated with producing animal-source foods, especially red meat. There are also long-standing ethical objections to eating animal-source food on animal welfare and animal rights grounds.

These recent efforts to promote plant-based diets for ethical reasons can be viewed against a background of two related movements that stretch back decades: first, the animal rights and animal welfare movement, which has opposed industrial animal agriculture and advocated vegetarianism and veganism; second, the alternative food movement, which has advocated sustainable agriculture and localized food systems. While both of these advocacy movements are motivated by ethical concerns, both have been criticized on ethical and social justice grounds.

The alternative food movement has been criticized as not meaningfully addressing the needs of low-income people—for example, not addressing food insecurity (the inability to reliably afford enough food) and not addressing the fact that low-income people may have difficultly affording healthier diets rich in fruits, vegetables, and whole grains (Guthman 2004, 2008, 2011). A related criticism is that the kinds of foods promoted by the alternative food movement are more expensive, making them unaffordable to low-income people (McEntee 2010). "The poor get diabetes; the rich get local and organic," in food advocate Mark Winne's words (Winne 2009: 125). Thus, the criticism goes, the food system changes advocated for by these movements are ones that would not address the basic needs of low-income people and could even exacerbate these needs if food were more expensive as a result. Furthermore, critics argue, the alternative food movement has failed to address these needs because it is homogenous—it has mostly white and middle-class adherents—and it resonates with these participants but does not reflect the experience, perspectives, or needs of people of color and low-income people (Hinrichs & Kremer 2002; Alkon & Agyeman 2011; Guthman 2011). The animal advocacy movement and vegan and vegetarian movements have been criticized in a similar vein, as exclusionary movements that reflect the experiences of white people (Harper 2009; Schlottman & Sebo 2018).

Given this experience, we might worry that efforts to promote plant-based diets, including by modifying recipes in a vegan or vegetarian direction, may take hold most strongly in the alternative food movement, animal rights, and vegetarian/vegan communities, and do so in ways that replicate existing ethical problems and limitations. Are efforts to promote plant-based diets—including modifying recipes to be vegan and vegetarian—sufficiently attuned to the needs of low-income people? Are they attuned to the perspectives and culinary preferences of nondominant cultural groups? If not, how can these efforts proceed without being exclusionary?

One potential solution is to include communities in the design of policies promoting plant-based diets, including the modification of recipes. True, the London pie shop example is not an instance of government policy. This case concerns instead the relationship between consumers and business owners, driven by the spirit of free market exchange. But as we have seen, the free market does not operate within a social vacuum. Various social norms concerning authenticity, for example, influence consumers' demands as well as the different ways in which food sellers respond to them. Furthermore, the state can play a role in influencing these social norms. More specifically, if as we have argued, the promotion of plant-based diets does not normally reflect the interests and values of more marginalized groups, governments could provide these groups with an opportunity to design and implement plant-based diet efforts that resonate with them. Policies and grantmaking could support these efforts. Existing efforts that are more inclusive could be encouraged and subsidized. This could help shape social norms about how a plant-based diet, or a diet respecting animal rights and animal welfare, could be promoted in ways that also reflect the interests of low-income and ethnic minority groups. Hopefully this could reduce the perceived bias underlying the demand for vegetarian or vegan variants of existing recipes, as in the London pie shop example.

Conclusion

In this chapter we have examined the modification of recipes. First, we considered different reasons for modifying traditional recipes: for health, to accommodate religious dietary restrictions, to accommodate other dietary restrictions such as veganism or vegetarianism that might not be religious, and to accommodate local preferences or tastes. Then we also addressed the question why one would want to consider these modifications of the same recipes rather than new recipes. Finally, we identified the ethical issues surrounding these cases, including cultural appropriation and authenticity; legitimacy and public justification; and the issues concerning the broader contexts of recipe modification. The latter point is important. Even if the specific modification of a recipe itself is deemed unproblematic, it can be part of a broader pattern of change that raises concerns—for example, gentrification. And, vice versa, even if there are issues associated with modifying a recipe, this modification may be part of a broader process of culinary change that is ethically important and in many ways desirable—for example, shifts toward more plant-based diets for sustainability-related and/or ethical reasons.

Is Social Gastronomy a Recipe for Peace?

Johanna Mendelson Forman

In the twenty-first century people around the world are connected by what they eat. The opportunities to taste the foods of distant cultures, either through travel, in ethnic restaurants, or by Internet cooking classes, are gaining more attention. Just as the invention of the Internet in the 1990s created a world of borderless connectivity, today food has been described as the new Internet, an edible way to share cultures, flavors, and recipes (see Musk 2015).

We are also experiencing a revolution in the way food has moved from its central role as a basic necessity for human survival to a way to connect people. Among millennials dining has become a substitute for formal religious gatherings. Coming around the table is a form of non-threatening interaction, or a reflection of modern commensality (see Thurston & ter Kuile 2018).

If culinary diplomacy is a tool of state-promoted soft power, we see the rise of gastrodiplomacy as a way for ordinary citizens to use food as a way to create agency. Both chefs and home cooks are transforming their kitchens to become platforms for a new form of public diplomacy. Gastrodiplomacy has also become known as a term that is used to describe the actions of states, the tourism industry, and trade ministries to promote national cuisines as brand. Nation-branding has become a very important way for middle powers to distinguish themselves in a competitive and globalized world.

Social gastronomy is emerging as a new subset of citizen-driven gastrodiplomacy. It has become a way for chefs to take on a new role as activists. Chefs have gone beyond the safety of their kitchens to address the needs of the poorest and most excluded members of society. In turn, they have transformed cooking and recipes into a powerful tool for building a more peaceful society.

In this chapter I will explore ways in which social gastronomy confronts global challenges—from refugees fleeing civil wars, to climate change, to youth empowerment and training, to helping prisoners find new ways to create a life after jail. By creating a community of practice around social gastronomy chefs and other food activists are involved in projects that share a common interest that goes beyond food preparation to supporting the most urgent needs of people.

Many of these projects have created cookbooks reflecting the experiences of sharing a kitchen. The process of compiling recipes, often translating them from food memories to written documents, has made social gastronomy projects a means of building trust and promoting social cohesion. Will the recipes of those being trained in culinary skills become a way to communicate personal histories? Will recipes from social gastronomy projects memorialize a culinary heritage that is at risk of being lost? I will give some recent examples.

Finally, we see a diverse community of chefs and activists who see in food a common bond and in recipes a lingua franca that unites rather than divides those coming around the table. Is social gastronomy, as practiced today, a tool of conflict prevention and peacebuilding? Does the existence of this community of practice represent another form of multilateralism that affords the rights of universal hospitality where a stranger is not treated as an enemy? Do food projects that focus on the inclusion of strangers to new countries, the refugees and migrants seeking a new start, lay a foundation for what Immanuel Kant believed was the basis for perpetual peace? Specifically, I ask whether food possesses a unique characteristic that makes it a perfect tool for social inclusion and dialogue? While I dare not suggest that I can answer all of these questions in one chapter, it is possible to examine the evolution of ways we have relied on food as a tool of soft power so we can understand why social gastronomy can serve as a unifying concept going forward.

Defining Culinary Diplomacy, Gastrodiplomacy, and Social Gastronomy

The vocabulary about food is dynamic and always evolving. It reflects food's political power and connection to international relations. While we see the kitchen as the new venue of foreign policy, it is also useful to understand what we mean by terms like "culinary diplomacy," "gastrodiplomacy," and "social gastronomy" in the context of the current political environment.

Culinary Diplomacy

Culinary diplomacy, one of the oldest tools of international relations, refers to "the use of food and cuisine as an instrument to create cross-cultural understanding in the hope of improving interactions and cooperation" (Chapple-Sokol 2013: 162). It is a subset of state-run diplomacy, considered a form of soft power (see Nye 2004: 5).

History is replete with stories of culinary diplomacy—from ancient times, when Roman armies used banquets to co-opt their enemies, to the French Court using their banquets that featured displays of large quantities of food and wine as ways to entice diplomats of rival states to negotiate. Lavish dinners reflected the wealth and the power of monarchs.

Modern culinary diplomacy started during the eighteenth century in France (Chapple-Sokol 2013: 162).[1] After the Napoleonic Wars during the Congress of Vienna (1814–15), the French diplomat Talleyrand brought his chef, Marie Antoine Carême, to prepare French-style cuisine for the assembled diplomats, literally buttering up other stakeholders as a way to negotiate with them (Chapple-Sokol n.d.).[2] By the twentieth century, at the height of the Second World War, the three allied powers—England, the United States, and Russia—used private dinners held in Moscow, Adana, Teheran, Yalta, and Potsdam, as a way to build trust among their respective leaders. Prime Minister Winston Churchill, President Franklin D. Roosevelt, and Chairman Joseph Stalin used these gatherings to discuss ways to purse an allied victory against Germany. It was remarkable that these summits happened at all. Each one required complicated logistics. The allied nations used their own militaries to transport chefs and elegant food supplies by air transport and by sea. The latter was especially risky in waters filled with Nazi submarines and landmines (see Stelzer 2013).

State dinners, a modern manifestation of culinary diplomacy, remain a mainstay of the diplomatic toolkit. One of the best documented dinners of the twentieth century, a banquet hosted by Chinese leader Zhou Enlai for President Richard Nixon, remains a singular event not only because it marked a major political breakthrough between the United States and China, but because the famous meal that featured many variations on duck launched a new appreciation of Chinese cuisine (Ewbank 2017).

A recent study about state dinners in the United States suggests that hosted dinners at the White House were losing their appeal based on the decline in the number of these formal events in the past decade. No reasons are offered for this change; in an age of growing informality, this comes as no surprise (Hickey 2019).

Culinary diplomacy took a new turn in 2015. US Secretary of State Hillary Clinton established a Chef's Corps, an assemblage of celebrity chefs who were sent around the world to become food ambassadors for American cuisine. This display of soft power had an interesting twist. It privatized culinary diplomacy through the Diplomatic Culinary Partnership with the James Beard Foundation, a not-for-profit organization dedicated to promoting American cuisine and the chefs who prepared it (see James Beard Foundation n.d.). This program can also be viewed as a transition to a more citizen-driven movement, gastrodiplomacy.

Gastrodiplomacy

If culinary diplomacy is about improving international relations through official contacts to demonstrate the power of food as the tool of soft power, gastrodiplomacy refers to a more democratic way to use food to achieve greater cultural awareness to a much broader audience. Gastrodiplomacy may be undertaken by a state or by an individual. Both fall within what we call public diplomacy. Gastrodiplomacy assumes that people first learn about different cultures through their palates. Eating different international cuisines can promote greater understanding among different groups of individuals by teaching them about the flavors and ingredients of heretofore unknown countries.[3]

Research about gastrodiplomacy reflects the term's dual meaning, first as a state-promoted program that features a nation's culinary heritage and second as a citizen-driven movement that uses the lens of food to create better intercultural communication (see Rockower 2012: 2). States that pursue gastrodiplomacy through nation-branding (see Zhang 2015: 569) hope to promote increased tourism and export of indigenous foods. Another related component of nation-branding occurs when countries seek international recognition of their unique culinary contributions to the world by soliciting that UNESCO designate a certain dish or food preparation part of the world's intangible cultural heritage.[4] Middle powers, in particular, see food-branding as a way to make them stand out in a highly competitive globalized environment (see Rockower 2012: 12).

In the last decade a growing literature has featured research about the nation-branding, including governments using cuisine to promote tourism. It has also demonstrated its use by middle powers (Pham 2013; Lipscomb 2019). Asian countries have been especially focused on using gastrodiplomacy to promote their food as part of their cultural diplomacy. Expanding a nation's culinary culture to other countries is a common practice of governments who invest in restaurants and food programs abroad to achieve this goal. The Global Thai program, started in 2005, where the government provided loans to citizens wanting to open Thai food restaurants abroad, is among the most well known (Frank 2001). In the Americas, Peru and Mexico have also invested in robust nation-branding programs that have been effective in promoting these states as important culinary tourism destinations.[5] These efforts have often been used as part of wider public campaigns to rebrand these countries as safe destinations for international travelers after all had experienced years of violent conflict.[6]

Gastrodiplomacy more generally "revolves around the people-to-people role [...] and the manner in which food is used to shape and expand perceptions and understanding" (Rockower 2014: 9). For example, Michael Rakowitz, a conceptual artist, created Enemy Kitchen, a cooking course that taught students his mother's Iraqi recipes "as a new route through which Iraq can be discussed." His goal was to make visible another dimension of Iraqi culture by expanding the political space and using food to promote local culture (see Rakowitz n.d.).[7]

Social Gastronomy

The growing interest in using food to address larger societal problems got a boost in the second decade of this century. A chef-led movement took activism from the kitchen to the world stage. Like gastrodiplomacy, social gastronomy is citizen driven and unofficial. But its goal is to use food as the means to achieve social impact through the programs that help diverse constituencies address specific needs. The concept is evolving, but the term "social gastronomy" refers to food training and education to provide solutions to deep-rooted social problems in communities that are frequently at the margin of society.

Specifically, social gastronomy projects use real-time solutions such as training or using food waste to help people survive. Impoverished people, women, prisoners, refugees, or youth at risk are all beneficiaries of this type of programming. Chefs say they are inspired to be activists because they see their work helping to alleviate crises arising from international conflicts, climate change, migration, child malnutrition, hunger, poverty, and inequality.[8]

Social gastronomy is not a new term, but its usage has changed over time. Nineteenth-century French epicure and gastronome, Jean Anthelme Brillat-Savarin, used it in his writing on gastronomy. Early in the twentieth century an Australian newspaper article described a dinner that featured members of different social classes coming around the same dinner table as social gastronomy (King 2018). By 1975 a short chapter on social gastronomy appeared in a book about everyday pleasures. In that volume the author referred to social gastronomy as a way to describe dining in New York City's expanding international ethnic food scene (Fast 1977: 140).

The Social Gastronomy Movement (SGM) as we know it today was officially launched in Davos, Switzerland, at the World Economic Forum in 2018. Commodity giant, Cargill International's Vice President, Devry Boughner Vorwerk, and David Hertz, a Brazilian chef, who in 2006 founded Gastromotiva, a culinary training program for young men and women in the favelas of Rio de Janeiro, formed a public-private partnership to elevate the concept to a global level.[9]

According to the SGM website,

> Social gastronomy uses the power of food and gastronomy to address social inequality, improve nutrition, educate consumers about healthy diets, and engage chefs in using their skills to do social good. The term is about using the food as a way to create a better, more inclusive and peaceful world. (Social Gastronomy Movement n.d.)

It may be a stretch to call this effort a movement. What Hertz and his followers are doing is more akin to a community of practice. This is actually a good thing. It created a global network of chefs and community activists who are dedicated to using their talents to empower others. This network helps teach culinary skills and entrepreneurship to people who have been unable to gain employment. Network members also share important values such as promoting dignity for the poor by serving food to those who are in need. Organizations who are part of the social gastronomy community have established local soup kitchens, trained street children in Cambodia, helped elderly men and women find careers in food production, and worked with refugees to provide training in culinary skills and entrepreneurship that can lead to employment.

The important achievement of the SGM is the creation of a network to bring awareness to a generation of young chefs, mostly in Latin America, Europe, and Asia, about the potential for the culinary arts to go beyond the kitchen to address local needs. This political awakening is also having a spillover effect connecting local problems and global issues. The hope is that eventually members of this network will create a real political movement with a strong international presence that uses food as a way to give agency to the voices of those trained in culinary arts.

SGM has a deep connection with recent projects that support chefs willing to create social change. The Chef's Manifesto, launched in 2018 as project of the United Nations World Food Program, has been a driving force in creating a set of eight thematic areas of practice aligned with Goal Two of the Sustainable Development Goals, Ending

World Hunger by 2030. In the last three years there has been a major push by chefs to work toward achieving this goal (see United Nations 2017). Today there are more than 600 chefs from seventy-seven countries who are putting into practice new ways to cook, reduce waste, and promote better nutrition. As part of a global community, these chefs are contributing to an international conversation about transforming the food system.[10]

Finally, by launching eleven Social Gastronomy Hubs in 2019 in cities in Europe, Asia, the United States, and Latin America, the Social Gastronomy network has provided a mechanism for chefs to put into practice the value-based programs fitted to the particular needs of each location.[11] It is difficult to keep track of all the organizations around the world that fall under the "social gastronomy" label. Some groups have joined the SGM's community of practice to form hubs, such as the Clink in London, which trains inmates in two jails in culinary skills and also runs a first-class restaurant staffed by the prisoner-chefs. Ultimately, those trained are placed in restaurants once they are released (see The Clink 2018). Others work with refugees in Sweden at the Malmo, while a hub in Minneapolis's inner city, Appetite for Change, trains youths-at-risk to find careers in the food sector.[12]

Chefs as Activists: Politicizing Food and Recipes

The chef-driven concept of social gastronomy has received greater notoriety because of the participation of celebrity chefs. One of the world's greatest chefs, Massimo Bottura, owner of Osteria Francescana, used his name to start collecting food waste from the Milan Food Expo in 2015 to feed homeless people and refugees in a church in Milan. The Refettorio Ambrosiano became the model for other feeding programs around the world (see Bottura and Friends 2017: "Introduction"). By using repurposed food to create meals for those in need, and serving people in venues that allow diners to enjoy the dignity of a restaurant, this project has evolved as a social gastronomy brand in many cities around the world (Adams 2017).[13]

British chef Jamie Oliver focused his cooking skills on training disadvantaged youth to learn to cook and find new careers through his Fifteen Foundation (see Jamie Oliver Foundation 2020).[14] Spanish-born American chef Jose Andres, in 2010, started World Central Kitchen, to bring food to Haiti, mobilizing others and using solar kitchens to feed the survivors of one of the most devastating earthquakes. Today his organization is among the leading players in offering food in humanitarian disasters.[15]

Claus Meyer, the Danish bread-maker and chef, launched his own program to help Indigenous communities in Bolivia by investing in a culinary academy and establishing a world-class restaurant in La Paz that featured a cuisine made from local products (Kormann 2016).

More recent accounts about Meyer's role in the creation of New Nordic Cuisine, his launching of Noma with Chef Rene Redzepi, and the focus of Nordic states on the social contributions of food to citizens' well-being are early expressions of what we are now calling social gastronomy (Morris 2020).

Since the 2015 refugee crisis in Europe, other groups have emerged to assist people fleeing the conflicts in Syria, Afghanistan, and North Africa. *Uberdentellerand*, "Make the World a Better Plate," started in Berlin by a Jordanian refugee, has used food production and communal dinners to bring people together during a time of deep political divides around refugees and migration in Germany (see Über den Tellerand n.d.). At the height of Syrian refugee migration in 2015, two French food entrepreneurs hired refugee chefs to cook their native cuisines at local restaurants. A year later Louis Martin and Marine Mandrila started Food Sweet Food, a charity to address the needs of refugees in France. They hosted a Refugee Food Festival in 2016, which has become a multi-European city program. Last year they brought it to the United Nations to coincide with the annual general assembly meetings (Rubin 2016; Medrano 2019).[16]

Chef activism in the United States is not new. There have always been vocal chefs such as Dan Barber and Alice Waters who have been advocated for locally sourced food and sustainable agriculture. Their efforts predated the concept of social gastronomy, but today we would characterize their actions that way (see Barber 2009).

Today chefs have moved from the kitchen onto the barricades. They have joined forces with lobbyists in Washington, DC, to demand changes in the food system (Godoy 2015). The Chef's Action Network, started by Chefs Tom Colicchio and Michel Nischan, and in partnership with the James Beard Foundation, works to educate politicians about the connection between food, business, and cooking, while also advocating legislation to address gaps in the food system.

Chef-activist Julia Turshen went even further in articulating the nexus of food and political action when she wrote *Feed the Resistance*, a combination of food manifesto and cookbook:

> To think deeply about food is to also think deeply about the environment, the economy, immigration education, community, culture, families, race, gender, and identify. Food is about people, all people. It is the most democratic thing in the world, lowercase "d," and affects all of us […]. It is the thing we, the entire world! have in common. It is no wonder that bread, fruit, wine and even water itself are symbols in just about every religion and culture. (Turshen 2017: 12)

Turshen adds that the universal act of cooking a meal, peeling an onion, and watching it cook in butter "might not be an answer to world peace," but she also thinks that millions of people around the world are "doing the exact thing at the same time. When we cook, we are in solidarity" (Turshen 2017: 12).

Unique to this work is her categorization of recipes for the resistance that links the preparation of food to a political outcome (Turshen 2017: 13–14): first, "Easy Meals for Folks Who Are Too Busy Resisting to Cook," quick, simple and healthy meals that anyone can cook—parents, students, multitaskers; second, "Feeding the Masses: Food for Crowds," geared for working with groups—community meals. She says that the recipes here are for getting food on the table "with lots of intention but without spending a fortune on ingredients or time"; third, "Baked Goods and Portable Snacks," mainly foods arising from earlier resistances movements—civil rights marches and boycotts used to raise money to help support earlier resistance movements in US history. Hence, if her activism is well grounded in earlier political movements, it is also a manifestation of what social gastronomy strives to achieve, a change in the political system that supports an improved social outcome around key issues such as climate change, immigration reform, and ending social inequality.[17] Moreover, it illustrates how the culinary community has acquired new leverage as central players in the efforts to promote a more peaceful and just world.

Peacebuilding through Food and Recipes

Even before the SGM was launched, the nexus of food and peacebuilding was well established in the first decade of the twenty-first century. Groups who worked on rebuilding war-torn societies were well aware of the food connections associated with immigrants and refugees fleeing conflict zones.[18] For example, British NGO International Alert, known for its work in post-conflict peacebuilding, was adding the use of food and culinary projects to their toolkit of programs in 2014, to help promote reconciliation and greater confidence among former enemies. One effort involved working with the Caucasus Business and Development Council in Armenia and a Turkish university. Together they hoped to overcome the negative narrative between Armenians and Turks by "exploring the emotional and cultural experience of preparing and sharing food, and by identifying the traditions, practices and stories associated with cuisine, which are common to both cultures" (Caucus Business Development Council n.d.).

Two years later they started a dinner series in London, Conflict Café, which "celebrated peacebuilding through food." These pop-up dinners became a source of cultural integration and education for anyone interested in learning more about the conflict, the stories of the foods prepared by refugee chefs, and engaging in important conversations about food memory, recipes, and the role that these acts had in promoting peace.[19]

International Alert also used its website to host *Recipes for Peace*, where people could easily access the dinner recipes. These posts provided the backstory of many of the recipes chosen by chefs as examples of food that were prepared as offerings of peace in their cultures.[20]

There has also been increased attention paid to a new term, "gastromediation," where food is used as a tool for dispute resolution (Avieli 2018: 7–9). This concept incorporates some of the broader objectives of social gastronomy in that food remains the means to resolve a difference, but with mediation the food is also at the center of a dispute.

Among the notable recent example of gastromediation is the much-cited hummus wars between Israel and Lebanon. The competition over who invented the chickpea-based recipe for a common dish prepared throughout the Middle East remains a very contentious matter. Without belaboring the details of this food fight, this ongoing debate over food ownership resulted in a mediation by Arab-Israelis who helped to diffuse a very heated challenge in a competition to prepare the world's largest dish of hummus for the Guinness Book of Records. Food anthropologist Nir Avieli, who studied this event, noted that "food is a perfect metaphor for building peace. It becomes a means to facilitate interaction and cooperation, during and after a meal. It is the perfect peacebuilding tool. It can be molded" (Avieli 2016: 19–30).[21]

Psychologists have explored how food can be used as mechanism for building trust (see Guendelman, Cheryan and Monin 2011). These studies merit consideration when asking whether social gastronomy is a tool for peacebuilding as any type of negotiations to resolve a conflict requires a minimum of trust to go forward.

A recent study in the *Journal of Consumer Psychology* asked whether incidental similar food consumption served as a cue of trust or used other types of cues to understand different types of group behavior. The authors concluded that food consumption increased trust and also improved negotiating outcomes when subjects consumed similar foods. Moreover, the authors concluded that "food serves as a social lubricant and is especially beneficial for new relationships where people have limited information about the other person and are forming first impressions […] leading to smoother transactions from the start" (Woolley & Fishbach 2017: 9). Although this work suggested that the findings were useful to direct consumer behavior, these results also show the role food can play in easing social tensions among different communities.

This observation has not been lost on the peacebuilding community. Sharing meals and understanding foods that were considered to support more peaceful relations were central to programs such as a Conflict Café in London. Today we see how social gastronomy projects around the world are being used to address the global refugee crisis. Food production and entrepreneurship training programs use communal kitchens as an important tool of economic integration and also as a way to promote greater social cohesion among diverse communities. From Istanbul to Berlin to New York City we see how women and men from different countries and cultures are thrown together in food-training programs.

Documenting Refugee Cuisines: Cookbooks

Cookbooks featuring the recipes of refugees and immigrants have become a growth industry. Between 2015 and 2020 a search on the bookseller Amazon revealed seventeen cookbooks featuring refugees and thirty written by immigrant chefs. The numbers underscore an interest in documenting the food of strangers and a market for these recipes.[22]

Immigrants quickly discover that recipes do not respect borders. This is especially true in the Levant region. LIFE, a recent social gastronomy project that was started in Turkey in 2017, used shared culinary traditions to help build greater social cohesion between Syrian refugees and the Turkish community. Program participants discovered the similarity of dishes, which differed only by their names in Arabic or Turkish. This sparked conversations about ingredients and cooking methods. More important, it eased tensions between both groups because it changed some preconceived notions about stereotypes of Syrian refugees.[23] It also led to the publication of a cookbook that shared the recipes of each group, providing documentation of these traditions and a tangible record of their recipes.[24]

Many of immigrant cookbooks break new ground by documenting recipes for the first time.[25] They are opening a window to the past and to the traditions that have been lost through migration. Memorializing recipes allows anyone to gain access to the special dishes that were once limited to families and close friends. *The Bread and Salt between Us*, a cookbook by Syrian refugee Mayada Anjari, explains that before the publication of the book, all the recipes had been in her head. "Transcribing a recipe by watching someone preparing a dish is hard work. You must list and measure the ingredients, and also order the steps necessary to prepare a dish" (Anjari & Sit 2018: 6).

Cookbooks published by immigrants create a codex of migration. They become a lasting contribution to the national cuisines of their new homelands (see Appadurai 1988: 17–18). They may also be one of the important collateral benefits of the ongoing migrations we are seeing around the globe.[26]

Conclusion

This chapter has examined the various ways food has been a tool of what we call a nation's soft power. In their various forms, culinary diplomacy (a practice of states and elites), gastrodiplomacy (a citizen-based approach to using food to help promote cuisines as unique to a specific country or national group), and social gastronomy (which uses food as a means to address social inequities) are all considered tools of public diplomacy.

I have explained why social gastronomy practitioners have considered their activities to be a form of advocacy. Whether to support peacebuilding and conflict prevention or to help immigrants gain a foothold in a new society, all see the power of food to support important social goals. This is because food and commensality provide a peaceful means for confronting difficult issues. Research suggests that eating together is a way to build trust among different groups of people. Programs that help refugees integrate into new homelands offer ways to bring together groups who may otherwise have been divided or polarized by preconceived notions about ethnicity and national identities. Recent experience shows that when these communities started interacting based on their participation in culinary training programs, or in dining together on food prepared by refugees, there was a greater willingness to work together and to find a common purpose in food as a way to create economic stability. It is possible that social gastronomy's community of practice may signal a new form of culinary multilateralism. It may also be possible for social gastronomy programs to offer a path toward what is considered perpetual peace.

What remains is the question of whether these social impact activities could have been achieved by other means instead of using food as the tool for engagement and activism. Based on what I have learned about social gastronomy it is clear that food-centered programs have a powerful, but nonthreatening quality when they are used to help achieve deeper social change.

First, chef-driven movements provide leadership by a class of people who enjoy a high degree of societal trust.[27] Chef activism is not new, but in today's highly polarized political environment the kitchen table provides a safe space for difficult conversations when the focus is on the preparation of meals and the creation of community entrepreneurship.

Second, chefs have established an important alliance with those who produce our food. Farm-to-market concept restaurants, a trend that remains very popular around the world, also allow the chef to build deep connections in the local community. It raises awareness about agriculture, food waste, climate, and labor conditions. The Slow Food movement, which began this way in 1989, had very similar objectives. It did not address many of the social issues such as youth unemployment or refugee reintegration that the SGM embraces in its agenda.[28] It did, however, establish a connection with the land and labor that has been embraced by chefs today.

Third, the global awakening around poverty and hunger, memorialized by the outcome document of the United Nations World Food Conference in 1974, declared that "every man, woman and child has an inalienable right to be free from hunger and malnutrition in order to develop their physical and mental faculties." This international meeting elevated food insecurity to a new level of multilateral action (United Nations 2002). The United Nations Millennium Development Goals of 2000 and its successor, the Sustainable Development Goals, seek to end global hunger by 2030. Chefs are driving part of this effort, reducing hunger, feeding people with dignity, reducing food waste, and preparing nutritious food, no matter what the socioeconomic status of the individual is. While the world has come a long way to reduce the threat of global hunger since 1974, it is precisely the connection between conflict and food that continues to leave almost 800,000 people at risk of starvation in 2020. Social gastronomy is considered a means of using food to help raise awareness to this problem through action-oriented projects that address the ongoing issues of food and peacebuilding.

Food is the Internet of the twenty-first century. It connects us all. In many cases it has become the only way to reach so many diverse communities. Organizing a rock concert to help refugees may be an excellent way to raise money and awareness for the United Nations organizations. It will not put food on the table unless people have a way to earn a living and have access to growing food. Social gastronomy uses food as a means to rebuild people's lives.

Both gastrodiplomacy and social gastronomy are multilateral mechanisms for managing global problems. Practitioners are organized globally and communicate through networks of NGOs. Groups come together around food. Chefs are emerging as the new interlocutors of this form of international engagement as we seek to prevent conflicts and address some of the most challenging problems of our times.

Finally, food can be a powerful lens to view challenges from global migration to climate change. Chefs can offer some of the practical solutions for managing the daily issues arising from these problems at a local level. So many projects described in this chapter support goals that are compatible with making this planet more sustainable. They can provide a recipe that makes peace with nature.[29]

A Philosophy of Meat in the Early Twenty-First Century

Benjamin Aldes Wurgaft

The phrase "philosophy of food" is a commonplace of menus, restaurant self-descriptions, cookbook author biographical statements, and other types of food world ephemera in the early twenty-first century. Usually preceded by "my" or "our," the convention seems to express seriousness of intent rather than a claim about the possible relationship between food and philosophical reflection. "My philosophy of food" often seems decorative or reflexive rather than thoughtful, although it could imply that a Tokyo turnip, sautéed with garlic, can raise philosophical questions or even represent a philosophical principle. One especially curious variation is "my philosophy of barbecue" or "my philosophy of grilling." No food raises philosophical issues more readily than meat because to get meat you must kill animals and often inflict suffering in the process. Said suffering is an intrinsic part of the industrial production of meat because of the conditions cows, pigs, chickens, and other animals experience in feedlots and slaughterhouses. The philosophical questions involved with meat clearly include moral ones. The expression "my philosophy of meat" implies a moral position on the value of the lives and pain of animals. Turkeys aren't turnips.

During the second decade of the twenty-first century, and ongoing as of this chapter written in 2020, a number of scientists and entrepreneurs have promoted a new kind of meat, made by an entirely new recipe, which they propose as a solution to the moral-philosophical problems with meat. The elements of that problem include animal suffering, as well as the meat industry's effects on our environment. No part of food production is as polluting, or as wasteful of natural resources, as industrial meat production. Derived from animal cells and grown via tissue culture techniques, laboratory-grown or "cultured meat" is also known by other names: "clean meat," "cultivated meat," and "in vitro meat" but also, and more pejoratively, "vat meat." It is not yet available to consumers as of this writing, but many of its champions promise that it soon will be. (Indeed, this dynamic of promise and delay has persisted for several years, now.) Cultured meat could be a way of eating meat, defined as animal protein and fat produced through the growth of animal cells, without killing animals. Hypothetically (but not certainly) it might consume fewer natural resources than conventional meat production. Cultured meat might be a moral boon on multiple fronts.

However, I do not think cultured meat's most interesting philosophical dimension is whether it helps us to eat meat without harming animals or our environment. In this chapter I review the philosophy of meat as understood by cultured meat's promoters, and I suggest that cultured meat raises philosophical questions beyond the intentions of the cultured meat movement itself. These include questions about the line between humans and other animals and thus questions about the nature of being human. Such questions may not seem as pressing as the moral one about the suffering and deaths of animals, but this should not make them less significant in philosophical terms. This chapter draws its empirical details from an extended period of ethnographic research I conducted in the culture meat movement between 2013 and 2019, research I describe elsewhere (see Wurgaft 2019).[1] I also follow a thought of the philosopher Christine M. Korsgaard, namely that living with nonhuman animals raises questions about what is distinctive about our humanity. As Korsgaard puts it, "Thinking about how we stand with respect to our fellow creatures is a way of thinking about the questions that draw most of us into philosophy in the first place" (2018: 5). I argue that the philosophy of meat contains complexities not exhausted by the moral-philosophical framing preferred by many actors within the cultured meat movement itself. Indeed, the cultured meat movement's moral framework has kept it from publicly grappling with the philosophical questions that meat, and the animals we take it from, raises. As an ethnographer, it was my role to try to understand those actors' moral beliefs as best as I could, but this posture of understanding is not the same as philosophical endorsement. This chapter establishes a certain difference of view on my part.

Here is a brief account of the recent past, and current condition, of cultured meat research with special attention to the way moral philosophy frames and inflects the conversation around cultured meat. The idea of growing meat using tissue culture techniques began to develop not long after the successful use of those techniques themselves; the American embryologist Ross Harrison grew amphibian cells under glass in 1907 and kept them alive and duplicating. Alexis Carrel managed to keep avian heart cells alive for a considerable time, and while tissue culture was used almost exclusively for biological and medical research, it nevertheless excited public imaginations beyond research institutions (on the history of tissue culture, see Landecker 2007). By the early 1930s, Winston Churchill entertained (most likely in the spirit of playful fantasy) the idea of growing not whole chickens, but their parts, as part of a future of abundance without waste. By mid-century, meat without animals became a staple of science fiction writers. It was not until the turn of the millennium, however, that a few scattered and unrelated teams of scientists and bio-artists began practical research into growing meat via tissue culture. From one group in the Netherlands, the Professor of Medicine and Cardiologist Mark Post emerged as a leader in the field in 2013, unveiling a cell-cultured burger at a carefully choreographed media event in London. A professional chef cooked the burger, a panel of expert tasters ate it and discussed its flavor, and Post answered questions from an audience of journalists who mixed enthusiasm with bemusement. This was certainly a turning point. Prior groups had pursued research into using animal cells grown in culture as a food source; around the year 2000, Morris Benjaminson's team at Touro College in New York attempted to grow goldfish cells, funded by a grant from NASA. The artists Oron Catts and Ionat

Zurr, working as "the Tissue Culture & Art Project," grew frog cells into tiny "cutlets" for an event in Nantes, France, in 2003, continuing work they had begun (with sheep cells) as visitors to Harvard University in the year 2000 (see Catts & Zurr 2004–2005). But, as Neil Stephens, Alexandra Sexton, and Clemens Driessen have described, these early experiments in growing animal cells in tissue culture with the goal of producing meat took place without a widespread agreement on the parts of researchers, commentators, or the public at large, regarding the nature of the cells produced (see Stephens, Sexton & Driessen 2019[2]). In other words, did these cells really count as meat? Was the ultimate goal to produce a meat product that did not require killing animals? Stephens, Sexton, and Driessen are careful to note the lack of consensus on these issues, although some onlookers did presume that "vat," "lab," or "cultured" meat could replace conventionally recognized meat taken from animal bodies. It was on that basis that People for the Ethical Treatment of Animals (PETA) announced a contest in 2008, offering a million US dollars to the team that produced the first marketable chicken nugget grown in a lab. The contest's deadline expired in 2014, the victory conditions unmet.

Mark Post and his team produced their hamburger by starting with a tiny biopsy of muscle tissue taken from a cow. The cow in question was a "Belgian Blue," a breed popular with meat producers because of a mutation in its myostatin gene MSTN, which causes it to produce twice as much muscle as most breeds. The Post team then isolated skeletal muscle stem cells, which proliferated in a set of T flasks, bathed in growth media. The technicians coaxed their cells to form strands, and those strands then became muscle fibers, which could be "exercised," expanding and contracting much like skeletal muscle in an animal. Several months of labor-intensive work produced enough muscle fibers to form several patties. Cultured meat scientists have been working steadily since 2013 to refine several important aspects of the existing process and to achieve a set of critical technical goals. These include growing fat cells (vital for carrying the flavor of meat) and finding a growth media that is not animal-derived but still relatively inexpensive; the industry standard in 2013 (and throughout the time of my fieldwork) included an ingredient called Fetal Bovine Serum or FBS, which contains beneficial growth factors. Non-animal-derived alternatives already exist but tend to be more expensive and less effective at encouraging cell growth than FBS. Another challenge has been growing three-dimensional tissue, which is important if scientists hope to produce anything resembling steak or a chicken breast. While producing single layers of cells is relatively easy, producing complex arrangements of muscle and fat cells in three dimensions is quite challenging. To get nutrients to all parts of a three-dimensional tissue culture, researchers have to develop a vascularized bioreactor that emulates the veins and capillaries in living tissue; mammalian cells cannot live more than about 200 micrometers from a nutrient source. From when I began my research in 2013, to when I completed it in 2018, the major technical hurdles (FBS and three-dimensional tissue) seemed unsurpassed. Nor had any laboratory devised a means by which to produce cultured meat on a vastly larger scale, as compared to the early work of the Post Lab, which would be necessary for industrial production. As of this writing in 2020, there are unconfirmed rumors that some laboratories have found an alternative to FBS, rumors that are difficult to investigate for reasons I explain below.

While the academic literature on cultured meat has been small, some influential early articles presumed that the goal of research into tissue-cultured meat was not only practical (which food biotechnology research usually is) but also moral. In an optimistic 2008 article in the *Journal of Agricultural and Environmental Ethics*, Patrick D. Hopkins and Austin Dacey wrote:

> What if we could have the best of both worlds in reality—eat meat and not harm animals? The nascent biotechnology of tissue culture, originally researched for medical applications, holds out just such a promise. Meat could be grown in vitro without killing animals. In fact, this technology may not just be an intriguing option, but might be our moral obligation to develop. (Hopkins & Dacey 2008)

Note that tissue culture was not a "nascent" biotechnology as of 2008, but a very well-established one, though its application to meat production certainly was nascent and is still only emerging as of this writing. Hopkins and Dacey closed their article by suggesting that moral philosophy need not simply respond to emerging technologies but might "champion and assist in the development of new technologies, as a step toward the production of a world that in fact, and not merely in ideal, mirrors the moral vision we possess for it." Such a statement introduces a slippage between the idea of a new technology helping us realize our moral vision of the world, and the idea that new technologies might change our very parameters for moral action, turning us into new kinds of moral actors. This slippage raises a significant question, one that has been long debated by moral philosophers: does morality reside in the nature of our actions or in their outcomes? And does being moral rely on our capacity for moral judgment and free action? This is an important question to keep in mind.

We can see the same slippage regarding morality—does it reside in the nature of our actions, in our capacities, or in the outcomes of our acts—in a 2013 promotional film released at Mark Post's cell-cultured burger demonstration. The first line of the film is "Sometimes a new technology comes along, and it has the capability to transform how we view our world," and it comes from Post's funder, Google cofounder Sergey Brin. Many of the film's arguments on behalf of cultured meat are technical in the sense that they present cultured meat as a potential solution to a set of specific problems. A series of experts appear on camera to describe population growth and our growing planetary appetite for meat, as well as the environmental and animal welfare costs of industrial meat production. But implicit in their arguments is an idea that follows from Brin's "how we view our world." Not only can cultured meat serve to resolve technical challenges, a world of cultured meat would be one in which we would have morally better options than we currently do. Post imagined a customer in a supermarket in 2033 encountering two essentially identical pieces of meat, one taken from an animal, the other grown in a lab. "So what are you going to choose? From an ethical point of view it has only benefits." The picture is one of moral growth, although again it remains unclear if moral growth is something that happens in human subjects or as the fruit of their deeds. Did Post ask "what are you going to choose" to suggest that consumers would retain their power to choose, and the option of consuming dead animals, or that the latter would become no choice at all, superseded by a future of moral meat?

If the first wave of cultured meat research largely took place in academic settings, and its participants understood themselves as engaging in "basic research" as opposed to research that targets a specific practical and commercial goal, the second wave, post-2013, has been very different, even if, as Stephens, Sexton, and Driessen point out, it has been continuous with the first wave in many ways, often including the same personnel. Cultured meat research has shifted venues, as scientists (some of whom participated in the first wave) and businesspeople found start-up companies with the financial support of venture capitalists. Post, for example, has cofounded a start-up company called Mosa Meats. The start-ups are explicit about their goal: growing meat to be marketed, sold, and consumed in lieu of conventional meat in the hopes of replacing as much of the conventional industrial meat system as possible. They are also usually very clear about what they see as the practical, and especially the moral, advantages of their approach, framing cultured meat as a product intended to alleviate animal suffering in the food system and reduce the environmental footprint of meat production. The latter goal depends on expectations that cultured meat would have a smaller environmental footprint than conventional meat, expectations that remain impossible to test as of this writing. Notably, assumptions about the practical and moral goal of cultured meat research have shaped the physical target of that research, or to put the point more simply, cultured meat workers seem to agree that if cultured meat is to replace conventional meat, it has to look and taste as much like it as possible. Mark Post's burger was the first highly mimetic form of cultured meat to appear in the media, copying a very familiar form of meat found in fast-food restaurants around the world.

I should also mention another feature of the second wave of cultured meat research: from the start of my research in 2013 to its conclusion in 2019, interviewing researchers and learning about their progress became more difficult. This was partly because the start-up model of cultured meat work relies on developing intellectual property, and researchers who would like to talk with social scientists and journalists are often not at liberty to do so. The result is that a certain non-transparency about the state of the art is a structural element of the current dominant funding model. Rather than criticizing this non-transparency because of the challenges it presents for our research, researchers such as myself are obliged to treat this as part of the social fabric of the field. In a sense, it is part of the "culture" of cultured meat research.

When I interviewed individuals involved in cultured meat work, and asked specifically about their moral-philosophical views, they almost always mentioned the utilitarian philosopher Peter Singer. In fact, some of my interviewees thought that their work might resolve the problem of meat as Singer has presented it. Utilitarians often emphasize the maximization of pleasure and the minimization of suffering, and it is hard to imagine a more utilitarian solution to the problem of animal agriculture than a technology that allows us to continue to enjoy meat without involving animals except as donors of small biopsies of cells. We might save animals and our environment without altering our appetites, minimizing suffering without sacrificing pleasure. For the cultured meat workers inspired by Singer, the difficulty does not lie in philosophical debate, but in a set of technical, regulatory, and business challenges. They often reminded me of this fact as I interviewed them, steering the conversation away from unresolved (and perhaps unresolvable) philosophical questions and toward what they saw as pragmatic ones.

Peter Singer, who himself supports the idea of cultured meat, has stated that he is a vegetarian because he is a utilitarian (see Singer 2013: Wurgaft 2019: ch. 12). To briefly review the essential points of that philosophical perspective, utilitarianism is consequentialist, meaning that it considers actions themselves neither morally right nor wrong, but instead judges them on the basis of their outcomes. It is universalist, weighing every being's interests equally, provided they fall within its circle of moral concern. Utilitarianism considers the welfare of each of those beings by looking at whether or not their needs are satisfied and is thus welfarist. It is also aggregative, meaning that it considers the welfare of a population together and not each member singly; it balances the happiness and suffering of all, hoping to ensure the happiness of the greatest number possible and keep suffering to a minimum. In that collective accounting, each individual only matters insofar as they contribute to the whole. For Singer, the fact that a nonhuman animal is capable of happiness, or suffering, is enough to place it within the circle of his moral concern.

The ideas of satisfaction, suffering, and happiness are critical to utilitarianism and to explaining how utilitarianism could have led Singer to vegetarianism. Satisfaction offers a way around the problem of the very different needs of different persons or beings. A wolf and a woman have different capacities for suffering and happiness, but both can experience both states. Jeremy Bentham himself used suffering as the criteria for drawing animals into the same moral circle as humans, writing in his *Introduction to the Principles of Morals and Legislation*: "the question is not, Can they reason? nor, Can they talk? but, Can they suffer?" (Bentham [1879] 1996). Using a term coined by an acquaintance he made while a student at Oxford, the psychologist and animal activist Richard Ryder, Singer called the denial of moral regard to nonhuman animals "speciesism." Significantly, moral regard here does not mean absolute equivalency— merely that animal suffering demands consideration just as human suffering does.

There is an oddly poetic fit between utilitarianism, a moral philosophy that seems to overcome "speciesism," and a technology that aspires to make biological things more malleable, producing meat out of cells rather than animal bodies, and making billions of animals in our food system effectively redundant. Both ask us to question assumptions that may be foundational to our lives (such as what kinds of creatures are worthy of moral treatment, or where meat comes from) with an eye toward a specific moral outcome. Both view the world from an administrative perch. Cultured meat could replace the unethical practice of treating animals as mere heaps of properties by replacing them with heaps of cells (a thing, rather than a being). It could enable us to eat meat without causing suffering—case closed. There are, of course, counterarguments to the utilitarian story about eating animals; Singer has his critics. One of the most important of these has been Tom Regan, a deontological philosopher who argued, in his book *The Case for Animal Rights*, that Singer and other utilitarians are wrong to think that "suffering" is the best term for summing up the harm we do to animals. Acknowledging that utilitarianism affords equality of a sort, Regan argued that this is "not the sort [of equality] an advocate for human or animal rights should have in mind. Utilitarianism has no room for the equal moral rights of different individuals because it has no room for their equal inherent value or worth." Regan suggested that the utilitarian perspective focuses on the suffering or happiness of beings rather than the beings themselves. If utilitarianism hedonistically identifies pleasure (and freedom from suffering) with the good, then it renders beings mere "receptacles" for the good rather than ends in themselves. His project was to base a theory of animal rights on animals' worth as beings—in his terms, "subjects of a life." Singer and Regan have agreed that we should not eat animals, but for very different reasons. Regan's reasons lead to a full-fledged account of rights, which Singer's do not. For Regan, the death of an animal, rather than the animal's suffering, is the greatest harm we can cause.

But the limitations of the utilitarian story about cultured meat have to do with more than philosophical arguments. They lie in the narrow scope of its vision. Bernard Williams wrote that utilitarianism "appeals to a frame of mind in which technical difficulty [...] is preferable to moral unclarity, no doubt because it is less alarming." In other words, the question of how to maximize happiness and minimize suffering is more pleasing to the utilitarian mind than the question of just what the moral good is, anyway. We could frame this still differently, as a preference for technical problems over potentially foggy interpretive ones, and a preference for an abstract story about maximizing the good in which actual beings (the creatures for whom things can be good) matter not at all. The larger problem, though, is that the utilitarian framing of cultured meat obscures a set of questions about what it means for humans and animals to be "subjects of a life," questions that have a more interpretive character.

It may seem unnecessary or beside the point to write about the nonmoral philosophical questions associated with meat or to depart from the utilitarian framing proposed by Singer and his supportive readers, including readers within the cultured meat movement. However, there are two good reasons to do so. One of these has to do with philosophical importance itself: a given philosophical question is not less important than another simply because it is not connected to a pressing situation, such as the mistreatment of animals; necessity may sweep us into addressing pressing questions first, but it is not clear that this nonphilosophical necessity makes them more important in philosophical terms. Another is that we simply do not know the future of cultured meat. Not only do we not know whether or not cultured meat products will meet the approval of regulatory bodies and make it to market, we do not know if customers will want to eat them or what debates we may hold in public about them. This fog of futurism means that we are well served by trying to understand cultured meat from all possible angles. We may not yet know what its true benefits may be— they may, in fact, be more philosophical than practical. In a world in which cultured meat never makes it to market, the thought experiments we stage around it may still help us to clarify our views on eating animals, and those views will have implications, regardless of the results of laboratory experiments. There are thus good reasons to resist the combination of philosophical and narrative closure that the "official future" of cultured meat presents.[3]

In his well-known 1977 essay on the images of animals that circulate in late capitalist societies, "Why Look at Animals?" the art critic and writer John Berger observed that zoos themselves are a kind of epitaph to a lost relationship between humans and other animals. At the zoo, Berger states, we get a subtle hint of the fact that our species has so constrained and controlled animals both wild and domestic that our only encounters with them in daily life come in the form of images; even the animal in a zoo cage becomes a kind of image, rather than the reality of that animal living in its natural environment. This is an interpretive claim, of course, but what it interprets is a set of empirically verifiable truths. The *longue durée* history of modernity certainly involves most humans—more urbanized and less directly involved with agriculture in every generation—spending less of their time with nonhuman animals, domesticated or wild, except in the case of pets. Berger does not answer his chapter's titular question. He leaves that to the reader. But his implication is that within the lost relationship between humans and other animals lay a set of insights not only into the independence of animals from ourselves but also into our own condition. These are what modernization and daily life without other animals have placed beyond our reach. He writes, "The 19th century, in western Europe and North America, saw the beginning of a process, today being completed by 20th century corporate capitalism, by which every tradition which has previously mediated between man and nature has been broken." Before this rupture, animals and man stood together at the center of the world. They could look at one another, and that exchange of gazes was (in Berger's view) crucially different from the exchange of gazes between two humans. It lacked the element of recognition, potentially mediated by language, present in human-to-human regard. But it carried a sense of common "creatureliness." All the forms of animal symbolism in human societies derive, Berger suggests, from the fundamental difference carried by the experience of looking at animals and finding that they look back, something that modernity has cost us.

Christine Korsgaard argues that when we live with animals, we find that they reveal aspects of human existence that might be hard to describe without them. As she puts it, they produce "a profound disturbance" in our thinking about the world (see Korsgaard 2012). We cannot "get them firmly into view" or "see them for what they really are." Korsgaard's claim is similar to Berger's, but what Berger described as the difference of the animal's gaze, Korsgaard sharpens to a philosophical challenge. What is different about animals? Partly, as Berger noted, that when we exchange a look with an animal we don't receive the kind of recognition a human might provide, the sense that we could draw near and understand one another through language. But the difference also has to do with how they live. Like us, animals organize their lives in relationship to the satisfaction of their needs. They have norms of a sort (is this a good bush in which to find berries?) but they do not seem to reflect on those norms in the same way that we reflect on ours; when I ask myself if I am a good son or a bad son, I can also ask what would qualify me as one and arrive at a kind of definition of "good son" or "bad son." This means that there is something fundamentally different about the way we organize our lives, even though the notion of "satisfaction" applies to human life just as it does to the lives of animals. Our ability to think reflectively about norms and ideals, Korsgaard argues, helps us to establish a sense that our lives are akin to projects, things we work on. Bears, tule elk, and sea otters don't seem to live like this.

It seems clear enough that one difference between humans and the other animals is that we can see our morality as a project that we work to perfect. In this way, morality is unlike other needs that get satisfied, though we could describe a given set of conditions for morality as being met or not met. Having a sense of morality thus distinguishes us from the other animals, which are simply amoral by nature. According to Korsgaard, arguing in her book *Fellow Creatures: Our Obligations to the Other Animals*, our morality does not make us superior (see Korsgaard 2018). Nor does it mean that we can do with the other animals whatever we wish. Immanuel Kant thought that the nonhuman animals are not ends in and of themselves. Thus we can use them for our own instrumental purposes—however, he also believed that we have substantial reasons not to mistreat animals unnecessarily in the process, reasons that are effectively duties to ourselves, seemingly because the possible analogy between animals and humans means that if I mistreat an animal, I may be capable of mistreating a human person too. Korsgaard thinks Kant was wrong to thus exclude animals from his Kingdom of Ends; he could have easily seen that animals must, if we can mistreat them, count as ends in and of themselves rather than mere things. But if that is the case, in what sense are the nonhuman animals ends in themselves?

Korsgaard wants to show that philosophy has had trouble understanding animals because comparisons between animals and humans become preoccupied with, and founder upon, the obvious differences that derive from human rationality, while missing something all creatures have in common: a sense of value that is "tethered" to their perspective. This is, in fact, true for such seemingly unsophisticated animals as banana slugs, even if it is more obviously true for animals that articulate their likes and dislikes in ways we easily grasp, such as golden retrievers. These sentient animals all engage in goal-oriented behaviors, ranging from finding food to finding a mate, and seek to avoid harm. When we say that humans are more important than other animals, we say something incoherent; important to whom? Importance is always tethered to a particular creature, a singular perspective. Korsgaard thinks that demonstrably greater intelligence or a capacity to think reflectively may distinguish us from other animals but rationality does not render us superior or make our lives more importantly meaningful. Except to us, and that "to us" matters enormously. Korsgaard wants to show that importance, or meaning, are not things that exist in the abstract, but rather always exist in relation to a particular being; again, this is tethering. In Korsgaard's account, human rationality is interesting, but it does not somehow elevate human beings above all other creatures, placing those creatures beyond humanity's moral regard. Indeed, it would be strange if it did so, since humanity is the only species that has something like moral regard, a notion of morality as subject to meditation, debate, and improvement. Responding to J. S. Mill's claim that it would be better to be Socrates dissatisfied than a pig satisfied, Korsgaard writes: "Would it be better for the *pig* if he were Socrates?" It's not clear that the pig is suffering from a lack of Socratic method. Again, animal difference is very hard to keep in view, and Mill's claim exemplifies this difficulty. As surprising an argument as this may seem, Socrates's life is not more inherently worthy than that of the pig. But the inherent worth of his life, like the pig's life, stems not from dialectic but from being a creature.

Korsgaard's claim that "we share the world with fellow creatures" has implications for the philosophy of meat in the early twenty-first century and for the special case of cultured meat. She argues that we are wrong to treat animals as thing-like; she agrees with Singer that nonhuman animals are worthy of our moral regard, although her reasons for thinking so are very different from his. Indeed, Korsgaard and Singer seem to agree that we should not conduct animal agriculture. What is strikingly different in Korsgaard's account is that she makes room for animals as beings as opposed to as sufferers or enjoyers. We should not imagine, she says against Singer and other hedonic utilitarians, that animals are mere receptacles for feelings, whose replacement with other receptacles would not alter the moral balance of the world. Animals can remind us that there are many ways for a creature to be an end in and of itself, and they can remind us of the differences between human reason and morality, and the way the other animals exist. But if the existence of other animals can remind us of what makes us distinctly human, this might make us skeptical about the wisdom of a morality that limits its goals to maximizing happiness and minimizing suffering. Earlier in this chapter, I suggested that the most philosophically interesting question about cultured meat might not be whether or not it resolves the moral issue of eating animals, but what it tells us about ourselves, as human creatures. If rationality (which lets us conduct science, and produce things like cultured meat, and engage in moral reflection too) distinguishes us from the other animals, what makes us "ends in and of ourselves" is something we share in common with them, namely animal existence.

It is for this reason that I have selected, as my favorite thought experiment from all the speculative thought experiments produced by people in the world of cultured meat research, the "Pig in the Backyard."[4] Unlike many visions of cultured meat production, it is not a vision devoid of animals. It was developed by the bioethicists Cor van der Weele and Clemens Driessen, drawing on a very real social experiment in which Dutch neighborhoods were given the opportunity to collectively raise a pig; they then had to debate and decide whether to kill and eat that pig (van der Weele & Driessen 2013). In the "Pig in the Backyard" scenario, cultured meat technology makes it possible for a community to raise an animal collectively, develop relationships with that animal, and also eat that animal's cells. What makes this thought experiment distinctive is that it asks how cultured meat might change our relationships with animals and our moral sense. Would we want to eat an animal's meat, if we knew them? Would the painlessness of turning their cells into meat sweeten the deal? Would it radically change what we think meat is and alter our willingness to eat it? Presumably, it would, and in ways that are impossible to predict. The future of the moral imagination is, well, difficult to imagine. But it seems also correct to assume that living with the animals whose cells we eat would keep their animal-ness in view in a way that the current meat-production system, or its replacement with a cultured meat system, would not. "The Pig in the Backyard" comes with built-in reminders that the pig is its own being, with its own satisfactions, rather than a means toward human ends. Looped into our instrumentalism by tissue culture, the pig would nevertheless be free to be a pig. That is to say, it would be a unified being rather than a bundle of measurable physical and emotional states. The possibilities for the philosophy of meat in the early twenty-first century are many, but it is worth remembering that every philosophical view we take of meat is also a view of the moral value of animals, including the surprisingly different animals that we are, ourselves.

Notes

Chapter 2

1 The ideas expressed in this chapter were first presented at the conference "Framing Recipes—Identities, Relationships, Norms" at the University of Milan in December 2018, organized by the Culinary Mind—Centre for the Philosophy of Food. Thanks to the audience for questions and comments. Special thanks to Andrea Borghini, Julien Dutant, and Patrik Engisch whose comments on the first draft helped to improve the chapter.

Chapter 3

1 This casts dishes as *tokens* and recipes as abstract entities of some sort (*types* or *kinds*). Thus, it departs from a view that some might find *prima facie* more intuitive—namely, the view that dishes are types of material objects that result from the application of certain types of procedures (see, e.g., Hirvonen in this volume). I cannot fully defend my choice here. However, reasons of ontological parsimony seem to preliminarily militate in its favor—after all, if we can commit to only two categories of entities (dishes and recipes) as opposed to three (recipe-types, dish-types, dish-tokens), this is preferable. Moreover, treating dishes as types introduces further complications, as it forces us to account for the relation between recipe-types and dish-types too.

2 It is a matter of dispute what is the best account of taste properties (see, e.g., Korsmeyer 1999; Smith 2009, 2013, 2015; Richardson 2013; Meskin and Robson 2015; Lycan 2018; Todd 2018b). Questions arise here that at least partially overlap with those raised by phenomenal properties of other sorts, such as colors, sounds, or odors. Though quite important, these issues are orthogonal to the present discussion. So, I will remain neutral on them, as much as possible (see also note 7).

3 This is a simplification. On this view, recipes are likely to be construed as *norm*-kinds, which have been largely discussed in philosophy of music (see e.g., Wolterstorff 1980; Anderson 1985; Dodd 2007). However, given the purposes of this chapter, we can safely ignore these complications. The substance of the points that I am going to raise will not change. I leave it up to the reader aware of the relevant complications to operate the relevant substitutions and adapt the discussion appropriately.

4 The reader familiar with the debate in philosophy of music might find this view similar to sonicism (Dodd 2007, 2010). This impression is not off target: to some extent, strong essentialism is modeled on sonicism. However, I do not mean to suggest here (a) that strong essentialism is the philosophy of food counterpart of sonicism or (b) that my criticisms can be applied, *mutatis mutandis*, across different domains to hit sonicism.

5 Of course, variations in taste among different instances of the same recipe are allowed as long as they are variations among *tokens* of the same *type*—recall, the taste of a recipe is a *type* of gustatory profile.

6 I am indebted to Patrik Engisch for pointing this out to me.
7 In the present context, this is an innocuous assumption concerning taste properties, insofar as it grants a point to the essentialist.
8 For a review of different version of realism and critiques, see Borghini (2015).
9 For very useful comments on previous drafts and fruitful discussions on this topic, I wish to thank Andrea Borghini and Patrik Engisch. For their feedbacks on the Introduction, I am grateful to a bunch of friends, inside and outside of philosophy—especially, Jo Ahlberg, Giulia Barison, Marco Coratolo, Enzo D'Armenio, Cristian Mariani, and Eleonora Tomo. Preparatory materials for this chapter were presented at a conference on recipes held in Milan in December 2018: I am grateful to the audience for their questions and remarks.

Chapter 7

1 In the relevant literature, there is considerable ambiguity in the terms used for these distinctions. Some authors use "flavor" to refer to mouth sensation and "flavor properties" to refer to the features of the objects we eat. Others use "tastings" for the former and "tastes" for the latter. I use "flavor" and "taste" interchangeably, because it is idiomatic to do so, but stipulate whether I mean mouth sensation or the properties that cause it.
2 An intriguing variation on this possibility arises when a cooking tradition changes in one place over time but is retained elsewhere. Food historian Massimo Montanari offers "a piece of personal advice: a voyage in space to the gastronomic traditions of North Africa can serve as a visa in time to our own [European] Middle Ages" (2015: 11).
3 For valuable comments on an earlier version of this chapter, I thank Mohan Matthen, Andrea Borghini, and Patrik Engisch.

Chapter 8

1 For the interested reader, there are many good introductions to the metaphysics of objects and properties. See, for example, Armstrong (1989) or Allen (2016).
2 Readers who wish to know more about representation can have a look at Crane (2016).
3 Reid (1983) is the historical source for such a line of argument. More recent defences of such a claim, in a variety of forms, can be found, *inter alia*, in Batty (2010), Richardson (2013), and Mizrahi (2017). A notable exception in the debate is Todd (2018a).
4 And what would the point be, one might ask? *Parmiggiano Reggiano* and *Grana Padano* are similar but different cheeses, with different areas and methods of production. But as Bottura is fond of saying, he's himself so much from the *Pargmiggiano Reggiano* region that his muscles are "made from *Parmiggiano Reggiano*" and the recipe has been developed in collaboration with producers of *Parmiggiano Reggiano* with the aim of becoming a "portrait of the Emilian countryside seen from ten kilometres away" (2014: 32). Accordingly, whatever the respective merits of the two cheeses, the intended expressive relation between the recipe and its core ingredient

that is an integral part of Bottura's culinary intention would be lost by substituting *Grana* for *Parmiggiano*. On this expressive relation, see Adams (2018).

5 For a philosophical discussion of culinary value and the role of recipes, see Engisch (2020, forthcoming). For a recent influential reflection and practice on the interaction between recipes and culinary and non-culinary values, see Bottura and Friends (2017). See also the chapters in this volume by Barnhill & Bonotti and Forman.

6 For a recent overview, see Morin (2016: ch. 1).

7 Researching "Alpabzug" on the Internet will acquaint one with many instances of the tradition.

8 See the chapter by Bordini in this volume for a detailed elaboration of this claim.

9 Earlier versions of this chapter were presented to (mostly skeptical) audiences at the "Framing Recipes" conference in Milan in December 2018, the half-baked seminar at the University of Milan in December 2019, and the EXRE research colloquium at the University of Fribourg in December 2019. Many thanks for questions and feedback to those who attended these events. In particular, thanks to Miloud Belkoniene, Philipp Blum, Andrea Borghini, Donatella Donati, Julia Langkau, Nicola Piras, Kristina Pucko, Beatrice Serini, Gianfranco Soldati, and Cain Todd.

Chapter 9

1 On the type/token distinction applied to recipes and dishes, see Bordini and Hirvonen, in this volume.

2 Engisch (personal communication) has expressed skepticism about this difference, arguing that chefs also have in mind the specific stages through which ingredients may pass and may try to display these differing properties. Nonetheless, insofar as the resulting dish necessarily depends on the same recurring developmental process, the standard wine recipe will not resemble the standard food recipe in this respect.

3 It's true that we speak of styles in cuisine—for example, Old French, New French, Modernist, and Nordic—and a chef may be expected to work in such a style. But I think this notion of style corresponds rather to the notion of "category" and not to "style" as I am using it here. These cuisine notions have a more taxonomic function. On the tricky difference between style and category, see the discussion below. It is also true that many chefs, particularly in higher-end establishments, will aim to express in their dishes and menus an individual style. Although it might seem that the notion of style plays a more determining and ubiquitous role in the world of wine than in the world of food generally, with the exception of certain "high-end" chefs, I will point out below that the difference is not so pronounced since "routine" wines too arguably have styles only in a category sense that can also be reduced to taste.

4 https://www.thewinecellarinsider.com/bordeaux-wine-producer-profiles/bordeaux/margaux/margaux/, accessed March 5, 2021.

5 Here I'm using "taste" broadly to refer to the experience of flavor and I'm assuming, controversially, that background cognitive influences, such as a knowledge of terroir and intention, can directly affect the experience of flavor. See Todd (2010) for discussion.

6 It is not that a fine wine like Chateau Margaux is thereby aiming to be unapproachable, but certainly fine wines aim to be complex, to express a unique terroir, and to that extent perhaps they can be a little challenging to non-connoisseurs.

7   I take this point to be in broad agreement with Bordini (in this volume) who argues that dishes come prior to recipes in terms of their taste.

8   Bordini argues that dishes have priority over recipes in determining taste, and I take it he would therefore agree with my view of wine recipes.

9   Many thanks to Andrea Borghini for helping me to clarify some of the ideas in this section concerning how recipe and style relate in wine.

Chapter 11

1   What we need to assume with respect to the existence of flavor is minimal, even an antirealist can accept that healthy human beings resemble each other in their psycho-physical properties at least insofar as the gustatory perception of certain chemical features will result in something that justifies us talking about a common taste (flavor) and a common taste experience.

2   Here and in what follows we will use "food" as an umbrella term for any solid or liquid nutrients that we taste and ingest while having a gustatory experience. We prefer to be a bit sloppy in the usage of an ordinary term rather than adopting the more pompous "victualia."

3   *Nota bene*: "taste" vs. "flavor." Usually the literature distinguishes between taste experiences, mono-sensorial experiences that we have by virtue of our taste receptor cells, and flavor, multisensorial experiences that combine taste, touch, smell, and retro-smell perceptions. Since we want to stay with the established term "aftertaste," we will speak about "aftertaste" and "primary taste" although, strictly speaking, we are talking about "primary flavor experiences" and "after flavor experiences." In other words, we do not intend aftertaste to be understood as restricted to taste perceptions.

4   Colman (2000: 42). And here is the definition of the more general term "aftereffect," to which both afterimages and aftertastes are deemed to belong: "Any phenomenon occurring some time after its cause, especially (in psychology) a delayed sensory or perceptual experience" (Colman 2000: 42). While in what follows we argue against the idea of putting together aftertaste and afterimage in the category of aftersensations, we grant that "aftereffect" is general enough to encompass both.

5   "Sensationalists" who think that afterimages are non-worldly purely sensational non-perceptual features of experience, include Boghossian & Velleman (1989), Block (1996), and Kind (2008).

6   The terms "sensationalists" and "purists" are taken from Phillips (2012). Although sensationalists are anti-representationalist in the sense who do not accept that the phenomenal character of our perceptual experience is exhausted by the representational content, not all purists are representationalists. Phillips himself defends a direct realist version of purism (see also note 14).

7   While we are fully aware of the dangers that lurk in opening the Pandora's box entailing the phrase "epistemic reliability" (see Goldman & Beddor [2015] for an overview), we are confident enough that our minimal definition will convey the intuitive understanding required for our purposes.

8   The fact that we talk about primary "percept" and after*sensations* merely reflect that the term "afterpercept" is not very common in the literature, and we prefer to follow usage.

9   Note that the epistemic superiority of primary percepts with regard to aftersensations even holds in cases where we have experiences of stars that are so far away that they

have ceased to exist during the time it took the light reflected from them to reach us. In such cases the light we are perceiving from the star, the proximal cause of our experience, maintains the core information about the distal cause. Since the proximal cause is the only constitutively responsible factor in producing the visual experience of the star, the fact that the star has ceased to exist does not decrease the epistemic reliability of the experience, at least not per se.

10 We do not want to make a stance as to whether odours are clouds of molecules. Our view is compatible also with a view like for example Richardson's, where odors are "parcels of stuff" (2018: 12) supervening on molecules.

11 Cf. Valberg (1992).

12 What we have in mind here is Dainton's model of specious present experiences in particular, although Dainton (2000) does not use a representational framework.

13 As Richardson (2013) points out, the fact that receptors that are usually dedicated to smell have an important role in the gustatory experience does not make the experience of taste an *olfactory* experience. As we will see in "Again the Received View: Aftertastes Are Not Aftersensations," if we are right, the so-called retro-smell may play a crucial role in explaining the epistemic import of aftertaste.

14 This is even clearer for Philipps's version of purism, in which afterimages present light phenomena and not concrete objects as often the "object source" is.

15 Specifically Loomis (1972) and Virsu & Laurinen (1977).

Chapter 12

1 I say that this atmosphere does characterize inquiry, though sometimes it might be more appropriate to say that I *wish* it characterized inquiry. Whatever the attitude that prevails between inquirers, there is a sense in which their activity is at least interactive. What I mean is that, despite the stories inquirers may tell themselves about being disinterested subjects, they are in fact in relations both with the things into which they inquire and with other inquirers.

2 I'm sure the sorts of cooking that go on in multi-star restaurants do or could manifest an element of abstracted theoreticity that would rival that of the sciences.

3 Thanks to Susan Heineman for this example.

4 There still may seem to be a troubling disparity between cooking and theorizing, however, because it seems that cooking produces food a lot more often than theories produce practical consequences in one's life in the world. Precisely. I think there is. And I think this is a failure of theorizing. I *am* willing to say that it would be very useful to try to make theories that matter to people in our lives, just as it's useful to create recipes that go on to get used. But again, I don't want to translate this into an essentialist assertion.

5 It's a brutal fact that this relationship of mystification is far more common than a cooperative one. In some respects, then, the recipe model is an idealistic one; it works best when the participants in inquiry are willing participants, anxious to reveal motives and strategies.

6 Evelyn Fox Keller has already given us an example, in Barbara McClintock, of a biologist who thinks of her research as a loving *communication* with her corn plants. And the work of some theoretical physicists, who utilize the notion of a "participatory universe," also point toward this way of thinking about inquiry.

Chapter 16

1   There is no single definition of public diplomacy, but there is a consensus that
    as a concept it is a key mechanism through which nations foster mutual trust
    and productive relationships and has become crucial to building a secure
    global environment. See USC Center for Public Diplomacy, https://www.
    uscpublicdiplomacy.org/page/what-is-pd, accessed April 20, 2020.
2   "To the Congress, he brought his refined French style, as well as a host of tributes to
    the gathered diplomats. His *gâteau Nesselrode*, a frozen treat made from chestnuts
    and boozy fruit, was created in honor of Count Karl Nesselrode, the Russian
    negotiator. The famous *Charlotte Rousse*, a molded dessert made from cream and
    ladyfingers, was supposedly a tribute to the Russian czar, Alexander I. Carême's
    buttering-up of the gathered diplomats likely aided Talleyrand's negotiating position,
    and in the end, the outcome was favorable to the French. Carême was subsequently
    invited for a European tour, and served under both the British Prince Regent, George
    IV, as well as Tzar Alexander I. He earned the nickname 'The King of Chefs and the
    Chef of Kings', truly an honorable title. His legacy in the kitchen remains, but we
    should not forget his larger contribution—peace in Europe, ushered in with chestnuts
    and ladyfingers" (Chapple-Sokol n.d.).
3   The *Journal of Public Diplomacy* dedicated an issue to this subject in 2014
    with articles on a wide range of issues falling under concept. http://static1.
    squarespace.com/static/5be3439285ede1f05a46dafe/t/5be3511daa4a996fcaa49
    8f3/1541624135259/GastroDiplomacy. See also Johanna Mendelson Forman, Salon
    27, Gastrodiplomacy, Museum of Modern Art, September 11, 2018, http://momarnd.
    moma.org/salons/salon-27-gastrodiplomacy/, accessed April 2, 2020.
4   UNESCO, *Convention for the Safeguarding of Intangible Cultural Heritage*, defined
    as the practices, representations, expressions, as well as the knowledge and skills
    (including instruments, objects, artifacts), which communities, groups, and in some
    cases, individuals recognize as part of their cultural heritage. Food is a category
    under this convention. UNESCO website https://ich.unesco.org/en/home, accessed
    April 16, 2020.
5   *Comida Peruana para el Mundo*, the brand name for Peru's efforts, has been
    especially helpful in altering the views of reluctant tourists who had been afraid to
    travel there in the 1990s because of a guerrilla group, the Sendero Luminoso, who
    terrorized both urban and rural locations. Peru also used the program to promote its
    biodiversity, being the home to 3,000 varieties of potatoes and creating a generation
    of chefs who were now developing recipes using indigenous product to create dishes
    of remarkable complexity of ingredients and techniques. https://www.peru.travel/
    gastronomia/pe/, accessed April 12, 2020. In 2015 the Mexican Secretary of Tourism
    and the Secretary of the Treasury issued a strategic plan for developing culinary
    tourism. See "Politica Nacional Gastronomica 2015–2018." Secretaria de Turismo
    Mexicana, 2015.
6   For example, in Colombia after the 2016 peace accord, both the government and
    business groups started to brand the country's diverse ecosystems as a source for new
    foods and recipes after the end of its 66-year civil war. Chefs were sent to remote
    areas that had once been held by guerrilla groups to explore with local home cooks
    ways to transform local flora and fauna into new recipes. Colombia's president
    even created the position of a culinary ambassador for peace to promote the plan

internationally. Alejandro Cuellar Suarez, *Cocina y Paz,* Medellin, Colombia 2016. Chef Cuellar was named Colombia's first culinary ambassador for peace.

7   Rakowitz also did similar projects using a food truck in Chicago to sell Iraqi meals. A similar project, Conflict Kitchen, in Pittsburgh, Pennsylvania, a take-out restaurant, also used cuisines of countries with adversarial relations with the United States to stimulate conversation.

8   The COVID-19 pandemic had a transformative effect on projects that supported training of food entrepreneurs. Many programs quickly geared up to become neighborhood feeding programs for those who had lost their income. "Should Social Gastronomy Be Part of the Restaurant Industry's New Normal?" *Un-Plated,* July 21, 2020, https://un-plated.com/should-social-gastronomy-be-part-of-the-restaurant-industrys-new-normal/.

9   The SGM was officially announced at the World Economic Forum in Davos in January 2018 by David Hertz and Devry Boughner Vorwerk, corporate vice president global corporate affairs at Cargill, and has since been growing rapidly. See https://www.socialgastronomy.org/our-events.

10   "We think chefs can be powerful advocates for a better food future—inspiring people to make changes in their kitchens and communities and empowering them to call on governments and companies to also play their part" (SDG2 Advocacy Hub n.d.). Member chefs have also created an online database of recipes, "Cooking the Manifesto," which features ways to prepare foods sustainably.

11   There are eleven hubs located in Latin America, the United States, Europe, and Asia. Each one operates independently. Hubs are a collective of existing SG projects that have taken on the responsibility to activate and mobilize toward greater impact in the fight against world hunger, social inequality, and food waste, making the movement tangible. https://www.socialgastronomy.org/faq, accessed April 20, 2020.

12   There are hubs in Malmo, London, Berlin, Phnom Penh, Minneapolis, Zurich, Santiago, Medellin, Rio de Janeiro, Santarem, and Miami, https://www.socialgastronomy.org/new-page, accessed April 2, 2020.

13   Boturra later opened a Refettorio in London and Paris and helped chef David Hertz create one in Rio de Janeiro in 2017 to use food leftover from the Olympic villages to serve the poor.

14   These restaurant training centers are no longer in operation.

15   Today World Central Kitchen is one of the main feeding agencies for hospital workers in many cities in the United States and Europe. He is also using his celebrity to advocate for people in the food sector who have been forced out of work because of the pandemic. https://www.eater.com/2017/11/10/16623204/world-central-kitchen-jose-andres-bahamas-puerto-rico-haiti-houston, accessed April 1, 2020.

16   The Refugee Food Festival is now a well-established annual event with a goal of demonstrating that newcomers work hard to earn a living and reducing the mistrust around "different" people.

17   In the United States, the newest and youngest member of Congress, Alexandra Ocasio-Cortez, attributed her political win in 2018 to food. "My campaign started in food, and in a lot of ways, evolved out of food." Food is political. "The food industry is the nexus of almost all the major forces in our politics today. Its super closely linked with climate change and ethics. It's the nexus of the minimum wage fights, of immigration law, of criminal justice reform, of health care debates, of education. You'd be hard pressed to find a political issue that doesn't have food implications." Hilary Cadigan, *Bon Appetit*, November 2018, www.bonappetit.com,

accessed December 1, 2018. See also Eve Turow, *A Taste of Generation Yum, How the Millennial Generation's Love for Organic Fare, Celebrity Chefs and Microbrews Will Make or Break the Future of Food* (Independent, 2015).

18   The connection between food and peacebuilding may even have deeper roots in the late eighteenth century in the work of Immanuel Kant whose treatise *Perpetual Peace: A Philosophical Sketch*, laid out the way hospitality would allow a stranger to not be treated as an enemy when he arrives in the land of another. Kant also noted the inhospitable actions of the civilized and commercial states where states trying to establish economic undertakings "excited widespread wars among the various states, spread famine, rebellion, perfidy, and the whole litany of evils which afflict mankind" https://www.mtholyoke.edu/acad/intrel/kant/kant1.htm, accessed April 10, 2020.

19   "Conflict Café" International Alert, https://www.international-alert.org/conflict-cafe, accessed April 20, 2020. Yotam Ottolenghi, the well-known Israeli chef and cookbook author, was quoted on the website as supporting these dinners because "there is something very significant about the act of bringing people together around a table to eat, whatever their differences: the very act of cooking and sharing food is a unifying one. It's true that this is not the only tool for peace, but it is a step in the right direction and a great reason to support Conflict Café."

20   "Conflict Kitchen." International Alert, https://www.international-alert.org/tags/conflict-kitchen, accessed April 20, 2020. Recipes were part of the site. For example, a Jordanian woman prepared a dish called Mansaf. This complex lamb stew was topped with a white yogurt sauce. Mansaf's white color was a symbol of peace, a way to indicate to those partaking of the feast that the dispute had been resolved. The woman recalled how her father would always ask her mother to prepare this dish and invite guests as a sign to others in the household and community that a dispute had been resolved.

21   There is also a documentary, *Hummus, the Movie*, using a subtitle, "It Unites, It Divides, It's Delicious." Holyland Productions, 2016 N: https://amzn.to/2GcN2wC

22   The number of books on Amazon featured only books, and not CDs, Kindle versions, or Audible. Otherwise the numbers would have been in the hundreds. One of the newest books to surface in 2019, *A Place at the Table: New American Recipes from the Nation's Top Foreign-Born Chefs*, combined both groups but focused on the contributions made by immigrants to American cuisines; Rick Kinsel and Gabrielle Langholtz, Editors, Prestel, Munich, London, New York, 2019. But the book that grabbed the most attention was *Together: Our Community Cookbook*, Hubb Community Kitchen (Clarkson Potter 2018), which was supported by Meghan, the Duchess of Sussex. It used the power of food to support the survivors of the Grenfell Tower fire in London in 2017, the majority of them being immigrants from Algeria, Egypt, India, Iraq, Russia, Uganda, and Yemen.

23   *The Cuisines of Life: Stories and Recipes from Turkey's New Food Entrepreneurs* (2019 Istanbul) cataloged recipes from a diverse group of men and women, refugees and residents, who came together around the common methods, spices, and tastes of their respective dishes. Co-editing this cookbook that memorialized the recipes of Syrian refugees and Turkish women demonstrated the power of food as a shared experience to create a community. Once trainees discovered similarities in their respective cuisines, each group was able to compare cooking methods and break down preconceived notions about each other's culture.

24   There are too many programs to list them all, but among the more successful ones that use a social gastronomy mindset are Newcomer Kitchen in Toronto,

https://thedepanneur.ca/newcomerkitchen/; Sanctuary Kitchen, in New Haven, Connecticut, https://faithandleadership.com/sanctuary-kitchen-transforms-refugees-lives-through-power-food; Eat Off Beat, started as a project of the International Refugee Commission in New York City, https://eatoffbeat.com/who-we-are; Mera Kitchen Collective in Baltimore, https://www.mera.kitchen/; LIFE Project in Turkey, https://lifeforentrepreneurs.com/.

25 The portability of recipes is a frequent topic of discussion in the academic literature about a refugee cuisine and immigration. There is an ongoing debate about whether committing a recipe to writing, something that was once part of an oral tradition, actually transforms the way a dish tastes or loses something in the act of preparation.

26 Gillian Crowther, *Eating Culture, An Anthropological Guide to Food* Toronto (2013). See chapter 5, "Recipes and Dishes." pp. 129–48, for a more in-depth discussion. In the United States there is a curious regulation from Office of Refugee Resettlement of the Department of Health and Human Services. It strongly recommends that groups working with newly arrived refugees in their communities provide the family or individuals with what they describe as a "Culturally Appropriate Home Meal" or CAHM. The regulation was enacted in 1980 when the Refugee Act was passed. Anna Lucente Sterling, "Resettling Refugees One 'Culturally Appropriate' Hot Meal at a Time." *HuffPost*, May 30, 2019, https://www.huffpost.com/entry/trump-administration-refugee-resettlement_n_5ceecb15e4b05a622337eb5a.

27 Edelman Trust, "Edelman Trust Barometer 2020 Global Report." 2020, https://www.edelman.com/sites/g/files/aatuss191/files/2020-01/2020%20Edelman%20Trust%20Barometer%20Global%20Report.pdf. Food Industry Trust Increases.

28 Slow Food International, 2015, https://www.slowfood.com/about-us/our-philosophy/. See the Slow Food Manifesto for details.

29 Ambassador Jan Eliasson, the Swedish diplomat and former UN Undersecretary General, suggested that to solve the food problem and create sustainability, we first had to "make peace with nature." Speech at EAT Forum, June 12, 2018, Stockholm, Sweden (available at: https://www.youtube.com/watch?v=fIXUdxiTXoI, accessed June 4, 2021).

Chapter 17

1 Much of this chapter explores themes I first took up in Wurgaft (2019: ch. 12), "Philosophers."

2 This chapter does not claim to present an all-inclusive history of cultured meat research, but I believe it offers the best balance of inclusion and concision available; readers may also be interested in the version I present in Wurgaft (2019).

3 I borrow the term "official future" from the futures consultant Peter Schwartz. See Schwartz (1991) and Gilman (2017).

4 I have written about this thought experiment elsewhere. See Wurgaft (2019: 187–9), and Wurgaft "Biotech Cockaigne of the Vegan Hopeful." in *The Hedgehog Review*, Spring 2019. You could be forgiven for thinking cultured meat was, as an idea, mostly an excuse to write thought experiments in moral philosophy.

References

Adams, M. (2009). "Empirical Evidence and the Knowledge-that/Knowledge-how Distinction." *Synthese*, 170: 97–114.

Adams, M. (2018). "The Aesthetic Value of Local Food." *The Monist*, 101 (3): 324–39.

Adams, T. (2017). "Massimo Bottura and His Global Movement to Feed the Hungry." *The Observer*. May 21. [online] Available at: https://www.theguardian.com/lifeandstyle/2017/may/21/massimo-bottura-feed-the-hungry-food-for-soul. Accessed April 20, 2020.

Alaimo, S. & Hekman, S. (eds.) (2008). *Material Feminisms*. Bloomington: Indiana University Press.

Alkon, A. H. & Agyeman, J. (2011). "Introduction: The Food Movement as Polyculture." In: Alison Hope Alkon & Julian Agyeman (eds.), *Cultivating Food Justice: Race, Class, and Sustainability*. Cambridge, MA: The MIT Press: 1–20.

Allen, S. R. (2016). *A Critical Introduction to Properties*. London: Bloomsbury.

America's Test Kitchen (2018). "Kitchen Smarts: How to Make Hard-Cooked Eggs so Easy to Peel That the Shells Practically Fall Off." July 13. [online] Available at: https://www.americastestkitchen.com/articles/1072-kitchen-smarts-how-to-make-hard-cooked-eggs-so-easy-to-peel-that-the-shells-practically-fall-off. Accessed March 7, 2021.

Anderson, J. (1985). "Musical Kinds." *British Journal of Aesthetics*, 25: 43–9.

Anjari, M. & Sit, J. (2018). *The Bread and Salt between Us: Recipes and Stories from a Syrian Refugee's Kitchen*. New York: Lake Isle Press.

Appadurai, A. (1988). "How to Make a National Cuisine: Cookbooks in Contemporary India." *Comparative Studies in Society and History*, 30 (1): 17–18.

Armstrong, D. M. (1989). *Universals: An Opiniated Introduction*. Boulder, CO: Westview Press.

Ashmolean Museum (2019). "Last Supper in Pompeii." May 7. [online] Available at: https://www.ashmolean.org/article/last-supper-in-pompeii. Accessed September 7, 2021.

Avieli, N. (2016). "The Hummus Wars Revisited: Israeli-Arab Food Politics and Gastromediation." *Gastronomica: The Journal of Critical Food Studies*, 16 (3): 19–30.

Avieli, N. (2018). *Food and Power: A Culinary Ethnography of Israel*. Oakland: University of California Press.

Bacchini, F. (2020). "Culinary Works Come in Three Ontological Flavours." *Humana. Mente*, 13 (38): 163–89.

Bamman, M. J. (2017). "Portland Burrito Spot Shutters amid Claims of Cultural Appropriation." *Eater Portland*. May 22. [online] Available at: https://pdx.eater.com/2017/5/22/15677760/portland-kooks-burrito-cultural-appropriation. Accessed June 4, 2021.

Barad, K. (2003). "Posthumanist Performativity: Toward an Understanding of How Matter Comes to Matter." *Signs: Journal of Women in Culture and Society*, 28 (31): 801–31.

Barad, K. (2007). *Meeting the Universe Halfway: Quantum Physics and the Entanglement of Matter and Meaning*. Durham, NC: Duke University Press.

Barber, D. (2009). "The Third Plate: Field Notes for the Future of Food." *The Third Plate*. [online] Available at: https://www.thethirdplate.com/.

Barr, S. (2018). "This Is How You Should Eat Sushi, According to an Expert." *The Independent*, May 11. [online] Available at: https://www.independent.co.uk/life-style/food-and-drink/how-to-eat-sushi-chef-nobu-matsuhisa-wasabi-chopsticks-soy-sauce-a8330611.html. Accessed September 7, 2021.

Batty, C. (2010). "A Representational Account of Olfactory Experience." *Canadian Journal of Philosophy*, 40 (4): 511–38.

Beckett, N. (2008). 1001 *Wines You Must Try Before You Die*. London: Cassell.

Begos, K. (2018). *Tasting the Past: One Man's Quest to Discover (and Drink!) the World's Original Wines*. Chapel Hill, NC: Algonquin Books.

Bentham, J. ([1879] 1996). *Introduction to the Principles of Morals and Legislation*. Oxford: Clarendon Press.

Berlant, L. (1998). "Intimacy: A Special Issue." *Intimacy*, 24 (2): 281–8.

Bernstein, R. (1983). *Beyond Objectivism and Relativism: Science, Hermeneutics and Praxis*. Philadelphia: University of Pennsylvania Press.

Bertinetto, A. (2020). "Dishes as Performances Authenticity, Normativity and Improvisation in the Kitchen." *Humana.Mente*, 13 (38): 111–42.

Biener, A., Cawley, J. & Meyerhoefer, C. (2017). "The High and Rising Costs of Obesity to the US Health Care System." *Journal of General Internal Medicine*, 32 (1): 6–8.

Block, N. (1990). "Inverted Earth." *Philosophical Perspectives*, 4: 53–79.

Block, N. (1996). "Mental Paint and Mental Latex." *Philosophical Issues*, 7: 19–49.

Bober, P. P. (1999). *Art, Culture, and Cuisine: Ancient and Medieval Gastronomy*. Chicago: University of Chicago Press.

Boghossian, P. A. & Velleman, J. D. (1989). "Colour as a Secondary Quality." *Mind*, 98 (389): 81–103.

Bon Appétit (n.d.). "Bon Appétit Magazine: Recipes, Cooking, Entertaining, Restaurants." *Bon Appétit*. [online] Available at: https://www.bonappetit.com. Accessed December 1, 2018.

Borghini, A. (2010). "Generals and Particulars." In: Tadeusz Czarnecki, Katarzyna Kijania-Placek, Olga Poller & Jan Wolenski (eds.), *Analytical Way: Proceedings of the Sixth European Conference of Analytic Philosophy*. London: College Publications (King's College): 379–95.

Borghini, A. (2011). "What Is a True Ribollita? Memory and the Quest for Authentic Food." In: T. Piazza (ed.), *Secret and Memory in the Information Age*. Porto: Afrontamento: 93–106.

Borghini, A. (2012). "On Being the Same Wine." *Rivista di Estetica*, 51: 175–92.

Borghini, A. (2014a). "Geographical Indications, Food, and Culture." In: P. B. Thomson & D. M. Kaplan (eds.), *Encyclopedia of Food and Agricultural Ethics*. Berlin: Springer: 1115–19.

Borghini, A. (2014b). "Authenticity in Food." In: P. B. Thomson & D. M. Kaplan (eds.), *Encyclopedia of Food and Agricultural Ethics*. Berlin: Springer: 180–5.

Borghini, A. (2014c). "Substantial Equivalence." In P. B. Thomson & D. M. Kaplan (eds.), *Encyclopedia of Food and Agricultural Ethics*. Berlin: Springer: 1169–73.

Borghini, A. (2015). "What Is a Recipe?" *Journal of Agricultural and Environmental Ethics*, 28: 719–38.

Borghini, A. (2017). "Hunger." In P. B. Thompson & D. M. Kaplan (eds.), *Encyclopedia of Food and Agricultural Ethics*, 2nd edition. Berlin: Springer. https://doi.org/10.1007/978-94-007-6167-4_563-1.

Borghini, A., Donati, D. & Piras, N. (2020). "Metaphysics at the Table." Special issue of *Argumenta*, 5 (2): 179–84.

Borghini, A. & Gandolini, M. (2020). "Recipes, Their Authors, and Their Names." *Humana.Mente*, 13 (38): 143–62.

Borghini, A. & Piazza, T. (2019). "The Aesthetic Properties of Wine." In: Lars Aagaard-Mogensen & Jane Forsey (eds.), *On Taste: Aesthetic Exchanges*. Newcastle upon Tyne: Cambridge Scholars Publishing, 101–22.

Borghini, A. & Piras, N. (2020a). "Introduction." In: *The Philosophy of Food: Recipes Between Arts and Algorithms, Humana.Mente*, 13 (38): 3–13.

Borghini, A. & Piras, N. (2020b). "The Philosophy of Food: Recipes between Arts and Algorithms." Special issue of *Humana.Mente*, 13 (38).

Borghini, A. & Piras, N. (2020c). "On Interpreting Something as Food." *Food Ethics*, 6 (1). https://doi.org/10.1007/s41055-020-00082-5.

Borghini, A. & Baldini, A. (2021). "Cooking and Dining as Forms of Public Art." *Food, Culture & Society* (scheduled publication for August 2022 issue). https://doi.org/10.1080/15528014.2021.1890891

Borkenhagen, C. (2017). "Evidence-based Creativity: Working between Art and Science in the Field of Fine Dining." *Social Studies of Science*, 47 (5): 630–54.

Bottura, M. (2014). *Never Trust a Skinny Italian Chef*. London: Phaidon.

Bottura, M. and Friends (2017). *Bread Is Gold: Extraordinary Meals with Ordinary Ingredients*. London: Phaidon.

Boucher, B. (2018). "'It's a Strange Communion,' Artist Michael Rakowitz on Why He Set up an Iraqi Food Truck Outside the MCA Chicago." *Artnet News*. January 15. Available at: https://news.artnet.com/art-world/iraq-cooking-michael-rakowitz-enemy-kitchen-1198394. Accessed 2019.

Bowen, S., Elliott, S. & Brenton, J. (2014). "The Joy of Cooking?" *Contexts*, 13 (3): 20–5.

Bower, A. (ed.) (1997). *Recipes for Reading: Community Cookbooks, Stories, Histories*. Amherst: University of Massachusetts Press.

Buccafusco, C. J. (2007). "On the Legal Consequences of Sauces: Should Thomas Keller's Recipes Be Per Se Copyrightable?" *Cardozo Law's Arts & Entertainment Law Journal*, 24: 1122–55.

Burgess, A., Cappelen, H. & Plunkett, D. (eds.) (2020). *Conceptual Engineering and Conceptual Ethics*. Oxford: Oxford University Press.

Burnston, D. C. (2017). "Interface Problems in the Explanation of Action." *Philosophical Explorations*, 20: 242–58.

Butterfill, S. A. & Sinigaglia, C. (2014). "Intention and Motor Representation in Purposive Action: Intention and Motor Representation in Purposive Action." *Philosophy and Phenomenological Research* 88 (1): 119–45.

Byrne, A. (2020). "Inverted Qualia." In: *The Stanford Encyclopedia of Philosophy* (Spring 2020 edition). Edited by E. N. Zalta. [online] Available at: https://plato.stanford.edu/archives/spr2020/entries/qualia-inverted/. Accessed September 7, 2021.

Cappon, L. (1988). *The Adams-Jefferson Letters: The Complete Correspondence between Thomas Jefferson and Abigail and John Adams*. Chapel Hill: University of North Carolina Press.

Caterina S. (2018). "The Notion of 'Work' in EU Copyright Law After Levola Hengelo: One Answer Given, Three Question Marks Ahead." *European Intellectual Property Review*, 7/41: 415–24.

Cates, T. (1981). *Infamous Santo Tomas*. San Marcos, CA: Pacific Press (1957. Reprinted).

Catts, O. & Zurr, I. (2004–2005). "Ingestion/Disembodied Cuisine: Toward Victimless meat." *Cabinet Magazine* (16): *The Sea* 13.

Caucus Business Development Council (n.d.). "Recipes for Peace." [online] Available at: http://caucasusbusiness.net/our-work-2/recipes-for-peace/. Accessed September 16, 2019.

Center for International Private Enterprise (2019). "The Cuisine of LIFE: Recipes and Stories of the New Food Entrepreneurs of Turkey."

Chapple-Sokol, S. (n.d.). "Five Meals That Changed the Course of History." Unpublished Manuscript shared by author, 2016.

Chapple-Sokol, S. (2013). "Culinary Diplomacy: Breaking Bread to Win Hearts and Minds." *The Hague Journal of Diplomacy*, 8 (2): 161–83.

Charsley, S. (1997). "Marriages, Weddings, and Their Cakes." In P. Caplan (ed.), *Food, Health, and Identity*. London: Routledge: 50–70.

Chemero, A. (2009). *Radical Embodied Cognitive Science*. Cambridge, MA: MIT Press.

Chisholm, R. (1969). "The Loose and Popular and the Strict and Philosophical Senses of Identity." In N. Care & H. Grimm (eds.), *Perception and Identity*. Cleveland, OH: Case Western Reserve University Press: 82–106.

Ciani, J. (2015). "Intellectual Property Rights and the Growing Interest in Legal Protection for Culinary Creations." In: M. Nobile (ed.), *World Food Trends and the Future of Food*. Milan: Ledizioni: 15–32.

Cohen, N. (2018). *Feeding or Starving Gentrification: The Role of Food Policy—Policy Brief*. New York: CUNY Urban Food Policy Institute. https://static1.squarespace.com/static/572d0fcc2b8dde9e10ab59d4/t/5aba9936575d1fe8933df34e/1522178358593/Policy-Brief-Feeding-or-Starving-Gentrification-20180327-Final.pdf. Accessed September 7, 2021.

Colman, A. M. (ed.) (2000). *Oxford Dictionary of Psychology*. Oxford: Oxford University Press.

Colquhoun, K. (2007). *Taste: The Story of Britain through Its Cooking*. New York: Bloomsbury.

Coole, D. (2005). "Rethinking Agency: A Phenomenological Approach to Embodiment and Agentic Capacities." *Political Studies*, 53: 124–42.

Crane, T. (2014). "Is Perception a Propositional Attitude?" In his: *Aspects of Pychologism*. Cambridge, MA: Harvard University Press.

Crane, T. (2016). *The Mechanical Mind*, 3rd edition. London: Routledge.

Cray, W. D. (2016). "Unperformable Works and the Ontology of Music." *British Journal of Aesthetics*, 56: 67–81.

Crouter, N. (n.d.). *Stark Family Papers*. Cambridge, MA: Harvard University. Schlesinger Library. Collection Identifier: MC 559.

Cunningham, E. (2009). "Protecting Food under the Rubric of Copyright: Should the Law Play a Bigger Role in the Kitchen?" *Journal of High Technology Law*, 9 (21): 22–51.

Dainton, B. (2000). *Stream of Consciousness: Unity and Continuity in Conscious Experience*. New York: Routledge.

Daniels, N. (2007). *Just Health: Meeting Health Needs Fairly*, 1st edition. Cambridge, New York: Cambridge University Press.

Davies, S. (2008). "Authenticity in Musical Performance." In: A. Neill & A. Ridley (eds.). *Arguing about Art: Contemporary Philosophical Debates*, 3rd edition. London and New York: Routledge: 59–70.

Derven, D. (2001). "A Feast of Gold." *Gastronomica*, 1 (3): 4–5.

Devitt, M. (2011). "Methodology and the Nature of Knowing How." *Journal of Philosophy*, 108: 205–18.

Dewey, J. (1929). *The Quest for Certainty*. New York: Perigree.

Dewey, J. (1938). *Logic: The Theory of Inquiry*. New York: Holt, Rinehart and Winston.

Dewey, J. (1958). *Experience and Nature*, 2nd edition. New York: Dover.

De Wit, M. M., De Vries, S., Van Der Kamp, J. & Withagen, R. (2017). "Affordances and Neuroscience: Steps towards a Successful Marriage." *Neuroscience and Biobehavioral Reviews*, 80: 622–9.

Di Stefano, G., King, A. & Verona, G. (2013). "Kitchen Confidential? Norms for the Use of Transferred Knowledge in Gourmet Cuisine." *Strategic Management Journal*, 35 (11): 1645–70.

Dodd, J. (2007). *Works of Music: An Essay in Ontology*. Oxford: Oxford University Press.

Dodd, J. (2010). "Confessions of an Unrepentant Timbral Sonicist." *British Journal of Aesthetics*, 50: 33–52.

Druckman, C. (2010). "Why Are There No Great Women Chefs?" *Gastronomica*, 10 (1): 24–31.

Edelman Trust (2020). "Edelman Trust Barometer 2020 Global Report." pp. 47–8. [online] Available at: https://www.edelman.com/sites/g/files/aatuss191/files/2020-01/2020%20 Edelman%20Trust%20Barometer%20Global%20Report.pdf. Accessed September 7, 2021.

Elias, M. (2017). *Food on the Page. Cookbooks and American Culture*. Philadelphia: University of Pennsylvania Press.

Eliasson, J. (2018). "Sustainability at Land and Sea." Speech at the *EAT Forum*. [online] Available at: https://www.youtube.com/watch?v=fIXUdxiTXoI. Accessed June 4, 2021.

Engell, J. (1981). *The Creative Imagination: Enlightenment to Romanticism*. Cambridge, MA: Harvard University Press.

Engisch, P. (n.d.). "Smell, Identification, and Attribution." Unpublished manuscript.

Engisch, P. (forthcoming). "Modelling Culinary Value." Unpublished manuscript.

Engisch, P. (2020). "Recipes and Culinary Creativity. The Noma Legacy." In: Andrea Borghini & Nicola Piras (eds.), "The Philosophy of Food. Recipes between Arts and Algorithms," Special issue of *Humana.Mente*, 13 (38): 61–82.

Ereshefsky, M. (2000). *The Poverty of the Linnaean Hierarchy: A Philosophical Study of Biological Taxonomy*. Cambridge: Cambridge University Press.

Evans, D. (2018). "Do You Even Bake, Bro? How the Silicon Valley Set Fell in Love with Sourdough and Decided to Disrupt the 6,000-year-old Craft of Making Bread, One Crumbshot at a Time." *Eater*. November 19, 2018. Available at: https://www.eater. com/2018/11/19/18099127/breadsilicon-valley-sourdough-tech-brostartine-chad-robertson. Accessed September 7, 2021.

Evans, G. (1982). *The Varieties of Reference*. Oxford: Oxford University Press.

Ewbank, A. (2017). "The Nixon Dinners That Taught Americans to Stop Worrying and Love Peking Duck." *Atlas Obscura*. [online] Available at: https://www.atlasobscura. com/articles/nixon-visit-china-1972-dinners-peking-duck. Accessed July 18, 2020.

Fantasia, R. (2018). *French Gastronomy and the Magic of Americanism*. Philadelphia: Temple University Press.

Fantl, J. (2016). "Knowledge How." *The Stanford Encyclopedia of Philosophy* (Spring 2016 edition). Edited by Edward N. Zalta. [online] Available at: https://plato.stanford.edu/ archives/spr2016/entries/knowledge-how/. Accessed September 7, 2021.

Fast, J. (1977). *The Pleasure Book*. New York: Stein and Day.

Fauchart, E. & Von Hippel, E. (2006). "Norms-Based Intellectual Property Systems: The Case of French Chefs." MIT Sloan Working Paper 4576-06.

Ferretti, G. (2016). "Through the Forest of Motor Representations." *Consciousness and Cognition*, 43: 177–96.

Ferretti, G. (2019). "Visual Phenomenology versus Visuomotor Imagery: How Can We Be Aware of Action Properties?" *Synthese*. https://doi.org/10.1007/s11229-019-02282-x.

Ferretti, G. (2020). "Anti-Intellectualist Motor Knowledge." *Synthese*. https://doi.org/10.1007/s11229-020-02750-9.

Ferretti, G. (2021). "A Distinction Concerning Vision-for-Action and Affordance Perception." *Consciousness and Cognition*, 87. https://doi.org/10.1016/j.concog.2020.103028.

Ferretti, G. & Zipoli Caiani, S. (2018). "Solving the Interface Problem without Translation: The Same Format Thesis." *Pacific Philosophical Quarterly*. https://doi.org/10.1111/papq.12243.

Ferretti, G. & Zipoli Caiani, S. (2019). "Between Vision and Action." Introduction to the Special Issue. *Synthese*. https://doi.org/10.1007/s11229-019-02518-w.

Ferretti, G. & Zipoli Caiani, S. (Forthcoming). "How Knowing-That and Knowing-How Interface in Action: The Intelligence of Motor Representations." *Erkenntnis*.

Fine, G. A. (1996). *Kitchens: The Culture of Restaurant Work*. Berkeley: University of California Press.

Fletcher, N. (2004). *Charlemagne's Tablecloth*. New York: St. Martin's Press.

Floyd, J. & Forster, L. (eds.) (2003). *The Recipe Reader: Narratives, Contexts, Traditions*. New York: Routledge.

Fowler, H. C. (1946). *Recipes Out of Bilibid*. Compiled by D. Wagner. New York: George W. Stewart.

Frank, R. (2001). "Thai Government Plans 3,000 Restaurants in U.S. and Elsewhere to Promote Nation." *Wall Street Journal*. February 6. [online] Available at: https://www.wsj.com/articles/SB981416480713537865. Accessed July 18, 2020.

Freedman, P. (ed.) (2007). *Food: The History of Taste*. Berkeley: University of California Press.

Fridland, E. (2016). "Skill and Motor Control: Intelligence All the Way Down." *Philosophical Studies*, 174: 1–22.

Friedersdorf, C. (2015). "Oberlin College's Food and Cultural Appropriation." *The Atlantic*, December 21. [online] Available at: https://www.theatlantic.com/politics/archive/2015/12/the-food-fight-at-oberlin-college/421401/. Accessed September 7, 2021.

Germain, C. (2019). "Don't Steal My Recipe! A Comparative Study of French and US Law on the Protection of Culinary Dishes against Copying." University of Florida Levin College of Law Working Papers.

Gibson, J. (1979). *The Ecological Approach to Visual Perception*. Hillsdale, NJ: Lawrence Erlbaum Associates.

Gilman, N. (2017). "The Official Future Is Dead! Long Live the Official Future." *The American Interest*, October 30.

Godoy, M. (2015). "Mr. Chef Goes to Washington: Cooks Learn to Lobby Congress on Food." *NPR.org*. [online] Available at: https://www.npr.org/sections/thesalt/2015/10/30/452559829/mr-chef-goes-to-washington-cooks-learn-to-lobby-congress-on-food. Accessed April 2, 2020.

Goldman, A. & Beddor, B. (2015). "Reliabilist Epistemology." *The Stanford Encyclopaedia of Philosophy*. [online] Available at: https://plato.stanford.edu/entries/reliabilism/. Accessed April 27, 2010.

Goldman, M. (2013). "Cooking and Copyright: When Chefs and Restaurateurs Should Receive Copyright Protection for Recipes and Aspects of Their Professional Reperoires." *Seton Hall Journal of Sports and Entertainment Law*, 23 (1): 154–86.

Goodman, N. (1976). *Languages of Arts: An Approach to a Theory of Symbols*. Indianapolis, IN: Hackett.

Goshen-Gottstein, A. (2017). *Religious Genius: Appreciating Inspiring Individuals across Traditions*. Cham, Switzerland: Palgrave Macmillan.

Grainger, S. (2006). *Cooking Apicius: Roman Recipes for Today*. London: Prospect Books.

Grasswick, H. E. (ed.) (2011). *Feminist Epistemology and Philosophy of Science: Power in Knowledge*. Berlin: Springer.

Gregory, R. & Zangwill, O. L. (eds.) (1987). *The Oxford Companion to the Mind*. New York: Oxford University Press.

Grosz, E. (1994). *Volatile Bodies: Towards a Corporeal Feminism*. Bloomington: Indiana University Press.

Guendelman, M., Cheryan, S. & Monin, B. (2010). "Fitting in but Getting Fat: Identity Threat and Dietary Choices among U.S. Immigrant Groups." *Psychological Science*, 22 (7). https://doi.org/10.1177/0956797611411585.

Guthman, J. (2004). *Agrarian Dreams: The Paradox of Organic Farming in California*. Berkeley: University of California Press.

Guthman, J. (2008). "Neoliberalism and the Making of Food Politics in California." *Rethinking Economy; Agro-Food Activism in California and the Politics of the Possible; Culture, Nature and Landscape in the Australian Region*, 39 (3): 1171–83.

Guthman, J. (2011). "If They Only Knew: The Unbearable Whiteness of Alternative Food." In: Alison Hope Alkon & Julian Agyeman (eds.), *Cultivating Food Justice: Race, Class, and Sustainability*. Cambridge, MA: MIT Press: 263–82.

Hales, S. (2007). *Beer and Philosophy: The Unexamined Beer Isn't Worth Drinking*. Malden, MA: Blackwell.

Haraway, D. J. (1999). *Simians, Cyborgs, and Women: The Reinvention of Nature*. New York: Routledge.

Haraway, D. J. (2008). *When Species Meet*. Minneapolis: University of Minnesota Press.

Haraway, D. J. (2016). *Staying with the Trouble*. Durham, NC: Duke University Press.

Harding, S. (1985). "Feminist Justificatory Strategies and the Epistemology of Science." Unpublished paper, delivered to Eastern Division Convention, American Philosophical Association.

Harper, A. B. (ed.) (2009). *Sistah Vegan: Black Female Vegans Speak on Food, Identity, Health, and Society*. New York: Lantern Books.

Hayes, T. (1987). *Bilibid Diary: The Secret Notebooks of Commander Thomas Hayes POW, the Philippines, 1942–45*. Edited by A. B. Feuer. Hamden. CT: Archon Books.

Heldke, L. (1988). "Recipes for Theory Making." *Hypathia*, 3 (2):15–29.

Heldke, L. (1992). "Foodmaking as a Thoughtful Practice." In: D. W. Curtin & L. M. Heldke (eds.), *Cooking, Eating, Thinking: Transformative Philosophies of Food*. Bloomington: Indiana University Press: 203–29.

Heldke, L. (2003). *Exotic Appetites: Ruminations of a Food Adventurer*. New York: Routledge.

Heldke, L. (2012). "An Alternative Ontology of Food: Beyond Metaphysics." *Radical Philosophy Review*, 15 (1): 67–88.

Heldke, L. (2018). "It's Chomping All the Way Down: Toward an Ontology of the Human Individual." *The Monist*, 101: 247–60.

Henry, C. (2016). *Terroir Champagne*. Self-Published Book.

Herald, S. M. (2006). "A Grain of Truth and A Pinch of Salt." *Smh.com*, April 1. [online] Available at: https://www.smh.com.au/lifestyle/a-grain-of-truth-and-a-pinch-of-salt-20060401-gdna7o.html. Accessed May 1, 2019.

Hey, M. (2019). "Fermenting Communications: Fermentation Praxis as Interspecies Communication." *Interspecies Communication*. Edited by Meredith Tromble & Patricia Olynyk. Special issue, *PUBLIC* 59: 149–57.

Hickey, C. K. (2019). "All the Presidents' Meals." *Foreign Policy*. [online] Available at: https://foreignpolicy.com/all-the-presidents-meals-state-dinners-white-house-infographic/. Accessed July 18, 2020.

Hinrichs, C. & Kremer, K. S. (2002). "Social Inclusion in a Midwest Local Food System Project." *Journal of Poverty*, 6 (1): 65–90.

Hirata, S., Watanabe, K. & Masao, K. (2001). "'Sweet-Potato Washing' Revisited." In: T. Matsuzawa (ed.), *Primate Origins of Human Cognition and Behavior*. Tokyo: Springer Japan: 487–508.

Hird, M. (2009). *The Origins of Sociable Life: Evolution after Science Studies*. New York: Palgrave Macmillan.

Hirvonen, S. (n.d.). "The Incompleteness of Recipes." Unpublished manuscript.

Hopkins, P. D. & Dacey, A. (2008). "Vegetarian Meat: Could Technology Save Animals and Satisfy Meat Eaters?" *The Journal of Agricultural and Environmental Ethics*, 21: 579–96.

Hubb Community Kitchen (2018). *Together: Our Community Cookbook*. New York: Clarkson Potter.

Huber, J. and Wolkenstein, F. (2018). "Gentrification and Occupancy Rights." *Politics, Philosophy & Economics*, 17 (4): 378–97.

Hutchins, E. (1995). *Cognition in the Wild*. Cambridge: MIT Press.

Hyland, J. (1984). *In the Shadow of the Rising Sun*. Minneapolis, MN: Augsburg Publishing House.

Irigaray, L. (1985). *This Sex Which Is Not One*. Translated by C. Power & C. Burke. Ithaca: Cornell University Press.

Isaacson, W. (2011). "The Genius of Jobs." *The New York Times*, October 29.

James Beard Foundation (n.d.). "The Diplomatic Culinary Partnership | James Beard Foundation." [online] Available at: https://www.jamesbeard.org/dcp. Accessed July 18, 2020.

Jamie Oliver Foundation. (2020). "Jamie Oliver Foundation—Fifteen." [online] Available at: http://www.icapcharityday.com/success-stories/2007-jamie-oliver-foundation-fifteen Accessed April 20, 2020.

Janssens, M. (2013). "Copyright for Culinary Creations: A Seven Course Tasting Menu With Accompanying Wines", *SSRN.com,* January. [online] Available at: https://papers.ssrn.com/sol3/papers.cfm?abstract_id=2538116. Accessed April 10, 2019.

Jefford, A. & Draper, P. R. (2005). "The Art and Craft of Wine." In: B. Smith (ed.), *Questions of Taste*. Oxford: Oxford University Press: 199–218.

Kant, I. (1903). *Perpetual Peace: A Philosophical Essay, 1795*. London: S. Sonnenschein. [online] Available at: https://www.mtholyoke.edu/acad/intrel/kant/kant1.htm. Accessed April 10, 2020.

Kember, S. & Zylinska, Z. (2012). *Life after New Media: Mediation as a Vital Process*. Cambridge, MA: MIT Press.

Kind, A. (2008). "How to Believe in Qualia." In: E. Wright (ed.), *The Case for Qualia*. Cambridge, MA: MIT Press: 285–98.

King, R. (2018). "Social Gastronomy: Can Food Change Society?" [online] Available at: https://www.finedininglovers.com/article/social-gastronomy-can-food-change-society Accessed April 2, 2020.

Kirksey, S. E. & Helmreich, S. (2010). "The Emergence of Multispecies Ethnography." *Cultural Anthropology*, 25 (4): 545–76.

Kivy, P. (1995). *Authenticities: Philosophical Reflections on Musical Performance*. Ithaca, NY: Cornell University Press.

Klein, L. F. (2020). *An Archive of Taste: Race and Eating in the Early United States*. Minneapolis: University of Minnesota Press.

Kohn, M. (2016). *The Death and Life of the Urban Commonwealth*. Oxford: Oxford University Press.

Kormann, C. (2016). "The Tasting Initiative: Can a Restaurant for the Rich Benefit the Poor?" *The New Yorker*, April 16.

Korsgaard, C. M. (2012). "Getting Animals into View." *The Point*, (6). [Online] Available at: https://thepointmag.com/examined-life/getting-animals-view/. Accessed September 7, 2021.

Korsgaard, C. M. (2018). *Fellow Creatures: Our Obligations to the Other Animals*. Oxford: Oxford University Press.

Korsmeyer, C. (1999). *Making Sense of Taste: Food and Philosophy*. Ithaca, NY: Cornell University Press.

Korsmeyer, C. (2011). *Savoring Disgust: The Foul and the Fair in Aesthetics*. New York: Oxford University Press.

Krause, S. R. (2011). "Corporeal Agency and Democratic Politics." *Political Theory*, 39 (3): 299–324.

Kurlansky, M. (2002). *Salt: A World History*. New York: Penguin Books.

Kyle, D. (In preparation). *Natural Talent: An Unnatural History*. Palo Alto, CA: Stanford University Press.

Kymlicka, W. (1995). *Multicultural Citizenship: A Liberal Theory of Minority Rights*. Oxford: Oxford University Press.

Landecker, H. (2007). *Culturing Life: How Cells Became Technologies*. Cambridge, MA: Harvard University Press.

Langholtz, G. & Kinsel, R. (2019). *A Place at the Table: New American Recipes from the Nation's Top Foreign-Born Chefs*. Munich: Prestel.

Latour, B. (1988). *The Pasteurization of France*. Translated by A. Sheridan & J. Law. Cambridge, MA: Harvard University Press.

Leong, E. (2018). *Recipes and Everyday Knowledge: Medicine, Science, and the Household in Early Modern England*. Chicago: University of Chicago Press.

Leschziner, V. (2015). *At the Chef's Table: Culinary Creativity in Elite Restaurants*. Palo Alto, CA: Stanford University Press.

Liem, D. G. & Russell, C. G. (2019). "The Influence of Taste Liking on the Consumption of Nutrient Rich and Nutrient Poor Foods." *Frontiers in Nutritions*, 6: 174.

LIFE. (2017). "LIFE." [online] Available at: https://lifeforentrepreneurs.com/. Accessed July 18, 2020.

Lipscomb, A. (2019). "Culinary Relations: Gastrodiplomacy in Thailand, South Korea, and Taiwan." *The Yale Review of International Studies*. Available at: http://yris.yira.org/essays/3080. Accessed September 7, 2021.

Littler, J. (2018). *Against Meritocracy*. London: Routledge.

Loar, B. (1997). "Phenomenal States: Second Version." In: N. Block, O. Flanagan, & G. Guzeldier (eds.), *Consciousness*. Cambridge, MA: MIT Press.

Loomis, J. M. (1972). "The Photopigment Bleaching Hypothesis of Complementary After-images: A Psychophysical Test." *Vision Research*, 12: 1587–94.

Lowenthal, D. (1985). *The Past Is a Foreign Country*. Cambridge: Cambridge University Press.

Lycan, W. (2001). "The Slighting of Smell." In: Nalini Bhushan & Stuart Rosenfeld (eds.), *Of Minds and Molecules: New Philosophical Perspectives on Chemistry*. New York: Oxford University Press.

Lycan, W. (2018). "What Does Taste Represent?" *Australasian Journal of Philosophy*, 96 (1): 28–37.

Markovits, D. (2019). *The Meritocracy Trap*. New York: Penguin Press.

Marx, K. (2000 [1867]). "The Fetishism of the Commodity and Its Secrets." In: J. Schor & D. B. Holt (eds.), *The Consumer Society Reader*. New York: New Press: 331–42.

Mary J. P. (2013). "Food as Communication: A Case Study of South Korea's Gastrodiplomacy." *Journal of International Service*. Available at: https://thediplomatistdotcom.files.wordpress.com/2013/01/jis-spring-2013-issue-gastrodiplomacy.pdf. Accessed September 7, 2021.

Masrour, F. (2013). "Phenomenal Objectivity and Phenomenal Intentionality: In Defense of a Kantian Account." In: U. Kriegel (ed.), *Phenomenal Intentionality*. Oxford: Oxford University Press.

Matwick, K. & Matwick, K. (2014). "Storytelling and Synthetic Personalization in Television Cooking Shows." *Journal of Pragmatics*, 71: 151–9.

Maynard, M. M. (2001). *My Faraway Home: An American Family's WWII Tale of Adventure and Survival in the Jungles of the Philippines*. Guilford, CT: The Lyons Press.

McBride, L. A. (2018). "Racial Imperialism and Food Traditions." In: A. Barnhill, M. Budolfson, & T. Doggett (eds.), *Oxford Handbook of Food Ethics*, Vol. 1. Oxford: Oxford University Press: 333–44.

McEntee, J. (2010). "Contemporary and Traditional Localism: A Conceptualisation of Rural Local Food." *Local Environment*, 15 (9–10): 785–803.

McGovern, P. (2003). *Ancient Wine: The Search for the Origins of Viniculture*. Princeton, NJ: Princeton University Press.

McGovern, P. (2017). *Ancient Brews Discovered and Recreated*. New York: W. W. Norton & Company.

McMahon, D. (2013). *Divine Fury: A History of Genius*. New York: Basic Books.

Medora, S. (2020). "Should Social Gastronomy Be Part of the Restaurant Industry's New Normal?" *Un-Plated*. [online] Available at: https://un-plated.com/should-social-gastronomy-be-part-of-the-restaurant-industrys-new-normal/. Accessed July 26, 2020.

Medrano, K. (2019). "Restaurants around the World Will Host a Giant Food Festival Celebrating Refugees." *Thrillist*. [online] Available at: https://www.thrillist.com/travel/nation/refugee-food-festival-2019. Accessed July 26, 2020.

Mera Kitchen Collective. (n.d.). "Mera Kitchen Collective." [online] Available at: https://www.mera.kitchen/. Accessed July 18, 2020.

Merleau-Ponty, M. (1968). *The Visible and Invisible*. Translated by A. Lingis. Evanston, IL: Northwestern University Press.

Meskin, A. and Robson, J. (2015). "Taste and Acquaintance." *Journal of Aesthetics and Art Criticism*, 73 (2): 127–39.

Mintz, S. (1996). *Tasting Food, Tasting Freedom: Excursions into Eating, Culture, and the Past*. Boston: Beacon Press.

Mizrahi, V. (2014). "Sniff, Smell, and Stuff." *Philosophical Studies*, 171 (2): 233–50.

Mizrahi, V. (2017). "Just a Matter of Taste." *Review of Philosophical Psychology*, 8: 411–31.

Mol, A. (2016). "Clafoutis as a Composite: On Hanging Together Felicitously." In: J. Law & E. Rupert (eds.), *Modes of Knowing: Resources from the Baroque*. Manchester: Mattering Press: 242–65.

Moniuszko, Sara M. (2020), "What to Bake During the Coronavirus Quarantine When You're Out of Eggs, Milk or Butter," *USA Today*, March 24, 2020. [online] Available at: https://eu.usatoday.com/story/life/food-dining/2020/03/24/coronavirus-quarantine-what-can-you-bake-without-eggs-milk-butter/2907496001/.

Monroe, D. (2007). "Can Food Be Art? The Problem of Consumption." In: F. Allhoff & D. Monroe (eds.), *Food and Philosophy*. Malden, MA: Blackwell: 133–44.

Montanari, M. (2015). *Medieval Tastes: Food, Cooking, and the Table*. Translated by B. A. Brombert. New York: Columbia University Press.

Morin, O. (2016). *How Traditions Live and Die*. Oxford: Oxford University Press.

Morris, K. (2020). "What Noma Did Next: How the 'New Nordic' Is Reshaping the Food World." *The Guardian*. February 28. [online] Available at: https://www.theguardian.com/food/2020/feb/28/what-noma-did-next-new-nordic-food-rene-redzepi-claus-meyer-locavore-foraging. Accessed March 17, 2020.

Moulier-Boutang, Y. (2011). *Cognitive Capitalism*. Malden, MA: Polity.

Murray, B. (2007). "Kant on Genius and Art." *The British Journal of Aesthetics*, 47 (2): 199–214.

Musk, K. TEDx Talks (2015). "Fertile Ground: Why Food Is the New Internet | Kimbal Musk | TEDxMemphis." YouTube. [online] Available at: https://www.youtube.com/watch?v=iUU1BffGon0. Accessed July 18, 2020.

Mylopoulos, M. and Pacherie, E. (2016). "Intentions and Motor Representations: The Interface Challenge." *Review of Philosophy and Psychology*. https://doi.org/10.1007/s13164-016-0311-6.

Naim, M., Nir, S., Spielman, A. I., Noble, A. C., Peri, I. et al. (2002). "Hypothesis of Receptor-Dependent and Receptor-Independent Mechanisms for Bitter and Sweet Taste Transduction: Implications for Slow Taste Onset and Lingering Aftertaste." In: P. Given & D. Parades (eds.), *Chemistry of Taste: Mechanisms, Behaviors, and Mimics*, ACS Symposium Series 825: 2–17, Washington, DC: American Chemical Society.

Nash, G. C. (1984). *That We Might Live*. Scottsdale, AZ: Shano.

Nash, J. (1984). "The Anthropology of Work." In: H. Applebaum (ed.), *Work in Non-market and Transitional Societies*. Albany: SUNY Press: 45–55.

National Heart, Lung and Blood Institute (NHLBI) (n.d.-a). "Heart Healthy Home Cooking African-American Style." [online] Available at: https://www.nhlbi.nih.gov/files/docs/public/heart/cooking.pdf. Accessed September 7, 2021.

National Heart, Lung and Blood Institute (NHLBI) (n.d.-b). "Soul Food Makeover—Heart Healthy African American Recipes." [online] Available at: https://www.nhlbi.nih.gov/health/educational/healthdisp/pdf/recipes/Recipes-African-American.pdf. Accessed September 7, 2021.

Neely, G. & Borg, G. (1999). "The Perceived Intensity of Caffeine Aftertaste: Tasters versus Nontasters." *Chemical Senses*, 24 (1): 19–21.

Nye, J. S. (2004). *Soft Power: The Means to Success in World Politics*. New York: Public Affairs; London: 5.

O'Callaghan, C. (2019). *A Multisensory Philosophy of Perception*. New York: Oxford University Press.

Ogle, M. (1958). *Worth the Price*. Washington, DC: Review and Herald Publishing Association.

Oliver, G. (2007). "The Beer Matrix: Reality vs Facsimile in Brewing." In: S. Hales (ed.), *Beer & Philosophy: The Unexamined Beer Isn't Worth Drinking*. Malden: Blackwell Publishing.

Opazo, M. P. (2016). *Appetite for Innovation: Creativity and Change at elBulli*. New York: Columbia University Press.

Orozco, T., De Mesa, J. L., Rodríguez, E. and Germán, M. and Prosperidad Social (2016). *Cocina y Paz*. Medellín: Cuellar Editores.

Osiurak, F., Rossetti, Y. & Badets, A. (2017). "What Is an Affordance? 40 Years Later!" *Neuroscience and Biobehavioral Reviews*, 77: 403–17.

Pavese, C. (2016). "Skill in Epistemology II: Skill and Know How." *Philosophy Compass*. https://doi.org/10.1111/phc3.12364.

Pavese, C. (2018). "Know-how, Action, and Luck." *Synthese*. https://doi.org/10.1007/s11229-018-1823-7.

Paxson, H. (2013). *The Life of Cheese: Crafting Food and Value in America*. Berkeley: University of California Press.

Peacocke, C. (1992). *A Study of Concepts*. Cambridge, MA: MIT Press.

Pearsall, S. L. (1925). *Words and Idioms*. London: Constable.

Pericoli, M. (2018). "The Laboratory of Literature Architecture. The Joy of Cardboard, Glue, and Storytelling. A Cross-Disciplinary Exploration of Literature as Architecture." In: J. Charley (ed.), *The Routledge Companion on Architecture, Literature, and the City*. New York: Routledge: 283–306.

Perú Ministerio de Comercio Exterior y Turismo. "Gastronomía Peruana | Perú Travel." [online] Available at: https://www.peru.travel/gastronomia/pe/. Accessed July 18, 2020.

Petrini, C. (2013). *Slow Food Nation*. New York: Rizzoli Ex Libris.

Phillips, I. (2012). "Afterimages and Sensations." *Philosophy and Phenomenological Research*, 87 (2): 417–53.

Pickering, M. (ed.) (2008). *Research Methods for Cultural Studies*. Edinburgh: Edinburgh University Press.

Pink, S. (2009). *Doing Sensory Ethnography*. London: SAGE.

Pink, S. (2012). *Situating Everyday Life: Practices and Places*. London: SAGE.

Pinsker, J. (2019). "The People Who Eat the Same Meal Every Day." *The Atlantic*, March 7. [online] Available at: https://www.theatlantic.com/family/archive/2019/03/eating-the-same-thing-lunch-meal/584347/. Accessed March 7, 2021.

Pollan, M. (2009). "Out of the Kitchen, onto the Couch." *The New York Times Magazine*, July 29. [online] Available at: https://www.nytimes.com/2009/08/02/magazine/02cooking-t.html. Accessed March 7, 2021.

Public Diplomacy Magazine (2014). *Gastrodiplomacy*. Issue 11, Winter 2014. [online] Available at: https://static1.squarespace.com/static/5be3439285ede1f05a46dafe/t/5be35 11daa4a996fcaa498f3/1541624135259/GastroDiplomacy. Accessed July 5, 2021.

Quong, J. (2011). *Liberalism Without Perfection*. Oxford: Oxford University Press.

Rakowitz, M. (n.d.). "Enemy Kitchen." *MICHAEL RAKOWITZ*. [online] Available at: http://www.michaelrakowitz.com/enemy-kitchen. Accessed July 18, 2020.

Ranta, R. (2018). "Gentrification, Vegans, and the Death of Historic London Pie Shops." *The Conversation*, October 9. [online] Available at: http://theconversation.com/gentrification-vegans-and-the-death-of-historic-london-pie-shops-104501. Accessed September 7, 2021.

Rawls, J. (2005). *Political Liberalism*. New York: Columbia University Press.

Reckwitz, A. (2017). *The Invention of Creativity: Modern Society and the Culture of the New*. Malden, MA: Polity Press.

Reid, T. (1983). *Inquiry and Essays*. London: Hackett Pub.

Revel, J.-F. (1982). *Culture and Cuisine: A Journey through the History of Food*. Translated by H. R. Lane. New York: Da Capo Press.

Richardson, L. (2013). "Flavour, Taste and Smell." *Mind and Language*, 28 (3): 322–41.

Richardson, L. (2018). "Odours as olfactibilia." In: T. Crowther & C. Mac Cumhaill (eds.), *Perceptual Ephemera*. Oxford: Oxford University Press.

Ritzer, G. (1993). *The McDonaldization of Society: An Investigation into the Changing Character of Contemporary Social Life*. Newbury Park, CA: Pine Forge Press.

Robinson, A. (2011). *Genius: A Very Short Introduction*. Oxford: Oxford University Press.

Rockower, P. S. (2012). "Recipes for Gastrodiplomacy." *Place Branding and Public Diplomacy*, 8 (3): 235–46.

Rombauer, I. and Becker, M. R. (1977). *Joy of Cooking*. Indianapolis, IN: Bobbs-Merrill.

Rose, D. B., Van Dooren, T., Chrulew, M., Cooke, S., Kearnes, M. & O'Gorman, E. (2010). "Thinking through the Environment, Unsettling the Humanities." *Environmental Humanities*, 1: 1–5.

Rubin, A. J. (2016). "From Refugee Chefs, a Taste of Home." *The New York Times*. July 5. [online] Available at: https://www.nytimes.com/2016/07/06/dining/refugees-chefs-paris.html. Accessed April 12, 2020.

Ryle, G. (1949). *The Concept of Mind*. London: Hutchinson.

Sakreida, K., Effnert, I., Thill, S., Menz, M. M., Jirak, D., Eickhoff, C. R. et al. (2016). "Affordance Processing in Segregated Parieto-frontal Dorsal Stream Sub-pathways." *Neuroscience and Biobehavioral Reviews*, 69: 89–112. https://doi.org/10.1016/j.neubiorev.2016.07.032.

Salz, B. R. (1984). "The Use of Time." In: H. Applebaum (ed.), *Work in Non-market and Transitional Societies*. Albany: SUNY Press: 203–18.

Schlottman, C. & Sebo, J. (2018). *Food, Animals, and the Environment: An Ethical Approach*. New York: Routledge.

Schopenhauer, A. ([1819] 1958). *The World as Will and Representation*. Indian Hills, CO: Falcon's Wing.

Schwartz, P. (1991). *The Art of the Long View: Planning for an Uncertain Future*. New York: Currency Doubleday.

SDG2 Advocacy Hub (n.d.). "Chefs' Manifesto: Join Our Community Today | SDG2 Advocacy Hub." [online] Available at: http://www.sdg2advocacyhub.org/chefmanifesto. Accessed April 20, 2020.

Shapin, S. (2012). "The Tastes of Wine: Towards a Cultural History." *Rivista di Estetica*, 51: 49–94.

Shapin, S. (2016). "A Taste of Science: Making the Subjective Objective in the California Wine World." *Social Studies of Science*, 46: 436–60.

Sharma, M. (2019). "How to Eat Dinner Like the Last Citizens of Pompeii." *New York Times T Magazine*, December 23. [online] Available at: https://www.nytimes.com/2019/12/23/t-magazine/heston-blumenthal-pompeii-dinner.html. Accessed September 7, 2021.

Shenhav, Y. (1999). *Manufacturing Rationality: The Engineering Foundations of the Managerial Revolution*. Oxford: Oxford University Press.

Shepherd, G. M. (2012). *Neurogastronomy: How the Brain Creates Flavor and Why It Matters*. New York: Columbia University Press.

Shepherd, J. (2017). "Skilled Action and the Double Life of Intention." *Philosophy and Phenomenological Research*: 1–20. https://doi.org/10.1111/phpr.12433.

Shibata, I. (2015). "Where Do Japanese Chefs Find Their Inspiration?" *Fool*, 6.

Shoemaker, S. (1982). "The Inverted Spectrum." *Journal of Philosophy*, 79: 357–81.

Shotwell, A. (2011). *Knowing Otherwise: Race, Gender, and Implicit Understanding*. University Park: The Pennsylvania State University Press.

Shotwell, A. (2016). *Against Purity: Living Ethically in Compromised Times*. Minneapolis: University of Minnesota Press.

Sibley, F. (2001). "Tastes, Smells, and Aesthetics." In: J. Benson, B. Redfern, & J. R. Cox (eds.), *Approach to Aesthetics: Collected Papers on Philosophical Aesthetics*. Oxford: Clarendon Press: 207–55.

Singer, P. (2013). "The World's First Cruelty-Free Hamburger." *The Guardian*. August 5.

Skeggs, B. (2001). "Feminist Ethnography." In: P. Atkinson, A. Coffey, S. Delamont, J. Lofland, & L. Lofland (eds.), *Handbook of Ethnography*. Thousand Oaks, CA: Sage Publications. http://dx.doi.org/10.4135/9781848608337.

Slow Food International (2015). "Our Philosophy – About Us – Slow Food International." [online] Available at: https://www.slowfood.com/about-us/our-philosophy/. Accessed September 7, 2021.

Smith, B. (2009). *Questions of Taste: The Philosophy of Wine*. Oxford: Oxford University Press.

Smith, B. (2013). "The Nature of Sensory Experience: The Case of Taste and Tasting." *Phenomenology and Mind*, 4: 293–313.

Smith, B. (2015). "The Chemical Senses." In: M. Matten (ed.), *The Oxford Handbook to Philosophy of Perception*. Oxford: Oxford University Press: 314–52.

Smith, B. C. (2017). "Tasting and Liking: Multisensory Flavor Perception and Hedonic Evaluation." In: C. Korsmeyer (ed.), *The Taste Culture Reader*, 2nd edition. Oxford: Bloomsbury: 250–60.

Smith, C. (2014). "Food Art: Protecting 'Food Presentation' under U.S. Intellectual Property Law." *John Marshall Review of Intellectual Property Law*, 14 (1): 2–23.

Smith, C. (2018). "Copyright in Culinary Presentation." In: E. Bonadio & N. Lucchi (eds.), *Non-Conventional Copyright: Do New and Atypical Works Deserve Protection*. Cheltenham, UK: Edward Elgar: 128–51.

Smith, W. (1961). *I Didn't Make a Million*. Manila: Lawrence R. Doran.

Social Gastronomy Movement (n.d.). "Social Gastronomy Movement." [online] Available at: https://www.socialgastronomy.org/. Accessed April 20, 2020.

Spence, C. (2017). *Gastrophysics: The New Science of Eating*. New York: Penguin.

Stanley, J. (2011). *Know How*. Oxford: Oxford University Press.

Stelzer, C. (2013). *Dinner with Churchill: Policy-Making at the Dinner Table*. New York: Pegasus Books.

Stephens, N., Sexton, A., & Driessen, C. (2019). "Making Sense of Making Meat: Analyzing Key Developments in the First Twenty Years of Tissue Engineering Muscle to Make Food." *Frontiers in Sustainable Food Systems*, 3. Available at: https://www.frontiersin.org/article/10.3389/fsufs.2019.00045. Accessed September 7, 2021.

Sterling, A. L. (2019). "Resettling Refugees One 'Culturally Appropriate' Hot Meal at a Time." *HuffPost*. [online] Available at: https://www.huffpost.com/entry/trump-administration-refugee-resettlement_n_5ceecb15e4b05a622337eb5a. Accessed July 18, 2020.

Stevens, F. H. (1946). *Santo Tomas Internment Camp: 1942–1945*. New York: Stratford House.

Straus, N. (2012). "Trade Dress Protection for Cuisine: Monetizing Creativity in a Low-IP Industry." *UCLA Law Review*, 60 (182): 184–260.

Strauss, A. & Corbin, J. M. (1997). *Grounded Theory in Practice*. Thousand Oaks, CA: Sage.

The Sydney Morning Herald (2006). "A Grain of Truth and A Pinch of Salt." *Smh.com*, April 1. [online] Available at: https://www.smh.com.au/lifestyle/a-grain-of-truth-and-a-pinch-of-salt-20060401-gdna7o.html. Accessed May 1, 2019.

The Clink Charity (2018). "Charity—The Clink Charity." [online] Available at: https://theclinkcharity.org/the-charity.

Theophano, J. (2002). *Eat My Words: Reading Women's Lives through the Cookbooks They Wrote*. New York: Palgrave.

Thurston, A. & Ter Kuile, C. (2018). *How We Gather*. Cambridge, MA: Harvard Divinity School.

Tillas, A., Vosgerau, G., Seuchter, T. & Zipoli Caiani, S. (2016). "Can Affordances Explain Behavior?" *Review of Philosophy and Psychology*: 1–21.

Todd, C. (2010). *The Philosophy of Wine*. London: Routledge.

Todd, C. (2018a). "Representation and Ephemerality in Olfaction." In: T. Crowther & C. Mac Cumhaill (eds.), *Perceptual Ephemera*. Oxford: Oxford University Press: 68–92.

Todd, C. (2018b). "Tasting in Time: The Affective and Temporal Dimensions of Flavour Perception." *The Monist*, 101 (3): 277–93.

Tran, C. L. (2015). "CDS Appropriates Asian Dishes, Students Say." *The Oberlin Review* (blog). November 6. [online] Available at: https://oberlinreview.org/9055/news/cds-appropriates-asian-dishes-students-say/. Accessed September 7, 2021.

Tsing, A. L. (2015). *Mushroom at the End of the World: On the Possibility of Life in Capitalist Ruins*. Princeton, NJ: Princeton University Press.

Tuccini, G., Corti, L., Baronti, L. & Ro., L. (2020). "Recipes, beyond Computational Procedures." *Humana.Mente*, 13 (38): 1–19.

Turow, E. (2015). *A Taste of Generation Yum: How the Millennial Generation's Love for Organic Fare, Celebrity Chefs and Microbrews Will Make or Break the Future of Food*. New York: Pronoun.

Turshen, J. (2017). *Feed the Resistance: Recipes + Ideas for Getting Involved*. San Francisco: Chronicle Books.

uber den tellerrand. "Make the World a Better Plate." [online] Available at: https://ueberdentellerrand.org. Accessed July 5, 2021.

Ulver, S. and Klasson, M. (2018). "Social Magic for Dinner? The Taste Script and Shaping of Foodieness in Netflix's *Chef's Table*." In: Z. Arsel & J. Bean. (eds.), *Taste, Consumption and Markets*. London: Routledge: 38–56.

UNESCO (2018). "UNESCO—Intangible Heritage Home." [online] Available at: https://ich.unesco.org/en/home. Accessed September 7, 2021.

United Nations (2002). "United Nations: Key Conference Outcomes in Food." [online] Available at: https://www.un.org/en/development/devagenda/food.shtml. Accessed July 26, 2020.

United Nations (2017). "Sustainable Development Goals: Sustainable Development Knowledge Platform." [online] Available at: https://sustainabledevelopment.un.org/?menu=1300. Accessed September 7, 2021.

Valberg, J. J. (1992). *The Puzzle of Experience*. Oxford: Oxford University Press.

Vallier, K. (2014). *Liberal Politics and Public Faith*. New York: Routledge.

Van Der Weele, C. & Driessen, C. (2013). "Emerging Profiles for Cultured Meat: Ethics through and as Design." *Animals: An Open Access Journal from MDPI*, 3 (3): 647–62.

Van Dooren, T., Kirksey, E. & Münster, U. (2016). "Multispecies Studies: Cultivating Arts of Attentiveness." *Environmental Humanities*, 8 (1): 1–23.

Van Sickle, E. (2007). *The Iron Gates of Santo Tomas: The Firsthand Account of an American Couple Interned by the Japanese in Manila, 1942–1945*. Chicago: Academy Chicago.

Vaughan, E. (1985). *The Ordeal of Elizabeth Vaughan: A Wartime Diary of the Philippines*. Edited by C. M. Petillo. Athens: University of Georgia Press.

Virsu, V. and Laurinen, P. (1977). "Long-lasting Afterimages Caused by Neural Adaptation." *Vision Research*, 17: 853–60.

Wallis, C. (2008). "Consciousness, Context and Know-how." *Synthese*, 160: 123–53.

Weber, M. (1905 [1958]). *The Protestant Ethic and the Spirit of Capitalism*. New York: Scribner.

Weber, M. (1964). *The Theory of Social and Economic Organization*. New York: Free Press.

Whitelaw, G. H. (2014). "Shelf Lives and the Labors of Loss: Food, Livelihoods and Japan's Convenience Stores." In: S. Kawano, G. S. Roberts, & S. Orpett Long (eds.), *Capturing Contemporary Japan: Differentiation and Uncertainty*. Honolulu: University of Hawai'i Press.

Whitfield, E. (1999). *Three Year Picnic: An American Woman's Life inside Japanese Prison Camps in the Philippines during WWII.* Corvallis: Premiere Editions International.

Winne, M. (2009). *Closing the Food Gap: Resetting the Table in the Land of Plenty.* Boston: Beacon Press.

Wolterstorff, N. (1980). *Works and Worlds of Art.* Oxford: Clarendon Press.

Woolley, K. & Fishbach, A. (2017). "A Recipe for Friendship: Similar Food Consumption Promotes Trust and Cooperation." *Journal of Consumer Psychology,* 27 (1): 1–10.

Wurgaft, B. (2019). *Meat Planet: Artificial Flesh and the Future of Food.* Oakland: University of California Press

Young, J. O. (2008). "The Concept of Authentic Performance." In: A. Neill & A. Ridley (eds.), *Arguing about Art: Contemporary Philosophical Debates,* 3rd edition. London: Routledge: 71–80.

Zhang, J. (2015). "The Foods of the World: Mapping and Comparing Contemporary Gastrodiplomacy Campaigns." *International Journal of Communication,* (9): 569.

Zipoli Caiani, S. (2013). "Extending the Notion of Affordance." *Phenomenology and the Cognitive Sciences,* 13: 275–93.

Zipoli Caiani, S. & Ferretti, G. (2017). "Semantic and Pragmatic Integration in Vision for Action." *Consciousness and Cognition,* 48: 40–54.

Zohar, N. J. (1993). "Collective War and Individualist Ethics: Against the Conscription of 'Self-Defense.'" *Political Theory,* 21 (4): 606–22.

Zylinska, J. (2014a). "Taking Responsibility for Life: Bioethics and Bioart." In: P. Macneill (ed.), *Ethics and the Arts.* Amsterdam: Springer: 191–200.

Zylinska, J. (2014b). *Minimal Ethics for the Anthropocene.* Ann Arbor: Open Humanities Press. [online] Available at: http://www.openhumanitiespress.org/books/titles/ minimal-ethics-for-the-anthropocene. Accessed September 7, 2021.

Contributors

Anne Barnhill is Core Faculty at the Johns Hopkins Berman Institute of Bioethics. Dr. Barnhill is a philosopher and bioethicist who works on the ethics of food and agriculture, among other topics.

Enrico Bonadio is Reader in Intellectual Property Law at City, University of London. His current research agenda focuses on the legal protection of non-conventional forms of creativity. He recently edited the *Cambridge Handbook of Copyright in Street Art and Graffiti* (2019) and *Non-Conventional Copyright: Do New and Atypical Works Deserve Protection?* (2018).

Matteo Bonotti is Senior Lecturer in the Department of Politics and International Relations at Monash University, having previously taught at Cardiff University, Queen's University Belfast, and the University of Edinburgh. Matteo's research interests include democratic theory, linguistic justice, free speech, political liberalism, and food justice. These interests are diverse but unified by a common underlying theme: ethical pluralism and cultural diversity in contemporary societies, and the question of how the state should respond to them.

Davide Bordini is Postdoctoral Research Fellow at the University of Liège. He works in philosophy of mind and is very interested in issues at the intersection between the latter and the philosophy of food. He is one of the members of Culinary Mind.

Andrea Borghini is Associate Professor of Philosophy at the University of Milan and Director of Culinary Mind, a research center fostering philosophical thinking on food.

Patrik Engisch is an adjunct lecturer at the University of Fribourg. He works mainly in philosophy of mind and the philosophy of food. He is a co-founder and member of Culinary Mind, a research center fostering philosophical thinking on food.

Gabriele Ferretti is Humboldt Fellow at the Institute for Philosophy II, Ruhr-University Bochum, Germany. His research is mostly about philosophy of perception and philosophy of action and is empirically informed by cognitive science. His main research interest is vision and its relation to the pictorial and the motoric.

Johanna Mendelson Forman is Adjunct Professor at American University's School of International Service. She is also a Distinguished Fellow at the Stimson Center, and Director of the Food Security Program. Her frontline experience as a policymaker on conflict and stabilization efforts drove her interest the role of food in conflict. In 2015 she created Conflict Cuisine®: An Introduction to War and Peace Around the Dinner Table.

Akiko Frischhut is Assistant Professor of Philosophy at Akita International University, Japan. Her main interests are in metaphysics and philosophy of mind, with a budding interest in aesthetics and the philosophy of food (possibly combined).

Rafi Grosglik is Lecturer in Sociology and Anthropology at Beit Berl College and Ben-Gurion University of the Negev, Israel. Previously, he served as Visiting Assistant Professor at the University of California, Davis, and taught at Brandeis University, Boston University, and Tufts University. He is an incoming assistant professor, the Department of Sociology and Anthropology at Ben-Gurion University of the Negev, Israel.

Barbara Haber is the former curator of books at the Schlesinger Library, the Radcliffe Institute, Harvard University where she oversaw the development of a large collection of cookbooks and other books and manuscripts related to food. Recognizing the connections between food studies and issues of gender, she published *From Hardtack to Home Fries: An Uncommon History of American Cooks and Meals*, and co-edited *From Betty Crocker to Feminist Studies: Critical Perspectives on Women and Food*. She was a recipient of the M.F.K. Fisher Award given by Les Dames d'Escoffier International to a woman who has made a major contribution to an understanding of food.

Lisa Maree Heldke is Professor of Philosophy at Gustavus Adolphus College in St. Peter, Minnesota and is the author of *Exotic Appetites: Ruminations of a Food Adventurer*.

Maya Hey is a Vanier scholar (Social Sciences and Humanities Research Council, Government of Canada) and PhD candidate at Concordia University. Her research combines the thinking and doing of food, feminism, and fermentation.

Sanna Hirvonen is a postdoctoral researcher in philosophy and a member of Culinary Mind. Her research is in philosophy of food, mind, and language with a focus on aesthetic and gustatory taste. She lives in Lisbon, Portugal.

Carolyn Korsmeyer is Research Professor of Philosophy at the University at Buffalo. Her areas of research include aesthetics, emotion theory, and the senses. Her most recent book is *Things: In Touch with the Past* (2019).

David Kyle is Associate Professor of Sociology at University of California, Davis. Building on several years of researching and considering the creativity of migrants as they imagine their future lives abroad, his research explores the social management of the imagination in the context of "meritocratic talentism" and institutional creativity.

Cain Todd is Senior Lecturer in Philosophy at Lancaster University. His main research interests are in aesthetics, the philosophy of mind, and philosophy of perception. He is the author of *The Philosophy of Wine* (2010) and has written several papers on wine and the nature of olfaction.

Giuliano Torrengo is Associate Professor of Philosophy at the University of Milan. He is the founder and coordinator of the Center for Philosophy of Time. His main interests are in metaphysics, philosophy of language, and philosophy of mind.

Natalie Weissenberger is a recent graduate of the University of Edinburgh where she obtained her LLM in Intellectual Property Law. She also holds an LLB in International and European Law from the University of Groningen. Her main areas of interest lie in the regulation of copyright and other IP rights in the online context, and the interaction between IP and new technologies.

Merry White is Professor of Anthropology at Boston University where she teaches Japanese studies and food anthropology. She writes on Japanese food, on coffee and social spaces in Japan, and on food workers. She also explores food, neighborhood, and social identity in Boston's communities.

Benjamin Aldes Wurgaft is a writer and historian. He has taught at the University of California, Berkeley; the New School for Social Research; and most recently at Wesleyan University. He was also a Visiting Scholar in Anthropology at MIT. His essays on food and other topics appear regularly in publications from *Gastronomica* to the *Los Angeles Review of Books* to the *Hedgehog Review*.

Index

Made in the USA
Las Vegas, NV
26 November 2023